Reading the Presidency

POLITICAL COMMUNICATION

FRONTIERS IN

Mitchell S. McKinney and Mary E. Stuckey
General Editors

Vol. 43

The Frontiers in Political Communication series
is part of the Peter Lang Media and Communication list.
Every volume is peer reviewed and meets
the highest quality standards for content and production.

PETER LANG
New York • Bern • Berlin
Brussels • Vienna • Oxford • Warsaw

Reading the Presidency

Advances in Presidential Rhetoric

Edited by Stephen J. Heidt
and Mary E. Stuckey

PETER LANG
New York • Bern • Berlin
Brussels • Vienna • Oxford • Warsaw

Library of Congress Cataloging-in-Publication Data

Names: Heidt, Stephen J., editor. | Stuckey, Mary E., editor.
Title: Reading the presidency: advances in presidential rhetoric /
edited by Stephen J. Heidt and Mary E. Stuckey.
Description: New York: Peter Lang, 2019.
Series: Frontiers in political communication; vol. 43 | ISSN 1525-9730
Includes bibliographical references.
Identifiers: LCCN 2018032137 | ISBN 978-1-4331-3542-2 (hardback: alk. paper)
ISBN 978-1-4331-6606-8 (paperback: alk. paper)
ISBN 978-1-4331-6053-0 (ebook pdf)
ISBN 978-1-4331-6054-7 (epub) | ISBN 978-1-4331-6055-4 (mobi)
Subjects: LCSH: Communication in politics—United States. |
Presidents—United States—Language. | Political oratory—United States. |
Rhetoric—Political aspects—United States. |
Executive power—United States.
Classification: LCC JA85.2.U6 R42 | DDC 352.2301/4—dc23
LC record available at https://lccn.loc.gov/2018032137
DOI 10.3726/b14831

Bibliographic information published by **Die Deutsche Nationalbibliothek**.
Die Deutsche Nationalbibliothek lists this publication in the "Deutsche
Nationalbibliografie"; detailed bibliographic data are available
on the Internet at http://dnb.d-nb.de/.

The paper in this book meets the guidelines for permanence and durability
of the Committee on Production Guidelines for Book Longevity
of the Council of Library Resources.

Contents

Acknowledgments

This book found its inspiration in Mary Stuckey's presidential rhetoric seminar. In the years since that ignominious foray into the study of presidential rhetoric, we have discussed, debated, and quarreled about many of the themes contained in this volume. Having finally decided to do something with our fervor for thinking about the presidency, this volume represents the outcome of that long-running conversation.

We are primarily grateful to our friend and conference dinner companion, Rob Mills, who was and is an indispensable part of many of our on-going arguments. We also thank the other members of that seminar, who are carrying on the conversation in their own ways.

We are also deeply indebted to the contributors to this volume. From inception to completion, they worked with us as we requested revisions, asked for additional information, and required patience. Through it all, they continued to believe in this project and the conversation it aims to further. This book would, literally, have been impossible without them.

The research for this book was supported by a Morrow Fund Endowment grant from the School of Communication and Multimedia Studies at Florida Atlantic University. We are deeply appreciative of all the ways our departments and universities have supported this work. Our gratitude goes first to Georgia State University, which was academic home to both of us for many years. Stephen is grateful for all the support he received from the faculty at FAU; he will finish this sentence as he sees fit. Mary thanks her colleagues at Penn State, and especially the department head, Denise Solomon, for what often seems like a magical academic environment.

We are also appreciate of the staff at Peter Lang who helped make this project a reality. We offer special thanks to Mary Savigar, Sophie Appel, Michael Doub, and Kathryn Harrison.

We would also like to thank each other. In inviting Stephen to co-edit this project, and indeed to take the lead on it, Mary knew he would do great work, but had no idea how much more than that he would contribute. Students always make us proud. But there aren't words for how proud I am of this one, who has certainly schooled me, and become a very good friend. Stephen thanks Mary for throwing a good party.

Finally, we wish to thank Diana Barreto, to whom this book is dedicated. Her unwavering support for Stephen's intellectual development, spanning from his years as a doctoral student to the present, has made this work possible. Without her, he would be lost.

Introduction

The Study of Presidential Rhetoric in Uncertain Times: Thoughts on Theory and Praxis

STEPHEN J. HEIDT

In 1996, Bruce Gronbeck declared that "electronic channels" had (or would) fundamentally alter the presidency and, in consequence, presidential rhetoric.[1] Contending that "electronics changed the essential nature of the presidency," Gronbeck identified three shifting "dynamics" that heralded a newly configured presidency "fundamentally different from the presidency as it has operated and been experienced in any other epoch."[2] Specifically, the rise of digital life "recast relationships between the presidency and its constituencies ... enlarged the role of spectacle ... [and] destroyed the traditional distance that has existed between leaders and the led."[3] Portending the ways digital life would capture public culture, Gronbeck heralded the rise of multimediated rhetoric, the speed at which that rhetoric would enter and exit public discourse, the increased importance *ethos* would play to the presidency in such a context, and the need to expand the definition of "presidential rhetoric" to include forms of presidential communication beyond those included in the official papers of the presidency.

We invoke Gronbeck's work to open this volume for two reasons. First, Gronbeck was the founding editor of the book series that is publishing this volume. We find it appropriate to recognize his contribution to the study of presidential rhetoric, via trenchant insights into the shifting landscapes that define and bound presidential discourse and by his efforts to create space for scholars to publish and circulate work related to presidential rhetoric and political communication.

Gronbeck is also an appropriate starting point, we believe, because in many respects his predictions about the presidency proved prescient. The rise of the Internet age shifted the context in which presidential discourse is constituted, uttered, and received. Advances in communication technology have enabled presidents to directly reach citizens, with advanced speed, about issues of national or personal importance. These shifts pose significant challenges for scholars seeking to make claims about the importance of presidential rhetoric, its significance inside and outside institutional contexts, and its deliberative function. While scholars have not abandoned their beliefs in the stability of presidential messages and the implications those messages have on publics and policy, recent trends have elevated concern about the utility of the rhetorical presidency thesis in a fragmented, digital media ecology.

The shifting media ecology is merely one component of an increasingly complex scene that frames and shapes the study of presidential rhetoric. At its base, the argument for the uniqueness of presidential rhetoric as a species of study—a separate speech genre unto itself—derives from the conviction in the universal importance of the presidency as an institution in a democratic culture. This assumption has, historically, implied that everything the president says matters.[4] Fundamentally, studies of presidential address hinge upon an institutional logic of the presidency—that rhetorical situations demand presidential address, that presidential success depends on individual persuasive ability, and that the person who holds the office is the focal point for inquiry. As scholars of the presidency, we are concerned this institutional logic has distanced work on the president from other important, relevant trends in rhetorical theory. This distance between method and theory matters a great deal because contextual shifts have decentered the chief executive. The president no longer commands the attention he once enjoyed.[5] Even as the person of the president remains a focal point for the mass public and the media, the nature and quality of that role is substantively different. And audiences of presidential address are increasingly diverse, fragmented, and heterogeneous, raising questions about the types of claims scholars can make about presidential rhetoric and its significance to political culture and public deliberation of policy issues. The audience problem is even thornier when considering transnational or foreign addresses and the myriad ways presidential speech is interpreted and reinterpreted by audiences difficult to identify and map.

Scholars of presidential rhetoric have not ignored the contextual complications and their impact on the types of claims available to be made about presidential speech. Yet, studies continue to measure presidents by the expectation their speech will lead to policy outcomes. Perhaps hamstrung by Roderick P. Hart's claim that "public speech … is governance," we believe scholars are grappling with how to articulate the significance of presidential address.[6] Concerned the expectation that presidential address determines policy outcomes is not a useful guide for measuring what presidents do rhetorically, especially since presidents who once relied on public comments to help them accomplish their policy goals now increasingly rely on administrative mechanisms,[7] we have crafted this volume as an initial effort to think about how presidential rhetoric develops in different contexts, serves different ends, and demands different methodological approaches.

Going Public, the Rhetorical Presidency, and the Waning Utility of Metatheory

The underlying premise behind most studies of presidential rhetoric relates to the significance of presidential address to issues of public deliberation. Jeffrey Tulis's *The Rhetorical Presidency,* which has become the dominant lens by which scholars have approached the study of presidential rhetoric,[8] contended that the advent of mass media technology enabled the president to reach mass audiences, fundamentally altering the constitutional arrangement that sought to balance power between the executive and the legislature.[9] Often conflated with the going public thesis, which explains how presidents look for levers of power to advance their agenda, with public appeals as one such mechanism, the rhetorical presidency thesis refers to the form of presidential address and its implications for the constitutional balance of power between the three branches of government. Commonly articulated as an increase in the quantity of presidential rhetoric, Tulis argued that mass media facilitated a generic shift in presidential speech—radio enabled the president to make deliberative appeals directly to the people, circumventing the requirements of negotiating with Congress. This thesis—beginning with its articulation by James W. Caeser et al—has undergone intense interrogation by scholars of presidential rhetoric.[10] That interrogation has undermined the original premise—that increases in presidential speech directed at the public has undermined the constitutional design—by criticizing the theorem's timelines, historical accuracy, and conception of rhetoric itself. In short, rhetorical critics have demonstrated that the presidency has always been rhetorical and that the shift perceived by Tulis relates more to the character and quantity of that rhetoric. While the early presidency may have been somewhat restrained in the content of public appeals, preferring epideictic forms over direct deliberation, presidents increasingly shifted to deliberative rhetoric as a means to achieve their agendas.[11]

While this volume does not abandon the rhetorical presidency thesis, we have begun to think of it as a heuristic. From the onset, the rhetorical presidency thesis focused on the constitutional arrangement between the president and Congress in a specific period of time (mainly the 20th century). While Tulis incited significant pushback from rhetorical scholars, many of whom contested not only his historical timeline but the very essence of the thesis, the post-Tulis conversation has consistently accepted the premise that presidential speech is purposeful, its purpose is to persuade, and its power is such that it has unbalanced the constitutional order and elevated the significance of the presidency in American national and political life. But, as media, culture, campaigns, and the doctrine of presidential leadership have shifted, the presidency's relationship to the constitution and Congress also shifts. Brandon Rottinghaus pointed to the evolution of these trends, noting that modern presidents "continually engage ... in order to explain or build support for policies," something made possible by technological developments in communication that enables presidents to "travel and stay connected to the apparatus of governing."[12] The facility with which presidents can directly communicate to the public, government, and foreign leaders has contributed to the omnipresence of the president in media—inclusive of journalism and fictional accounts—as well as in the national imaginary.

These trends have produced several outcomes. First, the current era has witnessed the proliferation of micro-texts. Historically, presidential address tended to be orchestrated speaking events, with planned and scripted remarks, delivered via broadcast mediums. The need to plan and stage speaking as an event limited the quantity of presidential speech. The shift from broadcast to cable television and the media glut that followed required presidents to speak more often, in less formal settings in order to find and reach audiences. From Bill Clinton playing the saxophone on the Arsenio Hall show to MTV Get out the Vote sessions, these trends have only intensified in the digital era. Now, presidents not only appear in popular culture settings, they also have digital presences that span Facebook, Twitter, and Instagram, among others. Heralding a dramatic shift in the tradition of presidential address, the massive uptick in the frequency of presidential speech has challenged traditional theories of persuasion, partially because the form and content of these addresses has departed from traditional genres of presidential speech. Given the contextual changes in audiences and transmission, Susan Herbst provocatively suggests that "the presidential voice matters, but perhaps not the content."[13] In other words, presidents now engage audiences in strange places, with quick bursts of content, to unknown outcomes.

Simultaneously, the shifting media landscape also resulted in the decline of textual integrity of presidential speech. Where citizens once listened to or viewed speeches in their entirely, contemporary audiences now hear or see snippets. From cable television shows like Jon Stewart's *The Daily Show* to real time meme creation and circulation, audiences exert greater control over presidential address than any time in history. In many cases, these efforts recirculate fragments of the original text in ways that convey alternative meanings from that intended by the president.

Herbst maintains these trends have altered "citizens' expectations, habits, preferences, and opinions," requiring presidents to do more to reach and connect with the public.[14] But the problem for presidents may be even more dire. The rhetorical presidency model, and its implicit assumption that presidential speech seek to persuade audiences to support presidential initiatives, depends upon notions of textual integrity. Stephen Heidt has written that a fragmented, atomized speech environment decenters the president and attempts at persuasion in favor of the discourse itself. His critique of the study of presidential address questions the utility of thinking of the president as a strategic actor, standing above the culture, searching for the perfect persuasive formula up to the task of captivating diverse audiences. While most presidents are strategic actors who attempt to design and deliver speeches to mass audiences to increase the prospects of securing their agendas, Heidt has pointed out that they are also subject to the discursive instability of the era.[15] Vulnerable to the streams of rhetoric that flow through and around the presidency, presidential outlook and speech is constituted from that discourse.

These developments have led scholars to think about presidential strategies for managing the complexity of the current era. For example, Scacco & Coe argue the goals of presidential speech have changed. During the rhetorical presidency era, they contend, presidents sought to influence policy with major or national addresses. Now, in response to media fragmentation, they claim presidents cultivate presence in political and non-political arenas—making presidential rhetoric accessible, personal, and pluralistic. In short, their "ubiquitous presidency" thesis claims that presidents are now incentivized to be seen governing, rather than just governing. By articulating the president as a stable subject, engaged in strategic rhetorical action designed to reach and persuade audiences about specific policy topics, the ubiquitous presidency model extends the fundamental premise of the rhetorical presidency thesis, rather than rewriting it. While it is too soon to test the veracity of claims to presidential intent, we suggest there are additional avenues to consider.

Toward that end, we have identified several trends in presidential speech, its fragmentation, and circulation. First, presidential rhetoric is more disentermediated than ever. Digital forms of communication enable presidents to bypass media and avoid exposure to tough questions and still reach target audiences. Heralding the return of interactivity, digital interaction with the president echoes the era when (white, male) citizens could walk into the White House to converse with the nation's leader. While presidents still must compete with new avenues of communication already clogged with popular culture, omitting media filters may heighten their capacities to frame issues. Second, presidential rhetorical strategy appears to be consolidating in the form of persona creation and embodiment. By this, we mean there is evidence that the persona presidents inhabit—lawyer, businessman—may have a greater impact on public perception of their agenda than the content of their speech.[16] Studies that adopt this methodological approach center their analytic efforts on the discourse that constitutes the public persona of the president, enabling claims about the significance of presidential speech even when partial, atomized, and incomplete. Third, presidents increasingly insert deliberative content into non-deliberative events. These trends suggest new capacities for presidential speech in terms of reaching diverse audiences, but also implicate governance in an era in which presidents discuss everything from disaster relief to football fields. Conflating substantive (policy) concerns and spectacle (popular culture), the penetration of presidential speech into popular culture raises questions about the quality and efficacy of such deliberative endeavors. Finally, the domain of "presidential" rhetoric has expanded to include diverse actors across the executive branch, but without theory to attend to the addition of non-presidential speakers. Pointing to the contours of institutional governance, this development recognizes the suasive potential of presidential speech in terms of administrative actors.

Presidents, Rhetoric, and the Quandary of Significance in the Absence of Metatheory

Traditionally, the presidency has been read through public and archival texts in an institutional setting that focuses on the person of the president. This approach advances claims about the persuasive capacities of the president, particularly by deploying public appeals to advance a policy agenda. Often analyzing single speeches, these inquiries seek to uncover the ways presidential rhetoric facilitates identification between the speaker and the audience,[17] constitutes versions of national identity,[18] deploys tropes to form specific appeals,[19] and elevates the primacy of place as a discursive marker.[20] Studies explore how rhetorical styles ranging from religious,[21] to the paranoid,[22] the demagogic,[23] and the authoritarian[24] constitute specific types of audiences or media responses. Others hone in on the ways presidents strategically maneuver to define,[25] equivocate,[26] dodge,[27] frame,[28] or mythologize situations.[29] An additional strand catalogues presidential rhetoric into specific genres, providing useful guidance for how to read presidential speeches in terms of their consistency or inconsistency with the rhetorical tradition of the presidency.[30] Ancillary approaches trace the ways presidents use props, anecdotes, and materiality as textual evidence, demonstrating how those developments alter speech genres.[31] These studies infer that presidential speech facilitates the president's ability to navigate the treacherous terrain of the 21st century media ecology in order to sustain or advance their agenda. Focused on the interiority of the text, this branch of scholarship makes claims about rhetoric's importance in the historical and contemporary analysis of politics by implicitly or explicitly judging presidential texts—as persuasive, artistic, significant, ethical, or none of the above.

Locating presidential rhetoric in its institutional setting raises the significance of presidential speech, not due to causal relationships, but rather as a resource that frames issues, creates institutional capacities, communicates with other elites, provides inventional resources, balances the institution off of cultural representations of the presidency, and performs a representative function. In specific form, this consideration has given rise to inquiries interested in the public policy potential of presidential discourse. Studies have focused on the place of presidential rhetoric in deliberative practices,[32] including how presidential policy rhetoric sustains even policy decisions,[33] how campaigns deploy policy talk as a sort of political alchemy to sustain candidacies,[34] how tropes orient policy debates with normative political reason,[35] how the anti-deliberative aspects of presidential actions can alter policy outcomes,[36] how speech can undermine policy,[37] and how speech institutionalizes policy practices.[38] Taking nuanced approaches to presidential audiences, these studies demonstrate the depth of research invested in understanding the policy implications of presidential speech.

Other approaches to the presidency have appeared in the years since Gronbeck's observations. One seeks to better understand the origins of presidential speech, tracing discourse from founding documents to speech[39] or from one president to another.[40] This genealogical approach to presidential rhetoric seeks to explain how presidential subjects themselves are constituted. Studies connect cultural experiences presidents had in their formative years to their political outlook to explain discursive and policy choices.[41] Others reveal how political, social, and cultural continuities manifest in presidential speech.[42] And some point to how presidents strategically embrace cultural narratives to rationalize their orientation to issues of national importance (in particular, foreign policy).[43] Studies that adopt a genealogical orientation understand discourse as something that exists externally to the presidency but is incorporated in presidential speech for instrumental and constitutive ends. At times foregrounding the discourse, these studies also represent the presidency as a window or vantage point from which a discourse can be perceived, parsed, or elucidated.

Scholars have also begun to engage comparative studies that examine presidential discourse in international contexts. Some studies articulate the significance of presidential rhetoric abroad, in formal or informal settings, and parse the different audiences involved in the speaking event.[44] Others compare the rhetoric of foreign presidents to that of the U.S. president.[45] A final approach applies current methodologies to foreign leaders to better theorize the ways those leaders constitute publics, politics, and personas.[46] As a nascent, but growing genre of presidential rhetoric, transnational studies infer an essential equivalence between and across democratic countries, their leadership, and the necessity, if not efficacy, of speech.

Scholars are also particularly interested in the ways these speech forms manifest during campaigns and elections. Over the last four presidential elections, studies have incorporated many of the traditional methodologies to explain the rise and fall of controversies, candidates, and platforms. Studies related to the 2004 election focused on the ways the war in Vietnam arose during the campaign,[47] the "cultural trauma" of 9/11 and its continuing cultural relevance,[48] and the reverberations of the 2000 recount.[49] After Obama's victory in 2008, scholars examined the rhetorical significance of Hillary Clinton's Iraq War vote,[50] the Reverend Wright controversy,[51] gendered and raced media coverage during the primaries and campaign,[52] and how John McCain crafted his political identity.[53] With the rise, if not dominance, of social media and other digital media, the focus of elections has also yielded numerous studies thinking through the ways technological innovations has altered creation, delivery, and reception of presidential messages.[54] Some have also turned to the significance of third party candidates to identify ways outsider discourse impacts the direction of the two major parties and their platforms.[55]

As with public culture itself, Obama's election shifted the focus of scholarly inquiry to focus more closely on issues of race or gender and the presidency. While post-election studies have continued their thematic focus, Mitt Romney's crafting of a political identity,[56] for example, significant inquiry has investigated the racial politics of a black president,[57] the gendered politics related to Obama's legislative centerpiece,[58] the gendered features of the 2016 campaign,[59] and the broader dynamics of a gendered, raced, and heteronormative political institution.[60] Perhaps heeding calls for presidential rhetoricians to address questions related to gender, race, and the implications of the poststructuralist turn,[61] these studies demonstrate collective efforts by scholars across the field to examine and articulate the ways the preeminent political institution designed to represent the people participates in white, patriarchal, and heteronormative notions about American political culture and society.

At the same time scholars have amplified and expanded the domain of the presidential "canon" and the "rhetorical archeology" enacted to delve and illuminate the meaning of presidential texts, as Martin Medhurst once wrote, scholars have also sought elaborate the contours of the "symbolic presidency."[62] This line of inquiry has produced studies elaborating the ways popular culture representations of the presidency influence public attitudes and expectations of the candidate and office holder. Studies of "presidentiality" have examined public culture constructs of the presidency, demonstrating how fictive portrayals reveal national anxieties about the institution while elaborating a mythos of the president as a (white) romantic hero, striving to work for the American people.[63] Others have discussed how those constructs produce racial and gendered stereotypes presidential aspirants must navigate.[64] Some have examined visual representations related to presidents to explain how media and voters shape presidential personas.[65] Finding that popular representations reflect back upon the presidency itself—altering how presidents constitute public personas and, in some cases, embody the role of president—these inquiries have synced with postmodern notions related to the instability of presidential subjectivities and the fragmentation of presidential texts. They have also examined the ways recent presidents have anticipated the atomization of speech to forge personas that can travel,[66] as well as begun to unravel similar patterns of image making and persona construction as a strategic action by presidents from previous eras.[67]

While these trends speak to a vibrant, diverse, and increasingly agile understanding of the presidency, virtually all of these studies rely on the going public or rhetorical presidency theses. Even while scholars have begun to rethink what it means to study the presidency, expanding the canon of presidential speech as well as the critical praxis leveled to examine that speech, they have yet to grapple with a shifting presidential role in which the president is no longer able to rise above an increasingly diverse and fragmented culture. This volume, then, asks: what happens to presidential speech when the president is enmeshed in culture? How do genres get constituted within and outside of political culture? How do the narratives that describe those genres influence presidential address and the media landscapes that attempt to govern political culture? What types of claims can be made about contemporary presidents, the body of their discourse, and its significance to culture, deliberation, and public policy?

We believe the time is ripe for discussion that brings together diverse theoretical diversity in the interest of advancing conceptions of presidential rhetoric in an era of radically shifting contexts. Bringing the study of presidential rhetoric and work in the wider field into closer conversation, this volume postulates a range of possibilities for how to conceive of the presidency and its significance to the national political landscape. In the spirit of amendment rather than critique, the collection combines scholarly approaches normally associated with the presidency and rhetorical studies with emergent approaches to the study of public discourse. For that reason, the volume contains a mix of authors not necessarily associated with the study of presidential rhetoric, but who apply their theoretical acumen to the presidency, and presidential scholars interested in reimagining disciplinary trends.

Chapter Summaries

While the chapters in this volume cannot answer all of the pertinent questions related to presidential rhetoric, they seek to begin a conversation for understanding the relational dynamics between the presidency and audiences in an era of media fragmentation and audience recirculation. The first section of this volume focuses on presidential communication and relationships. Chapters in this section forward cases that demonstrate the way the institution of the presidency incentivizes *rhetorical relationships* as a means for sustaining and intensifying the president's claim to knowledge, interpretation, and policy. Timothy Barney opens this section by focusing on presidential relationships to *place*. In this case, his study identifies the map as a sort of geopolitical guidepost for presidential audiences. Focusing on Cold War presidents who used maps for ideological claims, Barney demonstrates how the map enabled a sort of geographic thinking about world politics that naturalized realist assumptions about international relations during World War II. In his terms, maps serve as rhetorically powerful devices by extending and entrenching ideological worldviews. This power, he contends, derives from the implicit notion that maps are ideologically neutral—they show the world as it actually is—even while they facilitate and naturalize competitive notions of international relations. Urging public address scholars to "foreground" the ways presidential rhetoric constructs geopolitical dynamics that influence the ways foreign policy gets made, Barney's chapter points to the need for greater emphasis on the ways presidential props contribute to "geopolitical consent" in a mediated and networked world.

Allison Prasch adopts an alternative approach by isolating the ways presidents use physical spaces in public messages. For Prasch, thinking about place can explain why some presidential speeches are more powerful, persuasive, and long lasting. Examining Barack Obama's remarks on his visit to Cuba in 2016, she contends mass media technology has amplified the significance of place in presidential address. Her chapter offers a methodological guide for scholars interested in reading presidential rhetoric *in situ*.

Milene Ortega & Mary E. Stuckey write about presidential relationships between the *presidency* and *civil society*. Ortega and Stuckey intend to expand the definition of presidential rhetoric to include surrogates inside and outside the administration. Focusing on the "ensemble" of "political voices" that fragment, circulate, and orchestrate presidential discourse, they contend, sheds light on the ways presidents wield institutional power to achieve policy goals. Their study of the ratification of the Panama Canal treaties draws on archival and public materials to explain President Carter's success as the outcome of a coordinated and harmonized rhetorical strategy involving the president, institutional actors, and civil society. By synthesizing the criticism of presidential appeals with institutional and non-institutional actors aligned with the president, Ortega and Stuckey demonstrate treating presidential rhetoric as a dense ecosystem of discourse offers fertile ground for scholarly exploration.

Ryan Neville-Shepard's chapter addresses presidential relationships to *speech* itself. While many may have read Trump's addresses as violating the norms of presidential speech, in particular his inaugural, Neville-Shepard contends the best way to understand Donald Trump's rhetoric is by perceiving how his speech fits the genre of third party candidates. Characterizing Trump's discourse as aligned with that of outsider candidates, he advances the notion of "genre-busting" as a distinct rhetorical strategy at the core of Trump's political appeal. Offering an alternative, novel way of thinking about genre, Neville-Shepard suggests scholars think about the power of genre violations to generate media attention, captivate audiences, and advance political standing.

Jay Childers and Cassandra C. Bird attend to presidential relationships to *events*. Focusing on presidential responses to national tragedies from Ronald Reagan to the present, they argue presidential responses have constituted a persona they label "Comforter-in-Chief." This persona lives across administrations of differing partisan orientations, constructing and constricting the ways presidents speak after tragedy. Productive of media coverage that has come to expect a specific, empathetic form, Childers and Bird suggest this persona has shifted the role presidents play in the national imaginary and, potentially, amplified presidential rhetorical power to frame and shape the way events are articulated in the media. Foregrounding the persona and its interaction with political journalism, this chapter implies presidential scholars would be served by examining the interactive elements of presidential speech.

The second section of this volume reads the presidency through its *interactions* with diverse publics. Blake Abbott begins this section by describing the ways postmodern culture has fragmented the presidential subject. His chapter contends that circulating discourses influence and alter the president's identity, if not policy orientation. By focusing on the presidential subject, Abbott asks scholars of public address to think of the institution as a participant in a fragmented media culture.

Ronald Walter Greene and Jay Alexander Frank's chapter offers a unique case in which the discursive context of Obama's "red line" speech reframed the president's rhetoric toward Syria. Their approach demonstrates the ways social and international norms constitute the presidential subject. Pointing to the globalization of the presidency, the chapter highlights the ways the rise of global audiences coincided with the rise of the rhetorical presidency. Their findings suggest that public address scholars should attend to global audiences.

Belinda Stillion Southard's study of Michele Bachelet's rhetoric points to the inevitable interactivity between presidencies. Her chapter suggests that a key component for understanding the U.S. president as a global leader, scholars need to understand non-U.S. presidents, their rise, their rhetorical situations, and their rhetoric. That is, the self-serving motivation for studying foreign presidents is that, in doing so, scholars can better understand the rhetorical contexts that make up the American president and presidency.

The final two chapters in this section examine presidential interactions with specific audiences. Stephen J. Heidt and Damien Pfister grapple with Donald Trump's use of Twitter as his preferred form of communication. Urging critics of presidential rhetoric to take the microblogging form—if not the platform itself—seriously, they contend Trump's tweets can best be understood as a rhetorical form they call the "microdiatribe." Building off of Theodore Otto Windt Jr.'s theory of the diatribe, Heidt and Pfister argue that Trump's tweets channeled affective energies of outrage to sustain and bolster his candidacy by connecting with and mobilizing digital audiences who recirculated Trump's essential messages. The same rhetorical form, they suggest, undermines his ability to govern.

The last chapter in this section, by Leah Ceccarelli, focuses on the subtle reconfiguration of public attitudes over the course of a presidential term. Her study of the stem cell controversy during the first decade of the 2000s points to how differences between the ways Bill Clinton and George W. Bush addressed the science community altered the context that defined the stem cell debate. She asks scholars to understand rhetorical effect as how presidential speech shifts across administrations and how speech can box in or open up rhetorical opportunities.

The final section of this volume reads the presidency through *interruptions*. Paul Johnson opens this section with a critique of the presidency that begins with the premise that presidentialism itself suppresses inherent partisan dissensus by offering the presidential body as a singular representative site of national identity. He contends these compressed notions of the president produce two outcomes that complicate the political landscape and the study of presidential address. First, popular representations of what constitutes a president worsen policy deliberations by relegating the evaluation of complex issues to evaluations of the president's character or intent. Second, the accretion of institutional memory produces a narrow ethos of the president—as white, straight, male, and upper class—constituting an equally narrow range of expectations for presidential norms, practices, or habits. Johnson reads the 2011 debt ceiling controversy to highlight the ways Obama's blackness violated the normative expectations of the institution and channeled normally partisan deliberation into something much worse. By applying psychoanalytic theory to the presidency—particularly by extending Lauren Berlant's "cruel optimism" thesis—Johnson offers scholars a methodology for thinking through the complexity of presidentialism and its implications for deliberation.

Joel Lemuel's study of the war on drugs advances a genealogical framework for understanding the historical antecedents of an evolving discourse. His chapter distances the critic from the president to foreground the underlying discourse as the object of study. Delving into the historical arc of anti-drug discourse from the beginning of the 20th century to Richard Nixon, Lemuel demonstrates how medical and sociological discourses facilitated the criminalization of intoxicants in ways that specified a focus on racial minorities generally and African Americans particularly. His study isolates the contagion metaphor as the root of the medicalized approach to drugs and shows how the initial metaphoric framing moved the drug problem from a medical to a criminal problem. Marking the gradual integration of anti-drug discourse into legislative and juridical frameworks, Lemuel's chapter demonstrates how genealogical inquiry can expand the canon of presidential rhetoric while tracing the movement of specific tropes across political and institutional contexts.

Leslie Harris examines the rhetoric of the Progressive Era, particularly that of Theodore Roosevelt and Woodrow Wilson, to explain how presidential discourse naturalizes the political subjectivities of women. Emphasizing two tropes—home and nation—as participants in a broader discourse pushing back against notions of women as political subjects and women's suffrage, her chapter demonstrates how casual references unrelated to specific political controversies work to extend and deepen normative political reason. In this case, Harris points to the ways Roosevelt and Wilson amplified traditional, patriarchal notions of womanhood by articulating a spatial relationship between home and nation. This spatial relationship, she contends, synthesized into a regressive discourse that gendered and raced notions of the home to address issues related to national security, poverty, and immigration. Addressing presidential rhetoric as a sort of discursive matrix that speaks for a dominant element of political culture, Harris's contribution offers scholars of presidential rhetoric a method for discussing rhetorical absences and the naturalized outcomes they produce.

Rather than look at presidential speech as a site for instrumental or constitutive rhetoric, Lisa Corrigan sees the presidency as an agent capable of generating instrumental and constitutive discourses of resistance. That is, for Corrigan, the interesting thing about the presidency is the way that oppressed, marginalized, and raced bodies articulate themselves in relation to the prototypical locus of white, male hegemonic power. Rather than ignore the presidency and presidential rhetoric, Corrigan urges scholars of race and gender to think through the ways the figure of the president supplies resistant voices with a discursive target from which they can dis-identify. This innovative study inverts the examination of presidential rhetoric by thinking through the ways well meaning forms of presidential speech backfire, but in doing so, produce the possibility of unity and resistance, a particularly insightful focus in an era of presidential authoritarianism.

Notes

1. Bruce E. Gronbeck, "The Presidency in the Age of Secondary Orality," in *Beyond the Rhetorical Presidency, 2nd edition*, ed. Martin J. Medhurst (College Station: Texas A&M University Press, 2004), 30.
2. Gronbeck, 31.
3. Gronbeck, 35.
4. With all due apologies to Gerald Ford.
5. Donald Trump may prove the exception to the rule, but the jury is still out on the effectivity of his ability to garner constant attention. It certainly hasn't helped his policy agenda much.
6. Roderick Hart, *The Sound of Leadership: Presidential Communication in the Modern Age* (Chicago: University of Chicago Press, 1987), 14–17
7. On going public, see Samuel Kernell, *Going Public: New Strategies of Presidential Leadership* (Washington, DC: CQ Press, 2007). On the use of administrative strategies, see Vanessa B. Beasley, "The Rhetorical Presidency Meets the Unitary Executive: Implications for Presidential Rhetoric on Public Policy," *Rhetoric & Public Affairs* 13, no. 1 (2010): 7–36.
8. Joshua M. Scacco and Kevin Coe, "The Ubiquitous Presidency: Toward a New Paradigm for Studying Presidential Communication," *International Journal of Communication* 10 (2016): 2014–2037.
9. See: Jeffrey K. Tulis, *The Rhetorical Presidency* (Princeton, NJ: Princeton University Press, 1987).
10. James W. Ceaser, Glen E. Thurow, Jeffrey Tulis, and Joseph M. Bessette, "The Rise of the Rhetorical Presidency," *Presidential Studies Quarterly* 11, no. 2 (1981): 158–171.
11. Martin J. Medhurst, "Introduction," in *Before the Rhetorical Presidency*, ed. Martin J. Medhurst (College Station: Texas A&M University Press).
12. Brandon Rottinghaus, *The Provisional Pulpit: Modern Presidential Leadership of Public Opinion* (College Station: Texas A&M University Press, 2010), 29.
13. Herbst, 342.
14. Susan Herbst, "The Rhetorical Presidency and the Contemporary Media Environment," *Critical Review* 19, no. 2–3 (2007): 336.
15. Stephen J. Heidt, "Presidency as Pastiche: Atomization, Circulation, and Rhetorical Instability," *Rhetoric & Public Affairs* 15, no. 4 (2012): 623–634.
16. See: Don Waisanen, "Comedian-in-Chief: Presidential Jokes as Enthymematic Crisis Rhetoric," *Presidential Studies Quarterly* 45, no. 2 (2015): 335–360.
17. See: Robert C. Rowland and John M. Jones, "Reagan's Farewell Address: Redefining the American Dream," *Rhetoric & Public Affairs* 20, no. 4 (2017): 635–665.
18. See: Vanessa B. Beasley, *You, the People: American National Identity in Presidential Rhetoric* (College Station: Texas A&M University Press, 2004); and, Mary E. Stuckey, *Defining Americans: The Presidency and National Identity* (Lawrence: University of Kansas Press, 2004).
19. See: Michael J. Steudeman, "Entelechy and Irony in Political Time: The Preemptive Rhetoric of Nixon and Obama," *Rhetoric & Public Affairs* 16, no. 1 (2013): 59–96; and, Edward C. Appel, "Burlesque, Tragedy, and a (Potentially) 'Yuuuge' 'Breaking of a Frame': Donald Trump's Rhetoric as 'Early Warning'?" *Communication Quarterly* 66, no. 2 (2018): 157–175.

20. See: Allison M. Prasch, Reagan at Pointe du Hoc: Deictic Epideictic and the Persuasive Power of 'Bringing Before the Eyes'," *Rhetoric & Public Affairs* 18, no. 2 (2015): 247–276; and, Rachel Martin Harlow, "Souvenir Battlefields: How Presidents Use Rhetoric of Place to Shape the American Ethos," *American Communication Journal* 18, no.1 (2016): 45–62.

21. See, for example: Cindy Koenig Richards, "'To Restore the National Faith': Abraham Lincoln's 1854 Peoria Address and the Paradox of Moral Politics," *Southern Communication Journal* 76, no. 5 (2011): 401–423; John Murphy, "Barack Obama, the Exodus Tradition, and the Joshua Generation," *Quarterly Journal of Speech* 97, no. 4 (2011): 387–410; and, Joshua Gunn, "The Rhetoric of Exorcism: George W. Bush and the Return of Political Demonology," *Western Journal of Communication* 68, no. 1 (2004): 1–23.

22. See: Michelle Murray Yang, "At War with the Chinese Economic Yellow Peril: Mitt Romney's 2012 Presidential Campaign Rhetoric," *Journal of Intercultural Communication Research* 45, no. 1 (2016): 45–69.

23. See: Marnie Lawler McDonough, "The Evolution of Demagoguery: An Updated Understanding of Demagogic Rhetoric as Interactive and Ongoing," *Communication Quarterly* 66, no. 2 (2018): 138–156.

24. See: Douglas Kellner, "Donald Trump and the War on the Media: From Election '16 into the Trump Presidency," in *The Trump Presidency, Journalism, and Democracy,* ed. Robert E. Gutsche, Jr. (New York: Routledge, 2018); and, Matthew C. MacWilliams, *The Rise of Trump: America's Authoritarian Spring* (Amherst, MA: Amherst College Press, 2016).

25. See: David Zarefsky, "Strategic Maneuvering in Political Argumentation," *Argumentation* 22 (2008): 317–330; and, David Zarefsky, "Presidential Rhetoric and the Power of Definition," *Presidential Studies Quarterly* 34, no. 3 (2004): 607–619.

26. See: Robert L. Ivie, "Obama at West Point: A Study in Ambiguity of Purpose," *Rhetoric & Public Affairs* 14, no. 4 (2011): 727–759.

27. See: David Clementson & William P. Eveland, Jr., "When Politicians Dodge Questions: An Analysis of Presidential Press Conferences and Debates," *Mass Communication and Society* 19, no. 4 (2016): 411–429; and, Matthew A. Baum, "Going Private: Public Opinion, Presidential Rhetoric, and the *Domestic* Politics of Audience Costs in U.S. Foreign Policy Crises," *Journal of Conflict Resolution* 48, no. 5 (2004): 603–631.

28. See: Kathryn M. Olson, "Democratic Enlargement's Value Hierarchy and Rhetorical Forms: An Analysis of Clinton's Use of a Post-Cold War Symbolic Frame to Justify Military Interventions," *Presidential Studies Quarterly* 34, no. 2 (2004): 307–340; Christian Spielvogel, "'You Know Where I Stand': Moral Framing of the War on Terrorism and the Iraq War in the 2004 Presidential Campaign," *Rhetoric & Public Affairs* 8, no. 4 (2005): 549–569; and, Wesley W. Widmaier, "Constructing Foreign Policy Crises: Interpretative Leadership in the Cold War and War on Terrorism," *International Studies Quarterly* 51, no. 4 (2007): 779–794.

29. See: Robert L. Ivie & Oscar Giner, "More Good, Less Evil: Contesting the Mythos of National Insecurity in the 2008 Presidential Primaries," *Rhetoric & Public Affairs* 12, no. 2 (2009): 279–301.

30. Karlyn Kohrs Campbell & Kathleen Hall Jamieson, *Presidents Creating the Presidency: Deeds Done in Words* (Chicago: University of Chicago Press, 2008).

31. See: Allison M. Prasch & Julia Scatliff O'Grady, "Saluting the 'Skutnik': Special Guests, The First Lady's Box, and the Generic Evolution of the State of the Union Address," *Rhetoric & Public Affairs* 20, no. 4 (2017): 571–604; Christopher Oldenburg, "Re'characterizing' the Anecdote: Synecdoche and Ethotic Argument in Presidential Debate Rhetoric," *Communication Studies* 66, no. 1 (2015): 103–120; and, Jeffrey P. Mehltretter Drury, "Beyond 'Rhetorical Agency': Skutnik's Story in the 1982 State of the Union Address," *Western Journal of Communication* 82, no. 1 (2018): 40–58.

32. See: Robert Asen, "Introduction: Rhetoric and Public Policy," *Rhetoric & Public Affairs* 13, no. 1 (2010): 1–6.

33. See: Steven R. Goldzwig, "LBJ, the Rhetoric of Transcendence, and the Civil Rights Act of 1968," *Rhetoric & Public Affairs* 6, no. 1 (2003): 25–54.

34. See: Trevor Parry-Giles, "Resisting a 'Treacherous Piety': Issues, Images, and Public Policy Deliberation in Presidential Campaigns," *Rhetoric & Public Affairs* 13, no. 1 (2010): 37–64.

35. See: Megan Foley, "From Infantile Citizens to Infantile Institutions: The Metaphoric Transformation of Political Economy in the 2008 Housing Market Crisis," *Quarterly Journal of Speech* 98, no. 4 (2012): 386–410; and, Stephen J. Heidt, "Presidential Rhetoric, Metaphor, and the Emergence of the Democracy Promotion Industry," *Southern Communication Journal* 78, no. 3 (2013): 233–255.

36. See: Beasley, "The Rhetorical Presidency Meets the Unitary Executive."

37. See: David S. Birdsell, "George W. Bush's Signing Statements: The Assault on Deliberation," *Rhetoric & Public Affairs* 10, no.2 (2007): 335–360.

38. See: Mary E. Stuckey, *Jimmy Carter, Human Rights, and the National Agenda* (College Station: Texas A&M University Press, 2008); and, Stephen J. Heidt, "Presidential Power and National Violence: James K. Polk's Rhetorical Transfer of Savagery," *Rhetoric & Public Affairs* 19, no. 3 (2016): 365–396.

39. See: Stephen Howard Browne, "'Sacred Fire of liberty': The Constitutional Origins of Washington's First Inaugural Address," *Rhetoric & Public Affairs* 19, no. 3 (2016): 397–425.

40. See: Carol Winkler, "Parallels in Preemptive War Rhetoric: Reagan on Libya; Bush 43 on Iraq," *Rhetoric & Public Affairs* 10, no. 2 (2007): 303–334.

41. See: Philip Abbott, "A 'Long and Winding Road': Bill Clinton and the 1960s," *Rhetoric & Public Affairs* 9, no. 1 (2006): 1–20; David A. Frank, "Obama's Rhetorical Signature: Cosmopolitan Civil Religion in the Presidential Inaugural Address, January 20, 2009," *Rhetoric & Public Affairs* 14, no. 4 (2011): 605–630; and, Joseph Rhodes & Mark Hlavacik, "Imagining Moral Presidential Speech: Barack Obama's Niebuhrian Nobel," *Rhetoric & Public Affairs* 18, no. 3 (2015): 471–504.

42. See: John R. Butler, "Somalia and the Imperial Savage: Continuities in the Rhetoric of War," *Western Journal of Communication* 66, no. 1 (2002): 1–24.

43. See: Mark West & Chris Carey, "(Re)Enacting Frontier Justice: The Bush Administration's Tactical Narration of the Old West Fantasy after September 11," *Quarterly Journal of Speech* 92, no. 4 (2006): 379–412.

44. See: Michelle Murray Yang, "President Nixon's Speeches and Toasts during His 1972 Trip to China: A Study in Diplomatic Rhetoric," *Rhetoric & Public Affairs* 14, no. 1 (2011): 1–44; Amir H. Y. Salama, "The Rhetoric of Collocational, Intertextual and Institutional Pluralization in Obama's Cairo Speech: A Discourse-Analysis Approach," *Critical Discourse Studies* 9, no. 3 (2012): 211–229.

45. Mansup Heo & Jaeyung Park, "Presidential Rhetoric of South Korea and the United States: The Case of Lee and Obama," *Asian Journal of Communication* 26, no. 4 (2016): 301–318.

46. Timothy Barney, "Citizen Havel and the Construction of Czech Presidentiality," *Quarterly Journal of Speech* 101, no. 4 (2015): 585–611; and, Gene Segarra Navera, *The Rhetoric of PNoy: Image, Myth, and Rhetorical Citizenship in Philippine Presidential Speeches* (New York: Peter Lang, 2018).

47. See: Moya Ann Ball, "The Role of Vietnam in the 2004 Presidential Election," *Rhetoric & Public Affairs* 8, no. 4 (2005): 689–693; and, G. Mitchell Reyes, "The Swift Boat Veterans for Truth, the Politics of Realism, and the Manipulation of Vietnam Remembrance in the 2004 Presidential Election," *Rhetoric & Public Affairs* 9, no. 4 (2006): 571–600.

48. See: Shawn J. Parry-Giles and Trevor Parry-Giles, "Introduction: Campaign 2004: Looking to the Past for Ideological Certainty in a Period of National Anxiety," *Rhetoric & Public Affairs* 8, no. 4 (2005): 543–548; and, Diana B. Carlin, Dan Schill, David G. Levasseur, and Anthony S. King, "The Post-9/11 Public Sphere: Citizen Talk about the 2004 Presidential Debates," *Rhetoric & Public Affairs* 8, no. 4 (2005): 617–638.

49. See: Vanessa B. Beasley, "Of Mobs and Machines: Remembering the 2000 Florida Recount in 2004," *Rhetoric & Public Affairs* 8, no. 4 (2005): 679–698.

50. See: Denise M. Bostdorff, "Judgment, Experience, and Leadership: Candidate Debates on the Iraq War in the 2008 Presidential Primaries," *Rhetoric & Public Affairs* 12, no. 2 (2009): 223–277.

51. See: Susanna Dilliplane, "Race, Rhetoric, and Running for President: Unpacking the Significance of Barack Obama's 'A More Perfect Union' Speech," *Rhetoric & Public Affairs* 15, no. 1 (2012): 127–152; David A. Frank, "The Prophetic Voice and the Face of the Other in Barack Obama's 'A More Perfect Union' Address, March 18, 2008," *Rhetoric & Public Affairs* 12, no. 2 (2009): 167–194; and, William L. Benoit, "Barack Obama's 2008 Speech on Reverend Wright: Defending Self and Others," *Public Relations Review* 42, no. 5 (2016): 843–848.

52. See: Kherstin Khan & Diane Blair, "Writing Bill Clinton: Mediated Discourses on Hegemonic Masculinity and the 2008 Presidential Primary," *Women's Studies in Communication* 36 (2013): 56–71; and, Ronald Lee & Aysel Morin, "Using the 2008 Presidential Election to Think about 'Playing the Race Card'," *Communication Studies* 60, no. 4 (2009): 376–391.

53. See: Trevor Parry-Giles and Michael J. Steudeman, "Crafting Character, Moving History: John McCain's Political Identity in the 2008 Presidential Campaign," *Quarterly Journal of Speech* 103, no. 1–2 (2017): 66–89.

54. See: Deen Freelon & David Karpf, "Of Big Birds and Bayonets: Hybrid Twitter Interactivity in the 2012 Presidential Debates," *Information, Communication & Society* 18, no. 4 (2015): 390–406; Daniel Kreiss & Shannon C. McGregor, "Technology Firms Shape Political Communication: The Work of Microsoft, Facebook, Twitter, and Google With Campaigns During the 2016 U.S. Presidential Cycle," *Political Communication* 35, no. 2 (2017): 155–177; and, Brian L. Ott, "The Age of Twitter: Donald J. Trump and the Politics of Debasement," *Critical Studies in Media Communication* 34, no. 1 (2017): 59–68.

55. See: Christine Harold, "The Green Virus: Purity and Contamination in Ralph Nader's 2000 Presidential Campaign," *Rhetoric & Public Affairs* 4, no. 4 (2001): 581–603; Ryan Neville-Shepard, "Triumph in Defeat: The Genre of Third Party Presidential Concessions,"

Communication Quarterly 62, no. 2 (2014): 214–232; and, Ryan Neville-Shepard, "Unconventional: The Variant of Third-Party Nomination Acceptance Addresses," *Western Journal of Communication* 80, no. 2 (2016): 121–139.

56. See: Kristy Maddux, "Religious Dissociation in 2012 Campaign Discourse," *Rhetoric & Public Affairs* 16, no. 2 (2013): 355–368; and, Thomas A. Salek, "Faith Turns Political on the 2012 Campaign Trail: Mitt Romney, Franklin Graham, and the Stigma of Nontraditional Religions in American Politics," *Communication Studies* 65, no. 2 (2014): 174–188.

57. See: Darrel Enck-Wanzer, "Barack Obama, the Tea Party, and the Threat of Race: On Racial Neoliberalism and Born Again Racism," *Communication, Culture & Critique* 4, no. 1 (2011): 23–30; Matthew D. Luttig & Timothy H. Callaghan, "Is President Obama's Race Chronically Accessible? Racial Priming in the 2012 Presidential Election," *Political Communication* 33, no. 4 (2016): 628–650; and, Robert E. Terrill, ed., *Reconsidering Obama: Reflections on Rhetoric* (New York: Peter Lang, 2017).

58. See: Lora Arduser and Amy Koerber, "Splitting Women, Producing Biocitizens, and Vilifying Obamacare in the 2012 Presidential Campaign," *Women's Studies in Communication* 37, no. 2 (2014): 117–137.

59. See: Shawn Parry-Giles, *Hillary Clinton in the News: Gender and Authenticity in American Politics* (Chicago: University of Illinois Press, 2014); Sara A. Mehltretter Drury & Rebecca A. Kuehl, "Introduction to the Special Issue on the Rhetoric of the 2016 U.S. Election," *Communication Quarterly* 66, no. 2 (2018): 111–116; Mary E. Stuckey, "The Changing Face of Presidential Campaigns: Editor's Introduction," *Quarterly Journal of Speech* 103, no. 1–2 (2017): 1–6; and, Mary E. Stuckey, "American Elections and the Rhetoric of Political Change: Hyperbole, Anger, and Hope in U.S. Politics," *Rhetoric & Public Affairs* 20, no. 4 (2017): 667–694.

60. See: Karrin Vasby Anderson "Presidential Pioneer or Campaign Queen?: Hillary Clinton and the First-Timer/Frontrunner Double Bind," *Rhetoric & Public Affairs* 20, no. 3 (2017): 525–538; Joe Edward Hatfield, "Toxic Identification: #Twinks4Trump and the Homonationalist Rearticulation of Queer Vernacular Rhetoric," *Communication Culture & Critique* 11, no. 1 (2018): 147–161; Roseann M. Mandziuk, "Dressing Down Hillary," *Communication and Critical/Cultural Studies* 5, no. 3 (2008): 312–316; Leroy G. Dorsey, "Managing Women's Equality: Theodore Roosevelt, the Frontier Myth, and the Modern Woman," *Rhetoric & Public Affairs* 16, no. 3 (2013): 423–456; and, Roger C. Aden, Kelsey Crowley, Erin Phillips, and Gretchen Weger, "Doubling Down: President Barack Obama's Doubled Persona after the Zimmerman Verdict," *Communication Studies* 67, no. 5 (2016): 605–622.

61. See: Mary E. Stuckey, "Rethinking the Rhetorical Presidency and Presidential Rhetoric," *Review of Communication* 10, no. 1 (2010): 38–52; and, Stephen J. Heidt, "The Presidency as Pastiche: Atomization, Circulation, and Rhetorical Instability," *Rhetoric & Public Affairs* 15, no. 4 (2012): 623–634.

62. Martin J. Medhurst, "The Contemporary Study of Public Address: Renewal, Recovery, and Reconfiguration," *Rhetoric & Public Affairs* 4, no. 3 (2001): 495–511.

63. Trevor Parry-Giles and Shawn Parry-Giles, "*The West Wing's* Prime-Time Presidentiality: Mimesis and Catharsis in a Postmodern Romance," *Quarterly Journal of Speech* 88, no. 2 (2002): 209–227.

64. See: J. David Cisneros, "Racial Presidentialities: Narratives of Latinxs in the 2016 Campaign," *Rhetoric & Public Affairs* 20, no. 3 (2017): 511–523; and, J. David Cisneros, "Marco Rubio's Prospective Presidentiality: Latinx Politics, Race/Ethnicity, and the Presidency," *Quarterly Journal of Speech* 103, no. 1–2 (2017): 90–116.

65. See: Cara A. Finnegan and Anita J. Mixon, "Art Controversy in the Obama White House: Performing Tensions of Race in the Visual Politics of the Presidency," *Presidential Studies Quarterly* 44, no. 2 (2014): 244–266.

66. See: Don Waisanen, "Comedian-In-Chief: Presidential Jokes as Enthymematic Crisis Rhetoric," *Presidential Studies Quarterly* 45, no. 2 (2015): 335–360.

67. See: Bryan Blankfield, "'A Symbol of His Warmth and Humanity': Fala, Roosevelt, and the Personable Presidency," *Rhetoric & Public Affairs* 19, no. 2 (2016): 209–244.

Reading the President through Institutions

CHAPTER ONE

Cartographer-in-Chief

Maps in Televisual Addresses and the Cold War President as Geographic Educator

TIMOTHY BARNEY

During a 1942 fireside chat, President Roosevelt implored American citizens during World War II to "look" at their maps as they followed along over the airwaves with his presentation of the geography of a new world reality.[1] Since then, maps have provided a sense of fixity and truth for modern presidents, as cartography has accompanied them at the highest levels of both foreign policy decision-making and public communication in American culture.[2] Maps have not been just an accompaniment to presidents—presidents have thought and articulated *through* maps. They serve as both symbolic, abstract representations of world space *and* as actual material, tangible, and usable documents, passed around, debated upon, drawn upon, and re-drawn upon. In the process, maps become guarantors of authenticity, often so trusted that they recede into the background, already accepted as faithful to the landscapes they are abstracting. In fact, as scholars of geography and cartography have posited, maps create both *sites* and *sights*—they mark particular "places" with ideological importance but also offer modes of vision for how the world should be seen.[3]

The Cold War, with its particular sites and sights, represents an especially compelling long era of geographic concepts, geopolitical language, and spatial images. Geographer Anders Stephanson has written that the Cold War is "war as an ideological, political, and economic claim to universality, taking place not in the two-dimensional space of traditional battles but mediated through other realms when not, as universality, actually eliminating space altogether."[4] If this is correct, then maps seem especially fitting as a medium for communicating the parameters of the presidency during the Cold War. The map is not burdened by necessarily being a referent of the "real" space of, say, Cambodia. In the process, the map can exist as a space invented by the president that has a tenuous relationship to Cambodia on the ground. This is not to make some postmodern claim that there is no "real" Cambodia; the U.S. troops ordered into action that crossed its border, not to mention the tens of thousands of Cambodian civilians killed, were traversing the very real ground of Cambodia. But the Cold War itself is predicated on such abstractions—faraway parts of the world can be brought into a universalized Cold War. Certainly, many did not accept the presidential logics of intervention that each of these nations was somehow a vital strategic space for American national security. But the point here is that President Nixon was able to enhance his case because of cartography's singular power. As historian Walter Hixson has written, "Simply put, the Cold War always was and still is a narrative discourse, not a reality. While the Berlin Wall, nuclear weapons, and the deaths of millions of people were all too real, to be sure, the way in which these phenomena are framed and interpreted can only be determined by representation."[5] Maps provide an important form of that representation, and we can appreciate them not as accompaniments to Cold War exigencies but as part of spatial ideologies that are deeply rooted in American political culture.

In this essay, I use cartographic examples from public pronouncements by presidents Kennedy, Nixon, and Reagan to show that the abstractions and geographic divisions of presidential maps in the Cold War are used to build *consent*. These presidents did not bring forward maps for a debate about space and geopolitics; they used maps as evidentiary weapons to affirm tacit approval of interventionist Cold War policies. But more than mere evidence, however, maps set the sights—the terms of perception—for Cold War ideologies. These maps spoke to the ideological character of a Cold War marked by containments, dominoes, and arcs of crisis. I argue, in the process, that maps marked the powerful ability of presidents to become cartographers-in-chief, physically and ideologically setting the boundaries around global imaginaries of space. Maps, in these cases, are potent forms of public address—uniquely situated, not as visual aids to the somehow more important "speech," but as media that perform ideological work that speech cannot do. Certainly, the content of each map is important, but the very *act* of reaching for cartographic visual rhetoric to explicate these "places" and presidential policy positions represents a Cold War performance of spatial control and authority. The very form of the map shares with audiences a history of rationality, scienticity, and order.

This essay, then, is grounded in that often unspoken impulse for Cold War presidents to reach for maps. We have no reason to believe that their choice to reach for such maps was particularly contentious or deliberated on with much vigor. In fact, we have more of a reason to believe that maps simply made sense in the situation—that for these executive leaders to teach geography to American citizens, maps were *the* resource to do so. Thus maps are often seemingly innocuous inventive resources. For example, in Richard B. Gregg's and Gerard A. Hauser's important study of President Nixon's address on the incursion in Cambodia, one unfamiliar with the address would never know that the president spends key parts of his speech working in front of a map—nowhere does this visual aid get mentioned in their otherwise insightful critique.[6] The map, even by rhetorical critics like Gregg and Hauser who are sensitive to what they call the "dramaturgical" functions of presidential rhetoric, is seen as a fairly straightforward accompaniment to the all-important words of presidential policy, content to exist merely as an aid. Map historian Alan Henrikson believes we underestimate the importance of geopolitical factors in international politics because "geographical factors have been considered 'part of the landscape'—a parameter rather than a variable."[7] This study, then, situates these maps as contingent rhetorical choices on the part of presidents and their advisors to make in the realm of public opinion.

In the process, I invoke a particular approach called "critical geopolitics" that assumes the geopolitical rhetoric of important leaders like presidents is part of a contentious discursive and ideological process that constructs global imaginaries for publics to contend with.[8] In the following sections, I start by outlining the power of cartography within this notion of a "critical geopolitics." I use this framework to explore three important cases of the Cold War-era cartographer-in-chief: (1) Kennedy's press conference in 1961 about Laos; (2) Nixon's controversial 1970 announcement of the "incursion" into Cambodia; and (3) Reagan's address from the Oval Office in 1986 on his administration's new policies toward Nicaragua. The three cases are marked by important contrasts in their international contexts and in presidential styles, but they are linked by a geopolitical visual rhetoric that uses abstract cartographic space to evidence the encroachment of communist forces. With such arguments, we should not assume a truth/falsification dynamic in maps—the president is not necessarily being deceitful in their use of maps. The tendency to label these kinds of political maps that a president may use in official discourse as *propaganda* seems not particularly useful, since it implies that more seemingly scientific and objective maps are somehow bereft of ideology.[9] In fact, these cases are more compelling if we assume that these presidents drew on maps as reliable and necessary media and saw them as faithful in communicating their foreign policy goals to the American public.

Presidential Rhetoric and Critical Geopolitics

During Reagan's so-called Second Cold War, scholars in an interdisciplinary project called "critical geopolitics" saw the resurgence of the politics of nuclear fear and arms build-up as an opportunity to reflect on the erasure of spaces on a global scale. The technologization and speed of the nuclear missile dramatically shrunk the notion of distance, and they believed that shift necessitated a new way of critiquing how leaders conceived of world space.[10] As one of critical geopolitics' innovators, Gearóid Ó Tuathail, wrote, "The scripting of the global scene by the former B-movie-actor president produced a geopolitics that was markedly televisual in its presentation and articulation. The cartographic supports Reagan employed in addresses to the nation featured patriotic blue space ('democratic' Central America) in conflict with foreign red space (Nicaragua and Cuba). The Soviet Union was scripted as the 'Evil Empire' in a tale of conflict between the forces of light and the forces of darkness. This teletraditional revival of the Cold War as the dominant spectacle in international politics and rewriting of global space in the name of 'geopolitics' provoked new interest in the functioning of the problematic of geopolitics."[11] Geopolitics was traditionally treated as either a gentlemanly chess game of power balances or a pejorative pseudo-science related to Nazi geographers like Karl Haushofer.[12] In both of those cases, geopolitics involved a "systematic forgetting of the struggle over geography," and so the new scholars sought to situate geopolitics as a historical problem that required a more nuanced treatment of the relationship between time and space.[13] In the process, critical geopoliticians positioned geography itself as a discursive process.

In applying this lens of critical geopolitics to how presidents used maps in the Cold War, we must make a few assumptions. The first is that, over the course of the twentieth century, a "global imaginary" was constructed and articulated by U.S. leaders to ensure consent for foreign policies. Christina Klein has defined a global imaginary as an "ideological creation that maps the world conceptually and defines the primary relations among peoples, nations, and regions. As an imaginative, discursive construct, it represents the abstract entity of the 'world'; as a coherent, comprehensible whole and situates individual nations within that larger framework. … In reducing the infinite complexity of the world to comprehensible terms, it creates a common sense about how the world functions as a system and offers implicit instruction in how to maneuver within that system."[14] Through a consistent dissemination of geopolitical rhetoric and place-making images by leaders, Americans receive a kind of geographic education from both official and popular discourse that is infused with the ideological values of American national identity vis-à-vis the so-called rest of the world. Particular *places* such as Cambodia,

Laos, and Nicaragua are imbued with particular political purposes and characters that fit into coherent and progressive world narratives.[15]

A related assumption in this essay's analysis is the increasing capacity of the presidency to define geography and spatial meaning for U.S. citizens. The American president plays a uniquely important role in cultivating a global imaginary. John O'Loughlin and Richard Grant, for example, have empirically studied the post-WWII rise of presidential place-making and geographic education in State of the Union speeches and have found that "presidents attempt to define the 'vague and shifting environment' in their speeches and, through the use of adjectives, graphs, maps, historical analogies, and future scenarios, try to indicate by the facts as they see and present them."[16] But those "facts" are complex discourses, as "geopolitical images are important not because they accurately portray reality but because they interpret or express the intentions of certain powerful policymakers. The 'spheres,' 'dominos,' 'arcs,' and 'chains' that crop up as geographic images in international relations must be understood against the background of political images of individual states."[17] At the same time, presidential speeches on foreign policy that teach geography, according to Colin Flint et al, "are used to portray the United States as a benevolent political power," "identify particular threats or dangers, and classify regions and countries in colourful terms that imply particularly necessary, if not inevitable, actions."[18] Thus, portrayals of seemingly peripheral "places" such as Cambodia, Nicaragua, and Laos take on deeper significance, as each is cast with a broader ideological character. Robert J. McMahon has noted the tendency for Cold War presidents to equate American self-interests with the interests of the rest of the world, particularly in the areas that the U.S. deemed strategically important.[19] And increasingly, the Cold War's East/West orientations opened up to North/South ones. The landscapes of each strategic place were "fixed" by the president as having certain innate qualities, and that fixing took important rhetorical work on the president's part to reach back to geography's own narrative of itself as a natural science. For the three cases analyzed here, the president is making a case at least for international vigilance and elevated involvement, if not outright interventionist and military engagement in the Third World. And despite the internationalized orientation of postwar U.S. leaders, presidents still recognized that, in Klein's terms, "The American public needed to be schooled in internationalism: it needed to be persuaded to accept the nation's sustained engagement in world affairs, its participation in international organizations, and its long-range cooperation with other governments."[20] The president increasingly served that role during the Cold War.

What maps also do in this situation is reinforce Cold War "territorialities." Martin Lewis and Karen Wigen have written of the problematic "myth of continents" in the Cold War, where particular qualities are powerfully associated with the age-old groupings of Europe, Africa, Asia etc.[21] Within this geopolitical discourse of the Cold War, reinforced by centuries of increasingly statist thinking, was the fact that "new technology had so narrowed the gap between nations that developments half a world away could, as never before, vitally affect national security."[22] Dean Rusk understood this accepted geopolitical fact that "If you don't pay attention to the periphery, the periphery changes. And the first thing you know the periphery is the center."[23] The global imaginary of containment was, thus, a perfect fit for maps as a central medium, as it could forcefully portray, according to Klein, a "clear global identity and role for the U.S." while demarcating the spaces of infiltration and the systematic control of that infiltration.[24]

The three ensuing cases demonstrate how the president's position as an "official" interlocutor of American power and the employment of cartography enhance each other on the televisual stage. The map-making process is often concealed, in what map critics Ben and Marthalee Barton call the "suppression of the act of production"—only the immediacy of that cartographic image remains, and thus it can easily be "complicit with social-control mechanisms inextricably linked to power and authority."[25] Indeed, each time the presidents invoke maps as evidence, they construct the maps' usefulness as self-evident. The scientific, historical, and cultural power of the cartographic form weighs heavily before the viewer even engages with the idea of, say, Laos and its strategic position on the globe. In the process, the map's prestige is elevated by the prestigious image of the presidency.

Kennedy, Laos, and the "Victim of Geography"

At a State Department press conference on March 23, 1961, *The New York Times* noted that "Mr. Kennedy was unusually serious in manner," and he met reporters with a prepared statement rather than his usual improvisatory engagement with questions.[26] Not a little drama was involved, too, as a large metal map stand, mounted on rubber wheels, had been mysteriously cloaked in white cloth until seconds before Kennedy began. Uncovered by State Department press spokesman Lincoln White, the stand housed three enormous maps of Laos, six by eight feet apiece.[27] What brought Kennedy to the podium and screens that evening was a complex matrix of events. The Eisenhower administration had situated Laos as a kind of buffer zone between China and North Vietnam, but the position was more than precarious. A communist-dominated force called the Pathet Lao, led by Souphanouverong, was gaining a series of victories across the Laos/North Vietnam border, while Eisenhower had thrown in his lot with the unpopular General Nosavan Phoumi. A third force, led by the neutralist Souvanna Phouma (and

Souphanouverong's half-brother), was in exile but still commanded loyal support. The SEATO treaty was designed to aid in these situations, but the outgoing Eisenhower administration could not get the other main signatories like France and the U.K. to consider military action. In addition, the SEATO nations did not support Phoumi, and favored Phouma instead, leaving the U.S. in a potentially unilateral position. Before Kennedy stepped into the State Department auditorium, then, he had a lose-lose choice of taking unpopular military action or making an about-face and supporting a neutral Laos—the position he ultimately ended up taking at the press conference.[28] At the same time, the neutralist policy was to be backed, as William J. Rust put it, with a "thinly veiled threat of intervention."[29]

Enough substantial evidence suggests that Laos was of significant geopolitical, ideological, and security-related import, at least to Kennedy's inner circle. According to historian Usha Manajani, Kennedy saw Laos as a kind of "prestige project"—with the potential "humiliation of the West" as a prime motivator in the operative domino theory of his maps.[30] Theodore Sorensen suggested that Kennedy spent more time on Laos than any other issue in his first hundred days.[31] Seen in light of the concurrent and overlapping Vietnam crisis, Noam Kochavi noted the "seriousness of the challenge Laos posed for the New Frontiersmen. Mountainous, chaotic, and land-locked, Laos was a foreboding theater for American military intervention."[32] There was irony in a strong geographic argument being made for a nation that did not have a very strong geographic identity—it was no wonder the Office of the Historian of the Department of State referred to Laos as a "victim of geography."[33] Carved from the 1954 Geneva accords that partitioned a postcolonial Southeast Asia, the land of 91,000 square miles had less than 3 million people spread over its rural landscapes. A 1960 RAND study noted that Laos was only a "formal political entity" and was

> neither a geographic nor an ethnic unit and it does not constitute a viable economic entity. If it be assumed that among the essential characteristics of a modern national state are ethnic homogeneity, shared traditions, geographic unity, effective internal administration, economic viability, borders accepted by other nations, diplomatic recognition by neighboring states, representation in the United Nations, and the positive support of its inhabitants, it must be said that Laos lacks most of these characteristics.[34]

The Ambassador to Laos, Winthrop G. Brown, reflected bluntly that

> Laos was hopeless. It was described by one of my colleagues as being a classic example of a political and economic vacuum. It had no national identity. It was just a series of lines on a map, with more Lao in Thailand than there are in Laos. Plus, less than half the people speak Lao. They're charming, indolent, enchanting people, but they're just not very vigorous, nor are they very numerous, nor are they very well organized.[35]

The RAND report and Brown's words exemplify the era's liberal, paternalistic geopolitical discourses used by the president in his speech. In addition, those involved wondered, often in geographic terms, if Laos could truly be transformed into a place that was a convincing linchpin of the domino theory—Laos, in many ways, had to be actively constituted through media, like maps, as strategically significant in the Cold War.

On each of the three maps, the mass of Southeast Asia was a light brown, allowing nations like China, Burma, and Thailand to recede into the background. The majority of Laos is colored in a bright white, but is off-center, with the main focus, particularly on the last map of 22 March 1961, being the dark maroonish red of the communist advance in the country. The maps are unsophisticated but direct—the writing looks like it was neatly drawn in magic marker rather than printed through stencil, giving viewers at home a feeling of almost being in an intimate board room setting with the president. One must almost squint to see the red of the "rebel areas" on the first map (7 August 1960), with little dips in the northeast corners of Laos. The second map makes a significant leap (20 December 1960) by drawing in a large part of eastern Laos with dark red, as it looks as if North Vietnam is engulfing Laos in communism. However, the big "reveal" comes with the third map—less than four months later for 22 March 1961, an enormous portion of white-colored Laos is painted red. From the perspective of those seeing this revelation over black-and-white television, the black ink and the jagged lines of Laos borders resemble a rotting tooth getting worse. Luang Prabang appears next to fall—the country's symbolic royal heart—and the enthymematic reference is that another four months would see an exponential increase in communist red. An earlier draft of Kennedy's speech originally required only two maps showing the difference in communist advancement, but a marking by Kennedy's pen makes clear the preference for a third map to make the case of steady and alarming growth.[36]

In the speech, Kennedy points to the maps from his podium as his assistants dramatically turn his map displays. Importantly, despite the enormity of the displays, the focus remains on Kennedy, with the maps forming an evidentiary resource behind him. While the map is only referred to in one section, Kennedy draws on the maps' credibility for the rest of the speech, *inscribing* his policies onto the ground for viewers. Given the power of containment ideology and the promotion of American missionary internationalism abroad not just in policy circles but in popular culture, the president can merely show the advances of communism in one "place" and viewers will understand the argument that such movements can affect everyday Americans. Showing communism as a potent, mobile force, moving against allies asserts the need to redouble the national effort to contain and control the toxic ideology. While not all will agree on Laos's significance or the efficacy of intervention, the use of the map as a non-ideological symbol to depict the danger goes unquestioned. Kennedy was nationalizing Laos, writing it with the familiar qualities of nations, even though Laos was by no means acting as a typical nation at that point. Robert Amory, a deputy director of the CIA for Kennedy, worried that,

> I tried to point out to people how empty the damn country is. I wrote part of the speech that Kennedy gave to the nation very early in his administration where he used three maps of Laos ... and I put in it that everybody talked about "little Laos." Laos is actually as ... big as Italy. But whereas Italy has forty-five or fifty million people in it, Laos has two million. There are more tigers and water buffalo in Laos than there are people. So it's a great empty land; you've got to think in those terms. It isn't a nice little place. And Kennedy changed the analogy to three times as big as Austria. He wanted to pick a neutral country, he told me. And you know, his expertise of style, just what will be dramatic, and you pick up what is a fair simile or metaphor or figure of speech, and he had a better one.[37]

Even though the president explicitly says that he supports neutrality because he does not want Laos "to be a pawn in the cold war," his map presentation, with empty space steadily shaded in by communism, makes Laos precisely that.

Journalist and critic Bernard Fall, who covered the press conference, was unsparing in his critique of Kennedy's maps, believing that they grossly misrepresented what was actually a much worse situation in Laos.[38] As he wrote later,

> the three maps shown by President Kennedy at his press conference of March 23, 1961, which purported to show the progressively worsening situation in Laos, were so grossly inaccurate in their optimism as to be completely meaningless. At a time when most of the Laotian uplands were more or less under Communist control, the map purporting to show the "present" situation gave the Communists credit for holding only parts of three provinces and one small isolated spot around Kam Kheut. The question remains open as to whether the inaccuracy was deliberate (so as not to worry public opinion) or whether the research services which provided the maps for the President were fooled as well.[39]

While Fall holds the president to a particular standard of accuracy, his comments are perhaps more important in their assessment of cartography's role in the engagement with public opinion. What Fall misses is the idea that the very *display* of maps of Laos was just as important as the content. Kennedy's performance implied an understanding of cartography's role in the engagement with public opinion. Seeing the familiar lines of the maps, regardless of their accuracy, provided an educational anchor and an emotional immediacy to Kennedy's audiences—a certainty to hold onto in a complex and nebulous situation.

The very recourse of a president reaching for a map is ideologically important, as Cold War containment was an actual practice where lines had to be drawn. Kenneth Young, the ambassador to Thailand, was in the room for many discussions with Kennedy and other leaders, and he worried that

> the issue of Laos was being discussed in the Cabinet Room as just one piece of real estate plucked out of the map and stuck over there without much relationship to Vietnam or Thailand or China, and we didn't really ever bring China into this picture—you know, the interests of China, the whole thing. And Vietnam again became separate, just like Thailand. This has been the weakness of American policy in Southeast Asia from the very start.[40]

As Kennedy stood in front of his tripartite map stand, he transformed Laos into a repository for communist ideology and thus an affirmation of U.S. foreign policy. The problem of using maps as shorthand for dividing and re-drawing nations was that a state could become a decontextualized puzzle piece where powerful men have a simplified but profound bird's eye view over the material landscape and can synthesize unruly spaces into a coherent whole. Such an exchange – moving international problems from complex to simple – enabled the creation and justification of policies that fit the decontextualized parameters of the map but could never solve the problems that generated the need for maps in the first place.

"As You See Here on the Map": Nixon's Cartography of Cambodia

Nine years and a month after Kennedy's press conference, President Nixon reached for maps in a major national address, this time using them for the rollout of direct military escalation. Like Kennedy, Nixon saw what he called an "incursion" into Cambodia as a prestige project, one in which the image of his presidency loomed just as large as the image of the casualties that could result from his actions. But the context of Cambodia in the shambles of the Vietnam War dictated much greater stakes than what Kennedy faced in 1961. In March 1970, the neutralist Prince Norodom Sihanouk was overthrown in a coup by his own Prime Minister Lon Nol and his deputy Sisowath Sirik Matak. Nol's hard line was that the North Vietnamese must withdraw from their base camps along the South Vietnamese border, which plunged the country into Civil War and incited the North Vietnamese to move even farther west.[41] These actions forced a response by Nixon, who wanted to make a decisive show of support for the new pro-western regime of Nol and to effectively stop the North Vietnamese.[42]

Pat Buchanan wrote the initial draft of the speech, but the president took over in the drafting process and made it his own, despite vocal protest from his closest advisors.[43] The president had a resolute mission to make this speech a kind of symbolic line in the sand, an act that historian James A. Tyner has called a "performance of geopolitical machismo."[44] On the afternoon of April 30, hours before giving the speech, Secretary of Defense Melvin Laird strongly recommended that the president

> remove from the text all mention of COSVN (Hanoi's central office for South Vietnam) as a key target of the operation. Laird tried to explain to presidential aides that the COSVN shown on the map of Cambodia in the briefings given them by the Pentagon was no fortified bastion, no single entity, but a floating, amorphous command that slithered from one place to another in Cambodian jungles near the border of South Vietnam.[45]

However, according to Hal Bochin, Nixon "apparently felt that mentioning the headquarters dramatized his rationale for the operation" and he would not delete it from his speech.[46] President Nixon believed he had to instantiate the enemy, then, as a targetable geographic "place" for American viewers even if the reality was much more complex. This task helps explain why maps were seen as an essential accompaniment to the address, as they could help make this into a traditional strategic war when it was shaping up to be anything but.

The speech would reach an enormous audience of at least 60 million U.S. television viewers, giving presidential maps some of the biggest exposure they would ever receive.[47] The president becomes head geographer for the American people first when he instructs that "Cambodia—a small country of seven million people—has been a neutral nation since the Geneva Agreement of 1954, an agreement, incidentally, which was signed by the government of North Vietnam. ... North Vietnam, however, has not respected that neutrality." Then, Nixon gestures with his arm, and the camera cuts to a close-up of the map, as he notes: "For the past five years, as indicated on this map, that you see here, North Vietnam has occupied military sanctuaries all along the Cambodian frontier with South Vietnam. Some of these extend up to 20 miles into Cambodia." As he speaks next, the camera cuts to a wide shot of Nixon standing at the easel, indicating that "The sanctuaries are in red, and as you note, they are on both sides of the border." The camera cuts back to a close-up of the map, while Nixon moves to sit and adds that, "They are used for hit-and-run attacks on American and South Vietnamese forces in South Vietnam. These Communist-occupied territories contain major base camps, training sites, logistics facilities, weapons and ammunition factories, airstrips, and prisoner of war compounds."[48] By listing each of the extensive functions of the sanctuaries, the president is able to transform these bases into specific *places*, generating them not as loose blobs on the map, but instantiating them as highly systemic and organized.

The map of Cambodia is drawn in a deep, mustard-like color, with South Vietnam and Thailand in a more primary yellow, while Laos and North Vietnam are in a light brown, so as to fade them from view. The eye's focus goes to the dots of red along the border of Cambodia and South Vietnam. During Nixon's close-up, the viewers can see the red blobs on both sides of the border. The expected dividing lines of the map are violated by an almost sickly rash of unwanted invasions. Geographer Mark Monmonier has called color a "cartographic quagmire," where color contrasts between places on maps can create emotional connections—red, for example, can run the spectrum from "fire, warning, heat, blood anger, courage, power love, material force, and communism."[49] Whether or not the color of Nixon's maps had the same interpretations from audiences, Nixon was able to use color to stipulate an acceptable range of interpretations through contrasts.

As the president speaks with the map, he punctuates his geographic lesson several times with the pronouncement "as you see here on this map," a subtle but important appeal to the self-evidence of the map. Nixon draws on the often unquestioned power of the cartographic image to be read the same way by his diverse audiences, and does not open up the map to multiple interpretations or alternative evidence. In addition, the president's gestures become a key part of the presentation. Nixon rises from the protective armor of the desk to come forward and actually "teach" the map. At a crucial juncture in the speech where Nixon lays out the possible options, he implores Americans to "Let us go to the map again. Here is South Vietnam. Here is North Vietnam." Using his finger to trace, he says,

> North Vietnam already occupies this part of Laos. If North Vietnam also occupied this whole band of Cambodia, or the entire country, it would mean that South Vietnam was completely outflanked and the forces of Americans in this area as well as the South Vietnamese would be in an untenable military position.[50]

The map is not merely displayed behind him, but is, significantly, approached by and worked through the president. The abstract space of Cambodia is associated with Nixon's own corporeal presence—the concrete and the abstract combined together. He lets Americans *into* the spaces of strategy, thus creating the appearance of a kind of transparency.

The speech was one of the most controversial and peculiar of interventionist presidential addresses. In *The New Yorker*, Jonathan Schell offered that,

> On the evening of the invasion, when the President went to his map to show the American people where Cambodia is ('Here is South Vietnam, here is North Vietnam,' etc.), we felt that we were being given a geography lesson by military invasion. We don't want to learn about our brothers on the earth in this way.[51]

While in the space of that geographic lesson, Nixon commanded "perception" by situating maps as a rational actor drawing on the self-evident power of cartographic images. Outside that space the perception of those images did not necessarily correspond to the global imaginary that many Americans were formulating of the Vietnam War. The simplified presentation of this map belied a cartographic silence around the complicated position facing the U.S. mission in Southeast Asia during a period when public opinion was deeply divided. As Michael H. Hunt has written,

> The American tendency to see the world as simple and pliable has been reinforced by geopolitics, with its conception of the globe as a chessboard, neatly demarcated and easily controlled by anyone with enough strong pieces and the proper strategy. But the world, complex and slow to change, has resisted our efforts to impose our will and enforce our rules. We have known the bewilderment of the chess master who discovers that in fact no square is like another, that pawns often disturbingly assume a life of their own, and that few contests are neatly two-sided.[52]

A mere five days after Nixon's speech, four students at Kent State University lay dead from National Guard gunfire in the wake of a demonstration against U.S. actions in Cambodia. Certainly, cartography could still be marshaled at the highest levels for the purpose of strategy, but its ideological function as a contested discursive process had become, arguably, more complex in the U.S. move toward international intervention in the spaces of the so-called Third World. By this time, with the United States in the throes of the conflict in Vietnam, the weight of what maps *could not* order, classify, and simplify in the Cold War was just as heavy as the weight of what maps could.

The "Backyard" and Reagan's Mapping of Central America

One of President Reagan's central tasks was to be the chief geographic educator around all things Central America during his two terms. Again, like Nixon and Kennedy, Reagan associated his presidential prestige with particular *places*, and he reached for maps of Central America to the make the case for American strength. In 1981, Jeane Kirkpatrick, Reagan's ambassador to the United Nations, famously described Central America as "the most important place in the world for the United States today."[53] In many ways, during the so-called Second Cold War, Reagan revived the flagging geopolitical vocabulary of the Cold War, using Central America as a key test case for this rhetoric.[54] The resurgence of the domino theory marked the president's approach, as he drew on a longstanding hemispheric conception of Latin America as a "backyard" and coupled it with the frame of Soviet expansionism.[55] For historian Walter LaFeber,

> The rewriting of history was of special importance. After the experiences of Vietnam, many North Americans were reluctant to become involved in another indigenous revolution. The new administration and its supporters tried to circumvent that problem by declaring, in the president's words, that the Vietnam conflict was a 'noble cause,' and—more important—that the problems in Central America were not indigenous but caused by Castro and the Soviet Union.[56]

Maps were able to connote this ideological influence as being imposed by the outside, a much easier cartographic picture to frame than a homegrown revolution upending the region's entire socio-political system.

Reagan's 1986 national television address on Nicaragua affirmed this power. As Reagan constructed an argument about the need to fund anti-Sandinista movements in Nicaragua, he drew upon the familiar form of the map. But differently than Kennedy and Nixon, Reagan was able to draw on the increasingly technologized methods of cartography. Here, Reagan begins his appeal to the American public by explaining the deteriorating situation in Nicaragua and the increased geopolitical threat to the United States' national security. Then, he introduces a map, not by the usual standing and gesturing or using a pointer, but by having the camera transition to an animated map. Now, Reagan is more like the trusted news anchor bringing sophisticated graphics into his clear and self-evident presentation of geographic facts. It is no wonder political scientist Timothy W. Luke wrote of "screens of power" precisely during the Reagan era. He called Reagan "television's most consummate talking head," as the president was uniquely able to merge his own charismatic narrative into the spectacle of television—and the map was one vehicle for this.[57] The animation begins with North, Central and South America unmarked by text, except notably with the U.S. marked with a large "U.S.A." in white, and the continent in a neutral orange-brown color. Reagan, true to a hemispheric kind of perspective that was still operable even in the late Cold War, refers to what his audience is looking at as the "Western Hemisphere."[58] Then, the countries of Central America are brought forward into the foreground and the rest of the map drops away. Nicaragua is now notated with text and colored in an almost neon red. The president then proceeds to list the countries where Sandinista weapons have been found, and the map matches that list by a cascade of countries lighting up: Honduras, Costa Rica, El Salvador, Guatemala.

Shortly after, another map is shown that does the same kind of cascade of red across South America, as Reagan accuses Nicaraguan communists of providing "military training, safe haven, communications, false documents, safe transit, and sometimes, weapons to radicals" across Colombia, Ecuador, Brazil, Chile, and even the Dominican Republic.[59] Late in the address, Reagan returns to the map, with Nicaragua lit up, and both the U.S. and South America half visible—large white arrows are used to simply and starkly show how much trade, oil, and even military supplies cross through a dangerous area that could be closed off by communists. Such arrows powerfully control the directionality of America's economic, social, and political influence and that of, vice versa, Soviet influence.

Throughout the entire speech, and not just while the maps are shown, President Reagan uses a variety of "place" metaphors to describe the spread of communism across the region because of Nicaraguan influence: the Soviets are using Nicaragua as a "base," the U.S.S.R. will have a "beachhead" in North America, the arrival of terror at the "doorstep of the United States" is mentioned multiple times, and then "safehouse," "sanctuary," "command post" for harboring radicals.[60] As Paul A. Chilton has written, the container metaphors are a hallmark of explaining Cold War national security, and they are inherently spatial; in Reagan's address, the bleak images of these communist bulwarks in his verbal rhetoric work alongside the visuality of clearly defined statist borders being lit up entirely by red.[61] Each of these nations-as-bases becomes simplified, negative blank space on the map. For Roxanne Lynn Doty,

> Negation has constructed various regions making up the 'third world' as blank spaces waiting to be filled in by Western writing. ... Within these blank spaces the West may write such things as civilization, progress, modernization, and democracy. Imperial encounters become missions of deliverance and salvation rather than conquests and exploitation.[62]

In this sense, Reagan's concern for security, and his demonstration of this through maps, is much more than the protection of economic or military interests, it is ideological in nature, and is deeply felt and believed.

Finally, Reagan's address makes maps simply one part of a persuasive arsenal of evidentiary weapons. At one point, before launching into a list of incendiary quotes by Nicaraguan and Soviet leaders, the president says he uses these quotes only "if maps, statistics, and facts aren't persuasive enough."[63] Here, rather than just a background setting at which to occaisonally point, the map becomes part of the presidential storehouse of active images that the president can draw upon. Reagan's almost newsmanly quality draws maps into a kind of multimediated showcase in getting self-evident support for American foreign policy. Ronald Reagan has often been called the first "hyperreal" president, where the image of the actorly, rugged, and telegenic leader begins to lack a "real" referent behind his representation.[64] While all presidents can in some senses be considered hyperreal, the slippage between the real and the image with Reagan becomes particularly difficult for viewers and audiences to parse out, and thus much of what we react and engage with is the president's image. Again, Ó Tuathail sums up this concept well, in writing that

> The very shape of the post-war world was determined, in large part, on the basis of a fantastic reality organized around an immanent Soviet 'threat' to the West and an idealized vision of 'modernization' in what became known as the 'Third World.' The principle of hyperreality merely reached a grand apotheosis in the Reagan years with, on one hand, hyperreal *threats* from Nicaragua (a nation of 3 million), the window of vulnerability (a non-existent nuclear Achilles heel) and terrorism (which claimed fewer deaths than lightning in 1985) and, following on from these, the hyperreal *solutions* of the *contra* 'freedom-fighting founding fathers', the MX 'peacekeeper', 'Star Wars' and spectacular 'surgical strikes' (as if bombing were clean).[65]

While no doubt there were serious on-the-ground implications to the administration's policies in Central America, Reagan's mapping is part of a cleanly drawn, surface-driven image strategy to construct a particular arc that would affirm the rightness of Reagan's spatialization of the world.

Conclusion

In these brief moments of geopolitical education, the president enacts an idealized version of the statist model even in cases where that model may not be viable. For geographer Matthew Sparke, the "isolated, iconic space of the national map" is part of "the enframing effect of cartography" that "contributes to the concealment of the state's precariousness."[66] For the three cartographers-in-chief, their maps do not contain nuanced geographical information nor do they contain complex acknowledgments of the human costs of intervention. While Roosevelt asked Americans to grab their own maps and follow along over the audio waves of the radio, presidents Kennedy, Nixon, and Reagan curated and presented maps for public consumption specifically through TV, making the televisual experience in these cases a crucial part of the geopolitical power at play. The presidential office's authority of spatial definition combines with the disciplinary power of cartography to form unique rhetorical moments of geopolitical consent in the mass media.

For many viewers, their one experience of Laos or Nicaragua might be through a highly managed geopolitical definition given to them by the president over television. Cartography, thus, brings a degree of credibility and self-evidence, as if viewers are being drawn into the deliberations of the map-room with advisors. In the Cold War, presidents' use of maps allowed the public into the official spaces of diplomacy. Such use of maps simulates the foreign policy decision-making process, while stopping short of involving citizens in the actual process.

Within this simulation, a good portion of these maps are empty white space, as if this is an empty container to *fill* with American power, or a clean surface by which to traverse with military and economic might. The national territories presented by the president are divorced from anything beyond their regional networks, disembodied from their connections with the larger world. As Doreen Massey has noted, the problem with thinking of space as a "surface" on maps is that it allows geographic areas to be seen "without their own trajectories, their own particular histories, and the potential for their own, perhaps different futures. ... They are merely at an earlier stage in the one and only narrative it is possible to tell."[67] In this way, "surfaces" like Laos, Cambodia, and Nicaragua serve as blank and open spaces on the map that are always in the process of "becoming." In Roxanne Doty's terms,

> Many of the encounters between the North and the South have been occasions for the North to gather "facts," define and monitor situations and problems, and subsequently enact policies deriving from those "facts" and definitions. Surveillance renders subjects knowable, visible objects of disciplinary power.[68]

Within these presidential addresses, the map quite literally *surfaces* parts of the world and allows presidents to think of these areas as containable and classifiable.

These seemingly ephemeral moments in presidential communication are important precisely because they recede so easily into the background and become part of the taken-for-granted mythos of the presidency's power. Public address critics can reach back to these usually shadowed moments of a mere easel being uncovered, or a map being pointed at during a press conference, or a camera cutting to a close-up of a strategic region in the world. Rhetoricians certainly understand the contingency of those moments and can appreciate the politics of what it means to activate visual rhetoric into a presentation, but perhaps they can do more to foreground the constructed geopolitics of the modern world and the ways in which presidents call forward consent based on seemingly "natural" geographic precepts. Gearóid Ó Tuathail wrote that,

> The geopolitical gaze triangulates the world political map from a Western imperial vantage point, measures it using Western conceptual systems of identity/difference,

and records it in order to bring it within the scope of Western imaginings. … In sighting a world within the terms of Western forms of knowledge, geopolitics is siting it within the desires and fantasies of a privileged community of "wise men" and also citing it within the textual tropes and discursive contours of hegemonic centers of knowledge and learning.[69]

There is no better reminder that the world-making powers of U.S. presidents are constructed *with* and *through* the lines, shapes, and colors of maps and the knowledge they create on the page and in the world.

Notes

1. Franklin D. Roosevelt, "Fighting Defeatism: February 23, 1942," in *FDR's Fireside Chats*, eds. Russell D. Buhite and David W. Levy (Norman: University of Oklahoma Press, 1992), 207–208.

2. Besides the three examples of Kennedy, Nixon, and Reagan used in this essay, several other examples of presidents drawing on cartography have entered into political lore. The end of the Cold War, for example, saw George H. W. Bush using maps to make sense of a changing global landscape. During his November 1989 ad-hoc press conference in the Oval Office in response to the dismantling of the Berlin Wall, Bush gestured often to a State Department map of Cold War Germany, even tapping on the map to emphasize his points about a "whole and free Europe" coming to fruition. See James Der Derian, "All but War is Simulation," in *Rethinking Geopolitics*, eds. Gearóid Ó Tuathail and Simon Dalby (London: Routledge, 1998), 261–273. A month later, at the Malta Conference, Bush and Gorbachev fought about the accuracy of U.S. military encirclement of the Soviets over a world map. See Alan K. Henrikson, "The Power and Politics of Maps," in *Reordering the World: Geopolitical Perspectives on the 21st Century*, eds. George J. Demko and William B. Wood (Boulder, CO: Westview Press, 1994), 57. Years later, Bush's son, George W. Bush, was photographed at Camp David talking over a map of Afghanistan during a briefing with CIA Director George Tenet and National Security Adviser Condoleeza Rice. See Central Intelligence Agency, "CIA Cartography," Flickr Account, accessed June 1, 2017, https://www.flickr.com/photos/ciagov/collections/72157674854602812/. Finally, most recently, in a *New York Times* piece from February 2017, reporters profiled the kinds of changes to the intelligence briefing process that members of the new Trump administration were implementing. The *Times* noted, "And while Mr. Obama liked policy option papers that were three to six single-spaced pages, council staff members are now being told to keep papers to a single page, with lots of graphics and maps. 'The president likes maps,' one official said." See David E. Sanger, Eric Schmitt, and Peter Baker, "Turmoil at the National Security Council, From the Top Down," *New York Times*, 12 February 2017, https://www.nytimes.com/2017/02/12/us/politics/national-security-council-turmoil.html?_r=0.

3. These arguments are expanded in greater detail in Timothy Barney, *Mapping the Cold War: Cartography and the Framing of America's International Power* (Chapel Hill: University of North Carolina Press, 2015).

4. Anders Stephanson, "Fourteen Notes on the Very Concept of the Cold War," in *Rethinking Geopolitics*, 83.

5. Walter L. Hixson, *The Myth of American Diplomacy: National Identity and U.S. Foreign Policy* (New Haven, CT: Yale University Press, 2008), 166.

6. Richard B. Gregg and Gerard A. Hauser, "Richard Nixon's April 30, 1970 Address on Cambodia: The 'Ceremony' of Confrontation," *Speech Monographs* 40 (1973): 167-81.

7. Alan K. Henrikson, "The Geographical 'Mental Maps' of Foreign Policy Makers," *International Political Science Review* 1, no. 4 (1980): 495-530.

8. The classic text on "critical geopolitics" is Gearóid Ó Tuathail, *Critical Geopolitics* (Minneapolis: University of Minnesota Press, 1996), but a collection of essays published shortly after is important too: Gearóid Ó Tuathail and Simon Dalby, eds., *Rethinking Geopolitics* (London: Routledge, 1998). See also John Agnew, *Geopolitics: Re-visioning World Politics*, 2nd ed. (New York: Routledge, 2003).

9. John Pickles, "Text, Hermeneutics, and Propaganda Maps," in *Writing Worlds: Discourse, Text & Metaphor in the Representation of Landscape*, eds. Trevor J. Barnes and James S. Duncan (London: Routledge, 1992), 193–230.

10. See especially Simon Dalby, *Creating the Second Cold War: The Discourse of Politics* (London: Pinter, 1990).

11. Ó Tuathail, *Critical Geopolitics*, 59.

12. See James Sidaway, "Geopolitics: Twentieth Century Spectre," *Geography* 86, no.3 (2001): 225–234.

13. Ó Tuathail, *Critical Geopolitics*, 53.

14. Christina Klein, *Cold War Orientalism: Asia in the Middlebrow Imagination, 1945-1961* (Berkeley: University of California Press, 2003), 22–23.

15. See especially David J. Sylvan and Stephen J. Majeski, "Rhetorics of Place Characteristics in High-Level U.S. Foreign Policy Making," in *Post-Realism: The Rhetorical Turn in International Relations*, eds. Francis A. Beer and Robert Hariman (East Lansing: Michigan State University Press, 1996), 309–29.

16. John O'Loughlin and Richard Grant, "The Political Geography of Presidential Speeches, 1946-87," *Annals of the Association of American Geographers* 80, no.4 (1990): 504-530.

17. O'Loughlin and Grant, "The Political Geography of Presidential Speeches," 507.

18. Colin Flint, Michael Adduci, Michael Chen, and Sang-Hyun Chi, "Mapping the Dynamism of the United States' Geopolitical Code: The Geography of the State of the Union Speeches, 1988-2008," *Geopolitics* 14, no.4 (2009): 604-629.

19. See the overview in Robert J. McMahon, "'By Helping Others, We Help Ourselves': The Cold War Rhetoric of American Foreign Policy," in *Critical Reflections on the Cold War: Linking Rhetoric and History*, eds. Martin J. Medhurst and H. W. Brands (College Station: Texas A&M University Press, 2000), 233–246.

20. Klein, *Cold War Orientalism*, 28.

21. Martin W. Lewis and Karen E. Wigen, *The Myth of Continents: A Critique of Metageography* (Berkeley: University of California Press, 1997).

22. Michael H. Hunt, *Ideology and U.S. Foreign Policy* (New Haven: Yale University Press, 1987), 152.

23. Dean Rusk, "Rusk Press Conference May 4, 1961," *Department of State Bulletin* 44 (May 22, 1961): 763.

24. Klein, *Cold War Orientalism*, 36.
25. Ben F. Barton and Marthalee S. Barton, "Ideology and the Map: Toward a Postmodern Visual Design Practice," in *Professional Communication: The Social Perspective*, eds. Nancy Roundy Blyler and Charlotte Thralls (Newbury Park, CA: Sage, 1993), 53, 64.
26. W. H. Lawrence, "Kennedy Alerts Nation on Laos; Warns Soviet Bloc, Asks Truce; Stresses SEATO's Role in Crisis," *New York Times*, March 24, 1961, 1. https://www.nytimes.com/1961/03/24/archives/kennedy-alerts-nation-on-laos-warns-soviet-bloc-asks-truce-stresses.html.
27. W. H. Lawrence, "Kennedy Alerts Nation on Laos," 7.
28. See Office of the Historian of the Department of State, "The Laos Crisis, 1960–1963," October 31, 2013, https://history.state.gov/milestones/1961-1968/laos-crisis.
29. William J. Rust, *Before the Quagmire: American Intervention in Laos, 1954–1961* (Lexington, KY: University of Kentucky Press, 2012), 259.
30. Usha Mahajani, "President Kennedy and United States Policy in Laos, 1961-63," *Journal of Southeast Asian Studies* 2, no.2 (1971): 87–99.
31. Montague Kern, Patricia W. Levering, and Ralph B. Levering, *The Kennedy Crises: The Press, the Presidency, and Foreign Policy* (Chapel Hill: University of North Carolina Press, 1983), 29.
32. Noam Kochavi, "Limited Accommodation, Perpetuated Conflict: Kennedy, China, and the Laos Crisis, 1961–1963," *Diplomatic History* 26, no.1 (2002): 95-135.
33. Office of the Historian of the Department of State, "The Laos Crisis, 1960–1963."
34. J. M. Halpern, "The Lao Elite: A Study of Tradition and Innovation," U.S. Air Force, Project RAND, Research Memorandum, November 15, 1960, 3, http://www.rand.org/content/dam/rand/pubs/research_memoranda/2013/RM2636.pdf
35. Winthrop G. Brown, recorded interview by Larry J. Hackman, February 1, 1968, John F. Kennedy Library Oral History Program, 24.
36. "23 March 1961," folder, John F. Kennedy Library, http://www.jfklibrary.org/Asset-Viewer/Archives/JFKPOF-054-010.aspx.
37. Robert Amory, Jr., recorded interview by Joseph E. O'Connor, February 17, 1966, John F. Kennedy Library Oral History Program, 27.
38. Richard Patrick, "Presidential Leadership in Foreign Affairs Reexamined: Kennedy and Laos Without Radical Revisionism," *World Affairs* 140, no.3 (1978): 245-258.
39. Bernard B. Fall, *Anatomy of a Crisis: The Laotian Crisis of 1960–1961* (New York: Doubleday, 1969), 246–47.
40. Kenneth T. Young, recorded interview by Dennis J. O'Brien, February 25, 1969, John F. Kennedy Library Oral History Program, 39–40.
41. Office of the Historian of the Department of State, "Ending the Vietnam War, 1969–1973" October 31, 2013, https://history.state.gov/milestones/1969-1976/ending-vietnam.
42. Geoffrey Warner, "Review Article—Leaving Vietnam: Nixon, Kissinger and Ford, 1969–1975, Part One: January 1969–January 1972," *International Affairs* 87, no.6 (2011): 1485-1506.
43. Hal W. Bochin, *Richard Nixon: Rhetorical Strategist* (Westport, CT: Greenwood Press, 1990), 63.
44. James A. Tyner, *The Killing of Cambodia: Geography, Genocide, and the Unmaking of Space* (Farnham, UK: Ashgate, 2008), 70.

45. Rowland Evans and Robert D. Novak, *Nixon in the White House: The Frustration of Power* (New York: Random House, 1971), 246–247.

46. Bochin, *Richard Nixon*, 63.

47. Bochin, *Richard Nixon*, 63.

48. Richard Nixon, "Address to the Nation on the Situation in Southeast Asia, April 30, 1970" American Presidency Project, University of California, Santa Barbara, http://www.presidency.ucsb.edu/ws/?pid=2490.

49. Mark Monmonier, *How to Lie With Maps*, 2nd Edition (Chicago: University of Chicago Press, 1996), 163, 170.

50. Nixon, "Address to the Nation."

51. Jonathan Schell, "Notes and Comment," *The New Yorker*, May 23, 1970, 29.

52. Hunt, *Ideology and U.S. Foreign Policy*, 176.

53. Kirkpatrick's quote is in "The Reagan Administration and Revolutions in Central America," *Political Science Quarterly* 99 (1984): 1.

54. Gearóid Ó Tuathail, "Political Geography of Contemporary Events VIII: The Language and Nature of the 'New Geopolitics'—The Case of U.S.-El Salvador Relations," *Political Geography Quarterly* 5, no.1 (1986): 75.

55. Ó Tuathail, "Political Geography of Contemporary Events VIII," 73–85; LaFeber, "The Reagan Administration," 5.

56. LaFeber, "The Reagan Administration," 2.

57. Timothy W. Luke, *Screens of Power: Ideology, Domination, and Resistance in Informational Society* (Champaign, IL: University of Illinois, 1989), 125–149.

58. Ronald Reagan, "Address to the Nation on the Situation in Nicaragua," Washington, D.C., March 16, 1986, Ronald Reagan Presidential Library, http://www.reagan.utexas.edu/archives/speeches/1986/31686a.htm. The video clip was acquired through the Reagan Library, Tape #350, Control #: 06270-6T-W184-350, 0:00–23:21.

59. Reagan, "Address to the Nation."

60. Reagan, "Address to the Nation."

61. Paul A. Chilton, "The Meaning of *Security*," in *Post-Realism: The Rhetorical Turn in International Relations*, eds. Francis A. Beer and Robert Hariman (East Lansing: University of Michigan Press, 1996), 193–216.

62. Roxanne Lynn Doty, *Imperial Encounters: The Politics of Representation in North-South Relations* (Minneapolis: University of Minnesota Press, 1996), 11.

63. Reagan, "Address to the Nation."

64. Ó Tuathail, "Foreign Policy and the Hyperreal: The Reagan Administration and the Scripting of 'South Africa,'" in *Writing Worlds*, 157.

65. Ó Tuathail, "Foreign Policy and the Hyperreal," 157.

66. Matthew Sparke, *In the Space of Theory: Postfoundational Geographies of the Nation-State* (Minneapolis: University of Minnesota Press, 2005), 10.

67. Doreen Massey, *For Space* (Thousand Oaks, CA: Sage, 2005), 5.

68. Doty, *Imperial Encounters*, 11.

69. Ó Tuathail, *Critical Geopolitics*, 53.

CHAPTER TWO

Reading the Presidency *In Situ*

Obama in Cuba and the Significance of Place in U.S. Presidential Public Address

ALLISON M. PRASCH

On March 22, 2016, President Barack Obama spoke in Havana, Cuba, to an immediate audience of 1,100 (including Cuban president Raúl Castro) and to the 11 million people living on the island via national television.[1] As the first sitting U.S. president to visit the communist country in eighty-eight years, Obama invoked his presidential presence in Cuba as a symbolic gesture of his determination to reconcile the U.S.-Cuban relationship. In his opening remarks, the president declared, "I have come here to bury the last remnant of the Cold War in the Americas. I have come here to extend the hand of friendship to the Cuban people."[2] Obama described his trip in literal and metaphorical terms, stating, "Havana is only 90 miles from Florida, but to get here we had to travel a great distance—over barriers of history and ideology; barriers of pain and separation." This narrative recognized the tense history between the United States and Cuba, a history shaped by Cold War crises such as the 1961 Bay of Pigs incident and the 1962 Cuban Missile Crisis. And yet, Obama declared it "a new day—*es un nuevo día*" for the two countries, one that represented an end of Cold War diplomatic tensions and the beginning of what he hoped would be "a better and brighter future for both the Cuban people and the American people."[3]

Obama's landmark visit to Cuba is just one example of the persuasive power of presidential rhetoric in place. Since the earliest days of the republic, U.S. presidents have harnessed specific geographical locations and physical symbols as a means of rhetorical invention. Between 1789 and 1791, President George Washington, Secretary of State Thomas Jefferson, and French architect Pierre Charles L'Enfant worked to design a capital city that would impress foreign visitors from around the world and convince them of the United States' political influence on the world stage.[4] In the eighteenth and nineteenth centuries, chief executives most often used presidential tours throughout the nation as a way to connect with the citizenry, advocate for a particular policy, encourage national unity, or even make that place more relatable or salient to the wider U.S. public.[5] At Gettysburg, Abraham Lincoln delivered a stirring address that transformed a bloodied battlefield to a place that represented (and still represents) the ideals of the Declaration of Independence and the U.S. Constitution.[6]

Yet these situated rhetorical appeals had a limited audience; only those physically present could appreciate fully the symbolic aspects of the speech's location. With the advent of the modern presidency and the mediated coverage of a president's every word, chief executives began to appropriate the scene and setting of their speech for their rhetorical purposes, locating their public addresses in places that offered evidence for their claims. In 1906, when criticism of the United States' attempt to build the Panama Canal was at an all-time high because of reports of poor sanitary conditions and widespread disease, President Theodore Roosevelt sailed to Panama to take stock of the situation himself. The journey marked the first time a sitting president had traveled outside the United States. "The president is breaking precedents without mercy in connection with his Panama trip," wrote the *Chicago Daily Tribune*.

> A president of the United States has never placed his foot on foreign soil. ... Perhaps with the precedent of visiting foreign lands established a trip may be made by an American executive to Europe. This will come, however, only when the people are better educated in this direction.[7]

When he returned two weeks later, Roosevelt sent his own special message to Congress. The ninety-two-page document included the president's own assessment of the situation in Panama, a text of the speech he delivered to employees of the Isthmian Canal Commission, various reports from U.S. officials stationed in Panama addressing sanitary conditions and death rates, and twenty-six photos of the work camps in Panama—including one of TR disembarking from a steam shovel.[8] The *New York Times* printed the president's special message and fourteen of the accompanying photographs in an eleven-page spread the next day.[9] In this instance, TR's physical presence in Panama, his detailed report to Congress, and visual images from his trip provided powerful evidence that construction of the Isthmus should continue. "He feels that the entire responsibility of that gigantic work rests on his shoulders," noted the *New York Times*, "and all the resources of his tireless mind were devoted during that three days' visit to the business of assuring himself that all was well." The report—and the trip itself, in fact—carried "high value indeed for the American people. ... It will help them understand in a general way what is going on down there."[10]

Ever since Roosevelt's diplomatic mission to Panama, U.S. presidents have deployed geographical locales as rhetorical backdrops for various foreign policy initiatives in South America, Europe, Asia, and the Middle East. Consider the number of rhetorical acts that one immediately associates with a particular foreign location: Harry S. Truman's visit to Potsdam and subsequent report to the nation at the end of World War II (1945); Dwight D. Eisenhower's post-election visit to Korea in 1952; John F. Kennedy's 1963 "Ich bin ein Berliner" address in West Berlin; Richard Nixon's "opening to China" in 1972; Ronald Reagan's Cold War foreign policy addresses in Normandy (1984) and West Berlin (1987); Bill Clinton's speech at Goree Island in 1998 and, five years later, George W. Bush's memorable address in the same location; and Barack Obama's speeches in Cairo, Egypt (2009) and Havana, Cuba (2016). These rhetorical moments—among many others—offer critics the opportunity to consider how traditional "texts" of presidential speech operate within and as a product of their historical, temporal, and spatial contexts.[11] Attending to the material elements of the rhetorical situation—the place, the speech setting, the audience members, the objects located in the place—helps us understand how the verbal, the visual, and the spatial collide in U.S. presidential public address.

My aim in this chapter is to offer an entry point for thinking about what it means to read the presidency *in situ*—to analyze presidential rhetoric as designed for and delivered in place. The phrase *in situ* comes from the Latin "situ," a term that means "place, situated, present." It also suggests an intentionality behind where a person, object, or thing is located or placed.[12] To be *in situ* is to be in one's own place; to put a thing or object *in situ* is to return it to its original place.[13] Within rhetorical studies, the phrase *in situ* often describes scholarly participation in "'live' rhetorics"—rhetoric happening in the here and now.[14] This perspective, while valuable and important, leaves little room for considering how critics can examine the *in situ* elements of previous rhetorical action, specifically how the material and symbolic elements of the speech situation condition, shape, and (re)orient the rhetorical act. Although critics cannot recreate a particular moment of utterance, scholars can and must account for how rhetorical discourse—both historical texts and ongoing rhetorical performances—harnesses the material and symbolic elements of the speech setting as a means of evidence. The *in situ* orientation, then, must not be limited to rhetoric happening in the present moment, but should instead push critics to examine the "text in its historical, spatial, and temporal totality, as a speech act designed for and delivered in place, within a specific historical/temporal moment, to real people—bodies in their lived experiences."[15] To demonstrate how this perspective might enlarge and enrich our appreciation of presidential speech, I first outline six theoretical implications for this *in situ* orientation and then offer an analysis of Obama's 2016 visit to Cuba to demonstrate such an approach.

Reading U.S. Presidential Rhetoric *In Situ*

First, conceptualizing presidential rhetoric *in situ* emphasizes the inherent *placedness* of the rhetorical situation. Indeed, the very etymology of the term "situation" traces the term back to the Latin "situ," meaning "site." The *Oxford English Dictionary* defines situation as: "The place, position, or location of a city, country, etc., in relation to its surroundings."[16] In its most literal sense, then, a rhetorical situation should encompass "the place, position, or location" of a speech act. Of course, Bitzer's description continues to influence how scholars conceptualize (or redefine) just what this situation entails. "Let us regard rhetorical situation as a natural context of persons, events, objects, relations, and an exigence which strongly invites utterance," he famously wrote in 1967.[17] Yet more recent work theorizing the rhetorical situation reminds us that rhetoric can be much more than a communicative exchange between speaker and audience.[18] Instead, rhetoric shifts and moves and circulates within, between, and among persons, communities, organizations, campaigns, and social movements. It persuades through monuments and museums, flows through marches, protests, and rallies. It constitutes political actors and constrains political subjects. In short, rhetoric is a profoundly embodied experience, an exchange that is both material and symbolic. Reading U.S. presidential rhetoric *in situ*, therefore, asks the critic to include place as a defining element of the rhetorical situation and consider how speakers utilize their physical environment—and their situatedness within that environment—to address various exigencies, audiences, and constraints bound up in that location.

Second, to study presidential rhetoric *in situ* requires critics to consider the multiplicity of ways that places can function rhetorically. This orientation builds on the important work in the humanities broadly[19] and in rhetorical studies more specifically[20] that theorizes how certain spaces and/or places gain political and cultural significance and how, in turn, the material and symbolic dimensions of museums, monuments, and memorials shape how groups and political institutions collectively remember events. Much of the work connecting rhetoric and place considers how certain physical sites or geographical locations work persuasively in and of themselves.[21] Another perspective is that rhetoric constitutes and reconstitutes the meaning of a place even as that place enables and constrains human subjectivity.[22] Both concepts—"place-as-rhetoric" and the enabling and/or constraining function of place—are important, for when U.S. presidents (and rhetors more broadly) situate a speech act in a geographical location central to their argument, they activate the rhetorical resonances of that place, be it the argument that place makes in and of itself or the symbolic associations and limitations that place provides. In turn, these resonances condition the means of persuasion available to the president, means that are often associated with the rhetorical history of place. In fact, the very reason that a particular site or location can perform a "place-as-rhetoric" function is because it represents some shared history. It is precisely the physical, tangible, touchable nature of memory places that renders them a concrete manifestation of the past.[23] Simply being in—or speaking from—such a place triggers the memories and the histories we associate with that location. Thus, reading presidential rhetoric *in situ* asks the critic to analyze how the place of a rhetorical act has functioned within a much larger shared history. Critically analyzing how certain geographic locations have functioned persuasively throughout history reveals how places condition rhetorical acts even as rhetoric in place shapes, refashions, and even transforms the symbolic significance of that particular location.[24]

Third, when U.S. presidents speak *in situ*, they use their rhetorical authority to build upon a site's prior symbolic resonances even as they define the meaning of that place and (re)appropriate such resonances for present and future purposes. Because U.S. presidents speak to, for, and on behalf of the U.S. public, they are uniquely qualified to activate, constitute, and (re)define the memories, symbols, and ideologies located in place.[25] One of the ways that U.S. presidents recount this shared history is by tapping into the symbolic dimensions of particular locales through speech and recounting—and even redefining—why these places are significant for the U.S. public. When U.S. presidents invoke place as a rhetorical strategy, they demonstrate their innate understanding of U.S. political culture by situating their rhetorical act in a place that offers a powerful means of enthymematic proof for their argument. But describing, characterizing, or naming a place does much more than create a backdrop for a speech act or even define the symbolic significance of the place itself. When U.S. presidents speak *in situ* and link their rhetorical act to the symbols that are always already present in place, they contribute to the "dramas, subjects, histories and dilemmas" embedded in that locale.[26] Speaking *in situ*, therefore, is a rhetorical choice in itself, a persuasive strategy U.S. presidents (and rhetors more broadly) adopt to amplify the symbolic dimensions of that place while simultaneously contributing new meanings to that particular location.

Fourth, the embodied nature of presidential rhetoric *in situ* makes that location present, salient, relatable, and noticeable to the U.S. public. In fact, the very presence of the U.S. president works rhetorically and does not necessarily require spoken discourse to be persuasive. Within rhetorical studies, the concept of presence usually refers to the ways in which rhetors make certain pieces of evidence particularly salient for the audience.[27] Outside of this traditionally rhetorical interpretation, one of the most common understandings of presence is the embodiment of an individual or thing; the presence of someone or something denotes that they are physically there. The *Oxford English Dictionary* suggests that presence can also mean "[t]he place or space in front of or around a person."[28] When presidents travel to a particular location and speak in place, they make that place present—noticeable, relatable, salient—to the U.S. public even as their presidential presence marks the site as significant in U.S. political culture. When we see the president in a particular location, the simple fact that he is *there* suggests that this occasion (and this place) is important enough to warrant his attention. Ultimately, presidential presence in place reveals a co-constitutive relationship between presidential authority and rhetoric *in situ*, a reciprocal exchange between the persuasive potential of the president's presence and the rhetorical resonances of the place itself. In other words, speaking *in situ* contributes to the president's overall rhetorical authority even as the president makes the place more meaningful for the audience.

Fifth, the mediation and circulation of presidential rhetoric *in situ* fuses spoken discourse with the material elements of the speech situation. When presidential rhetoric extends beyond the immediate geographic location and moment in time and is circulated through radio, newspaper, television, and/or the Internet, audiences literally "see" the speech setting as an irreducible element of the rhetorical act—whether the rhetorical act happened yesterday or fifty years ago.[29] Because presidential rhetoric in place continues to circulate even after delivery, scholars of public address must account for the ways in which these verbal/visual texts extend over time and in/through place, often (re)making place for future rhetoric *in situ*.[30] It is essential to note that the mediation and circulation of presidential rhetoric in place quickly extends beyond its physical situatedness within spatial and geographical borders into the broader space of the global imaginary. In turn, the mediation and circulation of presidential rhetoric *in situ*—be it through photographs, radio broadcasts, newsreel footage, or live television—extended the local into the global. Speaking *in situ*, therefore, does not mean that rhetorical acts are bound to their location. Instead, it is the very *placedness* of these rhetorical encounters that makes them ripe for mediation, circulation, and extension over time and space. Presidential rhetoric in place, therefore, activates the material realities of the rhetorical situation as a means of evidence—including the visuals that accompany their body in place. When presidents speak *in situ*, the placement of their presidential body within a particular location triggers not only the symbolic dimensions of that place, but it also provides visual images to the immediate and extended audience of how and why that particular place is significant rhetorically. In turn, as images of the president speaking in place circulate in the United States and around the world, the president's rhetorical act extends beyond spoken discourse. It becomes a text that is simultaneously verbal and visual, one that circulates in place while simultaneously moving through place to (re)constitute the rhetorical significance of that place for present and future action.

Finally, reading presidential rhetoric *in situ* asks the critic to consider how speakers use language to activate the material realities of the rhetorical situation and link text with context. Identifying these linguistic cues—or deictic utterances such as "here," "now," or "you"—provides the critic with tangible evidence of the historical events, social relationships, symbolic places, shared communities, and dimensions of temporality the rhetor invokes through speech.[31] This orientation provides a framework for identifying how orators use language to invite their audiences to fuse the spoken text with its relational, spatial, and temporal contexts. Ultimately, this perspective pushes scholars to consider the ways in which these elements of context—bodies, places, temporalities, objects, and sensations—provide a material means of persuasion and to identify where and how the speakers use language to activate the scenic or situational elements of the immediate historical and socio-political context for their persuasive purposes.[32]

In this section, I have outlined six theoretical implications of reading U.S. presidential rhetoric *in situ*. To demonstrate how this approach works in practice, I now turn to analysis of President Barack Obama's historic visit to Cuba in March 2016.

Obama in Cuba: (Re)Visions of a Post-Cold War Foreign Policy

Obama's decision to visit Cuba represented a seismic shift in U.S. foreign policy and a radical attempt to redefine the discourse surrounding U.S.-Cuban relations.

As both a rhetorical trope and "place-as-rhetoric," "Cuba" triggers memories of multiple symbolic events during the Cold War. The most significant are the 1961 Bay of Pigs invasion, a CIA-backed attempt to overthrow Fidel Castro's government, and the 1962 Cuban Missile Crisis, the thirteen-day standoff between Kennedy and Soviet premier Nikita Khrushchev over Soviet nuclear missile sites secretly installed in Cuba. Throughout the 1960s and 1970s, the United States placed economic sanctions and trade embargos on Cuba, and in 1982, the Reagan administration added Cuba to the state sponsor of terrorism list. These sanctions only increased under Presidents George H. W. Bush, Bill Clinton, and George W. Bush.[33] As a presidential candidate in 2008, then-Senator Barack Obama announced he would "pursue direct diplomacy" with Cuban President Raúl Castro "at a time and place of my choosing."[34] In 2009, the Obama administration began to scale back restrictions on travel and sending financial assistance to family members living in Cuba. But the most remarkable change occurred in December 2014, when Obama and Cuban president Raúl Castro announced their intention to normalize diplomatic relations between the two countries. In May 2015, the U.S. State Department removed Cuba from the state sponsor of terrorism list. Two months later, the U.S. embassy reopened in Havana, Cuba, and the Cuban embassy reopened in Washington, D.C. Both had been closed since 1961, after the Eisenhower administration severed ties with Fidel Castro. In August, Secretary of State John Kerry traveled to Cuba to attend the flag raising ceremony at the U.S. Embassy in Havana.[35] But it was Obama's personal visit to Cuba in March 2016 that offered the most tangible evidence of this foreign policy shift, a move indicating the president's desire to redefine U.S.-Cuban relations for the 21st century.

Reading presidential rhetoric *in situ* directs the critic to the place-based nature of the rhetorical situation and the symbolic and material resources that place provides, Obama's decision to visit Cuba reveals the ways in which audiences (e.g. Castro; the U.S. public; the Cuban people), exigencies (e.g. Castro's willingness to restore diplomatic relations with the U.S.; the opportunity for the United States to encourage democratic reform in a communist country), and constraints (e.g. the Cold War-era U.S. foreign policy of isolation; historical/ideological baggage such as the Bay of Pigs or the Cuban Missile Crisis) can be bound up and rooted in a particular location or place. The president's trip to Cuba, therefore, can be read as an attempt to respond to the audiences, exigencies, and constraints of the dominant narrative surrounding the U.S.-Cuban rhetorical situation and to create or call forth a new set of social and political relationships between the two countries—a move that his presence in place helped accomplish.

On February 18, 2016, the president broke the news of his visit on Twitter: "Next month, I'll travel to Cuba to advance our progress and efforts that can improve the lives of the Cuban people."[36] The president linked to a lengthy article by Deputy National Security Advisor Ben Rhodes entitled, "President Obama is Going to Cuba. Here's Why." Here Rhodes offered a narrative of the tense history between the United States in Cuba, noting that

[f]or more than fifty years, the United States pursued a policy of isolating and pressuring Cuba. While that policy was rooted in the context of the Cold War, our efforts continued long after the rest of the world had changed. Put simply, U.S. Cuba policy wasn't working. … More importantly, our policy was not making life better for the Cuban people—in many ways, it was making it worse.[37]

But the White House's announcement garnered harsh criticism from both Democrats and Republicans who charged that Obama's visit would only reward Castro's government who, despite this new period of openness between the two countries, had done little to expand human rights.[38] The White House even acknowledged that the Cuban government had taken few steps toward democratic reform, and yet Rhodes argued that the best way to keep up the pressure on Castro's government was for the president to travel to Cuba himself. "We believe the best way to try and push this forward is for the president to go. The way to carry this policy forward is to keep leaning forward."[39] As the Obama White House prepared for the president's historic visit to Cuba, officials emphasized the symbolic significance of the trip and noted that Obama would "be the first American President since Calvin Coolidge in 1928 to visit Cuba; President Coolidge traveled to Cuba on a U.S. battleship, so this will be a very different kind of visit.[40] This historical narrative set the stage for Obama's public statements during the trip and suggested that traveling to and speaking in Cuba demonstrated a remarkable shift in U.S. foreign policy.

Before, during, and after the March 2016 visit, the Obama Administration used the president's physical presence in Cuba to make the place more relatable to the U.S. public, and the White House's strategic use of visual images, video recordings, and public statements shared via the Internet and social media invited those watching in the United States to come along for the ride. On March 20, the first day of Obama's visit to Cuba, White House press secretary Josh Earnest posted a video on Twitter of *Air Force One* landing in Havana, Cuba. "Air Force One makes history. #CubaVisit," the tweet read.[41] The next day, on March 21, Rhodes posted several pictures from Obama's first day in Cuba—including one of the president and members of his staff looking out the windows on the final approach to Cuba.

Photo of Obama looking out the window of Air Force One during final approach into Havana, Cuba, March 20, 2016. The White House circulated this photo in their photographic report of the president's first day in Cuba posted on Medium.com. The report was also shared by various White House staffers via official social media accounts.[42]

Images of the president and his family arriving in Cuba also circulated on social media, including this image taken by Pete Souza, the official White House photographer, of the First Family standing on the tarmac in Havana shortly after their arrival.

White House Instagram Post on March 20, 2016.[43]

Other images included photos of the president touring Old Havana with his family, dining at a restaurant, and greeting citizens on the street.

Photo from inside President Obama's Motorcade posted on White House Facebook page on March 22, 2016.[44]

The White House also released a forty-seven second video montage of live images captured during the president's first day in Cuba. The short film was shared via the official WhiteHouse.gov website, their YouTube channel, Medium.com, and other social media outlets.[45] With live images captured during the president's first day in Cuba, the video invited viewers to accompany the president as he landed in Cuba on *Air Force One* and walked through Old Havana in the pouring rain. These images and videos shared via social media made Cuba more relatable to the U.S. public as it invited them to participate—albeit virtually—in Obama's material rhetorical situation.

Obama's attempt to respond to the dominant narratives framing the U.S.-Cuban rhetorical situation and redefine this historical narrative becomes most clear in his address to the Cuban people at the Gran Teatro de la Habana Alicia Alonso. The speech came towards the end of his three-day visit to the island nation. This highly coordinated trip included a joint press conference between President Obama and Cuban president Raúl Castro, a nationally televised speech to the Cuban people, meetings with Cuban entrepreneurs, human rights activists, and government leaders, and a baseball game between the Tampa Bay Rays and the Cuban National team. But it was Obama's nationally-televised speech on March 22, 2016, that offered him the opportunity to address the Cuban people himself and articulate his vision for "a new day—*es un nuevo día*" between the United States and Cuba.[46] To do this, the president used spatial, temporal, and relational deictic indicators to build three rhetorical bridges connecting the United States and Cuba. These bridges, made possible by Obama's references to place, time, and the shared history of the two countries, simultaneously acknowledged past difficulties and gestured toward a new chapter in U.S.-Cuban relations.

Obama constructed the first bridge through his physical travel from the United States to the island nation of Cuba. In his March 22 speech, the president repeatedly emphasized the rhetorical significance of his presidential presence *in situ*. Obama began by thanking "President Castro" and "the people of Cuba" for "the warm welcome that I have received, that my family have received, and our delegation has received. It is an extraordinary honor to be here today." Here the president situated himself and his audience in time ("today") and place ("here") in relation to those who had welcomed him ("President Castro" and "the people of Cuba"). The president continued: "Havana is only 90 miles from Florida, but to get here we had to travel a great distance, over barriers of history and ideology, barriers of pain and separation." Here Obama described his own physical journey to Cuba through language that was both literal and metaphorical. Although it was "only 90 miles" from the southernmost tip of the United States to Cuba, the president argued that the journey was actually much longer and encompassed "barriers" that were historical and ideological. Yet, in this opening passage and throughout the rest of his speech, Obama repeatedly used his own physical presence in Cuba as physical proof that bridges could be built between the countries. This progression from physical (Obama's travel from the United States to Cuba) to metaphorical and historical (traveling "a great distance" over ideological barriers and a painful past) enabled Obama to link his own travels to Cuba as a direct response to and acknowledgement of the difficult diplomatic relations in previous years. The two nations had been separated by space and time, yes, but perhaps most importantly, by political conflict.

Obama's acknowledgement of these political tensions throughout history enabled him to build a second rhetorical bridge, one designed to cross the ideological gulf between the United States and Cuba. To do this, the president recounted other significant historical events that had taken place in "the blue waters beneath Air Force One," waters that "once carried American battleships to this island: to liberate, but also to exert control over Cuba." And yet, Obama explained, those waters

> also carried generations of Cuban revolutionaries to the United States, where they built support for their cause. And that short distance has been crossed by hundreds of thousands of Cuban exiles, on planes and makeshift rafts, who came to America in pursuit of freedom and opportunity.

The choppy waters between the United States and Cuba had been crossed by U.S. battleships steaming towards Cuba during the Bay of Pigs and, going the other direction, the overcrowded boats of Cuban refugees seeking a better life in the United States. Obama explicitly acknowledged this painful history in his speech, and even used his own personal narrative to frame his description, stating that he, like "so many people in both of our countries," could chart his "lifetime" in relation to the "time of isolation" between the two countries. Key moments in this "time of isolation," including the Cuban Revolution, the Bay of Pigs, and the Cuban Missile Crisis, carried their own ideological baggage for both the United States and Cuba because each event reflected both the United States' determination to defeat communism during the Cold War and the Cuban desire for independence and national sovereignty. And yet, despite the gradual changes in U.S. foreign policy and "a world that remade itself time and again," the "conflict between the United States and Cuba" still remained. The president then stated: "I have come here to bury the last remnant of the cold war in the Americas. I have come here to extend the hand of friendship to the Cuban people." With this impassioned declaration, Obama articulated the purpose for his visit through references to place, time, and social relations. He, the leader of the greatest democracy in the world, was implicitly rejecting the isolationist foreign policy of his predecessors and was instead extending a "hand of friendship" to the Cuban people. He, a child of the 1960s who could trace his own lifetime in relation to the moments of greatest tension between the two countries, had come here to bury that past, and begin anew.

The third rhetorical bridge Obama constructed through his rhetoric *in situ* was a relational bridge between the United States and the Cuban people. In his speech, the president noted that the most important reason for this foreign policy shift was the Cuban people—his immediate and extended audience—themselves. "*Creo en el pueblo Cubano*—I believe in the Cuban people," he said. This was not "just a policy of normalizing relations with the Cuban Government. The United States of America is normalizing relations with the Cuban people." Although Obama acknowledged clear ideological divisions between the United States and Cuba (such as Cuba's "one party system," "socialist economic model," and emphasis on "the role and rights of the state"), he also offered examples of similarities between the two nations, creating a symbolic identification with his audience by focusing on what the two countries had in common—warts and all. This decision to emphasize shared history despite competing political ideologies was significant, especially because it demonstrated Obama's focus on the citizens of Cuba. In fact, towards the middle of his speech, Obama shifted from speaking about "President Castro" and the "Cuban Government" and instead directed his remarks directly to the "Cuban people":

> I want the Cuban people—especially the young people—to understand why I believe that you should look to the future with hope. Not the false promise which insists that things are better than they really are, or the blind optimism that says all your problems can go away tomorrow; hope that is rooted in the future that you can choose and that you can shape and that you can build for your country. I'm hopeful because I believe that the Cuban people are as innovative as any people in the world.

Underscoring the individual agency of the "Cuban people" apart from their government, Obama told his audience that he saw

> an evolution taking place inside of Cuba, a generational change. Many suggested that I come here and ask the people of Cuba to tear something down, but I'm appealing to the young people of Cuba who will lift something up, build something new. *El futuro de Cuba tiene que estar en las manos del pueblo Cubano* [The future of Cuba must be in the hands of the Cuban people].

This reference to Ronald Reagan's 1987 call for Soviet premier Mikhail Gorbachev to "tear down this wall" was particularly appropriate, since President Reagan's declaration now often symbolizes the United States' victory over communism and the

Cold War.[47] But Obama was clear that he was not calling for political revolution or regime change. Instead, he argued, his desire was that the Cuban citizens act out of their own free will to "lift" and "build" a better, more democratic society.

Of course, Obama's claim that Cuban citizens could actively "choose … shape … [and] build" a new future could be described as naïve or unrealistic given Raúl Castro's authoritarian regime (and the White House's acknowledgement that few steps had been taken towards democratic reform). And yet, the president addressed Castro directly in his speech:

> And to President Castro, who I appreciate being here today, I wanted you to know, I believe my visit here demonstrates, you do not need to fear a threat from the United States. And given your commitment to Cuba's sovereignty and self-determination, I am also confident that you need not fear the different voices of the Cuban people and their capacity to speak and assemble and vote for their leaders.

Although Obama cited his visit as proof that the United States would stay out of Cuba's business, the clear implication was that the president expected Castro to hold up his end of the deal by allowing free elections and political expression. And as Obama had already made clear, this normalization of relations with Cuba was directed first and foremost toward the citizens of Cuba—not Castro.

To conclude his remarks, Obama reemphasized the physical, historical, ideological, and relational barriers that had separated the United States and Cuba for years, but argued that his visit symbolized an important step toward a new era of diplomatic relations.

> The history of the United States and Cuba encompass revolution and conflict; struggle and sacrifice; retribution and, now, reconciliation. It is time, now, for us to leave the past behind. It is time for us to look forward to the future together, *un futuro de esperanza* [a future of hope]. And it won't be easy, and there will be setbacks. It will take time. But my time here in Cuba renews my hope and my confidence in what the Cuban people will do. We can make this journey as friends and as neighbors and as family, together. *Sí, se puede. Muchas gracias* [Yes, you can. Many thanks].

In these final sentences of his speech, the president discursively constituted a Cuba that was active and alive, a Cuba comprised of engaged citizens, a Cuba eager to embrace the present moment, even despite its challenges and complexities. Obama used references to time ("now" and "it is time") to anchor his audience in the present moment ("now") while also reminding them of the history they shared and the history they hoped to create. "Now" represented the key temporal turning point between what had been and what could be even as Obama's physical presence in a nation who had threatened the United States with nuclear war symbolized a remarkable shift in diplomatic relations. Although the "journey" would "not be easy" and would include "setbacks," the president declared that the United States and Cuba could "make this journey as friends and as neighbors and as family, together. *Si, se puede.* [Yes, you can]." In a clear reference to his 2008 campaign theme, Obama underscored the agency and the responsibility of the Cuban people to take an active role in writing and rewriting their shared history. Their future, Obama said, was up to them.

Conclusion

President Barack Obama's 2016 visit to Cuba offers a poignant example of the power of reading U.S. presidential rhetoric *in situ*. As the first sitting U.S. president to visit the island nation in eighty-eight years, Obama undoubtedly understood the symbolic significance of his visit and, perhaps even more importantly, how his placement might reconcile diplomatic relations with this tiny island nation located just ninety miles from the United States. It is no accident that the White House repeatedly emphasized Obama's journey as a historic event. His presidential presence in place was a form of enactment, a material and symbolic embodiment of his overall foreign policy approach. Instead of distancing himself (and the United States) from the communist country through trade embargos and State Department blacklists, he had come to Cuba to (re)open the door himself.

In an interview with Jeffrey Goldberg of *The Atlantic*, the president cited the recent reestablishment of diplomatic relations with Cuba as, in Goldberg's words, "proof that his deliberate, non-threatening, diplomacy-centered approach to foreign relations is working."[48] In many ways, then, Obama's foreign policy shift was just one example of the Obama Doctrine, or a foreign policy approach emphasizing negotiation and collaboration rather than direct military intervention (the Bush Doctrine). Through his physical presence and rhetoric *in situ*, the president activated material elements of his literal rhetorical situation and called for a significant shift in U.S. foreign policy, one that he cemented through his physical travel to and rhetorical deployment of Cuba. This example also reveals how images and videos of Obama's rhetoric *in situ*—via official White House platforms and social media—invited the U.S. public to join the president for this historic journey. The presence of the president in place—and the mediation and circulation of his physical situatedness in that location—became a material means of persuasion.

More broadly, however, this case study offers a contemporary example of what it means to read presidential rhetoric *in situ*, a perspective that underscores both the significance of where a rhetorical act occurs and assumes that locating a speech act in a particular place is a rhetorical choice in itself—a means of invention. It suggests that the rhetorical act defines and, in some cases is defined by, the cultural and political symbols and memories associated with that place. It reveals that, just as rhetoric is placed and works rhetorically to transform a place, a rhetor can also draw on the physical and material elements of the speech setting to harness the power of place as a persuasive strategy. It communicates the idea that rhetorical acts respond to, negotiate with, (re)appropriate, and even transform the places in which rhetors speak. And finally, rhetoric *in situ* reminds the critic that all rhetorical acts are situated and performative—that is, they are emplaced.

Notes

1. Ryan Teague Beckwith, "Read President Obama's Speech to the Cuban People," March 22, 2016, http://time.com/4267933/barack-obama-cuba-speech-transcript-full-text/.
2. Barack Obama, "Remarks by President Obama to the People of Cuba," March 22, 2016, online by Gerhard Peters and John T. Woolley, *The American Presidency Project*, http://www.presidency.ucsb.edu/ws/index.php?pid=115045.
3. Barack Obama, "Remarks by President Obama and President Raúl Castro Ruz of Cuba in a Joint Press Conference," March 21, 2016, online by Gerhard Peters and John T. Woolley, *The American Presidency Project*, http://www.presidency.ucsb.edu/ws/index.php?pid=115063.
4. See, for example, Kenneth R. Bowling, *The Creation of Washington, D.C.: The Idea and Location of the American Capital* (Fairfax, VA: George Mason University Press, 1991); Fergus M. Bordewich, *Washington: The Making of the American Capital* (New York, NY: HarperCollins Publishers, 2008).
5. For further discussion of these presidential tours, see Richard Ellis, *Presidential Travel: The Journey from George Washington to George W. Bush* (Lawrence, KS: University Press of Kansas, 2008). See also Amy R. Slagell, "The Challenges of Reunification: Rutherford B. Hayes on the Close Race and the Racial Divide," in *Before the Rhetorical Presidency*, ed. Martin J. Medhurst (College Station, TX: Texas A&M University Press, 2008), 243–266.
6. Garry Wills, *Lincoln at Gettysburg: The Words that Remade America* (New York, NY: Simon & Schuster, 1992).
7. "Roosevelt to Say Adieu," *Chicago Daily Tribune*, November 5, 1906, p. 3.
8. To view a PDF of this report, visit http://www.theodore-roosevelt.com/images/research/txtspeeches/962.pdf. See also J. Michael Hogan, "Theodore Roosevelt and the Heroes of Panama," *Presidential Studies Quarterly* 19, no. 4 (1989): 79–94; David McCullough, *The Path Between the Seas: The Creation of the Panama Canal, 1870–1914* (New York: Simon & Schuster, 1977), 500–508.
9. See *New York Times*, December 18, 1906, pp. 17–27.
10. "The Panama Message," *New York Times*, December 18, 1906, p. 8.
11. To be sure, the advent of television and other technological changes have pushed scholars to consider the linkages between the verbal and the visual provide rich sites for rhetorical

analysis, particularly in thinking about how U.S. presidents utilize and even exploit the images that accompany their rhetorical acts. And yet, attending to the verbal and visual without a serious consideration of rhetoric's *placedness* limits our understanding of how U.S. presidents have harnessed the material and symbolic resonances of their speech situation as a means of persuasion. See, for example, Kathleen Hall Jamieson, *Eloquence in an Electronic Age: The Transformation of Political Speechmaking* (New York: Oxford University Press, 1988); Bruce E. Gronbeck, "The Presidency in the Age of Secondary Orality," in *Beyond the Rhetorical Presidency*, ed. Martin J. Medhurst (College Station, TX: Texas A&M University Press, 1996), 30–49.

12. Charlton T. Lewis and Charles Short, s.v. "Situ," *A Latin Dictionary* (Oxford: Clarendon Press, 1879), http://www.perseus.tufts.edu/hopper/morph?l=situ&la=la#lexicon.

13. *Oxford English Dictionary*, s.v. "in situ, prep.," http://www.oed.com.ezproxy2.library.colostate.edu:2048/view/Entry/92971.

14. Michael K. Middleton, Samantha Senda-Cook, and Danielle Endres, "Articulating Rhetorical Field Methods: Challenges and Tensions," *Western Journal of Communication* 75, no. 4 (2011): 386–406. For more on *in situ* rhetorical practices, see Michael K. Middleton, Aaron Hess, Danielle Endres, and Samantha Senda-Cook, *Participatory Critical Rhetoric: Theoretical and Methodological Foundations for Studying Rhetoric in Situ* (Lanham, MD: Lexington Books, 2015); Danielle Endres, Aaron Hess, Samantha Senda-Cook, Michael K. Middleton, "In Situ Rhetoric: Intersections Between Qualitative Inquiry, Fieldwork, and Rhetoric," *Cultural Studies   Critical Methodologies* 16, no. 6 (2016): 511–524; Sara L. McKinnon, Robert Asen, Karma R. Chavez, and Robert Glenn Howard, eds., *Text + Field: Innovations in Rhetorical Method* (University Park, PA: The Pennsylvania State University Press, 2016).

15. Allison M. Prasch, "Toward a Rhetorical Theory of Deixis," *Quarterly Journal of Speech* 102:2 (2016): 166–193.

16. *Oxford English Dictionary*, "Situation, n.," http://www.oed.com.ezproxy2.library.colostate.edu:2048/view/Entry/180520.

17. Lloyd F. Bitzer, "The Rhetorical Situation," *Philosophy & Rhetoric* 1, no. 1 (1968): 1–14.

18. See, for example, Richard E. Vatz, "The Myth of the Rhetorical Situation," *Philosophy & Rhetoric* 6:3 (1973): 154–161; Barbara A. Biesecker, "Rethinking the Rhetorical Situation from within the Thematic of *Différance*," *Philosophy & Rhetoric* 22, no. 2 (1989): 110130; Mary Garret and Xiaosui Xiao, "The Rhetorical Situation Revisited," *Rhetoric Society Quarterly* 23, no. 2 (1993): 30–40; Craig R. Smith and Scott Lybarger, "Bitzer's Model Reconstructed," *Communication Quarterly* 44, no. 2 (1996): 197–213; Jenny Edbauer, "Unframing Models of Public Distribution: From Rhetorical Situation to Rhetorical Ecologies," *Rhetoric Society Quarterly* 35, no. 4 (2005): 5–24; Catherine Chaput, "Rhetorical Circulation in Late Capitalism: Neoliberalism and the Overdetermination of Affective Energy," *Philosophy & Rhetoric* 43, no. 1 (2010): 1–25; Heather Ashley Hayes, *Violent Subjects and Rhetorical Cartography in the Age of the Terror Wars* (United Kingdom: Palgrave Macmillan, 2016).

19. See, for example, Yi-Fu Tuan, *Space and Place: The Perspective of Experience* (Minneapolis, MN: University of Minnesota Press, 1977); Michel de Certeau, *The Practice of Everyday Life* (Berkeley, CA: University of California Press, 1984); Edward Soja, *Postmodern Geographies: The Reassertion of Space in Critical Social Theory* (New York, NY: Verso, 1989);

Henri Lefebvre, *The Production of Space*, trans. Donald Nicholson-Smith (Malden, MA: Blackwell Publishing, 1991); Doreen Massey, *Space, Place, and Gender* (Minneapolis, MN: University of Minnesota Press, 1994); Michel Foucault, *Discipline and Punish: The Birth of the Prison*, trans. Alan Sheridan, 2nd ed. (New York: Vintage Books, 1995); Pierre Nora, *Realms of Memory: Rethinking the French Past* (New York: Columbia University Press, 1996); Doreen Massey, *For Space* (London: Sage Publications Ltd., 2005).

20. There are numerous studies that are important. For a helpful introduction to the relationship between rhetoric, memory, and place, see Carole Blair, Greg Dickinson, and Brian L. Ott, "Introduction: Rhetoric/Memory/Place," in *Places of Public Memory: The Rhetoric of Museums and Memorials*, ed. Greg Dickinson, Carole Blair, and Brian L. Ott (Tuscaloosa, AL: University of Alabama Press, 2010).

21. Daniel Endres and Samantha Senda-Cook use the term "place-as-rhetoric" to describe "the material (physical and embodied) aspects of a place having meaning and consequence." Danielle Endres and Samantha Senda-Cook, "Location Matters: The Rhetoric of Place in Protest," *Quarterly Journal of Speech* 97, no. 3 (2011): 257–282.

22. Kirt H. Wilson, *The Reconstruction Desegregation Debate: The Politics of Equality and the Rhetoric of Place, 1870–1875* (Lansing, MI: Michigan State University Press, 2002), 12. See also "The Politics of Place and Presidential Rhetoric in the United States, 1875–1901," in *Civil Rights Rhetoric and the American Presidency*, ed. James Arnt Aune and Enrique D. Rigsby (College Station, TX: Texas A&M University Press, 2005), 16–40.

23. See, for example, Pierre Nora, "General Introduction: Between Memory and History," in *Realms of Memory: Rethinking the French Past*, ed. Pierre Nora (New York: Columbia University Press, 1996), 1–20; Edward S. Casey, "Public Memory in Place and Time," in *Framing Public Memory*, ed. Kendall R. Phillips (Tuscaloosa, AL: University of Alabama Press, 2004).

24. For more on doing rhetorical history, see Kathleen J. Turner, ed. *Doing Rhetorical History: Cases and Concepts* (Tuscaloosa: The University of Alabama Press, 1998).

25. See, for example, Vanessa B. Beasley, *You, the People: American National Identity in Presidential Rhetoric* (College Station, TX: Texas A&M University Press, 2004); David Zarefsky, "Presidential Rhetoric and the Power of Definition," *Presidential Studies Quarterly* 34, no. 3 (2004): 607–619; Karlyn Kohrs Campbell and Kathleen Hall Jamieson, *Presidents Creating the Presidency: Deeds Done in Words* (Chicago, IL: University of Chicago Press, 2008).

26. Gearóid Ó Tuathail and John Agnew, "Geopolitics and Discourse: Practical Geopolitical Reasoning in American Foreign Policy," *Political Geography* 11, no. 2 (1992): 194, 95–96.

27. See Chaïm Perelman and Lucie Olbrechts-Tyteca, *The New Rhetoric: A Treatise on Argumentation* (Notre Dame, IN: University of Notre Dame Press, 1969); Robert E. Tucker, "Figure, Ground and Presence: A Phenomenology of Meaning in Rhetoric," *Quarterly Journal of Speech* 87, no. 4 (2001): 396–414.

28. *Oxford English Dictionary*, s.v. "presence, n.," http://www.oed.com.ezproxy2.library.colostate.edu:2048/view/Entry/150669.

29. For more on rhetorical circulation and the presidency, see Mary E. Stuckey, "On Rhetorical Circulation," *Rhetoric & Public Affairs* 15, no. 4 (2012): 609–612; Stephen Heidt, "The Presidency as Pastiche: Atomization, Circulation, and Rhetorical Instability," *Rhetoric & Public Affairs* 15, no. 4 (2012): 623–633.

30. Ronald Walter Greene, "Rhetorical Pedagogy as a Postal System: Circulating Subjects through Michael Warner's 'Publics and Counterpublics'," *Quarterly Journal of Speech* 88, no. 4 (2002): 434–443.

31. For more on the relationship between rhetoric and deixis, see Prasch, "Toward a Rhetorical Theory of Deixis"; Allison M. Prasch, "Reagan at Pointe du Hoc: Deictic Epideictic and the Persuasive Power of 'Bringing Before the Eyes,'" *Rhetoric and Public Affairs* 18, no. 2 (2015): 247–276.

32. Prasch, "Toward a Rhetorical Theory of Deixis."

33. Claire Felter, Brianna Lee, James McBride, and Danielle Renwick, "U.S.-Cuba Relations," *Council on Foreign Relations,* Backgrounder, last updated 19 January, 2018, https://www.cfr.org/backgrounder/us-cuba-relations.

34. Obama as quoted in Jeff Zeleny, "Obama, in Miami, Calls for Engaging with Cuba," *New York Times,* May 24, 2008, http://www.nytimes.com/2008/05/24/us/politics/24campaign.html.

35. See Azam Ahmed and Julie Hirschfeld Davis, "U.S. and Cuba Reopen Long-Closed Embassies," *New York Times,* July 20, 2015, http://www.nytimes.com/2015/07/21/world/americas/cuba-us-embassy-diplomatic-relations.html?_r=0; Patrick Oppmann, "Raising of Old Glory in Havana Expected to Help Heal Old Wounds," CNN.com, August 14, 2015, http://www.cnn.com/2015/08/14/world/u-s--embassy-reopens-cuba-havana and John Kerry, "Remarks at Flag Raising Ceremony," August 14, 2015, https://2009-2017.state.gov/secretary/remarks/2015/08/246121.htm.

36. Barack Obama, Twitter Post, February 18, 2016, 6:05 AM, https://twitter.com/potus44/status/700320240022921216.

37. Ben Rhodes, "President Obama is Going to Cuba. Here's Why," Medium.com, February 18, 2016, https://medium.com/@rhodes44/president-obama-is-going-to-cuba-here-s-why-41ecdc0586d8#.8s92nkn77.

38. Julie Hirschfeld Davis, "Obama Going to Cuba; First Visit by U.S. President in 88 Years," *New York Times,* February 18, 2016, https://www.nytimes.com/2016/02/19/world/americas/obama-cuba-trip.html?_r=0.

39. Rhodes as quoted in Davis, "Obama Going to Cuba."

40. Rhodes, "President Obama is Going to Cuba. Here's Why."

41. Josh Earnest, Twitter Post, March 20, 2016, 2:41 pm, accessed from https://twitter.com/PressSec44/status/711669087349432321.

42. "President Barack Obama joins others in looking out the window of Air Force One on final approach into Havana, Cuba, Sunday, March 20, 2016" (Official White House Photo by Pete Souza), public domain, accessed from https://medium.com/@rhodes44/day-one-in-photos-the-first-u-s-president-in-cuba-in-88-years-33da61622f7e.

43. White House Instagram Post, March 20, 2016, public domain, accessed at https://www.instagram.com/p/BDOFq6Ewirg/.

44. "President Barack Obama in Havana, Cuba, March 22, 2016" (Official White House Photo by Pete Souza), public domain, accessed from http://obamawhitehouse.gov.archivesocial.com.

45. The White House, "President Obama and the First Family Take a Walk in Old Havana," filmed March 2016, YouTube video, 00:47, posted March 21, 2016, https://www.youtube.com/watch?v=GdWWr4O2P04.

46. Obama, "Remarks at the Gran Teatro de la Habana." All successive quotations are from here unless otherwise noted.

47. Before, during, and after the president's trip, numerous columnists praised Obama's decision to end the Cold War-era policy of estrangement, with some even comparing Obama's action to Richard Nixon's 1972 opening to China and Ronald Reagan's engagement with the Soviet Union in the 1980s. See, for example, "Beijing, Hanoi—and Havana," *Chicago Tribune*, March 22, 2016, p. 2; Christi Parsons, "President Obama Considering Visit to Cuba to Shore Up Relations—and His Foreign Policy Legacy," *Los Angeles Times*, January 2, 2016, http://www.latimes.com/world/mexico-americas/la-na-obama-cuba-20160103-story.html.

48. Jeffrey Goldberg, "The Obama Doctrine," *The Atlantic*, April 2016, http://www.theatlantic.com/magazine/archive/2016/04/the-obama-doctrine/471525/.

CHAPTER THREE

The Other Presidential Rhetoric

Rhetorical Mobilization within the White House

MILENE ORTEGA AND MARY E. STUCKEY

'

When President Jimmy Carter signed the Panama Canal Treaties on September 7, 1977, public opinion was very much against them: 50% of those polled opposed the accords, and only 29% approved.[1] Yet within a matter of months, on April 18, 1978, the treaties were ratified by the Senate, an action approved by 44% of the American public.[2] In seven months, public opinion moved 15 points. While there is some evidence that these polls may be flawed,[3] both qualitative and quantitative evidence indicates that there was a remarkable shift in public opinion between the signing of the treaties and their ratification.[4] Traditionally, studies of presidential rhetoric analyze persuasive campaigns by focusing on texts produced by or on behalf of the president with particular focus on presidential speeches. This study takes a different approach to presidential rhetoric, one that allows us to analyze and understand presidential persuasion as administrative and institutional rather than as purely personal and individual.

We know, for instance, that it is hard for presidents, speaking as individuals, to change public sentiment, that a single speech has little effect on public opinion.[5] We also know that presidential efforts to move Congress by "going public" are generally ineffective; the mass public does not routinely lobby Congress, and when they do, these efforts have effects only at the margins.[6] It is at least possible that we understand presidential efforts to influence the public as ineffective because scholars focusing only on national presidential addresses are looking in the wrong place. Jeffrey Cohen, for instance, found that presidential efforts to move opinion may be more effective at the local than the national level,[7] and Brandon Rottinghaus argues that presidential speeches serve as signals to other elites rather than as efforts to persuade the mass public.[8] Finally, it is probably not useful to understand the public as a homogenous mass. It is more helpful to think of the public as fragmented, relatively inchoate, and organized on several levels: as members of racial and/ or ethnic groups, economic interests, regional identities, and so on. Moreover, when we look at presidential persuasion as coming only from the president, we ignore the institutional nature of the presidency. Presidential persuasion is both individual and collective. When we restrict the study of presidential rhetoric to presidential speech alone, we are ignoring the ways in which the president mobilizes the resources of the entire institution. This chapter, therefore, expands the province of presidential rhetoric and concentrates on the words and deeds of presidential surrogates.

The presidency is unquestionably a rhetorical institution.[9] Scholars of presidential rhetoric have argued the presidency has the power to shape discourse, narrow choices, and target specific audiences.[10] We have learned that if the presidency is ubiquitous, then its message is also fragmented.[11] In this chapter, we expand on the notion of presidential ubiquity by highlighting the power of the institution in fragmenting, mobilizing, and amplifying the voice of the president. We propose an amendment to the body of work on presidential persuasion. We expand our definition of presidential speech to include the actions and rhetoric of the entire administration. We argue that the act of "going public" should, in at least some cases, be understood not only as a single speech or set of speeches by the president, but also as a persuasive effort that extends across time and includes governmental actors.

In making this argument, we focus on ratification of the Panama Canal treaties. This case involved intensive lobbying efforts in which the administration sought to persuade both members of Congress and the mass public. They did so on a variety of fronts, including White House briefings for the press and for opinion leaders, the recruitment of celebrities and prominent political actors, efforts to engage editorial boards and prominent journalists, town hall meetings, congressional hearings, the creation and articulation of grass roots coalition, and direct appeals to the public through presidential addresses. They involved action by the president, administration officials, allies both within and outside of government, and the mass media. We contend the rhetorical campaign orchestrated by this composition of institutional and non-institutional actors proved successful in changing public opinion, mobilizing the public, and influencing congressional action.

Our argument proceeds in four parts. First, we lay out a brief history of the Panama Canal treaty debate. Second, we detail the president's persuasive efforts as he advocated for those treaties—the relatively traditional approach to the study of presidential persuasion. We then demonstrate the ways in which these efforts expanded and amplified that persuasion through administration actions, including the enlistment of Cabinet members, current and previous governmental officials and celebrities, press briefings, and town halls. We conclude by arguing that it is useful to examine presidential persuasion by understanding the president as an institutional as well as an individual political actor.

The Panama Canal Treaties

As early as 1514, there was interest in finding a way to connect the Atlantic with the Pacific Ocean in order to facilitate trade between the Old and the New World.[12] Modern efforts to construct a canal across the Panamanian isthmus began in 1880, but met considerable difficulty.[13] In 1903, the United States submitted a treaty to Colombia proposing the construction and American administration of the canal in the Panamanian region, then a Colombian territory. The Colombian government rejected the treaty and a few months later the U.S. sponsored a secession movement in what is now Panama. The U.S. offered military protection to the secessionists and promptly endorsed the revolutionaries, recognizing the sovereignty of Panama in exchange for the acceptance of the canal treaty first presented to and rejected by the Colombian government. In return for supporting Panamanian independence from Colombia, the U.S. received control of the Canal Zone.[14]

Article III of the treaty gave the United States "all the rights, power, and authority ... which the United States would possess if it were sovereign ... to the entire exclusion of the exercise by the Republic of Panama of any such sovereign rights, power, and Authority."[15] The treaty thus gave the U.S. sovereign status within the nation of Panama. While Panamanians agreed to the treaty under the impression that accepting help and support from the United States would allow them to develop the country and receive earnings from the canal, the terms of the treaty kept the Panamanians ineligible to profit from or to control the canal. Over the next hundred years, the continued U.S. presence in Panama and the economic disparities between Americans and Panamanians in the Canal Zone remained sources of tension both between the U.S. and Panama and between the U.S. and Latin America more generally.[16]

This tension concerned presidents as different as Woodrow Wilson, Dwight D. Eisenhower, John F. Kennedy, and Lyndon B. Johnson, all of whom tried to ameliorate the negative perception of the United States in Latin America. Wilson, for instance, offered $25 million to Colombia as a strategy to redress their grievances. Eisenhower signed a treaty in 1955 giving economic benefits to Panama, but the Senate failed to ratify it. Kennedy offered loans and grants and the promise of conciliatory dialogue between the American and Panamanian administrations. By the end of the Kennedy presidency, there remained considerable tension in the canal region, which manifested in bloody conflict between American soldiers and Panamanian citizens on January 10, 1964, when unarmed Panamanian students attempted to raise the Panamanian flag in the Canal Zone. The incident brought international attention to the canal when Panamanians requested support from the U.N. Security Council. In response, Lyndon Johnson proposed a treaty that would terminate the 1903 treaty and recognize Panamanian sovereignty. The treaty faced strong domestic opposition and never reached the Senate for a vote. During the Nixon administration, the U.S. and Panama negotiated the Kissinger-Tack Agreement on Principles, which outlined eight principles that would orient forthcoming negotiations. Chief among these principles was the promise that the U.S. would cede full control of the canal to Panama and that both parties would share the obligations related the canal in the meantime. Republicans criticized the agreement, and the administration, first occupied with a reelection campaign and then with Watergate, let the matter drop.[17]

The Carter administration had, among its foreign policy priorities, establishing better relations between the U.S. and South American nations.[18] Thus, Carter negotiated a treaty that attempted to remediate discontent with the canal arrangements by devolving control of the canal to the Panamanians. The administration depicted the treaty as a bipartisan measure that was both "the right thing to do" and in accordance with American geopolitical interests. Most Republicans, however, opposed the treaty. They stressed American ownership of the canal, and argued that Carter was allowing a "canal giveaway" ceding U.S. territory and interests to Panama.[19] They argued that such cession would weaken the U.S. politically, militarily, and economically. Press clippings document how the American Conservative Union (ACU) and others circulated these concerns through "mail campaigns, radio spots, a TV documentary, and "truth squads" of Senate and House members sent around the country to apply pressure on those senators whose votes were undertermined.[20] In the context of the Cold War, and especially following the traumas of Vietnam, abdicating control over any territory seemed to provide unwelcome evidence of the loss of American prestige and power.

While oppositional discourses circulated widely in diverse ways through including formal speeches, radio shows, press events, mass mailings, and others, we point to a letter signed by then-Governor Ronald Reagan as emblematic of the form and content of the oppositional discourse adopted. The letter was sent to millions of Americans by the Republican National Committee and the Carter administration gave it considerable attention.[21] The letter was used as a guiding document to structure official rebuttal to oppositional discourse.[22] As a result the language of the materials the administration crafted in support of the canal is reminiscent of the language and ideas present in Reagan's letter. The letter expressed three central ideas: in signing the treaty, the United States would become economically, politically and militarily vulnerable; the Panamanians were not qualified to control the canal; and Carter was failing to uphold American interests by relinquishing the rights to control the canal.

Additionally, the letter adopted military language to instill a sense of fear resulting from the imminent threat to American safety. Reflecting Cold War anxieties exacerbated by Vietnam, Reagan's argument underlined what he understood as the military and logistical impact of ceding control of the canal to Panama. For instance, he claimed ratifying the treaty would lead to the closure of military bases and that there would be "no guarantee the U.S. [could] intervene to protect and defend the neutrality of the Canal."[23] The choice of terms such as "intervene," "protect," and "defend" exemplify the martial terms that he adopted throughout the letter, underlining the military nature of the canal. For example, Reagan argued, "In the process of giving up our Canal, Mr. Carter has also surrendered our rights to build a new one if needed."[24] Terms such as "giving up" and especially "surrendered" evoked military consequences of political action, which highlighted the deleterious effects of the treaty on U.S. interests.

Reagan could consider the treaty as surrendering U.S. territory because in his view, the canal belonged to the United States. Throughout the letter, he referred to the canal as "ours." The possessive pronoun marks the territory of the canal as an American possession. This perception was troublesome because it erased Panamanian sovereignty by assuming a territory that has received American investment becomes a de facto part of America. In fact, the question of sovereignty generated considerable controversy, especially because the U.S. Supreme Court had been inconsistent in its rulings in cases that revolved around American interests and the Panamanian territory. But, legally and counter to popular perception, the Canal Zone had not been "acquired" by the United States as Louisiana, Florida, and Alaska had been in the past. The Canal Zone was administered by the United States but it was technically under the jurisdiction of Panama.

In fact, sovereignty was part of the problem. Reagan argued the treaty endangered the U.S. strategically since Panama had close ties with Fidel Castro. This claim combined the first and second arguments of the letter and of the anti-treaty constituency more generally: Panamanian politics augmented the military dangers inherent in the treaties. Reagan characterized Panama as "one of the most unstable countries in Latin America,"[25] a country led by a man who became leader through non-democratic means and who did not respect the rights of his own people (General Torrijos). For Reagan, as for many Republicans, ceding control of the canal undermined U.S. military capabilities while strengthening the capacities of its enemies—a weak Panama was susceptible to Communist influence and vulnerable to anti-democratic forces. The treaties endangered the U.S. on both the right and the left.

The third main argument against the treaty attacked Carter personally. Reagan claimed that Carter was not being transparent about the treaty. Claiming that Carter was rushing to have the treaty ratified, Reagan stated:

> from the beginning, Mr. Carter negotiated this treaty without consulting Congressional leaders. And then, to head off public opposition, he turned the treaty signing ceremony into an elaborately staged media event. Only after the treaty was signed did Mr. Carter reveal the terms to Congress and the public.[26]

Here, Reagan implied that Carter was abusing the powers of the presidency. This abuse was part of a larger pattern of behavior that caused bipartisan concern. Reagan wrote: "You see, the Panama Canal Treaty is only the latest item in a broad range of far-reaching foreign policy and defense decisions made by Mr. Carter that have Republicans, Democrats, and Independents in a state of alarm." Reagan thus argued that when Carter chose to use the considerable power of his office, he did so in ways that damaged U.S national interests.

In combination, these arguments exemplify two of the three types of narratives Thomas Hollihan identifies in the Panama Canal controversy. Reagan's letter illustrates both the "cold war drama," or a narrative of the treaty that highlighted the American vulnerability to Soviet and Cuban influence in the region, and the "power politics" drama, a narrative that read the treaty against the grain of American pragmatic interests.[27] The rhetorical strategies identified in this letter are common to most of the anti-treaty *topoi* that tended to approach the issue not in moralistic terms, but in pragmatic and militaristic terms.

Those who defended the treaty argued in moralistic and pragmatic terms that highlighted why the treaty "was the right thing to do" (as Carter emphasized in his speeches) given American politico-economic interests. Defenders of the treaty explained the historical conditions under which the first treaty had been established and why maintaining this treaty would be counter-productive to establish productive political relations to Latin American countries. These appeals relied on practical concerns related to the reduced use of the canal due to incompatibility between the size of the canal and American ships. Since their first iteration in 1903, the Panama Canal treaties generated controversy. Several presidents attempted to renegotiate treaties with no recognizable success. The Senate ratified the treaty, a persuasive deed that we argue required the efforts of the president, his administration, and its allies.

Carter's Communication

In between the signing of the treaties and their ratification, Carter spoke to the public on Panama forty-six times. Two of those occasions were at the signing itself; two were follow-up meetings in Honduras and Costa Rica. Another fifteen were responses to questions in press conferences dominated by other issues. Eight were on ceremonial occasions such as the celebration of Hispanic Heritage Week, in which he said nothing substantively related to the treaties. Ten were comments he made as part of local town hall meetings, various question-and-answer sessions with citizens, or at campaign events—only two of these Q&A sessions were dedicated specifically to the treaties. Carter also gave two major policy addresses in which he discussed the treaties—a State of the Union address and a speech at the United Nations. The treaties were the subject of three sentences in each of these addresses. He communicated five times to specific congressional audiences—he dedicated one sentence to the topic in a speech to the Black Caucus, made brief comments in his message transmitting the treaties for consideration, and he sent a letter to one member of Congress. He also sent messages after ratification. Finally, he gave one major address to the nation on the treaties advocating their ratification.

In all of this communication, he was remarkably consistent as well as remarkably brief. Five arguments dominated his discourse. First, he argued that the treaties were the product of a long process. In Denver, for instance, he stated that, "President Eisenhower, President Kennedy, President Johnson, President Nixon, President Ford, and myself have all seen the need to modify or amend the present treaty with Panama concerning the Panama Canal."[28] In one sentence, he underlined the longevity of the process, its bipartisan nature, and the dominance of the presidency in foreign policy. Given the weight that each of these elements would have, it is unsurprising that he would stress them.[29]

Second, he claimed that the treaties were important to national security interests and that those interests would be better protected with the treaties than without them. Writing to reassure Senator Richard Stone (D-FL), for instance, Carter argued, "Ratification of the Panama Canal Treaties should not be viewed by any power as signaling a retreat of the United States in Latin America. Our country will continue to play a visible and dynamic role in the Western Hemisphere." He then insisted that the U.S. would both oppose any Soviet presence in the region and would continue to maintain its bases there.[30] Carter claimed that if anyone attacked the canal the U.S. could and would defend it.[31] National security was one of the more frequent arguments used against ratification, and Carter consistently responded that the treaties posed no threat to our security.

In fact, he claimed that the treaties would improve our regional relationships, and thus enhance our security interests. Speaking to the UN, for instance, he said,

> The peaceful settlement of differences is, of course, essential. The United States is willing to abide by that principle, as in the case of the recently signed Panama Canal treaties. Once ratified, these treaties can transform the U.S.-Panama relationship into one that permanently protects the interests and respects the sovereignty of both our countries.[32]

Elsewhere, he called attention to the "new spirit of friendship" evident between the U.S. and Latin America because of the treaties.[33] These arguments responded to Republican concerns about national security by shifting the definition of security from one based in territory to one premised on strong, respectful relationships. Coupled with his commitment to maintain American military presence in the region, Carter's argument offered the treaties as a middle ground that could resolve tensions while also maintaining American interests in the region.

Fourth, he defended the treaties as consistent with our national identity. He connected the treaties with the long history of American support for human rights[34] and with our national willingness to forego bullying and behave in ways that were "strong and fair."[35] He argued,

> We Americans want a more humane and stable world. We believe in good will and fairness, as well as strength. This agreement with Panama is something we want because we know it is right. This is not merely the surest way to protect and save the canal, it's a strong, positive act of a people who are still confident, still creative, still great.[36]

Here, he sought to preempt the argument, already made in conservative circles, that surrendering the canal showed weakness. Instead, Carter claimed the treaties renewed American commitment to fairness and the higher principles that had always guided the nation. Embodying those principles by negotiating a return of the canal, he implied, demonstrated the nation's moral leadership and helped foster the conditions for a better world.

In the final response to his critics, Carter claimed opposition to the treaties relied on misconceptions and false parallels. He asserted the presidential responsibility to educate and inform. In his national address on the treaties, he argued, "Much of that opposition [to the treaties] is based on misunderstanding and misinformation."[37] This language implies that opposition was unreasonable—it was either the result of ignorance or delusion. Once he made the facts known, that disagreement would disappear. Here, of course, he also depicted his opponents as either deluded themselves or willing to delude others. In either instance, he evidenced a willingness to proceed on the basis that a well-informed public would support ratification.

In making these claims, Carter relied on institutional arguments about the nature of the presidency and its international responsibilities. He made none of them alone. These arguments were fragmented, mobilized, and amplified by other members of the administration and its allies in a well-organized and ultimately successful campaign to change public opinion and earn senatorial approval of the treaties.

Magnifying the President's Message

Amplifying President Carter's treaty ratification campaign required national and international orchestration of political voices shaping an ensemble endorsing the president's treaty. Similar to the inner workings of a choir, the ratification campaign garnered rhetorical force through the harmonization of multiple voices. The rhetoric of multiple organizations, businesses, politicians, celebrities, and grassroots efforts encapsulated, circulated, and expanded presidential treaty discourse. The unity of these various messages is evident in archival material that explains the orchestration of voices and in the peculiar prevalence of similar rhetorical strategies present in the majority of the speeches given by the administration's allies. We parse out this process in terms of three distinct but interrelated rhetorical moves: fragmentation, mobilization, and amplification.

Fragmentation

Through an elaborate process of fragmentation, the Carter administration broke down presidential rhetoric into specific talking points that were easily inserted in educational materials, speeches, and letters that various individuals could use across a variety of contexts. This process of fragmenting presidential rhetoric into messages delivered by citizens, celebrities, and political actors, allowed the Carter administration to expand the president's message and target various constituencies—many of whom never heard from the president directly.

Although the State Department and the administration-sponsored Committee of Americans for the Canal Treaties (COACT)offered a wide range of fragments for speakers to use in their own speeches, four arguments were central to the treaty ratification campaign: justifications defining the treaties as a matter of diplomacy; reference to America's role in the world; speculation of what would happen in case the treaties were rejected; and refutation strategies regarding both the sovereignty/payment controversy and the security of the canal. Speeches and statements referring to the canal would touch on at least three of the above *topoi*. We illustrate these claims with specific reference to the speeches delivered by former National Security Advisor and former Secretary of State Henry Kissinger, Ambassador Ellsworth Bunker, Ambassador Sol Linowitz, Consul General of Panama Juan Antonio Stagg, Archbishop of Philadelphia John Cardinal Krol, First Lady Rosalynn Carter, National Security Advisor Dr. Zbigniew Brzezinski, and Secretary of State Cyrus Vance. They spoke in a variety of settings such in front of Congress, the Senate, on college campuses, to the press, and directly to citizens. Taken together, these texts exemplify the rhetorical strategies permeating the discourse of administration allies, and they were widely seen and discussed during the debates.

In defining the treaties, Carter's supporters framed the issue as a matter that exceeded the canal issue. They explained that the treaties with Panama were a symbolic diplomatic effort displaying American goodwill to other Latin American countries and developing nations around the world. Ambassador Sol Linowitz, for example, introduced his comments by saying: "The Panama Canal issue is not an issue between the United States and Panama. It involves the United States on one hand and Latin America, and indeed a good part of the Third World, on the other."[38] Using a more subtle, yet similar approach, Henry Kissinger explained the treaties as "the essential foundation of a long-term relationship of friendship and cooperation with the nations in the Western Hemisphere."[39] By shaping the narrative of the treaties as something greater than the relations between the U.S. and Panama, Linowitz, Kissinger, and others were able to amplify the magnitude of the concrete action of ratifying the treaties towards its symbolic significance worldwide. The speakers defined ratification as a diplomatic move with worldwide repercussions, thus raising the stakes of ratification to the public. This rhetorical move is particularly evident in articulations like that of John Cardinal Kroll, Archbishop of Philadelphia. He explained the Panama Canal treaties as a "prismatic case" in the sense that Americans were being observed for the way they would respond to the dynamics between industrialized and developing nations. He concluded that there was "a significant opportunity (…) for the U.S. and Panama to signal a new kind of relationship between large and small, industrialized and developing nations."[40] Kroll's narrative of the treaties resembled the narrative of most religious leaders who spoke in support for the ratification of the treaties: instead of a speeches filled with arid facts, the speeches of religious leaders were based on values, morals, and emotional appeals.[41]

In addition to using defined narratives regarding the treaties, those who spoke on behalf of the White House often emphasized the American role in the world. Speakers who alluded to this theme explained that it behooved a powerful nation to choose peaceful solutions that sought international cooperation. Brzezinski used this rhetorical strategy in a White House briefing in Denver when he highlighted that the America's potential to negotiate foreign affairs. The "ability to pioneer a new global framework of cooperation on such matters as arms transfers and nuclear proliferation and on a variety of other issues," he claimed, depended on

> the ability of the U.S. to present itself to the world as a force that is dealing constructively with the world, that does have a sense of historical direction, and that recognizes the need for a much wider fabric of international operation.[42]

This passage touched on some well-known themes in presidential rhetoric. Brzezinski alluded to American exceptionalism, the belief that the U.S. is uniquely moral, and acts with consistent morality. His discourse on American morality also implied a concern on how others would perceive the country if their actions and words were incoherent. Others made moral arguments to strategically insinuate the guilt of those who opposed administration actions, in this case, the treaties. For example, Archbishop Kroll claimed that the U.S. was obligated "to provide an example in world affairs of how states of very different political, economic and military power can deal with each other in terms of equality, dignity, and mutual respect."[43] The choice of highlighting America's elevated moral standards resembles the strategy of alluding to America's manifest destiny, a powerful device to heighten the moral grounds in reading the case of the treaties' ratification against the grain of the American duty of upholding values of respect, cooperation, and historical fairness. This strategy raised the stakes of treaty ratification even higher by implying the decision implicates both America's commitment to diplomacy to resolve disputes and the nation's historic commitment to international leadership by example. In sum, these arguments suggested treaty ratification placed American diplomatic and moral credibility on the line and that only by acceding to the treaties could the nation live up to its true ideals.

These two strategies were often accompanied by warnings of what could happen to the country if the treaties were rejected. Such warnings were almost identical for most of the speakers: American diplomacy would be seriously jeopardized. Secretary of State Cyrus Vance mentioned in a Q&A session in Kentucky that given the deep feelings associated to the Panama case, if the treaties were not ratified, he was "fearful that this deep feeling could cause a very serious situation," which he thought was not "limited to Panama itself" because all Latin American countries were also paying attention to the matter.[44] Brzezinski highlighted

multiple times that he had no doubt that rejection of the treaties would incite radicalization in Panama, presenting countries such as Cuba and the Soviet Union an
opportunity to exploit a moment of destabilization to their advantage.[45] Kissinger
was also categorical in affirming:

> Rejection of the treaties would poison our relationship with all countries of Latin
> America on all other issues, and leave us, for the first time in our history, facing the
> unanimous hostility of all the nations to the south of us in our own Hemisphere.[46]

He also remarked that rejection of the treaties would undermine presidential
authority, because it would display lack of unity and thus vulnerability, further
jeopardizing the nation's standing in the region and world.

Finally, texts of supporters often contained rebuttal strategies addressing controversial themes. Two of them stood out for their frequency: the controversy surrounding Panamanian sovereignty and questions regarding security of the canal.
Panamanian sovereignty was often questioned in anti-treaty materials through the
mistaken idea that the canal territory had been acquired, like Alaska or Louisiana.
To address such questions, speakers explained that the treaty signed in 1903 did
not transfer sovereignty over the Canal Zone to the United States. Instead, as
Consul General of Panama Ing. Juan Antonio Stagg put it, the 1903 treaty only
gave the U.S the right to "to act as if it were sovereign for the specific purpose
of building, sanitizing, operating, maintaining, and protecting the Canal."[47] Like
Stagg, speakers highlighted that the new treaties were not "giving away" the canal,
because it had never been America's possession in the first place.

Some speakers reinforced this notion through rhetorical strategies that highlighted the inappropriateness of such colonial language. First Lady Rosalynn
Carter pinpointed this very issue in a speech delivered in Puerto Rico. While
mentioning the new "cooperative spirit" in relations between the United States
and Latin American countries, she claimed:

> Our past programs for our friends in Latin America –both successful and otherwise—
> have been based primarily on economic aid. With the Panama Canal treaty, a powerful
> and tangible new factor has been added: a spirit of equality, mutual respect, partner-
> ship, and an end to a damaging image of colonialism.[48]

Similarly, Archbishop Kroll adopted language that highlighted the need to dis-
solve the "vestiges of colonial politics of the nineteenth century."[49] This type of
message reinforced the unsuitability of the colonial mentality in referring to the
canal as American property in a moment when most industrialized countries
would no longer maintain colonial relations with developing nations. That was

one way of highlighting the inappropriateness of thinking of the Canal Zone as an American possession. Another way to refute the question of sovereignty relied on factual proofs such as the fact that babies born in the Canal Zone had the right to be Panamanians, not Americans—unless born of American parents.[50]

The other central point of criticism regarding security of the canal was addressed more subtly through articulations explaining that the best way to maintain the canal's security was not through military engagement but through diplomatic actions, namely, the ratification of the treaties. Kissinger noted the treaties would "improve the political environment for the protection of our interests" and that

> while the United States would, in any event, continue to have the physical means to defend the canal unilaterally, we could exercise that ability under the present 1903 treaty only at the risk of considerable cost to our other Western Hemisphere interests.[51]

Implicit in Kissinger's comment is the idea that the new treaties are the cheapest viable option for keeping the canal secure. In general, such comments were not typically detailed but drew a direct association between treaties' ratification and canal security through an implicit suggestion that without the treaties, turmoil would make the task of securing the canal very costly. By breaking the president's message into fragments, speakers could maintain the essential coherence of the administration's message while also tailoring that message to specific audiences. This element of the persuasive campaign was buttressed by the deployment of supportive speeches.

Mobilization

Mobilization, as a rhetorical mechanism, consists of orchestrating various fragments into a composition that best fits a specific audience. The administration mobilized individuals and organizations to circulate the presidential message by defining who would speak when and where. The ratification campaign was a concerted effort to reach different publics through voices that resonated with each specific audience.

Several individuals were important in organizing the people, organizations, and events that composed such an ensemble promoting the ratification of the treaty. Chief among them was Laurie Lucey, Executive Assistant to the Deputy Assistant to the President, who assumed a central role in organizing the rhetorical logistics of the persuasive effort. Among her voluminous memos, tracking reports, schedules of speakers and the like, we found a handwritten note scribbled in a page of a yellow legal pad, in which Lucey laid out the groups of individuals who would participate in the rhetorical campaign for treaty ratification.[52] This unassuming note was helpful in confirming the key political actors involved in amplifying presidential rhetoric. The ratification campaign depended upon the endorsement of key businesses and associations, along with the support of politicians and grassroots organizations, namely the Committee of Americans for the Canal Treaties (COACT).

Lucey's archives reveal a rich arsenal of educational materials related to COACT. Her files also contained COACT's extensive compilation of sample letters, speeches, and spot announcements (in 30, 50, or 60 second versions) for radio or television crafted for many of the officials in the initiative, including Senator Ernest Hollings, Senator Hubert Humphrey, John Wayne, President Gerald Ford, Secretary Henry Kissinger, General Brent Scowcroft, Secretary William D. Rogers, Senator John Sherman Cooper, General Robert J. Fleming, General Matthew B. Ridgway, General William C. Westmoreland, Governor W. Averell Harriman. COACT's packet also provided instructional materials for its members to write personalized and more effective letters to their communities, newspapers, and representatives, and lists of phone numbers of senators who could be urged to support the treaty.[53] Much of the content available in COACT's packet is identical to the educational materials put together by the State Department. Preparation for speakers and supporters was extensive both for citizens and political actors. If COACT compiled substantive communicative strategies to prepare supporters in their speeches, letters, and signs, the Bureau of Public Affairs of the Department of State invested twice as much in preparing political actors for their appearances.

Preparation ranged from informational materials, to seminars for Panama Speakers, to closely monitoring the content of speeches and interactions with the press. For example, a lengthy memo dated January 5, 1978 from Jill A. Schuker from the Bureau of Public Affairs—Department of State provided prepared information such as thematic background (including specific talking points) that political actors could include in their speeches, a compendium of "common misconceptions" regarding the canal, a compilation of "sample comments," and a list of organizations and public leaders endorsing the new treaties. A letter attached to this memo and signed by D.H. Popper, highlighted the importance of keeping messages consistent by claiming: "Department of State would appreciate the opportunity to read in advance a draft of all statements, to assist in avoiding inaccuracy and imbalance."[54] Close monitoring of officials' rhetorical strategies helped the Carter administration ensure that the fragmentation of the president's message did not lose the core characteristics planned by the campaign. In preparing political actors to speak, the administration organized a seminar containing the following schedule: "briefing/discussion on positive points to stress and answers to points commonly raised in opposition to treaty," "organization, presentation and audience analysis," "short presentation by speakers on Panama Treaty (2 minutes followed by 2 minute questions and answer)—Videotape playback and critique," and on the following day "speakers prepare 7-minute formal presentation advocating treaty. Presentation followed by 3 minute questions and answers—Videotape playback and critique."[55] Through such measures, the administration ensured uniformity among speakers who were to extend the rhetorical campaign nationwide. These efforts also allowed the administration to tailor speakers to specific audiences, which, along with the fragmentation of messages, meant that the president's message could be extended in the ways and to the places of the White House's choosing.

Amplification

The similarity in rhetorical strategies in surrogate speeches suggests the content derived from a common source, namely, the White House. Echoing the rhetorical strategies present in Carter's addresses on the subject, the speakers on behalf of the administration relied on narratives telling the history of the canal and drawing a conclusion that the new treaties were the right, fair thing to do. Furthermore, the speeches and statements of most officials speaking on behalf of the administration used language similar to the president's, highlighting words like "efficient," "open," "neutral," and "secure."

This strategy of amplifying the president's message was not unique to the Carter presidency. In fact, archival material of the presidential staff discussing the early stages of the ratification campaign reveal that their communication strategy was borrowed directly from Truman presidency aides who orchestrated the communication campaign for the Marshall Plan. Similar to the Marshall Plan, the executive's role in selling the treaties involved choosing individuals to speak on behalf of the presidency. Public opinion was to be influenced through "well-coordinated private efforts" that would generate a sense of objectivity and acceptability to the plan. As revealed in a memo to Joseph Aragon, Assistant to the President, regarding the usefulness in borrowing from the strategies used to "sell" the Marshall Plan, the effort to influence public opinion highlighted the need for grassroots support and entailed the following:

> Special committees of prominent citizens were formed at the direct invitation of President Truman, following the advice of Paul Hoffman and the ECA public affairs people. These private committees were asked to study the problem of European postwar economic recovery, to write reports, and prominent Administration officials were put in charge of coordinating such private efforts.[56]

The use of this as a persuasive template is evident in other materials gathered in documents describing the plans delineated for outreach strategies regarding the Panama Canal treaties.

While some memos highlighted the key areas of activity (as well as who would be involved in each), other memos laid down detailed strategies for each of the phases of the treaties. As laid out in June of 1977, the plans to change public perception towards the treaties relied heavily on Ambassador Linowitz and Ambassador Bunker to speak about the negotiations initially, but to also drawn on other surrogates. Emphasis on the speaking committees was given to the states that had been identified as "key areas of opposition (particularly as they relate to influential Senators and their positions on relevant Committees and in leadership)." Moreover, the plan was emphatic in claiming that "immediate considerations should be given to the formation of a prominent 'spontaneous' citizens' committee with some strong conservative/moderate names."[57] The "spontaneous" citizens' committee eventually became COACT which led many of the efforts in educating the public and supporting the treaties. All these efforts were essential to the fragmentation, mobilization, and amplification of presidential rhetoric; they all point to the importance of focusing on the administration rather than the person of the president in understanding White House efforts to affect public opinion and persuade Congress.

Conclusion: The President and the Presidency

This study demonstrates how presidential rhetoric works institutionally and individually. Through a concerted effort of multiple political voices, Carter's main message on the treaties was intentionally fragmented, mobilized, and amplified. The White House used a specific set of arguments, employed in various combinations by speakers who targeted narrow audiences, which extended the president's own communication. With the orchestration of messages between the president and important political actors, leaders from religious organizations and businesses, and COACT, the message in support of ratification was both narrowly and widely broadcast. Borrowing from the credibility of such key pieces in this rhetorical puzzle, the administration mobilized important institutional actors and earned senatorial support for ratification. Taken collectively, the communicative efforts to change public opinion and harness political support towards the treaties' ratification are displays of how presidential rhetoric encompasses institutional as well as individual efforts.

Finally, this chapter demonstrates contemporary concerns about message and media fragmentation have a long history and are not a recent phenomenon. By including the rhetorical efforts of the administration in how we define "presidential rhetoric," our understanding of presidential persuasion is more complete and more complicated because it accounts for the ways presidencies have addressed problems related to audience, mass media, and message fragmentation. Methodologically, this case provides good evidence for the centrality of archival research for the study of presidential rhetoric. Engaging presidential archives enables scholars to make claims about the desirability and effectivity of rhetorical campaigns in the modern era. Theoretically, this chapter points to the usefulness of placing an individual president in an institutional context, and to understand presidential rhetoric in a wider frame, both across time, and across the executive institution itself.

Notes

1. Associated Press poll on the Panama Canal, conducted on September 19, 1977, "Canal: Press, media, public affairs 7/77–9/77" Folder, Box 17, Assistant to the President—Joseph Aragon, Jimmy Carter Library.

2. Louis Harris, "Narrow Margin in U.S. Prefers Panama Canal Treaty Approval," *The Washington Post*, April 3, 1978, accessed February 24, 2016, https://www.washingtonpost.com/archive/politics/1978/04/03/narrow-margin-in-us-prefers-panama-canal-treaty-approval/ce5629a6-b1d3-4640-a881-2fc0df954525/?utm_term=.5210230d94bd.

3. Ted J. Smith III and J. Michael Hogan, "Public Opinion and the Panama Canal Treaties of 1977," *Public Opinion Quarterly* 51 (1987): 5–30.

4. Cambridge Survey Research—Panama Canal: Summary of Public Opinion, "Canal: Press, media, public affairs 10/77- 4/78" Folder, Box 18, Assistant to the President—Joseph Aragon, Jimmy Carter Library.

5. George C. Edwards, III, *On Deaf Ears: The Limits of the Bully Pulpit* (New Haven, CT: Yale University Press, 2003); George C. Edwards, III, *The Strategic President: Persuasion and Opportunity in Presidential Leadership* (Princeton, NJ: Princeton University Press, 2009).

6. George C. Edwards, III, *At the Margins: Presidential Leadership of Congress* (New Haven, CT: Yale University Press, 1990).

7. Jeffrey Cohen, *Going Local: Presidential Leadership in the Post-Broadcast Age* (Cambridge: Cambridge University Press, 2010).

8. Brandon Rottinghaus, *The Provisional Pulpit: Modern Presidential Leadership of Public Opinion* (College Station: Texas A&M University Press, 2010).

9. For more information on the rhetorical presidency, see: James W. Ceaser, Glen E. Thurow, Jeffrey Tulis, and Joseph M. Bessette, "The Rise of the Rhetorical Presidency," *Presidential Studies Quarterly* 11 (1981): 158–171; Jeffrey Tulis, *The Rhetorical Presidency* (Princeton, NJ: Princeton University Press, 1987); Mary E. Stuckey and Frederic J. Antczak, "The Rhetorical Presidency: Deepening Vision, Widening Exchange" *Annals of the International Communication Association* 21 (1998): 405–442; and Mary E. Stuckey, "Rethinking the Rhetorical Presidency and Presidential Rhetoric," *Review of Communication* 10 (2010): 38–52.

10. David Zarefsky, "Presidential Rhetoric and the Power of Definition," *Presidential Studies Quarterly* 34, no. 3 (2004): 607–619; Vanessa B. Beasley, "Making Diversity Safe for Democracy: American Pluralism and the Presidential Local Address, 1885–1992," *Quarterly Journal of Speech* 87 (2001): 25–40; Cohen, *Going Local: Presidential Leadership in the Post-Broadcast Age* (New York, NY: Cambridge University Press, 2010).

11. Joshua M. Scacco and Kevin Coe, "The Ubiquitous Presidency: Toward a New Paradigm for Studying Presidential Communication" *International Journal of Communication* 10 (2016): 2014–2037; Stephen Heidt, "The Presidency as Pastiche: Atomization, Circulation, and Rhetorical Instability," *Rhetoric & Public Affairs* 15, no. 4 (2012): 623–633.

12. No author, *Guide to the Panama Canal* (Panama City, Ediciones Balboa, 2010), 4.

13. For the best history of the canal and its construction, see David McCullough, *The Path Between the Seas: The Creation of the Panama Canal, 1870-1914* (New York: Simon and Schuster, 1977).

14. J. Michael Hogan, *The Panama Canal in American Politics: Domestic Advocacy and the Evolution of Policy* (Carbondale, IL: Southern Illinois University Press, 1986), 59. For additional details on how the United States orchestrated the secession in order to get the terms most convenient for the treaty approved, see: David Bushnell, *The Making of Modern Colombia: A Nation in Spite of Itself* (Berkeley, CA: University of California Press, 1993): 151-153.

15. "Text of the Canal Treaty," *New York Times*, November 21, 1903, accessed March 30, 2017, http://query.nytimes.com/mem/archive-free/pdf?res=9A0CEED91039E333A25752C2 A9679D946297D6CF

16. Paul B. Ryan, *The Panama Canal Controversy: U.S. Diplomacy and Defense Interests* (Stanford, CA: Hoover Institution Press), 16-17; 23-24.

17. Hogan, *The Panama Canal in American Politics:* 62; 69; 75-78; 85.

18. Michael Grow, *U.S. Presidents and Latin American Interventions: Pursuing Regime Change in the Cold War* (Lawrence, KS: University Press of Kansas, 2008), 120.

19. Memo, Hamilton Jordan to the President, 10/16/77, "Mailing Anti-Treaty" Folder, Box 254, WHCF—Laurie Lucey's Oversized Attachment Files, Jimmy Carter Library.

20. Press Clipping from Congressional Quarterly entitled 'Panama Canal: Groups Favoring Treaties Fight to Offset Opponents' Massive Lobbying Effort' published on January 21, 1978, "Newspaper Clippings, [CF OA 76]" Folder, Box 254, WHCF—Laurie Lucey's Oversized Attachment Files, Jimmy Carter Library.

21. Memo, Hamilton Jordan to the President, 10/16/77, "Mailing Anti-Treaty" Folder, Box 254, WHCF—Laurie Lucey's Oversized Attachment Files, Jimmy Carter Library.

22. See "Panama—Responses to Ronald Reagan," Box 256, WHCF—Laurie Lucey's Oversized Attachment Files, Jimmy Carter Library.

23. Memo, Hamilton Jordan to the President, 10/16/77, "Mailing Anti-Treaty" Folder, Box 254, WHCF—Laurie Lucey's Oversized Attachment Files, Jimmy Carter Library.

24. Memo, Hamilton Jordan to the President, 10/16/77, "Mailing Anti-Treaty" Folder, Box 254, WHCF—Laurie Lucey's Oversized Attachment Files, Jimmy Carter Library.

25. Memo, Hamilton Jordan to the President, 10/16/77, "Mailing Anti-Treaty" Folder, Box 254, WHCF—Laurie Lucey's Oversized Attachment Files, Jimmy Carter Library.

26. Memo, Hamilton Jordan to the President, 10/16/77, "Mailing Anti-Treaty" Folder, Box 254, WHCF—Laurie Lucey's Oversized Attachment Files, Jimmy Carter Library.

27. Thomas A. Hollihan, "The Public Controversy Over the Panama Canal Treaties: An Analysis of American Foreign Policy Rhetoric," *Western Journal of Speech Communication* 50, no. 4 (1986): 368–387.

28. Jimmy Carter, "Denver, Colorado, Remarks and a Question-and-Answer Session at a Briefing on the Panama Canal Treaties," October 22, 1977, online by Gerhard Peters and John T. Woolley, *The American Presidency Project*, http:// www.presidency.ucsb.edu/ ws/?pid=6836.

29. See also, Jimmy Carter, "Address to the Nation on the Panama Canal Treaties," February 1, 1978, online by Gerhard Peters and John T. Woolley, *The American Presidency Project*, http://www.presidency.ucsb.edu/ws/?pid=29995; Jimmy Carter, "Remarks at the Signing Ceremony of the Panama Canal Treaties," September 7, 1977, online by Gerhard Peters and John T. Woolley, *The American Presidency Project*, http:// www.presidency.ucsb.edu/ ws/?pid=6592.

30. Jimmy Carter, "Letter to Richard Stone," January 27, 1978, online by Gerhard Peters and John T. Woolley, *The American Presidency Project*, http://www.presidency.ucsb.edu/ ws/?pid=29784.

31. Carter, "Denver."

32. Jimmy Carter, "Address Before the United Nations General Assembly," October 4, 1977, online by Gerhard Peters and John T. Woolley, *The American Presidency Project*, http:// www.presidency.ucsb.edu/ws/?pid=

33. Carter, "Address to the Nation"; Jimmy Carter, "Signing Ceremony."

34. Jimmy Carter, "World Jewish Congress Remarks at the Meeting of the General Council," November 2, 1977, online by Gerhard Peters and John T. Woolley, *The American Presidency Project*, http:// www.presidency.ucsb.edu/ws/?pid=6875.

35. Carter, "Denver."

36. Carter, "National Address."

37. Carter, "National Address."

38. Comments by Ambassador Sol Linowitz—The Panama Canal, "Panama—Early Material" Folder, Box 254, WHCF—Laurie Lucey's Oversized Attachment Files, Jimmy Carter Library.

39. Statement of the Honorable Henry A. Kissinger with Respect to the Panama Canal Treaties Before the Committee on International Affairs of the United States House of Representatives, "Panama Background Material 8/30/77—10/12/77" Folder, Box 119, WHCF—Landon Butler's Transition Files, Jimmy Carter Library.

40. Testimony of John Cardinal Krol, Archbishop of Philadelphia on Behalf of the United States Catholic Conference on The Panama Canal Treaties—Presented to the Committee on Foreign Relations of the United States Senate, "[Panama Canal—Pros and Cons], 9/8/772/5/78" Folder, Box 121, WHCF—Butler, Jimmy Carter Library.

41. The liberal narrative is guided by logics of long-term thinking, and the political actors speaking on behalf of the president are coherent in highlighting that conservative thinking limited by its short-term nature.

42. Dr. Zbigniew Brzezinski's Remarks at the White House Briefing on the Panama Canal Treaties, "Panama—Senior Administration Speakers" Folder, Box 256, WHCF—Laurie Lucey's Oversized Attachment Files, Jimmy Carter Library.

43. Testimony of John Cardinal Krol, Archbishop of Philadelphia on Behalf of the United States Catholic Conference on The Panama Canal Treaties—Presented to the Committee on Foreign Relations of the United States Senate, "[Panama Canal—Pros and Cons], 9/8/77—2/5/78" Folder, Box 121, WHCF—Butler, Jimmy Carter Library.

44. Question and Answer Session Following the Address by the Honorable Cyrus R. Vance Secretary of State at Leadership Luncheon—Galt House Hotel, Louisville, Kentucky, January 13, 1978, "Panama—Senior Administration Speakers" Folder, Box 256, WHCF—Laurie Lucey's Oversized Attachment Files, Jimmy Carter Library.

45. Dr. Zbigniew Brzezinski's Remarks at the White House Briefing on the Panama Canal Treaties, "Panama—Senior Administration Speakers" Folder, Box 256, WHCF—Laurie Lucey's Oversized Attachment Files, Jimmy Carter Library.

46. Statement of the Honorable Henry A. Kissinger with Respect to the Panama Canal Treaties Before the Committee on International Affairs of the United States House of Representatives, "Panama Background Material 8/30/77—10/12/77" Folder, Box 119, WHCF—Landon Butler's Transition Files, Jimmy Carter Library.

47. Speech Given at: Auburn University, State of Alabama—January 11, 1978—By Consul General of Panama—New York Ing. Juan Antonio Stagg, "[Panama Background Material, 8/12/77—8/28/77]" Folder, Box 119, WHCF—Landon Butler's Transition Files, Jimmy Carter Library.

48. Office of the First Lady's Press Secretary, "[Panama Canal Treaty—Support Efforts]— 1/26/78 - 8/20/79" Folder, Box 123, WHCF—Butler.

49. Testimony of John Cardinal Krol, Archbishop of Philadelphia on Behalf of the United States Catholic Conference on The Panama Canal Treaties—Presented to the Committee on Foreign Relations of the United States Senate, "[Panama Canal—Pros and Cons], 9/8/77—2/5/78" Folder, Box 121, WHCF—Butler, Jimmy Carter Library.

50. Comments by Ambassador Sol Linowitz—The Panama Canal, "Panama—Early Material" Folder, Box 254, WHCF—Laurie Lucey's Oversized Attachment Files, Jimmy Carter Library.

51. Statement of the Honorable Henry A. Kissinger with Respect to the Panama Canal Treaties Before the Committee on International Affairs of the United States House of Representatives, "Panama Background Material 8/30/77—10/12/77" Folder, Box 119, WHCF—Landon Butler's Transition Files, Jimmy Carter Library.

52. Lucey wrote down that the first group would be composed by "Linowitz, President, Bunker, Vice President, Vance, Christopher, Brown, Duncan, Gen. Brown," while under cabinet she wrote "Blumenthal, Strauss, Kreps, Young, Sahlesinge, Marohal, Harris, Adams, Bell, Califano," the negotiating team would be composed by "Amb. David Popper, Gen Welborn Dolvin, Richard Wyrough, Ambler Moss, Todman, Cooper, Solomon, Scramton, Alexander, Stetson, Claytor," and a third group was composed by "Ford, Kissinger, Laird, Zumwalt, Lemnitzer, and Taylor." Laurie Lucey, "Panama—Early Material" Folder, Box 254, WHCF—Laurie Lucey's Oversized Attachment Files, Jimmy Carter Library.

53. COACT, "Committee of Americans for the Panama Canal Treaties (COACT)" Folder, Box 253, WHCF—Laurie Lucey's Oversized Attachment Files, Jimmy Carter Library.

54. David H. Popper, in compiled materials from Jill A. Schuker "[Panama Canal—Background Information], 12/1/77—1/12-78" Folder, Box 119, WHCF—Landon Butler's Transition Files, Jimmy Carter Library.

55. Memo, Peter B. Johnson (ARA/PPC) to Ambassador Todman (ARA), September 8, 1977, "Canal: Press, Media, Public Affairs 7/77—9/77" Folder, Box 17, Assistant to the President—Joseph Aragon, Jimmy Carter Library.

56. Memo, Pedro A. Sanjuan to Joseph Aragon, October 5, 1977, How the Marshall Plan Was Sold to the American People and to Congress, "Committee of Americans for the Canal Treaties (COACT) 9/77—12/77" Folder, Box 18, Assistant to the President—Joseph Aragon, Jimmy Carter Library

57. Memo, Jill A. Schuker to Joseph Aragon, June 17, 1977, Working Paper on Panama/Public and press Outreach Strategy, "Committee of Americans for the Canal Treaties (COACT) 9/77—12/77" Folder, Box 18, Assistant to the President—Joseph Aragon, Jimmy Carter Library.

CHAPTER FOUR

Genre-Busting

Campaign Speech Genres and the Rhetoric of Political Outsiders

RYAN NEVILLE-SHEPARD

When President Donald Trump delivered his inaugural address on January 20, 2017, the common response from members of the news media was that something was amiss, that the new president had given one of the most important kinds of speeches in American politics and radically deviated from long-established generic norms. Ed Kilgore of *New York* magazine wrote that the address was "belligerent, nationalist, and populist," and confessed he had "never heard anything like this one in terms of its divisive content and complete lack of uplift."[1] Similarly, David Von Drehle of *Time* stated that Trump delivered a speech that in "16 mostly harsh, mostly confrontational minutes" would "alienate his predecessors dating back to Theodore Roosevelt and beyond," marking an entrance to "office as a wrecking ball" with a "first message to the world [that] was as radical as they come, and as populist as a pitchfork."[2] Philip Bump of *The Washington Post* agreed, summarizing that Trump's inaugural address "stood out from the 57 prior in one way: It was bleaker. A lot bleaker."[3] This was not the first time Trump surprised critics by violating the spirit of an important speech genre. Although Trump's victory speech touched on all of the essential points of the genre, Sopan Deb of CBS News remarked that it felt insincere as he relied on a teleprompter, something he had previously "derided for being a tool of entrenched politicians."[4] Before his surprise victory, Trump claimed that should he lose, he might not even concede, and "he might consider the results illegitimate because the process is rigged."[5] His promise to keep America "in suspense" led *The Wall Street Journal*'s Bret Stephens to call it the "most disgraceful statement by a presidential candidate in 160 years."[6] Trump's nomination acceptance speech at the Republican National Convention fared no better, as he was criticized for using "dark imagery and an almost angry tone," departing "from the optimistic talk about American possibility."[7] Trump's rejection of generic norms actually began as early as his announcement speech when he characterized Mexican immigrants as drug lords and rapists. Reflecting on Trump's mistakes, CNN's Sally Kohn suggested he would ultimately be hurt by his rhetoric, claiming after his chaotic announcement "there's no way Trump will become president."[8]

Some countered the impulse to criticize Trump for deviating from generic norms by suggesting he might actually represent a different tradition of political communication. Trump, some argued, resembled a third party candidate. Journalist Dan Balz, for instance, called Trump "the country's first independent president."[9] Likewise, Jonathan Martin of *The New York Times* said Trump "ran as a Republican, but he was effectively a third party candidate."[10] It may not be a coincidence that Trump sounded like a blend of George Wallace and Ross Perot. After all, Trump first flirted with a presidential campaign in 2000 when he ran in the primary for the Reform Party's nomination.[11] His violations of political norms certainly seem in line with the rhetorical practices of third party candidates. In my recent research on third party announcement speeches, nomination acceptance addresses, and concession statements, I have found that the recurring situational barriers, perceived strategic constraints, and overall purposes of minor party campaigns means that the formal characteristics of the genres differ substantially when one comes from outside the two major parties.[12] The similarities between Trump and those representing minor parties are likely to mean one of two things: either Trump was a third party candidate infiltrating the system while temporarily carrying the banner of a major party, or third party candidates and Trump practice some sort of common outsider style. This chapter addresses that second possibility.

I contend that candidate Trump and third party candidates share an outsider style that became clearest in performing formal campaign speech genres. I suggest that neither Trump nor third party candidates are the sloppy violators of generic norms as some imply, but that they act as "genre-busters," purposefully violating expectations of a class of discourse in order to achieve the complicated goals of fringe political leaders. This argument develops over several sections. First, I suggest that the political outsider's practice of genre-busting requires a fresh look at how genre scholars treat violators of generic norms. In the spirit of this collection of essays, what I am advocating is a close reading of the language of those who do not meet our expectations of rhetorical leadership in order to advance our understanding of the rhetoric of those who challenge institutions and conventions. Second, instead of tracing the functions and formal characteristics of an outsider variant of an individual speech genre, as I have in previous work, I focus on the performance of various speech genres by eleven prominent third party presidential hopefuls, including all those who have received at least one percent of the popular vote in the post-war era. Identifying what they have in common, I argue that genre-busting draws media coverage, creates public spectacle to maintain that coverage, while crafting a form of nontraditional political authenticity. I analyze how this task is accomplished through several strategies, including an explicit rejection of generic norms, a series of odd policy proposals, and a reliance on polarizing rhetoric. Third, I explain how the function and formal features of genre-busting move beyond third-parties by offering a case study of the rhetoric of Donald Trump, specifically a close reading of his campaign announcement speech. I end by discussing how this chapter suggests a need to revisit the value and practice of genre criticism, especially as they pertain to understanding political oddballs and outsiders.

Advancing Genre Studies: "Violators" versus "Outsiders"

While genre analysis has been essential to understanding the ways presidents and presidential candidates have defined the executive branch, this study seeks to expand the usefulness of genre criticism in understanding individuals who do not fit neatly into these imagined molds. Any political speech tends to fall into some established genre. As Karlyn Kohrs Campbell and Kathleen Hall Jamieson argued, "To deal with anything at all without classifying or typing it, without remarking on its similarities or dissimilarities to other like or unlike things, is simply not possible."[13] However, the grouping of similar speeches into a familiar class for purposes of evaluation can happen prematurely, sometimes rendering those who do not fall in line with generic norms as ignorant or careless. In this section I seek to amend understanding of political campaign speech genres to account for actions of political outsiders. I begin by reviewing key definitions of genre, and I then explain how genre criticism often misunderstands those who deviate from generic norms

The lack of a nuanced understanding of how political outsiders use genres of political discourse stems from the way genre has been defined. In an early effort, Ed Black defined genre situationally, arguing that there are a "limited number of situations in which a rhetor can find himself," "a limited number of ways in which a rhetor can and will respond rhetorically to any given situation type," and that the "recurrence of a given situational type through history will provide the critic with information on the rhetorical responses available in that situation."[14] Black's notion of genre advanced the idea that situation type determines generic constraints and content, that any campaign announcement, for instance, would sound similar due to a common rhetorical situation. Attempting to avoid over-simplification, other scholars more narrowly defined the forces that lead to the limitations on acceptable responses, suggesting that the situation dictating similar formal characteristics may be limited to very specific situations. Campbell and Jamieson agreed that generic forms "are stylistic and substantive responses to perceived situational demands," but added that form defines "the unique qualities of any rhetorical act" and that "they are the means through which we come to understand how an act works to achieve its ends."[15] Crucially, Campbell and Jamieson elaborated, the formal characteristics of a genre "appear in other discourses," but they make a genre unique when they are "together in constellation,"[16] or when they satisfy the same function. Robert Rowland referred to such an approach to genre as the ontological/empirical perspective, which is "based on the assumption that genres are empirical categories of discourse that possess underlying (ontological) defining principles distinguishing them from other works."[17] Revising this approach Rowland added that the internal dynamic that leads to recurring formal characteristics is created from the forces of the exigence and constraints, plus "needs, limiting purpose in confronting those needs, and societal limitations on appropriate rhetorical responses."[18] Thus, by this definition there would be very few situations requiring similar responses.

Even when the internal dynamic is strong, and the formal characteristics are consistent, theorists see genre more as a critical tool than providing hard and fast rules. Campbell and Jamieson argued "there will always be other ways to approach [presidential addresses]," especially since the "categories [critics] are using are only one set among many."[19] Yet critical attention seems to gravitate toward "links between function and form." That is, generic critics are pragmatists "interested in those similarities that make works rhetorically absorbing and consequential," the way a purpose is satisfied with common language strategies.[20] Explaining the way genre criticism serves as a tool, Rowland wrote that it seeks to "increase our understanding of form, structure, and content" of rhetorical acts, to achieve "explanation aimed at increasing the subtlety and sensitivity with which we appreciate the communication."[21] Urging critics to embrace a form of generic classification that is "most useful in situations that are highly constrained,"[22] Rowland suggested that such an approach means revisiting the usefulness of an imagined genre by making sure that categories adequately explain the discourse, but that the discourse advances our knowledge of the category as well. The ultimate goal is to avoid oversimplification.

Despite genre criticism's flexibility as a method, evaluations of campaign speech genres may exhibit significant flaws. First, critics occasionally make mistakes when analyzing a performance through an inappropriate categorization. As Rowland warned, "If a work is inappropriately placed in a given category the analysis of it inevitably will be flawed."[23] Campbell and Jamieson warned of something similar, arguing that sometimes a "generic 'fit' is asserted although certain essential characteristics are absent or significant dissimilarities exist."[24] Second, critics may engage in an automatic classification, producing a kind of cookie cutter criticism without much of a desire to learn from the individual performance of a genre.[25] Third, and relatedly, Campbell and Jamieson argued, sometimes genre criticism is flawed because understanding of the genre itself is flawed. "The critic may fail to delineate the essential characteristics of the model," they suggested, "so that the basis for comparison is faulty."[26] Carolyn Miller similarly cautioned that genre claims are sometimes made though "there may fail to be significant substantive or formal similarities at the lower levels of the hierarchy," or even worse, that the similarities exist only in the exigence or the audience.[27] Finally, and perhaps most importantly, genre criticism can miss its mark when "there is no pragmatic component, no way to understand the genre as a social action,"[28] or when the social action of a dominant genre may be mistakenly assumed in its variants.

When it comes to political rhetoric, genre criticism can be most problematic in its treatment of those who deviate from generic norms. Ultimately, genre criticism serves "explanatory, predictive, and evaluative aims,"[29] but there is little agreement about how to handle those who appear to go their own way. At some level, critics have suggested that those who do not satisfy the expectations of a genre usually fall short. While Rowland suggested there are many ways to evaluate a speech like a eulogy, he added "the assumption here is that acts which fail to fulfill generic norms are likely to be of poor quality."[30] Simons and Aghazarian agreed, writing, "One could … legitimately criticize a eulogist if his or her rhetoric failed to fulfill the demands of eulogistic situations."[31] In a separate study, Simons said a lack of conformity usually means that one is responding "inappropriately."[32] Yet genre scholars simultaneously recognize that deviating from generic prescriptions may be necessary "in exceptional cases … [when] there was clear and compelling reason to do [so]."[33] "Exigencies may be violated," Rowland concluded, "and in some cases successfully violated, in part because it is sometimes strategic to do the unexpected."[34] Such deviations, Campbell and Jamieson noted, most likely respond "to the conditions at a particular moment," and require "special comment."[35] Carolyn Miller has opined that violations may not be special cases, however. "Genres change, evolve, and decay," she noted, and "the number of genres current in any society is indeterminate and depends upon the complexity and diversity of the society."[36]

At best, scholarly approaches to generic violations are split—in some cases they are considered failed opportunities, and in others they are said to succeed because they are special cases. In reality, though, the abrasive and bleak rhetoric of someone like Donald Trump, especially in moments that are usually formal, scripted, and hopeful, still leave many critics scratching their heads and predicting backlash for what is perceived to be a poorly-considered style. I submit this confusion reflects an uncritical read of Trump and political outsiders like him. As, Simons and Aghazarian argued, "generic criticism often serves uncritically as an implicit endorsement of existing ways of doing things." Explaining the impact of this tendency, they noted, "What begins as a rule-of-thumb description of what it takes to succeed rhetorically in a given role easily becomes an ironclad prescription that implicitly sanctions and further legitimizes pervading societal norms." Genre criticism, therefore, is usually a defense of tradition, a conservative practice. "Although we ourselves would prefer to remain neutrals," Simons and Aghazarian confessed, "we recognize that, by training if not by inclination, the genericist tends to tilt in a conservatizing direction."[37] Rather than gravitating toward approaches that defend tradition, I suggest that critics should understand consistent violations of generic expectations as a practice completely on its own. As Simons and Aghazarian urged almost three decades ago, genericists should seek to discover

> how rhetors play off of existing genres, deviating ever so slightly from generic rules in some cases, breaking violently with them in others, but always, in effect, engaging in conversation with the past, and with their own cultures, while setting new precedents and helping to create new conventions in the process.[38]

To better understand the rhetoric of political outsiders, we must begin to see them not as misguided violators of rhetorical norms, but as cleverly practicing a tradition that addresses their unique goals of disrupting the political system.

For the remainder of this chapter, I use third party candidates as an example to understand the practice of genre-busting. In particular, and to narrow the scope of my analysis, I limit examples to campaigns that received at least one-percent of the popular vote, indicating a serious enough ground game, appearance on several state ballots, and—most importantly—attention to political messaging.[39] I also limit my analysis to three campaign genres that are fairly fixed in their function and form. After describing the unique functions and strategies of genre-busting for third parties, I move to an analysis of Donald Trump's announcement speech from June 16, 2015, to understand how the genre-busting style of third party candidates may be shared by outsiders more generally.

Third Party Genre-Busting

Third party candidates are by definition political outsiders. In short, they sound different from mainstream Democratic and Republican candidates for the simple fact that they have little hope of winning presidential elections due to a host of constraints. Such candidates face a form of political socialization that steers most voters toward the two major parties.[40] Furthermore, they face enormous barriers due to the dominance of single member plurality systems, restrictive ballot access laws, inadequate campaign financing, limited media coverage, exclusion from televised debates, and a belief among even their supporters that they are a wasted ballot.[41] As a result, most third party candidates give up the dream of winning, and instead run with agenda setting in mind, specifically through agitating for political change by "stimulating a response from the major parties."[42] In this sense, many candidates simply hope to be influential enough to receive five percent of the popular vote, which would guarantee federally matching funds, or to become relevant by appearing to spoil the election for one of the major party candidates. Thus, when delivering major political addresses, the rhetorical situation for third party candidates is shaped by conditions that are not shared by most mainstream candidates. Consequently, this tends to lead to a purposeful violation of generic norms.

Genre-busting serves at least three functions. Because political outsiders are often blockaded from news coverage, the first function of violating generic norms is to use rare moments when even a fringe campaign might be covered to get the public to pay attention. This attempt to force media coverage is obviously desperate. Unless candidates are already widely known millionaires who self-fund their campaigns, they are unlikely to be considered newsworthy. After all, political scientists John Zaller and Mark Hunt noted, "the press tends to cover candidates in multicandidate races in proportion to how well it expects them to do."[43] Third party candidates, Ralph Nader lamented after the 2000 election, should "count on receiving almost no media coverage" unless they are able to "speak in eight-second sound bites."[44] Since media coverage of third party candidates typically ranges from ignoring them completely to emphasizing their odd distinctiveness,[45] genre-busting functions to give reporters what they want by being as distinct as possible.

A second function of genre-busting is to create a public spectacle as a way of gaining, and even keeping, media attention. As a kind of theatre, Jonathan Matusitz argued, public spectacle is "a performance to be seen," a way of "commanding the audience's gaze" through an "exceedingly shocking violation of long-established rules."[46] Television spectacles, Michael Gurevitch and Anandam Kavoori wrote, create a "unified mass audience" at a time "when audiences are increasingly fragmented."[47] Moreover, public spectacles are especially useful for outsiders, as "they allow for the emergence into public discourse of perspectives, frames of reference that are not usually present."[48] In the political arena, Gurevitch and Kavoori emphasized, this means "[departing] from the old style of campaign communication" by "[breaking] down the barrier between 'high' and 'popular' political discourse and to reach out to voters through seemingly direct, quasi-intimate appeals."[49]

Finally, genre-busting creates an image of authenticity. Shawn Parry-Giles defined political authenticity as a "symbolic, mediated, interactional, and highly contested process by which political candidates attempt to 'make real' a vision of self and political character to the electorate."[50] One of the important symbols of authenticity is an unrehearsed style. Martin Montgomery argued that "ordinary" people communicate authenticity "not by fluency or eloquence (although such qualities may help) but by virtue of an unstudied naturalness of delivery."[51] This "naturalness" is an alternative form of political legitimacy, a way of proving that one is as normal as the people they represent. Tamar Liebes argued, "Authenticity is performed, live, on stage, and can be watched, in action, and everyone can see and judge for themselves … if [the speaker] is for real or just faking."[52] In other words, authenticity serves as a form of "emotional trust."[53] That trust is earned over time. Liebes argued,

> As everyone is aware of the rules (and assumes that any show of sincerity or spontaneity is phony), and the politicians know that everyone knows, the challenge is to persuade the public against their better judgment because they want to believe.[54]

That happens when speakers violate norms, especially in the face of possible backlash. As Parry-Giles noted, markers of authenticity include consistency and oppositional opinions, "especially ones that counter public opinion."[55] With the news media watching the performance of important campaign speech genres, third party candidates can have their outsider status confirmed by violating the standards of political pundits, who essentially serve as the "authenticating agents in this image-making exercise."[56]

In order to receive media attention, create a public spectacle, and build an image of authenticity, third party genre-busters often resort to three common strategies regardless of the speech genre. The first, and perhaps most obvious strategy, is a purposeful rejection of generic form or function. While the other strategies I discuss violate each genre in some way, genre-busters like third party candidates often intentionally violate one of the most obvious requirements of a genre. This becomes clearest in the case of concessions, which require a candidate to admit that they lost and appeal for unity.[57] Many third party candidates, however, suggest their campaign was a success and that the election was an example of widespread corruption. Libertarian Ed Clark in 1980 emphasized an optimistic vision despite receiving around one percent of the vote, saying he was "very, very successful" and, in extreme hyperbole, claimed that his campaign marked "the beginning of the three party system in the United States."[58] In 2000, for instance, Ralph Nader closed his campaign by complaining, "most of the coverage on the horse race was between these two horses." Beyond blaming the media, Nader added, "the two parties control the debate commission which is really a private company. And they exclude Third Party candidates, so really it's a quite amazing and varied system of rigging the election for the two major parties."[59] Similarly, George Wallace ended his campaign in 1968 by emphasizing his success, saying, "We ran well. Ten million votes are a lot of votes." However, he trashed the news media, joking that his one regret was "I probably would have left the press at home."[60] Ultimately, the obvious violation of a genre invites criticism and news coverage, and when done in various moments throughout the campaign it can contribute to the image of an authentic outsider.

Furthermore, third party candidates often deviate from generic norms by discussing odd policy proposals, often leading to charges of delusional thinking. George Wallace, for example, launched his campaign in February 1968, promising that he would do whatever it takes to make the streets safe from "the activist, the militants, the anarchists, [and] the Communists," even if it meant "30,000 troops stationed every 30 feet with 2-foot bayonets." Attacking anti-war protesters, Wallace added, "I would ask the attorney general to proceed with indictments against every person in this country who advocated victory for the enemy."[61] Jill Stein repeatedly referenced impractical policies throughout her key speeches in 2016. In her announcement statement, Stein introduced her "Power to the People Plan" that "ensures economic rights for everyone—the right to a job, the right to complete healthcare through a Medicare for All" and a right to "free public higher education and abolishing student debt."[62] In addition to announcing efforts to achieve "100% renewable energy by 2030," Stein suggested she would create a "Truth and Reconciliation Commission" to "get to the bottom of the crisis of racism" and also "provide reparations to acknowledge the enormous debt owed to the African American community."[63] Stein's motives may have been altruistic, but her policies were not common among 2016 hopefuls, and her plans contained few details. Stein was quotable, though, and sounded like a possible spoiler for Hillary Clinton, and was the most popular—and perhaps widely covered—Green Party candidate since Ralph Nader.

Finally, third party genre-busters frequently employ strategies of polarization, arousing discontent with negative rhetoric in moments that tend to be some of the most positive of the campaign. Describing the rhetoric of polarization to make sense of the Wallace campaign in 1968, Richard Raum and James Measell described a range of strategies, including what they term "concrete description devices" like god and devil terms, *reductio ad absurdum*, and exaggeration, and "copula tactics" including artificial dichotomies, we/they distinctions, monolithic opposition, motive disparagement, and self-assertion.[64] While all political candidates use polarization in some form, third party candidates use it as their main strategy in an attempt to exacerbate frustration with the two-party system and to justify the cause of outsiders. In their embrace of negative messaging, often very early in the campaign, they also embrace frank talk, the key to appearing authentic. The strategy of exaggeration, for instance, often paints an apocalyptic crisis. Henry Wallace of the Progressive Party used his nomination acceptance to describe "the great betrayal" of Harry Truman, contending, "Instead of the promised years of harvest, the years of the locust are upon us." When they buried Roosevelt, he claimed, "they buried our dreams."[65] Ross Perot in 1996 went so far as to warn about the death of American democracy. Quoting Scottish historian Alexander Tyler in his acceptance speech, Perot said "the average age of the world's democracies has been 200 years," before reminding viewers, "George Washington, our first president, was sworn in 207 years ago. The clock is ticking."[66] Jill Stein had similar warnings in 2016, telling the audience for her acceptance speech, "The clock is ticking, and this is the Hail Mary moment," adding, "The day of reckoning is drawing closer—on climate change, on endless war, on nuclear weapons, and the next economic meltdown."[67]

Continuing to build an image of hopelessness, third party candidates stay on the attack by creating a monolithic opposition out of the two major parties, producing some the best eight-second sound bites of their campaigns. Henry Wallace called both parties two degrees of the same evil, insisting in his announcement speech, "There is no real fight between a Truman and a Republican. Both stand for a policy which opens the door to war in our lifetime and makes war certain for our children."[68] John Schmitz of the American Independent Party stated in his 1972 announcement speech, "The only choice the old parties offer now is between Democratic disaster and Republican decay."[69] Other candidates attacked both parties for being too closely tied to special interests. In his announcement speech in 2000, Ralph Nader railed against "corporate government," and insisted that "voters find themselves asked to choose between look-a-like candidates from two-parties vying to see who takes the marching orders from their campaign paymasters."[70] Portraying the two parties as the same duopoly, Jill Stein in announcing her 2016 campaign claimed that both major parties were "bought out by the big money," while her own party "does not accept corporate money," "does not accept money from lobbyists nor from corporate CEOs or surrogates of corporations."[71]

Closely related to this strategy is the we/they distinction. Claiming to be a voice for pure democracy and a commitment to bring the government under the control of citizens, Nader said in his announcement that government leaders "turn their backs, or worse, actively block fair treatment for citizens."[72] For Nader, the two parties represented a hostile corporate takeover of government, while he represented a citizen-led movement. Stein spoke on the same themes in her nomination acceptance speech in 2016, claiming that the two parties represented the "super-rich" and the "political elite" who are now richer and more powerful than ever, while the Green Party shows "the courage of our convictions" and represents "the vision and values of the American people."[73] While there are various methods of polarization, they all ultimately add up to this we/they distinction, a strategy employed by those like Nader and Stein to imagine candidates in binary terms, with every race representing a battle between insider elites and authentic outsiders.

Third party candidates, as quintessential outsiders, approach the fixed situations of campaign speech genres with an aim to create controversy, embracing authenticity over traditional markers of legitimacy. Rather than presenting an uplifting message of optimism in their announcements, they are far more likely to create an apocalyptic vision of an America controlled by the two parties. Rather than delegating the harshest attacks in their conventions to surrogates, they embrace negativity. And instead of uniting Americans behind the victor in their concession statements, they are more likely to resist admitting defeat and blame the corporate parties for rigging yet another election. And as they lose by large margins, their rejection of generic norms may be the only reason we hear about them in the first place. In the next section, I argue that the tactic of genre-busting need not be limited to third party candidates, and that outsiders within the two-party system may put the strategy to use and perhaps with better results. Failing to recognize this point, I conclude, strips genre criticism of its explanatory value, and privileges tradition over innovation when assessing presidential discourse.

Donald Trump's Genre-Busting in the 2016 GOP Primary

Launching his campaign in June 2015, Donald Trump may not have been the typical outsider. After years of being one of the most recognizable names in American business and hosting *The Apprentice*, he was undeserving of the "other candidate" tag that is often placed on third party candidates. Alexander Burns of *The New York Times* correctly predicted that his "enormous media profile" gave him a "good chance of qualifying for nationally televised debates." Although he might have been guaranteed some attention from the news media, favorable attention was not certain. Burns added, "Trump's presidential posturing has seldom been taken seriously, and for good reason: Before the 2000 and 2012 elections, he hyped up the possibility of seeking the White House before abandoning the idea."[74] Trump's announcement speech was the perfect example of how he would speak as an outsider for the rest of the campaign. It was clearly public spectacle. *Politico's* Adam Lerner called it a "discursive, pugnacious announcement [that] was one of the more bizarre spectacles of the 2016 political season." So bizarre was the speech, Lerner claimed, that it was "hard to pick just one sound bite."[75] In the end, Trump achieved the goal of appearing authentic. Brian Doherty of *Reason* wrote that Trump displayed a "certain unbridled American id," and exhibited "a sort of middle-American arrogant bluster."[76] David Graham of *The Atlantic* wrote on the one-year anniversary of the speech that it became "the template for Trump's standard stump speech, which usually includes a few key highlights but is otherwise mostly improvised and disorganized." Graham concluded that while traditional politicians zig zag throughout the campaign to appeal to various audiences, "Trump is like a massive arctic icebreaker, steaming forward along a set course regardless of what comes up."[77] Steaming forward, despite generic norms, is the characteristic of the genre-busting I have described in this chapter. In the analysis that follows, I describe how Trump illustrated the characteristics of genre-busting in his announcement speech.

To understand how Trump rejected an obvious characteristic of the genre, it is important to understand the formal characteristics of traditional announcements. The speech usually contains a clear statement that a candidate is entering a race, a rationale for running, the themes of their campaign, and an argument that winning is possible. Finally, with the goal of presenting an optimistic vision of America and the campaign ahead, announcements tend to avoid negative attacks, remaining fairly positive in tone.[78] Trump, however, presented a hopeless description of the world. In a line repeated throughout the campaign, Trump complained, "Our country is in serious trouble. We don't have victories anymore." When the United States competes against China and Japan, he insisted "they kill us … they beat us all the time."[79] Complaining about the nation's economy, Trump argued, "We're dying. We're dying. We need money." Although the economy had been rebounding since the recession and unemployment had fallen, Trump declared, "Sadly, the American dream is dead." It was not just the negative tone that was a rejection of the norms of the announcement speech. Announcements show that a candidate is capable of being a steady leader. Trump clearly violated this purpose when announcing that when Mexico sends immigrants, "they're not sending their best. They're not sending you." He continued, "They're sending people that have lots of problems, and they're bringing those problems with us. They're bringing drugs. They're bringing crime. They're rapists. And some, I assume, are good peo-ple." The blanket characterization of a group of immigrants as mostly rapists and criminals shows such a level of carelessness, both for human beings and for creat-ing the impression of careful leadership. But that was really the point of Trump's speech—to make him look unlike any of the standard political leaders jumping into the race.

Continuing to build authenticity, Trump proposed odd policy after odd policy. Most of the policies actually remained a staple of his campaign, and even his pres-idency. In promising to crack down on immigration, Trump declared the threats as "coming from all over South and Latin America, and it's coming probably—probably—from the Middle East." Though admitting, "we don't know what's hap-pening," Trump declared "I will build a great, great wall on our southern border. And I will have Mexico pay for that wall." Trump also promised to set things right in the Middle East. Complaining that countries in the region, as well as ISIS, "took the oil" when the United States left Iraq, Trump added, "we should've taken" it. Somehow, he insinuated, if the United States committed to a war, a war he mis-leadingly claimed he never approved of in the first place, they should have at least got the oil. Again, the policy lacked detail or any kind of legal basis. Trump was rather forthcoming about what else he would propose during the campaign. After repealing Obamacare, he said, "it can be replaced with something much better for everybody. Let it be for everybody. But much better and much less expensive." And in promising to create better American jobs, Trump promised a 35 percent tax on "every car and every truck and every part manufactured in this plant that comes across the border." Like his other policies, the specifics of the tax might not have made sense, but again that was not the point. The point of Trump's policy propos-als was to create quotable moments, policies that targeted the emotions.

In an announcement that ran over fifty minutes and was filled with tangents, Trump proved to be a master at polarization. His speech was filled with exaggera-tions as he made points that were easily refuted. Trump complained that America's gross domestic product was "below zero," our "GDP below zero, horrible labor participation rate," and he claimed that the real unemployment in the country was "anywhere from 18 to 20 percent." Beyond the economy, the military was said to be failing. America's enemies "are getting stronger and stronger by the way, and we as a country are getting weaker," despite the country's military spending being higher than for any other nation. Particularly, Trump added, "our nuclear arsenal doesn't work" and we are stuck with "equipment that is 30 years old" that may or may not work. Obamacare was failing, too. In a flurry of numbers, Trump claimed "costs are going for people up 29, 39, 49, and even 55 percent, and deductibles are through the roof." And, apparently, the Obamacare website cost $5 billion and "to this day it doesn't work." The highest estimates of the website's cost were less than half of Trump's figure, and the website was functional, but Trump's points succeeded in producing a spectacle of falsehoods that instantly made him an obsession of media pundits.

Much like third party candidates, Donald Trump frequently belittled members of the two major parties, even though he was running for the Republican nomination. Making use of *reductio ad absurdum*, Trump began the announcement by ridiculing his primary opponents. "They didn't know the air-conditioner didn't work" when they announced, he said, and "they sweated like dogs." Linking their sweat to their weakness, and only sort of making sense, Trump added, "They didn't know the room was too big, because they didn't have anybody there. How are they going to beat ISIS?" Trump's use of creating a monolithic opposition, or grouping the parties into one group of "losers," stood out the most. The problem with both parties' candidates, Trump argued, was that they were all politicians. "Politicians are all talk, no action," he stated, adding, "Nothing's gonna get done." Politicians make false promises, he contended, "I watch the speeches of these people, and they say the sun will rise, the moon will set, all sorts of wonderful things will happen. And people are saying … 'I don't need the rhetoric. I want a job.'" Much like Jill Stein, Ralph Nader, and others, Trump argued that politicians cannot be trusted because they represent the interests of elites. "They will never make America great again," he warned, adding, "they're controlled fully by the lobbyists, by the donors, and by the special interests." All of our leaders were "stupid," he insisted, and the country could be stronger through free trade "if you have smart people, but we have people that are stupid. We have people that aren't smart."

Among the other examples of polarization featured in Trump's announcement, he used the tactic of "self-assertion," the idea that meaningful reform was only possible through electing a single person. In what many critics saw as Trump's signature bluster, he offered himself as a sacrifice to the nation. "Our country needs a truly great leader," he announced, "and we need a truly great leader now. We need a leader that wrote 'The Art of the Deal.'" That leader, he said, could "bring back jobs, can bring back our manufacturing, can bring back our military, can take care of our vets." All of that was possible because of Trump's uniqueness. He would be "the greatest jobs president that God ever created," thanks especially to his ability to stand up to special interest groups. Explaining his special qualities, Trump stated, "I don't need anybody's money. I'm using my own money. I'm not using the lobbyists. I'm not using donors. I don't care. I'm really rich." Continuing to talk about his personal wealth, Trump put the figure at $8.7 billion, saying, "I'm not doing that to brag … I'm doing that to say that that's the kind of thinking our country needs." Instead, he suggested, "We have losers. We have losers. We have people that don't have it. We have people that are morally corrupt. We have people that are selling this country down the drain."

It is easy to see why so many critics dismissed Trump's campaign after his announcement. He offered no hint of humility and an apocalyptic vision of public life that would send fact checkers into fits. Moreover, he proposed that he was the only person capable of producing sensible policy, but repeatedly offered unrealistic solutions with vague details. For a candidate so frequently dismissed while dabbling in previous campaigns, however, Trump's announcement speech was widely circulated. Moreover, the immediate criticism of his campaign fed into his purpose—he was an outsider.

Conclusion

I have argued throughout this chapter that a speaker's violation of generic norms is not necessarily a sign of failure. When genres are defined, and tied to recurring situations, it often becomes a knee jerk reaction to use knowledge of that genre to critique any speech delivered in a seemingly similar situation. However, political leaders are not all united in a goal of winning elections, and many others do not seek the same path to victory. This study calls on critics to recognize those who consistently violate our expectations not as special cases, but as skilled rhetors breaking rules to enhance their credibility as outsiders.

This study has several implications. First, it suggests that generic rules have a way of calcifying, thus blinding critics to alternative practices. Thus, this study answers the call of Simons and Aghazarian to discover how speakers evolve existing genres, appropriating some aspects, but changing others, for their unique purposes. Above all, this suggests critics should reject the impulse to evaluate, and instead aim to first explain. Second, this chapter suggests that Trump was a master in his campaign at using major speech genres to create a public spectacle and craft his image as a plain-spoken outsider. Since his inaugural address indicated a continuation of that strategy, the question as we move further into his presidency is how that strategy works in governing rhetoric. He has shown a desire to be the authentic outsider ruling over "the politicians," but how long can the head of state continue to violate the rhetorical traditions of the office he holds? Finally, this chapter suggests that the political construction of authenticity is fairly ironic. Outsiders craft their image through continued persuasive attempts, but committing to such a strategy outsiders not only show that being authentic is actually an insincere enterprise, but that its believability hangs on keeping up the act. If and when Trump ever pivots to resemble a traditional president, it is likely that the public will be "reading the presidency" to determine whether his authenticity is the mark of a true outsider, or simply the act of yet another scheming politician.

Notes

1. Ed Kilgore, "Trump's Dark, Weird, Inaugural Campaign Speech," *Daily Intelligencer*, January 20, 2017, http://nymag.com/daily/intelligencer/2017/01/trumps-dark-weird-inaugural-campaign-speech.html.
2. David Von Drehle, "Donald Trump's Unprecedented, Divisive Speech," *Time*, January 20, 2017, http://time.com/magazine/us/4642992/january-30th-2017-vol-189-no-3-u-s/.
3. Philip Bump, "Trump's Inaugural Address was Demonstrably Bleak," *Washington Post*, January 20, 2017, https://www.washingtonpost.com/pb/news/the-fix/wp/2017/01/20/trumps-inaugural-address-was-demonstrably-bleak/?outputType=accessibility&nid=menu_nav_accessibilityforscreenreader.
4. Sopan Deb, "Trump Delivers Restrained Victory Speech with Teleprompter," CBS News, June 8, 2016, http://www.cbsnews.com/news/trump-delivers-restrained-victory-speech-with-teleprompter/.
5. Karen Tumulty and Philip Rucker, "At Third Debate, Trump Won't Commit to Accepting Election Results if He Loses," *Washington Post*, October 19, 2016, https://www.washingtonpost.com/politics/trump-wont-commit-to-accepting-election-results-if-he-loses/2016/10/19/9c9672e6-9609-11e6-bc79-af1cd3d2984b_story.html?utm_term=.3f04e57e4041.
6. Quoted in Edward B. Foley, "What Happens if Trump Keeps Us 'in Suspense' on Election Night?" *Politico Magazine*, October 21, 2016, http://www.politico.com/magazine/story/2016/10/trump-election-night-concede-214379.
7. Patrick Healy and Jonathan Martin, "His Tone Dark, Donald Trump Takes G.O.P. Mantle," *The New York Times*, July 21, 2016, https://www.nytimes.com/2016/07/22/us/politics/donald-trump-rnc-speech.html?_r=1.
8. Sally Kohn, "Trump's Outrageous Mexico Remarks," *CNN.com*, June 18, 2015, http://www.cnn.com/2015/06/17/opinions/kohn-donald-trump-announcement/.
9. Dan Balz, "Donald Trump, America's First Independent President," *The Washington Post*, November 19, 2016, https://www.washingtonpost.com/politics/donald-trump-americas-first-independent-president/2016/11/19/b09e1cc6-ade2-11e6-8b45-f8e493f06fcd_story.html?utm_term=.8c1898596871.
10. Jonathan Martin, "Donald Trump Was Essentially a Third Party Candidate on a G.O.P. Ticket," *The New York Times*, November 9, 2016, https://www.nytimes.com/2016/11/10/us/politics/donald-trump-gop.html.
11. See Eleanor Clift, "The Last Time Trump Wrecked a Party," *The Daily Beast*, July 18, 2016, http://www.thedailybeast.com/articles/2016/07/18/the-last-time-trump-wrecked-a-party.html.
12. See Ryan Neville-Shepard, "Presidential Campaign Announcements: A Third Party Variant," *Southern Communication Journal* 79, no. 2 (2014): 130–146, doi: 10.1080/1041794X.2013.866157; Ryan Neville-Shepard, "Triumph in Defeat: The Genre of Third

Party Presidential Concessions," *Communication Quarterly* 62, no. 2 (2014): 214–232, doi: 10.1080/01463373.2014.890119; Ryan Neville-Shepard, "Unconventional: The Variant of Third Party Nomination Acceptance Addresses," *Western Journal of Communication* 80, no. 2 (2016): 121–139, doi: 10.1080/10570314.2015.1128560.

13. Karlyn Kohrs Campbell and Kathleen Hall Jamieson, *Presidents Creating the Presidency: Deeds Done in Words* (Chicago: University of Chicago Press, 2008), 14.

14. Edwin Black, *Rhetorical Criticism: A Study in Method* (Madison: University of Wisconsin Press, 1965), 133.

15. Karlyn Kohrs Campbell and Kathleen Hall Jamieson, "Form and Genre in Rhetorical Criticism: An Introduction," *Form and Genre: Shaping Rhetorical Action*, eds. Karlyn Kohrs Campbell and Kathleen Hall Jamieson (Falls Church, VA: Speech Communication Association, 1978), 19.

16. Campbell and Jamieson, "Form and Genre," 20.

17. Robert C. Rowland, "On Generic Categorization," *Communication Theory* 1 (1991): 128–144, doi: 10.1111/j.1468-2885.1991.tb00009.x

18. Rowland, "On Generic Categorization," 134.

19. Campbell and Jamieson, *Presidents Creating the Presidency*, 14.

20. Campbell and Jamieson, *Presidents Creating the Presidency*, 15.

21. Rowland, "On Generic Categorization," 134.

22. Rowland, "On Generic Categorization," 138.

23. Rowland, "On Generic Categorization," 129.

24. Campbell and Jamieson, "Form and Genre," 22.

25. Rowland, "On Generic Categorization," 129.

26. Campbell and Jamieson, "Form and Genre," 22.

27. Carolyn R. Miller, "Genre as Social Action," *Quarterly Journal of Speech* 70, no. 2 (1984): 151–167. doi: 10.1080/00335638409383686.

28. Miller, "Genre as Social Action," 164.

29. Rowland, "On Generic Categorization," 130.

30. Rowland, "On Generic Categorization," 130–131.

31. Herbert W. Simons and Aram A. Aghazarian, "Introduction," *Form, Genre, and the Study of Political Discourse*, eds. Herbert W. Simons and Aram A. Aghazarian (Columbia: University of South Carolina, 1986), 15.

32. Herbert W. Simons, "'Genre-alizing About Rhetoric: A Scientific Approach," *Form and Genre: Shaping Rhetorical Action*, eds. Karlyn Kohrs Campbell and Kathleen Hall Jamieson (Falls Church, VA: Speech Communication Association, 1978), 33–50.

33. Simons and Aghazarian, "Introduction, 15.

34. Rowland, "On Generic Categorization," 137.

35. Campbell and Jamieson, *Presidents Creating the Presidency*, 16.

36. Miller, "Genre as Social Action," 164.

37. Herbert W. Simons and Aram A. Aghazarian, "Genres, Rules, and Political Rhetoric: Toward a Sociology of Rhetorical Choice," *Form, Genre, and the Study of Political Discourse*, eds. Herbert W. Simons and Aram A. Aghazarian (Columbia: University of South Carolina, 1986), 54.

38. Simons and Aghazarian, "Genres, Rules, and Political Rhetoric, 54.

39. This list includes the campaigns led by the following third party candidates: Strom Thurmond of the National States Rights Party (1948), Henry Wallace of the Progressive Party (1948), George Wallace of the American Independent Party (1968), John Schmitz of the American Independent Party (1972), independent John Anderson (1980), Ed Clark of the Libertarian Party (1980), Ross Perot's independent campaign (1992), Ross Perot's campaign under the Reform Party (1996), Ralph Nader of the Green Party (2000), Gary Johnson of the Libertarian Party (2016), and Jill Stein of the Green Party (2016).

40. J. David Gillespie, *Politics at the Periphery: Third Parties in Two-Party America* (Columbia, SC: University of South Carolina Press, 1993), 29.

41. For more on these constraints, see: J. David Gillespie, *Politics at the Periphery: Third Parties in Two-Party America* (Columbia, SC: University of South Carolina Press, 1993), 25–36; Steven J. Rosenstone, Roy L. Behr, and Edward H. Lazarus, *Third Parties in America: Citizen Response to Major Party Failure*, 2nd ed. (Princeton, NJ: Princeton University Press, 1996), 15–47.

42. Ronald B. Rapoport and Walter Stone, *Three's a Crowd: The Dynamic of Third Parties, Ross Perot, & Republican Resurgence* (Ann Arbor, MI: University of Michigan Press, 2008), 5.

43. John Zaller and Mark Hunt, "The Rise and Fall of Candidate Perot: Unmediated Versus Political System —Part 2," *Political Communication* 12 (1995): 97–123, doi: 10.1080/10584609.1995.9963057.

44. Ralph Nader and Theresa Amato, "So You Want to Run for President? Ha! Barriers to Third Party Entry," *National Civic Review* 90 (2001): 164.

45. For more, see James G. Stovall, "The Third Party Challenge of 1980: News Coverage of the Presidential Candidates," *Journalism Quarterly* 62, no. 2 (1985): 266–271, doi: 10.1177/107769908506200206.

46. Jonathan Matusitz, "Terrorism as Spectacle: It's All for the Audience," *Explorations in Media Ecology* 14 (2015): 161, 163.

47. Michael Gurevitch and Anandam P. Kavoori, "Television Spectacles as Politics," *Communication Monographs* 59, no. 4 (1992): 415–420, doi: 10.1080/03637759209376284.

48. Gurevitch and Kavoori, "Television Spectacles as Politics," 416.

49. Gurevitch and Kavoori, "Television Spectacles as Politics," 419.

50. Shawn J. Parry-Giles, "Political Authenticity, Television News, and Hillary Rodham Clinton," in *Politics, Discourse, and American Society: New Agendas*, eds. Roderick P. Hart and Bartholomew Sparrow (Lanham, MD: Rowman & Littlefield, 2001), 212.

51. Martin Montgomery, "The Uses of Authenticity: 'Speaking from Experience' in a U.K. Election Broadcast," *The Communication Review* 4, no. 4 (2001): 447–462, doi: 10.1080/10714420109359479.

52. Tamar Liebes, "'Look Me Straight in the Eye': The Political Discourse of Authenticity, Spontaneity, and Sincerity," *The Communication Review* 4, no. 4 (2001): 499–510, doi: 10.1080/10714420109359482.

53. Liebes, "Look Me Straight in the Eye," 499.

54. Liebes, "Look Me Straight in the Eye," 503.

55. Parry-Giles, "Political Authenticity, Television News," 215–216.

56. Parry-Giles, "Political Authenticity, Television News," 214.

57. See Ruth Ann Weaver, "Acknowledgement of Victory and Defeat: The Reciprocal Ritual," *Central States Speech Journal* 33 (1982): 480–489.

58. United Press International, November 5, 1980.

59. Ralph Nader, "Speech on Election Night, Nov. 7, 2000," in *Presidential Winners and Losers: Words of Victory and Concession*, ed. John Vile (Washington, D.C.: CQ Press, 2002): 326.

60. William Kling, "Wallace Sees Third Party Bid as Success," *Chicago Tribune*, November 7, 1968.

61. Thomas J. Foley, "Wallace Announces Candidacy, Plans 5—State Campaign," *Los Angeles Times*, February 9, 1968.

62. Jill Stein, "Exclusive: Green Party's Jill Stein Announces She is Running for President on Democracy Now!," *Democracy Now!* June 22, 2015, https://www.democracynow.org/2015/6/22/exclusive_green_partys_jill_stein_announces.

63. Jill Stein, "Transcript: Jill Stein Accepts the Green Party Nomination," *Jill 2016*, August 6, 2016, http://www.jill2016.com/transcript_jill_stein_accepts_the_green_party_nomination.

64. Richard D. Raum and James S. Measell, "Wallace and His Ways: A Study of the Rhetorical Genre of Polarization," *Central States Speech Journal* 25 (1974): 38–25, doi: 10.1080/10510977409367765.

65. *Washington Post*, "Text of Henry Wallace's Acceptance of Presidential Nomination," July 25, 1948.

66. Ross Perot, "Text of Perot's Speech," *Wall Street Journal*, August 19, 1996, https://www.wsj.com/articles/SB840468324557197000.

67. Stein, "Transcript: Jill Stein Accepts."

68. "Text of Wallace's Radio Talk Announcing His Candidacy," *The New York Times*, December 30, 1947.

69. John G. Schmitz, "Statement to the Press," August 2, 1972, Congressional Papers of John G. Schmitz, Special Collections & University Archives, Wichita State University.

70. Ralph Nader, "Statement of Ralph Nader, Announcing his Candidacy for the Green Party's Nomination for President," February 21, 2000, *4President.org*, http://www.4president.org/speeches/2000/ralphnader2000announcement.htm.

71. Stein, "Exclusive: Green Party's Jill Stein Announces."

72. Nader, "Statement of Ralph Nader, Announcing."

73. Stein, "Transcript: Jill Stein Accepts

74. Alexander Burns, "Donald Trump, Pushing Someone Rich, Offers Himself," *The New York Times*, June 16, 2015, https://www.nytimes.com/2015/06/17/us/politics/donald-trump-runs-for-president-this-time-for-real-he-says.html.

75. Adam B. Lerner, "The 10 Best Lines from Donald Trump's Announcement Speech," *Politico*, June 16, 2015, http://www.politico.com/story/2015/06/donald-trump-2016-announcement-10-best-lines-119066.

76. Brian Doherty, "Donald Trump, great American, Seeks Presidency of a Not-Great-Enough America, for a Greater America," *Reason*, June 16, 2015, http://reason.com/blog/2015/06/16/donald-trump-great-american-seeks-presid.

77. David A. Graham, "What the Press Got Right About Trump's Candidacy," *The Atlantic*, June 16, 2016, https://www.theatlantic.com/politics/archive/2016/06/what-the-press-got-right-about-trumps-announcement/487247/.

78. See William L. Benoit, Jayne R. Goode, Sheri Whalen, and Penni M. Pier. "'I am a Candidate for President': A Functional Analysis of Presidential Announcement Speeches, 1960-2004," *Speaker & Gavel* 45 (2008): 3–18; Daniel J. Palazzolo and Sean M. Theriault, "Candidate Announcement Addresses: Campaign Strategies and Voting Behavior," *Presidential Studies Quarterly* 26, no. 2 (1996): 350–363, http://www.jstor.org/stable/27551582.

79. For the remainder this section, all quotations from Trump's announcement come from the following source: Donald J. Trump, "Announcement Speech," *Time*, June 16, 2015, http://time.com/3923128/donald-trump-announcement-speech/.

CHAPTER FIVE

The Rise of Comforter-in-Chief

Presidential Responses to Violence Since Reagan

JAY P. CHILDERS AND CASSANDRA C. BIRD

In the early morning hours of June 12, 2016, a lone gunman walked inside a gay nightclub in Orlando, Florida, and opened fire. By the time police killed the gunman three hours later, 49 people were dead and another 53 were injured. Although the shooter's motivation remains unclear, that he was Muslim and the victims were mostly gay men led to assertions that the shooting should be viewed as either a terrorist attack or hate crime. Either way, it was the deadliest mass shooting in American history. Given this, it was little surprise that President Barack Obama visited Orlando four days after the shooting and gave a speech to mourners and community leaders gathered near the makeshift memorial that had been erected outside the Dr. Phillips Center for the Performing Arts.

That Obama was expected to speak after the shooting may be a little surprising for those who study the American presidency. On August 1, 1966, when a lone gunman opened fire on the campus of the University of Texas at Austin, killing 16 and wounding another 30, President Lyndon Johnson did no more than send a short statement of support to the university's Chancellor. President Ronald Reagan addressed neither a shooting on July 18, 1984 at a McDonald's in San Ysidro, California that left 21 dead nor the shooting in Edmond, Oklahoma on August 20, 1986 that left 14 postal workers dead. And George H. W. Bush did not speak after another lone gunman crashed his pickup truck through the front of a Luby's Cafeteria in Killeen, Texas and then shot and killed 23 people on October 16, 1991.

Despite these historical precedents, it would have been unimaginable to most Americans for Obama not to address the shooting in Orlando. Indeed, the expectation that presidents speak after mass shootings and other tragedies has become so common that there is now a term for when they do—comforter-in-chief. In the days following the Orlando shooting, several news outlets referred to Obama with the moniker, including the *Los Angeles Times* and *USA Today*.[1] In its article on Obama's trip to Orlando, the *Washington Post* began with this lead:

> For the eighth time during his presidency, President Obama will arrive Thursday in another grieving American city to assume the role of comforter in chief after a mass shooting, to console the victims and their families, and to offer a message of national solidarity and resilience.[2]

As the *Washington Post* used it, there was nothing clever in the title, which suggests how well-established the role had become.

Although Obama was most certainly called into the role often, he was not the first American president to be identified as comforter-in-chief. That honor goes to Bill Clinton. On October 9, 1996, President Clinton signed the Federal Aviation Reauthorization Act into law at a small ceremony attended by relatives of the victims of previous airline disasters. Reporting on that event the following day in the *Washington Post*, Peter Baker wrote that the event "allowed Clinton to resume his familiar role as comforter-in-chief, demonstrating his empathy for suffering Americans in a visible setting less than four weeks before Election Day."[3] Three years later, writing in *USA Today*, Laurence McQiullan wrote, "President Clinton, who has picked up the moniker 'comforter in chief,' visits North Carolina today to meet with victims of Hurricane Floyd and confer with state and local officials to coordinate federal relief efforts."[4] Clearly, the new label had stuck.

More importantly, the appellation survived the transition from one president to another. In the days following the terrorist attacks of September 11, 2001, the label transferred to First Lady Laura Bush. Just eight days after the attacks, a *Washington Post* article exploring the emergence of her new role ran under the headline, "Laura Bush, Comforter In Chief: First Lady Works to Sooth a Shaken Nation."[5] By February 2003, the epithet had transferred to the president himself. The day after the space shuttle *Columbia* disaster, the *New York Times* noted, "President Bush rushed back to the White House today from Camp David to assume once more the role of comforter in chief."[6] In fact, speaking at an event in 2014 promoting his biography of his father, *41: A Portrait of My Father*, the younger Bush, reflecting back on his eight years in office, noted, "one of the most difficult aspects of the presidency is to be comforter-in-chief."[7] From Clinton to Bush to Obama, the new moniker has found its way into the American political consciousness.

In this chapter, we argue that the role of comforter-in-chief began with Ronald Reagan's responses to the *Challenger* space shuttle explosion. We further posit that Bill Clinton firmly established and greatly expanded the persona in a series of speeches delivered after several school shootings in 1998 and 1999. In making this argument, we suggest that the rhetorical genre Karlyn Kohrs Campbell and Kathleen Hall Jamieson refer to as the national eulogy has been broadened through the expanding role of comforter-in-chief. Indeed, we argue that Clinton's decision to deliver speeches similar to national eulogies in response to events outside the direct scope of the federal government set new expectations for the presidency. It also shifted the roles presidents play in the American imaginary and, potentially, expanded the power of the presidency. Through their new role as comforters-in-chief, presidents increasingly have the power to transform localized accidents and shootings into national tragedies. When they do so, presidents gain the ability to more frequently act as the nation's moral leader by defining the nation's values through the epideictic rhetoric that accompanies such moments. Such a discursive power only amplifies the ability for presidents to play an outsized central role in contemporary American politics. To make this argument, we begin by revisiting ways in which the American presidency has changed over time before moving on to examine, first, Reagan's *Challenger* address and, second, several speeches by Clinton in response to gun violence in 1998 and 1999.

How Presidents Expand the Presidency

While the name comforter-in-chief was an obvious journalistic play on the president's role as commander-in-chief of the U.S. military, there is something more important going on in the emergence of the term. After all, the use of comforter-in-chief is a rhetorical trope that calls attention to something specific about the contemporary presidency and, consequently, influences cultural understandings of the American presidency. In rhetorical terms, comforter-in-chief is an antonomasia, which Jeanne Fahnestock argues, "is the device of replacing a proper name with a descriptive label that characterizes while renaming."[8] Essentially a type of metonymy, in antonomasia, "the new name selects and highlights some feature of the person named, and that selected feature foregrounds the person's value in the immediate context."[9] Since the term comforter-in-chief has been used to refer to Clinton, Bush, and Obama, the renaming in this instance references the office itself. Just as with commander-in-chief, the president shall be comforter-in-chief of a troubled nation when called upon.

As stated in Article II of the Constitution of the United States, the proper name of the nation's executive leader is President of the United States of America.

Employing the antonomasia comforter-in-chief, therefore, emphasizes a perceived characteristic of the responsibilities of the office itself. That is, the existence of the moniker suggests that many people believe that it is part of a president's job to console the American people following disasters and tragedies that have caused collective distress. In recent years, it has become routine for presidents to speak after shootings, natural disasters, and even some industrial accidents. Indeed, George H. W. Bush was roundly criticized for not responding effectively to Hurricane Hugo in 1989, and his son was similarly rebuked for his handling of the federal response to Hurricane Katrina in 2005.[10]

However, such expectations have not always been the norm. After the bombing and riot at Haymarket Square in Chicago on May 4, 1886, there is no record that Grover Cleveland addressed the event that left 11 dead and 130 injured even though around half the dead and injured were police officers. In April 1906, Theodore Roosevelt did acknowledge the San Francisco earthquake that killed approximately 3,000 people. However, he did so primarily through sending two telegrams to the governor of California, which asked the governor to let Roosevelt "know if there is anything that the national government can do."[11] And on April 16, 1947, when a ship carrying nearly 2,200 pounds of ammonium nitrate exploded while at port in Texas City, Texas, killing nearly 600 and injuring thousands of others, President Truman promised federal assistance and mentioned the incident at least once, in an address he delivered several weeks after the disaster at the opening of a Conference on Fire Prevention.[12] However, even as recently as 1947, Truman delivered no address on the disaster itself. Much has changed.

That the American presidency saw dramatic changes during the twentieth century is well documented. Put simply, the power of the presidency and its place in the American imaginary grew dramatically across that century. Whether referred to as the plebiscitary presidency or rhetorical presidency, the basic explanation for this dramatic growth has been the ability and willingness of presidents to appeal directly to the American people, bypassing both Congress and political parties.[13] As Theodore Lowi put it, across the twentieth century presidents increasingly "approached an unmediated relationship with the masses."[14] In noting these changes, most scholars have focused on how this new relationship has shifted the balance of power in the federal government. Extending this work, a focus on the emergence of the comforter-in-chief role reveals a deepening relationship between presidents and national mores, which only increases the presidents' already extensive powers.

The Constitution says relatively little about what presidents should do in exercising their executive powers. Therefore, much of what contemporary presidents do is predicated on precedents of former chief executives. As Karlyn Kohrs Campbell and Kathleen Hall Jamieson have argued, when presidents are expected to speak and what they are expected to say results directly from the rhetorical actions taken by individual presidents responding to their contemporary situations.[15] For instance, there is no constitutionally mandated reason presidents deliver a State of the Union address in person each year before Congress. All the U.S. Constitution has to say on the matter is that the nation's top executive "shall from time to time give to the Congress information of the state of the union, and recommend to their consideration such measures as he shall judge necessary and expedient." That the American people now expect presidents to deliver such addresses is a direct result of historical choices, most notably made by George Washington and Woodrow Wilson in this instance.

That presidents define what the presidency means through their rhetorical actions makes the appearance of new rhetorical patterns particularly important. Campbell and Jamieson are aware of this themselves. In their original *Deeds Done in Words*, published in 1990, there is no mention of the types of national eulogies or memorial addresses being discussed in this chapter. However, in their 2008 revised version of that book, *Presidents Creating the Presidency*, Campbell and Jamieson do include a new chapter on what they call "National Eulogies," which they suggest are "recent forms of epideictic discourse" distinct from historic speeches like Abraham Lincoln's Gettysburg Address or Franklin Delano Roosevelt's call to war following the attacks on Pearl Harbor.[16] Specifically, they argue, "the national eulogy emerges only when someone must make sense of a catastrophic event that unexpectedly kills U.S. civilians while also assaulting a national symbol."[17] It is, in part, because of this definition that Campbell and Jamieson focus their analysis on five specific catastrophes: the *Challenger* space shuttle explosion, the Oklahoma City bombing, the terrorist attacks of September 11, the *Columbia* space shuttle disaster, and Hurricane Katrina.

While we believe Campbell and Jamieson are right to begin their analysis with Reagan's response to the *Challenger* space shuttle explosion, we disagree with the scope of their generic category. Specifically, we argue that for a president to be called into the role of comforter-in-chief the tragedy does not have to reach catastrophic proportions and the assault does not have to be upon a national symbol. It is for these reasons that we resist employing a term like national eulogy, choosing instead to focus on the rhetorical persona of comforter-in-chief. Understood as such, it is a role that has expanded greatly in the past few decades.

An Emergent Role

When choosing to speak after tragedy, presidents find themselves in a rhetorically difficult situation. First, a president must interpret the tragedy, offering an explanation of why it happened and what it should mean. Second, the president must reassure a troubled audience that the tragedy is an aberration not likely to happen again so long as change occurs. However, in achieving these rhetorical goals, presidents must avoid the appearance of politicizing the tragedy in order to promote some administrative agenda. Therefore, choosing to speak after a tragedy is never a decision made lightly. As others have noted, presidents choose to speak because they decide to for some reason, or they do so because the scale of the event or the scope of the media coverage leaves them little choice.[18]

When the NASA space shuttle *Challenger* exploded on live television just 73 seconds into its flight on January 28, 1986, killing all seven astronauts onboard, most have agreed that President Ronald Reagan had no choice but to address the nation. As Mary Stuckey has argued,

> as soon as the explosion occurred, it was obvious that the president had to speak. Such an event— on such a scale and with such a large audience— demanded some sort of explanation, and only the president was positioned to offer it.[19]

That Reagan realized this almost immediately is clear in several decisions that were made in the hours following the disaster.

It should be remembered that Reagan was scheduled to deliver his annual State of the Union address on the day of the *Challenger* explosion. Reagan could have, therefore, chosen to revise that address and open with a tribute to the *Challenger* astronauts. After all, no previous NASA tragedy or one similar to it had demanded an immediate, separate speech. Nevertheless, Reagan's first important decision was to postpone the State of the Union address, which was a clear indication of the perceived significance of the explosion. The second important decision Reagan made was to speak at 5 pm, just a little more than five hours after the tragedy occurred. Speaking so soon after the explosion indicated an awareness of how upsetting the explosion had been. This awareness was especially pertinent because the launch had been watched in thousands of classrooms around the nation since the flight crew included Christa McAuliffe, who had been chosen to be the first teacher in space as part of NASA's Teacher in Space Project. Third, Reagan chose to speak from the Oval Office. As the president's official office, the Oval Office carries a weight of significance few other spaces do for the president. Once again, the choice of where to speak said something about the importance of the occasion.

And then there was what President Reagan had to say. In just four minutes and ten seconds, Reagan delivered one of the more powerful speeches in American history.[20] In those few minutes, Reagan both transformed the seven victims of an accident caused by a mechanical error into American heroes and elevated the NASA space program to the very embodiment of American freedom and the American people's pioneering spirit. Put simply, he gave the potentially senseless accident significant national meaning and offered calming reassurance to the American people.

As is widely known in rhetorical studies, Reagan accomplished his feat by characterizing the seven astronauts as heroic adventurers exploring the frontiers of space for the good of the nation. Reagan called the crew "seven heroes" who had "served all of us," and then he transitioned to referring to them as "pioneers" who were "pulling us into the future."[21] Because the nation had an obligation to follow them, Reagan promised that NASA would help "continue our quest in space. There will be more here; our hopes and our journeys continue."[22] And finally, Reagan envisioned the dead astronauts ascending to heaven in the speech's famous last line: "We will never forget them, nor the last time we saw them, this morning, as they prepared for their journey and waved goodbye and 'slipped the surly bonds of earth' to 'touch the face of God.'"[23]

To suggest that Reagan's response to the *Challenger* explosion is a pivotal moment is not to suggest that he did something no other president had ever done before. Lyndon Johnson eulogized John F. Kennedy after the latter's assassination on several occasions in different situations, and he addressed the nation following the deaths of both Martin Luther King, Jr and Robert Kennedy. Richard Nixon gave several eulogies of public officials during his time in office, including one for Senator Everett Dirksen in 1969 and another for former FBI Director J. Edgar Hoover in 1972. Jimmy Carter spoke at a memorial service for American soldiers killed in a failed attempt to rescue hostages being held at the U.S. Embassy in Tehran, Iran, two weeks after their deaths. Even Ronald Reagan had addressed the nation after disasters and deaths. In September 1983, Reagan gave a national address to the American people about the Soviet downing of a Korean civilian airliner and the deaths of passengers that included Americans, most notably a U. S. Representative from Georgia.

Despite all this, no speech by a sitting president in the immediate aftermath of tragedy had ever been as eloquent and powerful as Reagan's *Challenger* address. That he attended the memorial service in Houston, Texas days later and repeated the themes of his initial address only amplified his initial speech. In responding so quickly to the *Challenger* explosion, Reagan showed the power a president can have in shaping the way an event is understood and remembered. It is a power subsequent presidents seem increasingly aware of, even with its obvious limits.

An Expanding Role

If Ronald Reagan showed the true power of the president to comfort a nation and help interpret and define tragedies, Bill Clinton is the president who ought to get credit for fully establishing and expanding the role of comforter-in-chief, a moniker we noted above he was the first to earn. Perhaps this should be of little surprise for a president who famously told multiple audiences that he could "feel their pain."[24] Indeed, Clinton had a gift for making audiences believe that he understood their experiences and their struggles. It was that ability to express emotion and connect with citizens that helped Clinton overcome numerous problems during his presidency.[25]

One well-noted instance in which Clinton was able to masterfully create the appropriate emotional tenor was in his speech at the memorial service for victims of the Oklahoma City bombing. Delivered on April 23, 1995, four days after the bombing, with search and rescue missions still underway, the speech effectively revived a failing presidency that was reeling from the Republican takeover of Congress in 1994. As Campbell and Jamieson report it, "the immediate effect of Clinton's handling of the bombing was a 5 percentage point jump in the Gallup poll. Indeed, 84 percent of the public approved of Clinton's response to the calamity."[26] Such assertions are in-line with more contemporaneous assessments of Clinton's performance. Writing a year after the bombing and speech, Mark Shields argued the following in a *Washington Post* opinion piece about its impact on American politics:

> Clinton brilliantly seized the moment to make a persuasive defense of the legitimacy of government. He became comforter to the suffering innocent and the voice of national community. In an instant, the president seemed to go from being a precocious graduate student to being as mature as he was magnanimous. Ever since, the rabid anti-government conservative tide has been receding in the nation.[27]

Clinton's response to the Oklahoma City bombing demonstrated the potential benefits of effectively responding to tragedy. As chief executive of the federal government, Clinton had an obvious obligation to respond to the Oklahoma City bombing. The act of domestic terrorism had targeted a federal building in response to what Timothy McVeigh, the bomber, perceived as the federal government's crimes against the American people. However, a series of speeches following school shootings that Clinton delivered later in his presidency show how he expanded the role of comforter-in-chief in important ways.

Jonesboro, Arkansas

On March 24, 1998, two middle school boys set a trap for their classmates at Westside Middle School near Jonesboro, Arkansas.[28] While one of the boys, 13-year-old Mitchell Johnson, waited near trees lining the side of the school, the other, 11-year-old Andrew Golden, pulled the school's fire alarm and then ran to meet his waiting accomplice. As the school's students and teachers began evacuating the building, the two boys opened fire. Within minutes, four students and one teacher lay dead, with another 10 students injured. At the time, it was one of the worst school shootings in American history and remains the worst school shooting at a middle school.

There are several reasons Clinton might have chosen to speak to the grieving community near Jonesboro, but one of those reasons was not because of precedent. When a student killed two classmates and wounded seven others at Pearl High School in Pearl, Mississippi on October 1, 1997, Clinton did not choose to give a speech in response to it. Nor did he speak out after a 14-year-old student at Heath High School in West Paducah, Kentucky opened fire on a group of praying students just before the start of the school day, killing three and wounding another five.

Despite a lack of precedent, there are several reasons why Clinton might have chosen to speak out after the Jonesboro shooting. First, there is the simple matter of numbers. As already noted, it was one of the deadliest school shootings in America at the time. Second, there was the young age of the shooters and most of the victims. Put simply, the death of the very young is always more shocking because of their age. Third, there was the reality that the Westside shooting marked the third school shooting to take multiple lives in a single academic year. Finally, there was the simple fact that the shooting took place in Arkansas, the state where Clinton had been governor before running for president. In fact, Clinton suggested this himself the following year when he addressed the students from Columbine High School a month after the shooting that happened at their school. Briefly referencing the shooting that happened in his "home state" the previous year, Clinton told his Columbine audience, "I was Governor there 12 years. I knew the people involved; it was heartbreaking."[29]

Whatever the reason, Clinton did choose to speak out after the shooting at Westside Middle School, although he had to do so from Africa where he was on an 11-day trip. Clinton's first response was a short statement in which he suggested, "we may never fully understand what could have driven two youths to deliberately shoot into a crowd of their classmates" and offered "thoughts and prayers."[30] Then, in advance of a memorial to be held on March 31 in Jonesboro, Clinton recorded a short video to be broadcast there. Less than 250 words in length, the speech does not offer much. In addition to naming the victims and encouraging mourners to cherish their memories of the dead, Clinton suggested that the true reason for the shootings would likely remain a mystery. After stating that the tragedy was difficult to grasp, Clinton added,

> Saint Paul reminds us that we all see things in this life through a dark glass, that we only partly understand what is happening to us. But one day, face to face with God, we will see all things, even as He sees us.[31]

He then suggested that the dead now had that ability to see all things and asked that God bless both the victims' families and everyone else in Jonesboro.

The videotaped speech was, by almost every measure, incredibly unremarkable. It does not even attempt to soar to lofty heights, perhaps because it was recorded. The speech fails to have the kind of empathy and connection Clinton could have surely created in person. Ultimately, the speech does the bare minimum of what it was designed to do—acknowledge the tragedy and offer condolences. In fact, the speech makes no reference to the American people or the nation. It simply states that he and Hillary are offering their prayers.

And yet, the speech had an important effect—it set a precedent for future tragedies. Of course, Clinton could not have known the tragic events that would occur in the final two and a half years of his presidency, but several more events would call out the comforter-in-chief in him. Therefore, his decision to speak by recorded video to the memorial for the victims of the Westside Middle School had a lasting impact.

Springfield, Oregon

On the morning of May 21, 1998, just two months after the Jonesboro shooting, a 15-year-old student who had recently been expelled from Thurston High School in Springfield, Oregon entered the cafeteria, jumped up on a table, and fired more than fifty shots from a .22-caliber semiautomatic rifle into a crowd of students. He left two dead and more than 20 injured, and this was following the killing of his mother and father, which he had done the afternoon before. It was, by any account, a horrific crime, and the number of injured was certainly alarming. However, there was no requirement that Clinton go to Springfield or speak at any memorial events. Indeed, as we showed above, he had already mostly ignored two school shootings that had left two and three students killed. However, the precedent set just two months earlier put such a possibility out of the question.

So on June 13, 1998, having accepted an invitation to visit the community and school, Clinton addressed the student body after meeting with families of the victims. Unlike the Jonesboro address, on this occasion Clinton did talk about what the tragedy meant for America writ large. Indeed, Clinton connected the shooting in Springfield to both the nation and a series of shootings that had happened in the previous academic year:

> Let me say that this has been not only a horrible and traumatic experience for you; this has been a traumatic experience for all of America. As all of you know, there have been a series of these school shootings with terrible consequences, in Paducah, Kentucky; in Pearl, Mississippi; in Edinboro, Pennsylvania; and in my home State, in Jonesboro, Arkansas.[32]

In these two sentences, Clinton asserted the shooting was a national concern by making it one of a series of shootings that had happened around the country. That is, the importance of the shooting at Thurston High was set within a thematic frame that suggested a national gun violence problem in the country's schools. The shooting itself might not be a national tragedy, but it was certainly part of a national issue.

Having connected the Springfield shooting to a series of shootings around the country, Clinton then transitioned back to the immediate context and the two dead victims because "as so many of the families said to me today, including the fathers of Mikael and Ben, we want something constructive to come out of this."[33] To make something constructive happen in response to the tragedy, Clinton suggested that the primary problem was the result of three interrelated issues—a small minority of troubled youth, easy access to guns, and a culture that glamorized violence. Having identified these issues, Clinton then emphasized the need to identify troubled youth in the hope that "we can find them out, before they get out of hand." Beyond this broad goal of stopping troubled youth before they turn violent, Clinton then offered two specific policy proposals. First, he acknowledged a bill that had recently been introduced into the United States Senate that would require any student who brought a gun to school to be held for a 72-hour evaluation. The President then told his audience that he had

> instructed the Secretary of Education and the Attorney General to prepare a guide-book to be ready when school opens next year in every school in America, for teachers and parents and for students as well, to describe all the kinds of early warning signals that deeply troubled young people sometimes give.

After offering the two policy proposals to help identify and deal with troubled students, Clinton did little with the rest of the speech. He offered to do whatever he could to help the community heal and thanked the community for his time there, saying he had found his conversations with families and community leaders inspiring. So after bringing policy into the speech, Clinton ended the short address without giving the Springfield community either a clear sense of closure or a purpose moving forward.

Obviously, Clinton's speech in Springfield, Oregon did not fit the model of what most would consider a successful eulogy or memorial speech. He was not attending a funeral or official memorial service. He mentioned the two victims killed in the shooting rampage only in passing by their first names and made no attempt to suggest a meaning to explain their deaths. He even brought policy into the speech. And yet, Clinton did make the shooting at Thurston High part of a national issue, and he was there to help offer comfort to the victims' families and the Springfield community. So while he was not there to deliver a more formal national eulogy, Clinton was there in his role as comforter-in-chief. In performing that role, Clinton redefined a local or state matter into a national problem. The following spring Clinton more intimately combined attributes of national eulogies with his role as comforter-in-chief when he transformed the shooting at Columbine High School from part of a series of such shootings to a singular national event felt by all Americans.

Littleton, Colorado

As he did with Springfield, Oregon, President Clinton did not attend any official memorial services or funerals following the shooting that took place on April 20, 1999 at Columbine High School. Despite the fact that it was the deadliest high school shooting in U. S. history, the White House sent Vice President Al Gore to the official memorial on April 25, 1999, to honor the 13 dead and offer support to the 21 injured. Speaking to reporters, Clinton did address the shootings shortly after news broke about the massacre, and Columbine was the subject of his weekly radio address a few days later. However, as the *Denver Post* reported at the time, Clinton was hosting the 50th anniversary celebration for NATO.[34] That NATO was then also involved in a U. S.-led bombing campaign in Yugoslavia to stop the ethnic cleansing of Albanian's in Kosovo may also have played a role in his decision. Clinton met with the Columbine community for the one-month anniversary of the shooting.

It is worth remembering that the shooting at Columbine High School was a major news media event. As news helicopters from Denver were on sight shortly after the shooting rampage began, images of frightened students streaming out of the school were shown on cable and nightly news for days, if not weeks. As information emerged about how the two shooters, Eric Harris and Dylan Klebold, had planned the attack, which involved improvised bombs, several different firearms, and knives, the nation seemed obsessed with trying to make sense of their carnage. Stories about the two shooters and how to identify troubled youth appeared on the covers of *Time* magazine for weeks.[35] And if the news media's attention had shifted elsewhere in early and mid-May, there was a renewed focus on the students from Columbine High School as the one-month anniversary approached, with the school's commencement scheduled to follow just two days later on Saturday, May 22. Therefore, Clinton's speech on May 20 was an important moment for the President to help the community cope. As the *Denver Post* described it on the front page the following day,

President Clinton consoled grief-stricken victims and survivors of the Columbine High School massacre Thursday and asked them to help heal America with their inspirational faith, love and courage. Commemorating the one-month anniversary of the rampage that killed 15, injured 23 and shocked the nation, the president and first lady moved a crowd of 2,200 through pep-rally cheers and painful tears.[36]

The Columbine community was clearly still struggling to cope with the shooting rampage. The nation was still paying attention. Perhaps sensing this attention, Clinton's speech at Columbine is twice as long as the one he gave in Springfield, Oregon. It is also a far better speech, aligning more closely with what one might expect from a memorial service.

In the speech, Clinton began by claiming the Columbine shooting as a national event, saying that while "this has been a long, hard month for all of you, ... it's been a hard month for America."[37] Explaining what he meant by this, Clinton begins by calling attention to his role as comforter-in-chief by noting, "You heard [Hillary] say that part of our job in these last 6 years, more than we ever could have imagined when we moved to Washington after the election in 1992, has been to be with grieving people." Highlighting many of the violent episodes noted above, Clinton then emphasizes the singular importance of the Columbine shooting by a comparison to all those prior incidents that included the Oklahoma City bombing. He argued, "but something profound has happened to your country because of this. ... I'm not even sure I can explain it to you." It is here, in suggesting that there is some ineffable quality to the Columbine shooting that has shaken the American people, that Clinton effectively transforms a mass shooting in the Denver suburbs into a national tragedy that could be used as an inventional resource for defining the country's values.

The news media had already done a great deal of the work to make a school shooting in the Denver suburbs feel like a collective, national act of violence. That the school was in a decidedly upper middle-class area and attended by mostly white students surely played into normative assumptions about class and race as they are portrayed in much popular culture and news media. Still, Clinton worked in his speech to make the local tragedy a national tragedy, something he would not have had to do if the target or victims were part of the federal government. So Clinton told students, families, and community leaders from Columbine that he hoped "you have been comforted by the caring not only of your neighbors but of your country," and he added, "all America has looked and listened with shared grief and enormous affection and admiration for you."[38] He also suggested that there was something about the shooting at Columbine that made people realize that such shootings could happen at any school in the nation. Because Clinton felt the American people writ large could so easily identify with the Columbine community and imagine such violence happening in their own towns, he told his audience, "what happened to you has pierced the soul of America."

Having established that the violence in Columbine was very much an act that had affected the entire nation, Clinton then offered an explanation of why the shooting had happened and what it should mean moving forward. The core of his argument was summarized in one line: "You can give us a culture of values instead of a culture of violence."[39] According to Clinton, people act out in violence because they succumb to the fear of their "own smallness" and grow angry towards others because they cannot accept their own "shortcomings or ... fears." Therefore, Clinton asked the students and families from Columbine to inspire all Americans to become better people who can move past "all the political and religious and racial and cultural lines that divide us." For Clinton, these divisions and the way they were negatively represented through media caused the shooting, which is why he then asked the Columbine community to help the nation face "a demon we have to do more to fight." In asking the students and families at Columbine to rise above their anger and fear as a way to remember and honor the dead, Clinton was asking the nation to do the same.

Although Clinton's speech to the Columbine High School community certainly did not reach the rhetorical heights of Reagan's *Challenger* address, it did more closely align with that speech than either of Clinton's previous responses to school shootings. Clinton did not name the victims the way one would expect in a eulogy delivered at an official memorial event. Nor did he transform the victims into heroes. Nevertheless, he made the attack on Columbine High School an attack on all American schools and called on those most directly impacted by the shooting to lead the country forward toward a "culture of values." What we find so significant here is that Clinton did this for a shooting that happened at a modestly sized high school run by a county, Jefferson County Public Schools, and overseen by a state, the Colorado State Board of Education.

One could argue that Clinton had no institutional obligation to speak to the Columbine community on the one-month anniversary of the shooting. As chief executive, the president oversees the federal government, not state and local matters, and schools are most certainly a local and state government matter, even if the federal government does have an interest in promoting education. The U. S. Department of Education acknowledges this:

> Education is primarily a State and local responsibility in the United States. It is States and communities, as well as public and private organizations of all kinds, that establish schools and colleges, develop curricula, and determine requirements for enrollment and graduation.[40]

Even in his role of commander in chief, Clinton had no direct reason to be there since the nation was not under attack and the structure damaged was not a federal building.

Of course, such arguments do not take into account the symbolic value of the presidency and the expanded role the chief executive now plays in the national imagination. Nor does it account for the power of mass media to promote national connections to events that happen all around the country. In response to such moments, the president has the unique ability to represent the nation, to offer the American people meaning and reassurance, to serve, that is, as comforter-in-chief. By choice and by demand, it was certainly a role Clinton was willing to play.

An Established Role

As was noted in the introduction of this chapter, the moniker first attributed to Bill Clinton was transferred to both George W. Bush and Barack Obama. It has also already been brought up in reference to recently elected Donald Trump. As president-elect in December 2016, Trump visited with victims and families of an attack on Ohio State University's campus. On November 28, 2016, an Ohio State student plowed his car into a crowd and then got out with a butcher knife and began slashing at people. Before police shot the attacker dead, he left 11 people injured. Describing Trump's visit, one Associated Press reporter wrote,

> Trump met with the families privately and aides did not immediately provide an accounting of what was discussed. But, in his brief statement to reporters, he took on the role of comforter-in-chief, avoiding the inflammatory rhetoric that has marked his response to other attacks.[41]

Not known for his calming presence, it says a great deal about contemporary expectations of presidents being able to take on the role of comforter-in-chief that even Trump can be described with that moniker. Whether he likes it or not and whether he is particularly good at it or not, the role of comforter-in-chief has been established, and it seems Trump, as well as future presidents, will be expected to perform it.

Although the chapter's opening and our analysis of Clinton focused on responses to gun violence, it should be noted here that presidents can or must step into the role of comforter-in-chief for an increasingly broad range of events that have little direct connection to the federal government. Clinton chose to eulogize six firefighters in Worcester, Massachusetts who were killed while battling a fire in an abandoned warehouse that was accidently started by two homeless people.[42]

In the face of growing criticism of how the federal government was handling its response to the devastating Hurricane Katrina, Bush was all but forced to give a national address from New Orleans to both defend himself and try to calm the nation. And in addition to the many memorials he spoke at following gun violence, Barack Obama also spoke at a memorial service for the 29 victims of the Upper Big Branch Mine accident that occurred in Beckley, West Virginia on April 5, 2010.[43] Indeed, the different types of potential situations that a president might be called upon to respond to as comforter-in-chief is quite vast when the role is divorced from any direct connection to the federal government.

One of the reasons for such possible demands upon the president is that presidents are but one player in the complex struggle to define and shape the nation. Technology and the news media play a significant role in constructing national events in ways that would have been nearly impossible a century ago. When an angry town member and school board treasurer in Bath Township, Michigan detonated bombs that destroyed the Bath Consolidated School on May 18, 1927, Americans across the nation read about the deaths of the 38 elementary schoolchildren and 6 adults.[44] Many of those readers were surely concerned about the nearly 60 injured and horrified to learn that the bomber compounded the initial destruction by driving to the scene of the crime in order to detonate the truck he was driving in the manner of a suicide bomber. Nevertheless, they could not have shared in the immediacy and intensity of the event in the same way contemporary Americans can through video and breaking news updates as events are still unfolding. Perhaps it is at least in part for that reason that President Coolidge never publicly said a word about the Bath School bombing. Today, however, it is unthinkable that a president would not offer some comfort to the nation following the murder of 38 children.

Conclusion

For good or ill, the president's new and expanding role as comforter-in-chief seems to be here to stay.[45] This strikes us as both a good and bad thing. As citizens of a diverse nation who decreasingly share the same news media sources or watch the same television programs, the American people need ways to collectively identify with one another. Tragic events seem to offer that potential, and presidents are uniquely positioned to construct the rhetorical resources for a nation to come together in response to death and disaster. Given that such events are not suddenly going to stop happening, acknowledging the role the president plays in responding to them would be a good thing.

Alternatively, there is something worrisome in the potential power presidents can gain from successful responses to violence. Although each of these events carries with it the burden of the many pitfalls that can come from politicizing tragedy or striking the wrong tone, they can also, as Clinton's response to the Oklahoma City bombing shows, allow a president to build a significant amount of political capital. The role of comforter-in-chief also offers presidents a particularly effective way of controlling the way events are understood and the subsequent political ends they could be used for. With a president's party in control of Congress, such opportunities could lead to major policy initiatives, which might not represent what people would prefer during calmer times.

Of course, like most things, the comforter-in-chief role has both positive and negative potential. What matters is how individual presidents use it and how much support they have to use it in ways that build upon past performances. Regardless, there really is nobody else who can play the role. The authors of the United States Constitution did not see fit to divide the executive branch into different roles, with one serving a more symbolic purpose and the other a more political purpose. Nor does the United States have an official religion and, thus, no religious leader to turn to in times of crisis. We believe these are good things. However, as the nation has garnered more and more of the American people's attention and allegiance over the past century at the expense of local communities and states, this has given the presidency increasing weight. Giving that office an increasing amount of control over how people interpret and respond to violence seems a double-edged sword. At the very least, rhetorical scholars should pay very close attention to how individual presidents choose to use their role as comforters-in-chief. Each time a president does so, it presents a powerful opportunity to employ epideictic rhetoric that (re)defines the nation's values. Such a power does more than create an imbalance of power in the federal government; at least potentially, it could redefine an entire nation in subtle ways unnoticed at more deliberative times.

Notes

1. See, Gregory Korte, "Obama Renews Call for Gun Control: President Visits Orlando Victims, Families," *USA Today*, June 17, 2016, 3A; and, Christi Parsons & Michael A. Memoli, "In Orlando, Obama Reprises Role As Comforter-in-Chief," *Los Angeles Times*, June 16, 2016, http://www.latimes.com/nation/la-na-obama-orlando-shooting-20160616-snap-story.html.
2. David Nakamura & Juliet Eilperin, "Partisan Politics Will Test Obama's Call for Unity in Wake of Orlando Shootings," *Washington Post*, June 16, 1016, A10.

3. Peter Baker, "Clinton Approves Tough Airline Safety Bill; More Sophisticated Equipment to Be Installed in Airports to Combat Terrorist Threat," *Washington Post*, Oct. 10, 1996, A23.

4. Laurence McQuillan, "Clinton's Visit to N.C. Part of Comfort Pattern," *USA Today*, Sep. 20, 1999, 2A.

5. Ann Gerhart, "Laura Bush, Comforter In Chief; First Lady Works to Soothe a Shaken Nation," *Washington Post*, Sep. 19, 2001, C1.

6. Richard W. Stevenson, "Bush's Words to the Nation Mix Sadness and Resolve," *New York Times*, Feb 2, 2003, A32.

7. Eric Bradner, "George W. Bush 'Wanted Dad to Be Alive' to Read Biography," *CNN*, Nov. 11, 2014, http://www.cnn.com/2014/11/11/politics/bush-family-book/.

8. Jeanne Fahnestock, *Rhetorical Style: The Uses of Language in Persuasion* (New York: Oxford University Press, 2011), 103.

9. Fahnestock, *Rhetorical*, 104.

10. See, Mary Stuckey, *Political Rhetoric* (New Brunswick, NJ: Transaction Publishers, 2015), 52–53.

11. Theodore Roosevelt, "Aid for San Francisco," April 18, 1906, Online Archive of California, http://oac.cdlib.org/ark:/13030/hb0c6003sf/?brand=oac4.

12. See, "Truman Promises All Federal Aid," *New York Times*, April 18, 1947, A1; and, Harry Truman, "Address at the Opening of the Conference on Fire Prevention," May 5, 1947, American Presidency Project, http://www.presidency.ucsb.edu/ws/index.php?pid=12879.

13. See, James W. Ceaser, Glen E. Thuerow, Jeffrey Tulis, and Joseph M. Bessette, "The Rise of the Rhetorical Presidency," *Presidential Studies Quarterly* 11, no. 2 (1981): 158-171; and, Theodore J. Lowi, *The Personal President: Power Invested, Promise Unfulfilled* (Ithaca, NY: Cornell University Press, 1985).

14. Lowi, *Personal President*, 121.

15. See, Karlyn Kohrs Campbell & Kathleen Hall Jamieson, *Presidents Creating the Presidency: Deeds Done in Words* (Chicago: University of Chicago Press, 2008).

16. Campbell & Jamieson, *Presidents*, 73.

17. Campbell & Jamieson, *Presidents*, 73.

18. See, Stuckey, *Political Rhetoric*, 54.

19. Mary E. Stuckey, *Slipping the Surly Bonds: Reagan's Challenger Address* (College Station, TX: Texas A&M University Press, 2006), 6.

20. According to one prominent list, Reagan's address ranks 8th out of the top 100 speeches of the twentieth century in the U. S. See Stephen E. Lucas and Martin J. Medhurst, *Words of a Century: The Top 100 American Speeches, 1900-1999* (New York: Oxford University Press, 2008).

21. Ronald Reagan, "Address to the Nation on the Explosion of the Space Shuttle Challenger," Jan. 28, 1986, American Presidency Project, http://www.presidency.ucsb.edu/ws/?pid=37646.

22. Reagan, "Address to the Nation on the Explosion."

23. Reagan, "Address to the Nation on the Explosion."

24. According to Shogan, the first time Clinton publicly stated "I feel your pain" was at a fundraiser on March 28, 1992 when confronted with an AIDS activist that AIDS victims were

suffering from years of government neglect. See footnote 6 in, Colleen J. Shogan, "The Political Utility of Empathy in Presidential Leadership," *Presidential Studies Quarterly* 39, no. 4 (2009): 859–877.

25. For an example of Clinton's rhetorical abilities, see, Roderick P. Hart, Jay P. Childers, and Colene J. Lind, *Political Tone: How Leaders Talk and Why* (Chicago: University of Chicago Press, 2013), 129–149.

26. Campbell & Jamieson, *Presidents*, 79.

27. Mark Shields, "With Foes Like These," *Washington Post*, May 22, 1996, A21.

28. The following details come from two in-depth reports written in the days following the shooting. See, John Kifner et al., "From Wild Talk and Friendship to Five Deaths in a Schoolyard," *New York Times*, March 29, 1998, A1; and John Schwartz, "Pupils Return to Arkansas School Where Five Were Slain," *Washington Post*, Mar. 27, 1998, A3.

29. William J. Clinton, "Remarks to the Columbine High School Community in Littleton," May 20, 1999, American Presidency Project, http://www.presidency.ucsb.edu/ws/index.php?pid=57605.

30. William J. Clinton, "Statement on the Attacks of Westside Middle School in Jonesboro, Arkansas," March 24, 1998, American Presidency Project, http://www.presidency.ucsb.edu/ws/index.php?pid=55675.

31. William J. Clinton, "Videotaped Remarks for the Memorial Service in Jonesboro, Arkansas," March 29, 1998, *American Presidency Project*, http://www.presidency.ucsb.edu/ws/index.php?pid=55717.

32. William J. Clinton, "Remarks at Thurston High School in Springfield, Oregon," June 13, 1998, *American Presidency Project*, http://www.presidency.ucsb.edu/ws/index.php?pid=56142.

33. Clinton, "Remarks at Thurston."

34. Fred Brown, "Columbine, Tragedy and Recovery: Gores to Attend Service," *Denver Post*, April 24, 1999. http://extras.denverpost.com/news/shot0424r.htm.

35. One can find all the covers of *Time* magazine in 1999 here: http://time.com/vault/year/1999/.

36. Mark Obmascik & Patricia Callahan, "'You Can Help America Heal' Clinton Speaks to Columbine Community," *Denver Post*, May 21, 1999, A1.

37. Clinton, "Remarks to the Columbine."

38. Clinton, "Remarks to the Columbine."

39. Clinton, "Remarks to the Columbine."

40. "The Federal Role in Education," U.S. Department of Education, Accessed January 10, 2017, https://www2.ed.gov/about/overview/fed/role.html.

41. Jonathan Lemire, "Trump Meets with Ohio State Victims," *Bismarck Tribune*, December 9, 2016, A2.

42. See, Somini Sengupta, "Thousands Mourn Six Who Died in Warehouse Fire," *New York Times*, December 10, 1999, A20.

43. Barack Obama, "Remarks at a Memorial Service for the Victims of the Upper Big Branch Mine Accident in Beckley, West Virginia," Apr. 25, 2010, American Presidency Project, http://www.presidency.ucsb.edu/ws/index.php?pid=87795.

44. For a detailed account of the bombing, see, Arnie Bernstein, *Bath Massacre: America's First School Bombing* (Ann Arbor: University of Michigan Press, 2009).

45. Indeed, at least one blogger for the popular conservative site RedState uses Coolidge's lack of response to the Bath School disaster of evidence that the federal government has grown too intrusive in the lives of the American people. See, Conservativecurmudgeon, "May 18th, 1927—The Story Of Little Ralphie Cushman's Tulips, and How They Bloom Today," *RedState*, May 9, 2011, http://www.redstate.com/diary/conservativecurmudgeon/2011/05/09/may-18th-1927-the-story-of-little-ralphie-cushmans-tulips-and-how-they-bloom-today/.

Reading the Presidency through Interactions

CHAPTER SIX

Obama's Command

Chemical Weapons in Syria and the Global Duties of a Rhetorical Presidency

RONALD WALTER GREENE AND JAY ALEXANDER FRANK

On the night of April 6, 2017—two days after a chemical weapons attack in Khan Shaykun—President Donald Trump ordered 59 cruise missiles to strike the Al Shayrat Airfield in Syria. Several hours later he issued a rationale for the attack. "There can be no dispute," he said, "that Syria used banned chemical weapons, violated its obligations under the Chemical Weapons Convention, and ignored the urging of the U.N. Security Council."[1] The next morning, Fareed Zakaria assessed Trump's decision and his justification for the use military force. He claimed that "Donald Trump became President of the United States last night" and that, "for the first time really as president, he talked about international norms, international rules, about America's role in enforcing justice in the world."[2] Zakaria's comments are instructive. They suggest that one does not truly become the president simply by winning an election or occupying the office. What is necessary is talk. Furthermore, this talk is, first and foremost, about "international norms," "international rules," and America's role "in enforcing justice in the world."

If one must speak—and speak about particular things—in order to truly become "the president," then the institution of the presidency is rhetorical in material ways that exceed the traditional notion of presidential leadership that is manifested in attempts to persuade the public. Becoming a president, in other words, is a way of becoming a rhetorical subject. It is a rhetorical effect of speaking and being spoken to.[3] That effect relies on the inscription of discourse that "fixes norms, elaborates criteria, and hence makes it possible to speak of and treat a given problem at a particular time."⁴ It also relies on speech as a rhetorical technology to transform an individual that occupies a constitutional role into a rhetorical subject known as "a president." As a rhetorical subject, then, a president is an ideal type that is both governed by discourse and governs in and through discourse. We often use the word "presidential" to designate our sense of whether any given president has the appropriate orientation to this ideal type. The rhetorical presidency therefore describes how the institution enacts an ethical process by which one can form oneself into a "presidential subject" that is judged, evaluated, and imitated by oneself and others.

Zakaria's comments also illustrate a crucial problem to which a president must address his ethical becoming: a president cannot become "presidential," Zakaria claims, without embedding international rules and norms into his decisions to use military force. This international element of a president's ethical self-fashioning positions the rhetorical presidency as a global subject. But Trump's public justification for the use of military force came *after* his decision to strike Al Shayrat. His justification therefore reveals that he is implicated in a regime of international rules and norms at the same time as it obscures many of the processes that constitute his presidency as a global subject. In order to better flesh out these processes, we instead turn to president Barack Obama's speech on August 31, 2013. In this speech Obama attempted to persuade Congress to authorize the use of military force in Syria. He also asserted his capacity as commander-in-chief to initiate a military intervention even without congressional authorization. We suggest that Obama's articulation to a global order is twice glimpsed through this speech—first through his willingness to order a strike as commander-in-chief of the United States' military and second through his appeal to Congress as a proxy for the American people. The former, we argue, reveals the performative duties of the rhetorical presidency, while the latter reveals the distribution of the forms of subjectivity those duties entail. In both cases an ethical norm embeds the use of state violence into the international police powers of the rhetorical presidency. The first part of this chapter will therefore provide a theoretical argument for why the rhetorical presidency is an apparatus of ethical becoming or an "ethical machine." The second and third parts of the chapter activate this theoretical intervention as a materialist method for assessing, respectively, the roles of command and deliberation/debate as rhetorical techniques of ethical becoming.⁵

The Rhetorical Presidency is an Ethical Machine

By January 2011, the "Arab Spring" had come to Syria. Syrian President Bashar al-Assad, however, quickly made clear that he had no intention of negotiating a peaceful transition to a more democratic polity. In March, Assad's forces opened fire in Darra, killing four. Some in the military refused Assad's orders to use force against their own people, and defectors from the Syrian Army soon took up arms against Assad as the Free Syrian Army. Thus, the uprising in Syria became a civil war. It did not take long before "both factions, the Bashar Al-Assad regime and the Syrian opposition, were accusing each other of [chemical weapons] use."[6] As the civil war unfolded, the use of chemical weapons became a matter of "special concern" for the "Chemical Defense Community."[7] Syria's failure to sign the Chemical Weapons Convention—making it one of only six counties to resist ratification—intensified the concern that the effectiveness of the international norm against the use of chemical weapons might be threatened. In August 2012 Obama made clear that chemical weapons use in Syria was a "red line" that, if crossed, would prompt an armed intervention.[8]

By the end of the summer of 2013, the United States stood on the brink of military action in Syria. Little more than a week had passed following a devastating attack on the Syrian city of Ghouta—an attack in which the use of chemical weapons left hundreds of Syrians dead or in dire need of medical attention. The United Nations, as well as intelligence agencies from around the world, rushed to determine who was responsible. The UN's investigation found "clear and convincing evidence" that sarin gas had been used in Ghouta, but it also remained silent on the question of the weapons' origin.[9] The American intelligence community, however, was far more decisive. By August 30th, the White House had released a statement that claimed "with high confidence that the Syrian government carried out a chemical weapons attack in the Damascus suburbs on August 21, 2013."[10] Plans for an airstrike were soon made, and later reports indicated that the United States' planned attack may have had as many as 43 targets.[11] But the attack on Damascus never came. In its stead, Obama delivered a striking and peculiar oration. Rather than a post-hoc justification for a military intervention that was already begun, Obama appealed to Congress and to the American people to authorize the use of force.

Obama's decision to appeal to the American people in order to gain support for military action in Syria should not, however, come as a surprise to scholars of presidential rhetoric. Indeed, Roderick Hart explains, "modern" presidential speech is magnified and conditioned by changes in media technologies and news media practices.[12] Presidents now govern—particularly on matters of war and peace—through speechmaking. Rhetoric, the argument goes, allows presidents to shape the national agenda.[13] It allows them to "'go over the heads' of Congress to the people at large in support of legislation and other initiatives."[14] It is through the people, then, that rhetoric takes on its *instrumental* capacity as a "principle tool of presidential governance." There is, however, considerable dispute concerning the efficacy of presidential rhetoric. George Edwards suspects that "the real influence of rhetoric may be on elite debate, journalistic coverage, and congressional deliberation."[15] He worries that exhortations from the bully pulpit, if their aim really is popular leadership, often fall on deaf ears.[16] Martin Medhurst's rebuttal reminds us that rhetoric is more than "a causative factor in persuasion," and Hart adds that presidential rhetoric falls on "slow ears, busy ears, and elite ears, but a good deal of listening still gets done."[17]

On that, at least, most everyone agrees. "Presidents," as Karlyn Kohrs Campbell and Kathleen Hall Jamieson put it, may "address many audiences, but 'the people' are always watching."[18] We may, in other words, debate the utility of rhetorical leadership as an *instrument* of executive governance. But few doubt that "the people" are the *products* of presidential rhetoric. Indeed, the American people are often constituted and reconstituted as such by presidents, who "have shaped addresses in order to give the people a particular identity." Even when presidents fail to "lead"—that is, to create policy—through rhetoric, their attempts leave lasting impressions on the instruments of their leadership. The people themselves are cast as speakers with political agency. They become capable of exerting their influence on Congress. Whether or not they actually do so is beside the point. The fact that a rhetorical presidency creates rhetorical subjects is significant in itself because it transforms the prospect of executive governance. The concept of a rhetorical presidency thus ceases to measure only the instrumental capacities of presidential speech and begins to measure the ways the institutional power of the presidency itself is prefigured by and exercised over speech.

The president, too, is thus subject to the power of the rhetorical presidency. He is no exception. Instead, the president is set against an institution that draws, as Shawn and Trevor Parry-Giles write, from a "larger political and cultural understanding of the presidency."[19] Presidents are, moreover, bound by the history of their predecessors. Even "idiosyncratic" orations contribute to and are eventually transcended by generic patterns of presidential rhetoric. "Label a piece of presidential discourse a farewell," Campbell and Jamieson explain, "and Washington's final instructions from the presidency and the summative statement by Dwight Eisenhower come into play."[20] Presidents are, in other words, *compelled* to speak, and to look and sound "presidential" when they do so. They must, as John Murphy puts it, be invested with the power of the office.[21] Their authority must be the authority of the institution itself. But therein lies the rub. By shifting the focus from the president himself onto the institution, we risk missing a "story of cultural value and political struggle"—a history of techniques and practices through which the office comes into being as an *institution of speech*.[22] If scholars of rhetoric hope to assess how the rhetorical presidency can generate rhetorical subjects, then it is worth our time to ask how the institution itself comes to be a rhetorical subject—how it, and not merely the person occupying the office, comes to speak and be spoken to.

We are not the first to explore this problem. Jeffrey Tulis' famous account of the rhetorical presidency attempts to trace its *historical* emergence as a rhetorical institution by situating the presidency within the broader configuration of the American state apparatus. In Tulis' account, the rhetorical presidency emerges as a part of a radical transformation in the principles of republican governance following Woodrow Wilson's reinterpretation of executive power in his attacks on *The Federalist*. This argument is worth recalling in greater detail. The founders, Tulis writes, "worried especially about the danger that a powerful executive might pose to the system if power were derived from the role of popular leader."[23] The founders, in other words, associated rhetorical leadership with the problem of demagoguery. But they did not believe that the problem of demagoguery was reliably solved by the promise of good men speaking well. Instead, Tulis explains, they proscribed demagoguery through the administration of governing institutions:

> Like the liberal theorists, the founders seldom wrote about rhetoric directly … Because liberal theorists and the founders were so concerned to circumscribe politics, to narrow the public sphere, they generally addressed problems of rhetoric indirectly, through discussions of institutions … Aristotle, Quintilian, and Cicero, all of whom lived in polities whose governments deeply penetrated into what we call the private sphere, wrote treatises on rhetoric and addressed them directly to rhetoricians … in order to control tendencies toward demagoguery. There are no comparable treatises on rhetoric by the political philosophers most consulted by the founders (Locke, Hume, Montesquieu, etc.). Replacing a doctrine of rhetoric or a theory of persuasion addressed directly to political actors are sets of teachings on the building of institutions. It is primarily in discussions of the principles underlying the major national institutions that the founders addressed problems of rhetoric.[24]

This is the core of Tulis' argument. He thinks that the founders conceived of our governing institutions as such—of the separation of powers and the independence of the executive—because they believed that strong executive leadership through public address would impede quality deliberation among the people and in the halls of Congress. In fact, it is precisely because Woodrow Wilson reinterpreted—and, further, *reversed*—the relationship between leadership and deliberation that Tulis believes his critiques of *The Federalist* were so profound and transformative. "Unlike the founders, who saw these two functions [leadership and deliberation] in conflict, Wilson regarded them as dependent upon each other."[25]

Wilson worried that the founders' formula for the separation of powers—which he reinterpreted as "checks and balances"—"hindered efficient, coordinated, well-led policy."[26] He thought that the founders gave the president "no means of attack and few effective weapons of defense," and that under such conditions "the president cannot lead."[27] Moreover, Tulis explains that Wilson believed Congress was ill suited for "true" deliberation because its debates were overly technical and poorly publicized. "For the founders," Tulis writes, "this would not have been disturbing, but for Wilson, the very heart of representative government was the principle of publicity."[28] Wilson therefore prescribed a presidency that could lead public opinion. He would use public address as a means of both "energizing" the executive (by providing the president with the resources to direct the creation of policy) and "elevating" congressional debate to the level of "true deliberation" (which would demand the attention of the public).

Where Wilson favored a president that could lead through speech, Tulis argues that the founders believed that a "strong executive was compatible with, indeed *required*, a limit on most of the rhetorical practices that have now come to signify leadership."[29] Tulis thus believes that the rhetorical presidency could not have existed prior to Wilson in the way that it does today because the institutional configuration of American democracy proscribed the leadership of mass public opinion through popular rhetoric. Insofar as a rhetorical presidency now exists—and, moreover, dominates our conceptual understanding of the presidency's place in American politics—it was written into being through a re-organization of our governing institutions. Tulis thus offers one possible account of the rhetorical presidency's emergence as a form of rhetorical subjectivity: it emerges historically as a result of the shifting institutional configurations of the state apparatus. We believe this explanation is unsatisfactory because it, too, displaces the problem of subjectification onto the state apparatus itself—in this case onto the Constitution and the way it organizes the branches of American government.

We will be more specific. Tulis' basic argument is that the institutional shifts in the American state apparatus constituted a *radical historical break*. An era without a rhetorical presidency (at least in its "modern" or contemporary form) was followed by an era with a rhetorical presidency. On one side of this historical break, "the people" (and their representatives in Congress) are constituted as rhetorical subjects precisely insofar as the rhetorical leadership of public opinion by the president is proscribed by the separation of powers outlined in the Constitution. On the other side of the break, the people are constituted as rhetorical subjects by a president—a popular leader capable of identifying and unifying the public will through the awesome power of speech. But in this latter case the president himself is *assumed to be a speaker* only once the "separation of powers" is reinterpreted as "checks and balances," and, further, that the state apparatus itself is reorganized around a critique of that reinterpretation. Tulis does not, in other words, believe in the *ex nihilo* emergence of a rhetorical presidency from within a state apparatus otherwise devoid of rhetoric. "Political rhetoric is," for him "simultaneously, a practical result of basic doctrines of governance, and an avenue to the meaning of alternative constitutional understandings."[30] The internal movements of the state apparatus itself—its institutional shifts and administrative reorganizations—are thus rhetorical processes carried out by rhetorical subjects. Tulis' "historical break," in other words, posits the constitution of rhetorical subjects by and through the state apparatus at the same time as it assumes that such an apparatus is already populated by rhetorical subjects.

We believe that this reveals something crucial about the difficulty of thinking of the presidency as a rhetorical subject. Too often scholars of rhetoric assume that the power to constitute concrete individuals as subjects resides within the constitutive and instrumental dimensions of presidential speech (or, more generally, in the state apparatus itself). As an institution, the rhetorical presidency promotes a bureaucratic infrastructure to assist the president in producing, circulating, and testing his message. It encourages the president to speak. In so doing, the president's rhetoric becomes an exercise in power and political agency. So, too, with the publics to which modern presidents speak. These publics hear the call and are granted rhetorical agency as "the people." They are subjects because they are *made to appear*. But if subjectivity is not merely a constitutive effect of instrumental rhetorical practices, then presidential speech requires a closer alliance with its performative dimensions. Pierre Clastres informed us of this very point by contrasting the president's capacity to "command" (to exert political agency and constitute rhetorical subjects through instrumental rhetorical practices) with an account of the speeches of "chiefs" in "primitive societies."[31]

The primitive chief, Clastres observed, is never *obeyed* because in primitive society there is no institution (there is no State) that detaches power from the society as a whole. "An order? Now there is something the chief would be unable to give; that is the kind of fullness his speech is denied."[32] The speech of the chief is thus precisely the opposite of a command. It does not represent power, but rather *signifies nothing*.[33] It does not, however, *do* nothing. Clastres notes that the speech of the chief carries a ritual value. "Almost without exception," he writes, "the leader addresses the group daily, at daybreak and at dusk … in a loud voice" because "there is no gathering … no hush falls, everybody goes about their business as if nothing was happening."[34] The point of this ritual, Clastres explains, is to "make certain that all things remain in their place"—that power remains attached to society and is not consolidated in the word of a chief.[35] Speech is therefore what a chief does to guarantee that *society* (and not a State) remains in power. Speech is a chief's *duty*.

But Clastres' concept of duty is limited by his account of society. He thought society was *primitive*—that it existed only in those remote regions that had not yet encountered the State. Moreover, he believed that the State emerged (historically, in an evolutionary sense) from society and that the State would eventually *absorb* society. From within Clastres' "evolutionary" perspective, then, the concept of duty can never describe the nature of presidential speech, which is tied to our "evolutionary" tendency to govern through a State. We will offer a more contemporary concept of duty. In order to do so, however, we must first refigure much of Clastres' conceptual apparatus. The problem with his "evolutionary" perspective is that it does not accurately depict society, the State, or their relationship. The State—particularly as Clastres encountered it in the twentieth century—is neither divine nor imperial. Its law is, as Gilles Deleuze and Felix Guattari write, "not the law of All or Nothing (State societies *or* counter-State societies) but that of interior and exterior."[36] States, in other words, are *sovereign*. They govern territories which they internalize through the production and maintenance of borders. What Clastres' called "society"—the "primitive world" of his ethnographic voyages—is not a precursor to the State. It is its *exterior*. It is precisely this distinction between anteriority and exteriority that allows Deleuze and Guattari to reimagine "society:"

> Not only is there no universal State, but the outside of States cannot be reduced to "foreign policy," that is, to a set of relations among States. The outside appears simultaneously in two directions: huge worldwide machines branched out over the entire *ecumenon* at a given moment, which enjoy a large measure of autonomy in relation to the States (for example, commercial organization of the "multinational" type, or industrial complexes, or even religious formations like Christianity, Islam, certain prophetic or messianic movements, etc.); but also the local mechanisms of bands, margins, minorities, which continue to affirm the rights of segmentary societies in opposition to the organs of State power.[37]

Society, in other words, is greater than Clastres imagined. It runs through the State. It envelops the State. It exceeds the State. And for these reasons the exercise of State power—one form of which is the rhetorical leadership of public opinion by the President of the United States—can be viewed as the site of a struggle between many conflicting aspects of society. Duty, then, becomes an ethical machine. It is a way of understanding the locus of power (society) as it flows through the State and the body of the president, a way of glimpsing the shape of power in society as a whole. It is therefore important to emphasize just what this concept of duty does to something like "command." We believe that the concept of duty allows us to view presidential command in two distinct ways.

On the one hand, presidential command can be viewed as a symbolic effect—one which rhetorical scholars have often identified with the constitutive force of presidential leadership. The president speaks and produces subjects. But as we have already shown, scholars of presidential rhetoric have been saying as much for years. Our point is that in order to truly investigate the presidency as a site of rhetorical subjectivity we will need to explore how the presidency's ways of speaking work as techniques for the ethical becoming of both a president and a people through the performance of a duty toward a particular norm. Here it is useful to recall that duty manifests itself through speech—that ethical subjects *feel* compelled to speak. On the other hand, then, command can be understood as a dutiful speech act or "duty-ritual." A presidential command is a speech act that is most commonly associated with the president's role as commander in chief and that links his speech to the military and police arms of a state apparatus. When presidents utter commands, then, they articulate themselves to a complex assemblage of duties—to the lives of soldiers and officers but also to moral codes, industrial complexes, pro and anti-war movements, and international regimes. It is through what we call a "duty-ritual" that the nature of presidential subjectivity can thus be glimpsed. In the next section, we will demonstrate precisely how this process occurs. Specifically, we will show how Obama's repeated assertion of the power of command reveals how he sutures presidential subjectivity to the international norm against chemical weapons, thus reconstituting the presidency as a global subject.

Command is an Ethical Technology

Many contemporary scholars of presidential rhetoric are hard-pressed to see recent presidential discourse as a manifestation of social duty. No longer is it, as Tulis wrote, "taken for granted that presidents have a *duty* constantly to defend themselves publicly, to promote policy initiatives nationwide, and to inspirit the population."[38] This is the era, we are told, of the "post-rhetorical presidency" and the "unitary executive."[39] Indeed, recent efforts to bolster executive power—coupled with the fact that "the Constitution mandates not a single oratorical duty of an American president"—have given presidents both a means (absolute command over the executive branch) and an incentive (political power) to "bypass more traditional opportunities for public deliberation."[40] Even worse, when contemporary presidents *do* speak, they are apt to "confuse public opinion, prevent citizen action, and frustrate citizen deliberation."[41] Presidential speech, conceived in this way, is "post-rhetorical" and contributes to society's degradation. It *effaces* the president's social duty to public deliberation and, as Stephen Hartnett and Jennifer Mercieca argue, subsequently impedes democratic practice.

We are less sure, however, that the rhetorical presidency requires an ethical commitment to any one ideological purpose (let alone to deliberative democracy in particular). We suggest that the rhetorical presidency *does* generate an ethical mode of becoming—what Toby Miller calls a "determinate indeterminacy"—for subjects (regardless of whether those subjects are academics, media pundits, the people, or presidents themselves) to judge a president as more or less "presidential."[42] What makes the rhetorical presidency an ethical machine is therefore the different ways the speechmaking activities of a president activate and align the truth of rhetorical subjects (including the presidency) with some actions and not others. In Clastres' account this process is clear. The chief speaks because a normative commitment to society (as opposed to the State) obliges him not only to speak but to say nothing. Presidents have a similar personal capacity to draw on normative discourses as ethical means of becoming "presidential." But a broader (Deleuzian) notion of society means that a president's duty to speak subjects him to *all* of the political struggles associated with the production of social norms (and, concretely, to the political struggles internal to a given norm).

The norm against the use of chemical weapons, in particular, was asserted before the weapons were even invented. Indeed, the aftermath of World War I codified a prohibition on chemical weapons use, but it was The Hague Peace Conferences of 1899 that initiated the norm when delegates agreed "to abstain from the use of projectiles the sole object of which is the diffusion of asphyxiating or deleterious gases."[43] That agreement, moreover, belongs to a nineteenth century history of peace movement advocacy. As David Nicholas explains, "the nineteenth-century peace movement effectively began with the establishment toward the end of the Napoleonic Wars, independently and virtually simultaneously, of peace societies in the United States and Britain."[44] By mid-century these peace societies had inaugurated a "peace congress movement" by holding congresses in Belgium, Great Britain, Germany, and France.[45] These "peace congresses" were especially influenced by the American Peace Society's idea of a "Congress of Nations and an arbitration clause in international treaties."[46] Many 19th century peace movements, especially those with Christian (often Quaker inspired) and middle-class ties, subsequently cultivated the very idea of international law as a way to end or mitigate the horrors of war.

If early nineteenth century peace societies invented the idea of the peace conference, they were not the alone in their antimilitarism. Nineteenth century antimilitarism was also pushed along by socialists and anarchists calling for class solidarity across national lines and a class struggle against militarism and war.[47]

The norm against chemical weapons is thus, as Richard Price claims, a political construct and as such is affected by the contingencies of history and political struggle.[48] That political struggle, in particular, was defined by forces working above and below state actors toward what we now call international law. Indeed, the nineteenth century peace movements that created the opportunity for The Hague Conferences to actualize a norm against chemical weapons were largely forces external to the State. Contemporary prohibitions on chemical weapons use are similarly attached to "social" forces. In the United States' ratification of the Chemical Weapons Convention, for example, one discovers the role of non-governmental organizations as societal proxies rhetorically serving as "force multipliers" to secure ratification from Congress.[49] States, in other words, take to governing problems when the struggles of society attach themselves to the powers of a state apparatus. As a state apparatus, the rhetorical presidency is one site at which those struggles attach themselves to the president.

Obama's speech on August 31, 2013 thus marks a normative commitment to the international prohibition against chemical weapons that obliges him not only to speak but to utter *commands*. In it, Obama makes two core claims. First, he provides a rationale for why, "after careful deliberation," he has "decided that the United States should take military action against Syrian regime targets."[50] Second, he argues that Congress should grant him the authorization to use military force. These two moves require two different sorts of analysis. The first claim, we argue, must be approached as a duty-ritual in order to understand how the speech positions military command as a rhetorical technique of ethical becoming. The second, by contrast, must be approached as a discursive distribution of Obama's duty—a distribution that implicates both Congress and the American people in the presidency's emergence as a global subject.

Obama began the speech with a reference to the attack on Ghouta. "Ten days ago," he claimed, "the world watched in horror as men, women and children were massacred in Syria in the worst chemical weapons attack of the 21st century."[51] Further, he assigned responsibility to the Assad regime, describing the deaths of "over 1000 people … several hundred of them … children" as an act of murder carried out "by their government." He then wove both his reference to the victims of the attack and his claim about Assad's culpability into a rationale for military intervention:

> This attack is an assault on human dignity. It also presents a serious danger to our national security. It risks making a mockery of the global prohibition on the use of chemical weapons. It endangers our friends and partners along Syria's border, including Israel, Jordan, Turkey, Lebanon, and Iraq. It could lead to escalating use of chemical weapons, or their proliferation to terrorist groups who would do our people harm. In a world with many dangers, this menace must be confronted.[52]

It is worth dwelling on the complexity of this explanation. The claim that the attack was an "assault on human dignity" gestures toward a humanitarian justification for military intervention. Assad's action, meanwhile, disrespects the international norm against the use of chemical weapons, thus gesturing toward military interventions organized around the "police" functions of an international community. It also destabilizes American national security in two ways. On the one hand, the attack threatens regional allies by making it easier for Assad or other actors to use chemical weapons. Obama's justification is, in this sense, organized not only around American national security, but also around the American national security *regime*—around the network of international alliances and agreements that imbricate American national security and *global* security. On the other hand, the attack increases the risk of terrorism by provoking both the proliferation of chemical weapons and escalations beyond conventional warfare. In this latter sense, then, Obama's justification sutures military intervention to the activities of a set of transnational non-state actors.

Assad's attack, in other words, activated a number of global contexts in which an American president felt duty-bound to respond. Embracing these global duties, for Obama, required more than negotiating international agreements, it required a commitment to enforce them.[53] That commitment, he argued, entailed "hard decisions."[54] But Obama also argued that the consequences of not making those decisions—namely the potential downfall of an international regime of governance—were dire. He underscored that point with a series of rhetorical questions:

> What message will we send if a dictator can gas hundreds of children to death in plain sight and pay no price? What's the purpose of the international system that we've built if a prohibition on the use of chemical weapons that has been agreed to by the governments of 98 percent of the world's people and approved overwhelmingly by the Congress of the United States is not enforced? Make no mistake—this has implications beyond chemical warfare. If we won't enforce accountability in the face of this heinous act, what does it say about our resolve to stand up to others who flout fundamental international rules? To governments who would choose to build nuclear arms? To [terrorists] who would spread biological weapons? To armies who carry out genocide?[55]

These questions emphasized the need to "send a message"—to *speak* to and for a global order in the face of an atrocity. Since the nature of that message was bound up in the impetus to intervene militarily in Syria, Obama's rhetorical questions activated a form of "military persuasion" called deterrence credibility—they deployed the threat and/or use of military action and coercive bargaining to manage an international crisis situation.[56] While deterrence credibility has been a mainstay of U.S. foreign policy since World War II, our point is that it appears here as a discursive norm linking a number of disparate global contexts.[57] Insofar as a president is obliged to speak—to carry out a duty to those various global contexts—by adhering to that norm, he becomes "presidential" by *giving the order* to authorize military action. In order *speak* to and for the international order, in other words, a president must make missiles into messages.

Obama proposed precisely this sort of message. He expressed his confidence that a military action "limited in duration and scope … can hold the Assad regime accountable for their use of chemical weapons, deter this kind of behavior, and degrade their capacity to carry it out."[58] He assured his audience that "assets are in place" and that "we are prepared to strike any time we choose." He emphasized that he had made his decision as "Commander-in Chief" and that he believed he had the "authority to carry out this military action without specific congressional authorization"—a claim he would make repeatedly in the weeks following this speech.[59] Our point here is that deterrence credibility is a discourse that affects the institutional logics of the rhetorical presidency by providing an ethical norm (global security) with which a president can identify. We suggest that the repeated assertion of command thus enabled Obama to fulfill a duty to the various contexts that make up the global norm against chemical weapons. It was a display of power, but not one that was reducible to the consolidation of political agency in a commander-in-chief. Instead, these assertions reveal the particular (global) contexts in which a president can become a man of power by performing certain duties. Within those contexts, moreover, he can become presidential by actually commanding a military intervention.

But if that is the case, then why not just initiate a unilateral strike? Why appeal to Congress and the American people? Obama's argument is that the international order cannot survive a president's unilateral command—that is, it cannot survive an American military intervention that is not supported by Congress and the American people—any more than it can survive presidential silence. Obama's duty to the norm that calls forth his decision to give the order for military action thus also calls forth his request to have Congress authorize that action. Further, as we shall show, it provides him an opportunity to help others (Congress and "the people") align themselves with the global norm against chemical weapons. It is therefore not enough to attend to the ways that the global norm against chemical weapons allows presidents to govern their own ethical becoming. We must also attend to the ways that they *govern others* by distributing that norm.

Command is a Distributive Technology

An important feature of Obama's appeal to Congress and to the American people was his claim that an American military intervention was not time sensitive.

The Chairman of the Joint Chiefs," he explained, "has informed me that we are pre-pared to strike whenever we choose. Moreover, the Chairman has indicated to me that our capacity to execute this mission is not time-sensitive; it will be effective tomorrow, or next week, or one month from now. And I'm prepared to give that order.[60]

Obama followed this claim with an explicit appeal to Congress. As the head of "the world's oldest constitutional democracy," he began, "I've long believed that our power is rooted not just in our military might, but in our example as a govern-ment of the people, by the people, and for the people."[61] Thus, he claimed, he had made a *second* decision (beyond the decision to command a military intervention) to "seek authorization for the use of force from the American people's representa-tives in Congress."

This move is worthy of considerable attention. Scholars of rhetoric have often remarked that appeals to Congress and to the people provide constitutional legit-imacy for the president's decisions as commander-in-chief.[62] But Obama's tem-porally ambiguous assertion of command—of the authority to use force with or without congressional authorization—complicated his appeal to Congress, who, as Ezra Klein and Evan Sotas write, believed that "the way the White House chose to go to Congress didn't signal respect for the institution."[63] Kentucky Senator Rand Paul famously concurred, calling Obama's speech an exercise in "Constitu-tional theater."[64] Eric Posner, moreover, wrote that Obama's "motive is both self-serving and easy to understand" and that "Obama has reaffirmed the primacy of the executive in matters of war and peace"—that "the war powers of the presidency remain as mighty as ever."[65] The common feature of these interpretations is that they position the appeal to Congress as a sort of Machiavellian ploy. The appeal, in other words, hides Obama's real political agenda, which is to usurp power from Congress (and, accordingly, from the American people).

Our attention to duty reverses that interpretation. Obama's appeal to Con-gress was, indeed, genuine. Our evidence for this claim, however, is not a reading of Obama's intent or the constitutive effects of his instrumental leadership of public opinion. It is that he did not—despite his duty to a global order, despite the awesome power of the United States military, and despite his authority as commander-in-chief—order an attack on the Assad regime. The very fact that he *gave the speech* reveals that Obama was not only duty bound to uphold the global prohibition on chemical weapons (via a strike which would have, in its own way, sent a "message"), but also to *distribute* the global prohibition through the presi-dency. Indeed, Obama argued that the very same global prohibition on chemical weapons that obligated him to command a military intervention also obligated him to fulfill his constitutional duty to obtain war powers via a congressional authorization:

[Many] people have advised against taking this decision to Congress, and undoubtedly, they were impacted by what we saw happen in the United Kingdom this week when the Parliament of our closest ally failed to pass a resolution with a similar goal, even as the Prime Minister supported taking action. Yet, while I believe I have the authority to carry out this military action without specific congressional authorization, I know that the country will be stronger if we take this course, and our actions will be even more effective.[66]

This claim about efficacy is an important one because it is what ties American constitutional legitimacy to the type of speech (command) Obama must give to the international community. It also signals that an assertion of command before the international community might be perceived as (geopolitically) unilateral if it is not constitutionally legitimate. Obama was not, in other words, speaking in a vacuum. Upon entering office, he found himself embroiled in not one, but two wars after nearly a decade of largely unilateral (both geopolitically and constitutionally) executive governance. "Although," Jason Edwards writes, "global opinion of the United States has never been as glowing as Americans have believed it to be, the invasion of Iraq and President Bush's unilateralist foreign policy agenda created even more hostility for the United States abroad."[67] Obama himself did much to contribute to this problem.[68] But he was also quick to note its impact on the American people. "I know well," he claimed, "that we are weary of war. We've ended one war in Iraq. We're ending another in Afghanistan. And the American people have the good sense to know we cannot resolve the underlying conflict in Syria with our military."[69]

Obama's duty to the global prohibition against chemical weapons is therefore double. He must, on the one hand, command a military intervention against Assad. The prohibition itself must be enforced. But he must, on the other hand, also be wary of unilateral intervention. The global prohibition against chemical weapons is not made by the might of presidents and militaries. It itself *obliges those presidents and militaries to be mighty*. Obama made precisely this point when he claimed that "now is the time to show the world that America keeps our commitments. We do what we say. And we lead with the belief that right makes might—not the other way around."[70] But "right" is determined here by the global prohibition—it is a particular international norm. Congress and "the people" were thus Obama's means of balancing between these two obligations. His duty was not simply his own ethical becoming, but also the ethical becoming of the whole of the American polity. As a result, he had to make an attempt (albeit one that failed) not only to command but also to *lead*—to galvanize Congress and the people through the obligation to speak.

This is why Obama can explicitly admit that the people are weary of war. His speech is less about instrumentally constituting subjects that are prepared to go to war (in the sense that they will advocate it to their governing institutions) than it is about getting people to debate the prospect of war. *Deliberation* is what Obama asked of Congress and the American people. "We should have this debate," he claimed, "because the issues are too big for business as usual. And this morning, John Boehner, Harry Reid, Nancy Pelosi and Mitch McConnell agreed that this is the right thing to do for our democracy."[71] There was, in other words, always a possibility that Congress and the people might resist Obama's command. But debate would still function as the rhetorical technology by which Congress and the people might affirm the global norm against chemical weapons. Indeed, debating the issue would articulate both Congress and the people to the aftermath of the attack in Syria. It would articulate them to the Chemical Weapons Convention and to the Syria Act. It would articulate them to the same global contexts that obliged Obama to justify a military intervention. And it is by debating, Obama claims, that the American polity might affirm the "writ of the international community." A writ, of course, is a legal command—a speech act—made felicitous, in this case, by the normative framework of the international community's prohibition on the use of chemical weapons. The rhetorical effect of a global rhetorical presidency, then, is a globalized American citizenry if not also a globalized American state apparatus.

Conclusion

We have argued that command, as a speech act, is not merely a consolidation of executive power, but also a means of positioning the president as an ethical subject responsible for navigating and distributing shifts in a 21st century global order. These shifts are historical phenomena affected by political struggles waged at least since World War II. The end of the Cold War, moreover, set loose new forces that implicate a president's ethical orientation to the world. The prospect of a global presidency—and, further, a globalized American citizenry or a globalized American state apparatus—therefore presents a daunting task for 21st century scholars of presidential rhetoric. Insofar as the presidency has become a "global subject" because it internalizes and distributes global norms in the government of itself (presidents) and others (populations and other institutions), it is bound up in the complex political struggles that produce and perpetuate those norms. The rhetorical presidency, in other words, is not *merely* a global subject, since it is also a subject of the myriad processes of *globalization* that produce and organize an international regime. A global presidency, in other words, is also a rhetorical presidency in the midst of a class struggle, a rhetorical presidency in the midst of a colonial struggle, and so on. A global presidency is, moreover, not merely "in the midst" of these struggles—it is not their only effect. Indeed, a dutiful president will continue to speak and to distribute global norms throughout the polity, composing and recomposing the American citizenry as different kinds of global subjects.

Obama's articulation to a global order was frequently clear because he was often explicit about his duties. The early days of Donald Trump's presidency, however, might give us pause as to how we might imagine his global becoming. Trump campaigned (and has so far governed) vehemently against global trade.[72] He has withdrawn the United States from international agreements from the Trans-Pacific Partnership to the Paris Climate Agreement. He has demonstrated a propensity for violent rhetoric at home and abroad, and has—as he proved after the attack on Khan Shaykun—shown a willingness to exercise (both geopolitically and constitutionally) unilateral authority over the US military. Indeed, Trump's "presidentiality" may be short lived if it requires a sincere or sustained commitment to the international norms and rules he used to justify bombing an air base in Syria. His reluctance to affirm the mutual protection norm in Article 5 of the NATO treaty, for example, has already led conservative columnists to question his commitment to deterrence credibility.[73] "America first" may have, in other words, reemerged as an ethical orientation opposed to either liberal or neoconservative desires for a (new) "American Century."[74] But this is not to suggest that Trump lacks any "worldly ethos."[75] We suspect that his ethical becoming is deeply tied to his brand and his multinational real estate corporation. And if Trump's rhetorical presidency *is* stitched to the state apparatus at the same time as it performs duties to the "social forces" exterior to it, then the concept of a rhetorical presidency itself might be fruitfully reimagined as a practical site for investigating the nature of how a president internalizes and externalizes norms of ethical becoming to govern himself and others.

Notes

1. Donald Trump, "Statement by President Trump on Syria [Transcript]," *Office of the White House Press Secretary*, April 6, 2017. Accessed August 26, 2018 from https://web.archive.org/web/20170407184627/www.whitehouse.gov/the-press-office/2017/04/06/statement-president-trump-syria.

2. *New Day*, "Global Markets Mixed After Syria Strikes; Jobs Report Released; Trump Launches Strike Against Syria; U.S. Strikes Syria After Chemical Attack [Transcript]," aired April 7, 2017, on Cable News Network, accessed August 26, 2018 from http://transcripts.cnn.com/TRANSCRIPTS/1704/07/nday.08.html.

3. Ronald Walter Greene, "Rhetorical Materialism: The Rhetorical Subject and the General Intellect," in *Rhetoric, Materiality, and Politics*, eds. Barbara A. Biesecker and John Louis Lucaites (New York: Peter Lang, 2009), 43-65.

4. Toby Miller, *The Well-Tempered Self* (Baltimore: Johns Hopkins University Press, 1993), xiv.

5. Greene, "Rhetorical Materialism," 50–53. See also Ronald Walter Greene and Darrin Hicks, "Lost Convictions: Debating Both Sides and the Ethical Self-fashioning of Liberal Citizens," *Cultural Studies* 19, no. 1 (2006): 100–126.

6. René Pita and Juan Domingo, "The Use of Chemical Weapons in the Syrian Civil War," *Toxics* 2, no. 3 (2014): 391–402.

7. Ibid., 391–392.

8. Barack Obama, "Remarks by the President to the White House Press Corps," *Office of the White House Press Secretary*, August 20, 2012. Accessed August 26, 2018 from https://obamawhitehouse.archives.gov/the-press-office/2012/08/20/remarks-president-white-house-press-corps.

9. Åke Sellström, Scott Cairns, and Maurizio Barbeschi, "United Nations Mission to Investigate Allegations of the Use of Chemical Weapons in the Syrian Arab Republic: Report on the Allegations of the Use of Chemical Weapons in the Ghouta Area of Damascus on 21 August 2013," *United Nations*, September 13, 2013. Accessed August 26, 2018 from https://www.un.org/zh/focus/northafrica/cwinvestigation.pdf.

10. "Government Assessment of the Syrian Government's Use of Chemical Weapons on August 21, 2013," *Office of the White House Press Secretary*, August 30, 2013. Accessed August 26, 2018 from https://obamawhitehouse.archives.gov/the-press-office/2013/08/30/government-assessment-syrian-government-s-use-chemical-weapons-august-21.

11. Edward Luce, "A Trap of the President's Making," *Financial Times,* September 8, 2013. Accessed August 26, 2018 from https://www.ft.com/content/66b63f8c-1653-11e3-a57d-00144feabdc0.

12. Roderick P. Hart, *The Sound of Leadership: Presidential Communication in the Modern Age* (Chicago: University of Chicago Press, 1987), 2–3.

13. Mary Stuckey, *Jimmy Carter, Human Rights, and the National Agenda* (College Station: Texas A&M University Press, 2008).

14. Jeffrey K. Tulis, *The Rhetorical Presidency* (Princeton: Princeton University Press 1987), 4.

15. George C. Edwards, "Presidential Rhetoric: What Difference Does It Make?," in *Beyond the Rhetorical Presidency*, Martin J. Medhurst (College Station: Texas A&M University Press, 1996), 199–217.

16. George C. Edwards, *On Deaf Ears: The Limits of the Bully Pulpit* (New Haven: Yale University Press, 2008).

17. Martin J. Medhurst, "Afterward: The Ways of Rhetoric," in *Beyond the Rhetorical Presidency*, Martin J. Medhurst (College Station: Texas A&M University Press, 1996), 218–226. See also Roderick P. Hart, "Thinking Harder About Presidential Discourse: The Question of Efficacy," in *The Prospect of Presidential Rhetoric*, eds. James A. Aune and Martin J. Medhurst (College Station: Texas A&M University Press, 2008), 238–248.

18. Karlyn Kohrs Campbell and Kathleen Hall Jamieson, *Presidents Creating the Presidency: Deeds Done in Words* (Chicago: Chicago University Press, 2008), 7.

19. Trevor Parry-Giles and Shawn J. Parry-Giles, "The West Wing's Prime-Time Presidentiality: Mimesis and Catharsis in a Postmodern Romance," *Quarterly Journal of Speech* 88, no. 2 (2002): 209–227.

20. Campbell and Jamieson, *Presidents Creating the Presidency*, 11.
21. John M. Murphy, "Power and Authority in a Postmodern Presidency," in *The Prospect of Presidential Rhetoric*, eds. James A. Aune and Martin J. Medhurst (College Station: Texas A&M University Press, 2008), 28–45.
22. Greene, "Rhetorical Materialism," 49.
23. Tulis, *The Rhetorical Presidency*, 27.
24. Ibid., 32–33.
25. Ibid., 123.
26. Ibid.
27. Woodrow Wilson, "Leaderless Government," *Virginia Law Register* 3, no. 5 (1897): 337–354.
28. Tulis, *The Rhetorical Presidency*, 126–127.
29. Ibid., 26–27 (emphasis in original).
30. Ibid., 13–14.
31. Pierre Clastres, *Society Against the State*, trans. Robert Hurley and Abe Stein (New York: Zone Books, 1989), 152.
32. Ibid., 154.
33. Ibid., 153–154.
34. Ibid., 153.
35. Ibid., 154.
36. Gilles Deleuze and Felix Guattari, *A Thousand Plateaus: Capitalism and Schizophrenia*, trans. Brian Massumi (Minneapolis, University of Minnesota Press, 1987), 360 (emphasis in original).
37. Ibid. (emphasis in original).
38. Tulis, *The Rhetorical Presidency*, 4 (emphasis in original).
39. Stephen J. Hartnett and Jennifer R. Mercieca, "A Discovered Dissembler Can Achieve Nothing Great; or, Four Theses on the Death of Presidential Rhetoric in an Age of Empire," *Presidential Studies Quarterly* 37, no. 4 (2007); 599–621. See also, Vanessa B. Beasley, "The Rhetorical Presidency Meets the Unitary Executive: Implications for Presidential Rhetoric on Public Policy," *Rhetoric and Public Affairs* 13, no. 1 (2010): 7–36.
40. Hart, *The Sound of Leadership*, 2. See also, Beasley, "The Rhetorical Presidency," 12.
41. Hartnett and Mercieca, "A Discovered Dissembler," 600.
42. Miller, *The Well-Tempered Self*, xii.
43. Richard M. Price, *The Chemical Weapons Taboo* (Ithaca: Cornell University Press, 1997), 15.
44. David Nicholls, "Richard Cobden and the International Peace Congress Movement, 1848–1853," *Journal of British Studies* 30, no. 4 (1991): 351–376.
45. Ibid., 351.
46. Ibid., 352).
47. Jørgen Johansen, "Antimilitarism in the Nineteenth Century," in *Oxford International Encyclopedia of Peace*, ed. Nigel J. Young (Oxford: Oxford University Press, 2010), 65–67.
48. Price, *The Chemical Weapons Taboo*, 11–12.
49. John V. Parachini, "NGOs: Force Multipliers in the CWC Ratification Debate," in *The Battle to Obtain US Ratification of the Chemical Weapons Convention*, eds. Michael Krepon, John V. Parachini, and Amy E. Smithson (Washington, D.C.: The Stimson Center, 1997), 37–58.

50. Barack Obama, "Remarks by the President in Address to the Nation on Syria [Transcript]," *Office of the White House Press Secretary*, September 10, 2013. Accessed August 26, 2018 from https://obamawhitehouse.archives.gov/the-press-office/2013/09/10/remarks-president-address-nation-syria.

51. Ibid.

52. Ibid.

53. Barack Obama, "Statement by the President on Syria [Transcript]," *Office of the White House Press Secretary*, August 31, 2013. Accessed August 26, 2018 from https://obamawhitehouse. archives.gov/the-press-office/2013/08/31/statement-president-syria.

54. Obama, "Remarks by the President in Address."

55. Ibid.

56. Stephen Cimbala, *Military Persuasion: Deterrence and Provocation in Crisis and War* (University Park: Pennsylvania State University Press, 1994).

57. Jennifer L. Milliken, "Metaphors of Prestige and Reputation in American Foreign Policy and American Realism," in *Post-Realism: The Rhetorical Turn in International Relations*, eds. Francis A. Beer and Robert Hariman (East Lansing: Michigan State University Press, 1996), 217–238.

58. Obama, "Remarks by the President in Address."

59. Ibid. See also, Obama, "Statement by the President;" Jonathan Karl, "No Syria Attack Without Congressional Approval, Obama Aide Says," *ABC News*, September 6, 2013. Accessed August 26, 2018 from https://abcnews.go.com/Politics/no-syria-attack-without-congressional-approval-obama-aide-says/blogEntry?id=20176582; Michael Scherer, "Obama Admits Public Opposition to Syria Strike (Transcript)," *Time*, September 6, 2013. Accessed August 26, 2018 from https://archive.fo/GJfMA; Sabrina Siddiqui, "Rand Paul Accuses Obama of Reducing Congress' Role in Syria to 'Constitutional Theater," *Huffington Post*, September 4, 2013. Accessed August 26, 2018 from https://www.huffingtonpost. com/2013/09/03/rand-paul-syria_n_3862624.html.

60. Obama, "Remarks by the President in Address."

61. Ibid.

62. Campbell an Jamieson, *Presidents Creating the Presidency*, 217–219.

63. Ezra Klein and Evan Sotas, "Wonkbook: Seven Hard Truths for the White House on Syria," *The Washington Post* (Washington, D.C.), September 9, 2013.

64. Siddiqui, "Rand Paul Accuses Obama."

65. Eric Posner, "Obama is Only Making His War Powers Mightier," *Slate*, September 3, 2013. Accessed August 26, 2018 from https://www.slate.com/articles/news_and_politics/view_ from_chicago/2013/09/obama_going_to_congress_on_syria_he_s_actually_strengthening_ the_war_powers.html.

66. Obama, "Remarks by the President in Address."

67. Jason A. Edwards, "Resetting America's Role in the World: President Obama's Rhetoric of (Re)conciliation and Partnership," in *The Rhetoric of Heroic Expectations: Establishing the Obama Presidency*, eds. Justin S. Vaughn and Jennifer R. Mercieca (College Station: Texas A&M University Press, 2014), 130–150.

68. Heather Ashley Hayes, *Violent Subjects and Rhetorical Cartography in the Age of the Terror Wars* (London: Palgrave MacMillan, 2016).

69. Obama, "Remarks by the President in Address."
70. Ibid.
71. Ibid.
72. Mark Landler, "Trump Roars Again on Trade, Reviewing Steel and Chiding China," *The New York Times* (New York, NY), April 20, 2017.
73. Charles Krauthammer, "Trump Undermined NATO's Deterrent Effect," *National Review*, June 2, 2017. Accessed August 26, 2018 from https://www.nationalreview.com/2017/06/trump-refuses-affirm-nato-article-5/.
74. Henry Luce, *The American Century* (New York: Farrar and Rinehart, 1941).
75. Ronald Walter Greene, *Malthusian Worlds: U.S. Leadership and the Governing of the Population Crisis* (Boulder: Westview Press, 1999), 116.

CHAPTER SEVEN

Unpresidented

Articulating the Presidency in the Age of Trump

BLAKE ABBOTT

The first few months of the Trump administration have been incredibly hectic. Each new order, act, incident, scandal, or revelation has confounded traditional concepts of American political life and the presidency.[1] Cultural representations of the presidency have undergone their most significant shift in recent memory due to the candidacy and presidency of Donald Trump. In a stark departure from coverage of previous presidents, multiple national news outlets have employed terms like "authoritarian"[2] and "demagogue"[3] to describe Trump. Many outlets called Trump's behavior "unpresidential," even after he took office.[4]

In going from an abnormal candidate to an atypical president, Trump reconfigured the cultural representations of the presidency. The Trump campaign was notable more for the ways that it departed from a traditional presidential campaign than for the ways that it resembled one, and the Trump presidency has followed a similar fashion. While tempting to presume that this shift is the result of either Trump's prowess or sheer dumb luck, this chapter contends it only became possible under certain conditions. Identifying those conditions gives scholars an opportunity to examine not only the way that presidential subjects are produced but how they affect cultural representations of the presidency.

I argue that the rise of Trump rearticulated the presidency to traditional lines of privilege—white, male privilege in particular—via a reassertion of authoritarianism. This reassertion constituted a backlash against the Democratic Party's articulation of the presidency to pluralist democracy. In response to the Obama administration and the candidacy of Hillary Clinton, Trump's rhetoric and its acceptance by a significant portion of the electorate rearticulated the presidency to lines of privilege through a connection to authoritarianism.[5] Discourses of racism, sexism, and authoritarianism coalesced to construct a subject, Trump, in relation to the presidency. This articulation risks solidifying hegemonic lines of power by undermining many of the democratic mechanisms designed to protect the disempowered.

In what follows, I examine Trump's self-fashioning rhetoric in two ways. First, I examine the way that Trump's various statements undermine the notion of Trump as a stable presidential subject. Second, using a logic of articulation, I analyze the way that Trump's authoritarian rhetoric reacts to pluralist tendencies and constitutes a return to the presidency as a site of social privilege.

An Unstable President

Since he announced his candidacy for president in June 2015, many of Donald Trump's statements, tweets, interviews, and actions have been either false or wildly inconsistent.[6] Jane Timm of NBC News noted that during his presidential campaign, Trump took "141 distinct stances on 23 major issues."[7] One of his signature proposals was a wall on the border between the United States and Mexico. When he promoted it during the campaign, he claimed that he would build the wall and insisted that he would get Mexico to pay for its construction. When he met with President Enrique Peña Nieto of Mexico during the campaign, however, Trump reportedly did not insist on making Mexico pay for the wall.[8] Later, his position on the wall shifted, with surrogates insisting that the wall could be "digital" and that it was a "metaphor" for border security.[9] Despite taking design proposals for the wall and insisting that construction would go forward, Trump backed down from his initial insistence that funding for the wall be included in the short-term government spending bill in April 2017.[10] As of this writing, it is unclear whether the wall will be built.

Trump has also contradicted himself on other significant issues. On health care, Trump insisted on repealing and replacing the Affordable Care Act after being critical of it for years. In his first televised interview after the general election, Trump suggested that he would keep some parts of the law.[11] During the campaign, he claimed that in his health care plan, "there will be no cuts to Social Security, Medicare & Medicaid,"[12] but the American Health Care Act that he endorsed included $880 billion in cuts to Medicaid.[13] With regard to the firing of

FBI Director James Comey, Trump initially claimed that he did so at the recommendation of his Attorney General.[14] A few days later, in an interview with NBC's Lester Holt, Trump claimed that his decision to fire Comey was independent of the recommendation his letter cited.[15] Trump has decried the use of anonymous sources in news reports that were unfavorable to him, asserting that such reports are "fake news,"[16] but also he re-tweeted an unbylined article from Fox News citing anonymous sources defending his advisor/son-in-law Jared Kushner.[17] He has also cited anonymous sources of his own to support his claim that president Obama's birth certificate was fake.[18] Trump criticized Hillary Clinton for her use of a private email server while Secretary of State, claiming that it would compromise classified information, possibly making it available to enemies and adversaries, yet as president, Trump personally revealed highly classified information to foreign officials, including to members of the Russian government.[19] Trump criticized Obama for playing golf, but in his first hundred days in office Trump played golf nineteen times.[20] Trump criticized President Obama for taking vacations at taxpayer expense, but he was on pace to spend as much on travel in his first year as Obama did in eight.[21] One of the starker examples comes from a campaign rally when Donald Trump's speech was briefly interrupted by a crying baby. Trump reassured the mother of the child that he did not mind because he like the sound of a baby crying, but less than two minutes later, he said, "Actually, I was only kidding, you can get the baby out of here … I think she really believed me that I love having a baby crying while I'm speaking."[22]

One interpretation of this behavior is that it signifies blatant hypocrisy on Trump's part.[23] Another is that it signifies mental illness.[24] A third interpretation suggests that Trump's behavior points to a tendency to speak carelessly about virtually any subject he sees fit, which gives him free rein to say things that are factually inaccurate, offensive, or contradictory with little compulsion to apologize or correct himself. To restate the latter interpretation in Matt Yglesias' words, Trump is "a bullshitter who simply doesn't care."[25] While some or all of these interpretations may have merit, they do little to account for the rhetorical subjectivity of the president of the United States. How do the American people decipher Trump's actions, beliefs, or temperament if he is perpetually inconsistent? How can we know whether Trump is sincere in anything he says? Selena Zito, writing in *The Atlantic*, suggested an answer by claiming that Trump's supporters take Trump "seriously, but not literally," while the news media take him "literally, but not seriously"[26] As confusing and problematic as this explanation is,[27] it reveals a more fundamental issue of the presidential speaking subject. Rather than presume that Trump's rhetoric indicates planning, (in)competence, or deception, I read Trump's rhetoric as a signifier of the instability of the presidential subject itself. Seen this way, I present Trump not as outlier, but rather as an extreme version of an always already present embodiment of the presidential subject.

The Instability of the Presidential Subject

I begin with the premise that the president is not a stable speaking subject. This instability is not unique to the presidential subject; in fact, scholars have argued for years that the speaking subject is not enduring, static, or independent of the discourse that makes it intelligible.[28] Despite the decentering of the subject thanks to the poststructuralist turn in rhetorical criticism, many studies of presidential rhetoric have treated presidential discourse as intentional, strategic maneuvers crafted by candidates along with advisors or speechwriters for core audiences.[29] Barbara Biesecker calls this perspective "a logic of influence."[30] Presidents, in this view, craft discourse to achieve a particular goal: pass legislation, comfort the nation, justify an order or directive, etc. Scholarship from this perspective suggests that presidents are influential rhetors because their occupancy of the office places them in a unique position to speak to the nation in favor of their agenda.

While a logic of influence can provide useful analysis of presidential rhetoric from a certain perspective, its utility is limited because it remains rooted to a speaking subject that approaches the crafting and delivery of discourse from without, which produces a "certain blindness in rhetorical criticism" by relying on a limited set of perspectives for presidential rhetoric.[31] A logic of influence treats the 2016 election, for instance, as a product of Trump's persuasive appeals, which constructs Trump as a transparent, stable subject with identifiable qualities. Trump's instability, however, undermines any hope of stability in the presidential subject. A president's persona is neither stable nor entirely within his/her control. For instance, Matt Yglesias concedes that Trump's tendency toward bullshit is not necessarily "a strategic choice."[32] As Don Waisanen and Amy Becker note, discursive fragments distributed throughout the social produce multiple "circulating personae" that presidents navigate when they speak.[33] Combine their observation with Stephen Heidt's argument for viewing the presidency as pastiche, and the need for a different approach to analyzing presidential rhetoric more broadly and Trump's rhetoric more specifically is palpable.[34]

Instead of a logic of influence, I suggest analyzing the election of Donald Trump from what Biesecker calls a "logic of articulation."[35] Articulation is a process whereby disparate elements that have no natural relation to one another come together to produce a unity taken temporarily as an intelligible subject, object, or message.[36] A logic of articulation focuses on both the linkages among elements and the conditions for selecting or rejecting elements of a message rather than presuming that those elements are "defined by prior ontological distinctions."[37] It suggests that the presidency is a subject position—rhetorically constructed from multiple disparate elements—that bestows qualities onto an individual president in a particular moment, not "a persistent 'self.'"[38] Rhetorics of patriotism, hierarchy, bureaucracy, capitalism, leadership, humanism, rationality, race, gender, and territory (just to name a few) can articulate the ethos of a president differently in any given moment, and each of these rhetorics constantly shifts in both meaning and force. A logic of articulation examines practices that join various cultural and political elements to craft (new) discourses.[39]

Adopting a framework of presidential rhetoric premised on a logic of articulation allows scholars to approach the presidency without the compulsion to privilege the presidential subject as the primary agent. This framework recognizes the contingent connections between the personae of individual presidents and the discourses that articulate the presidency to the nation, its citizens, its institutions, and its traditions.[40] A logic of articulation takes seriously Anne Norton's crucial point that presidents are products of the individual occupant (who is him/herself the product of a variety of forces, discourses, and events), the history and stature of the office, and "the plurality of referents in the image of the President."[41] The presidency is constantly articulated and rearticulated in relation to other agents, forces, and discourses throughout the government and the nation. The articulation of the presidency is an ongoing process, and it constitutes presidential subjects differently in different moments as various forces coalesce in a moment, event, or situation. By emphasizing the inevitable instability of presidential subjects, this approach helps scholars gain purchase on understanding the reasons for shifts in presidential discourse.

Applying a logic of articulation to the presidency has far reaching implications for the study of presidential rhetoric. Analyses of presidential rhetoric that identify and illuminate the rhetorical conditions that constitute the presidential subject and articulate it to a given moment provide valuable supplements to more traditional approaches by asking how rhetoric produces the president. If the presidency is articulated—contingent, volatile, and perpetually made, remade, and negotiated—how do scholars analyze and evaluate presidential rhetoric? One approach involves mapping the rhetorical landscape that produces the president's persona and makes it intelligible.[42] Rather than consider a singular speech as the production of rhetoric, a logic of articulation considers it as a product of various forces and discourses that come together to articulate the presidency to the nation, event, citizenry, etc. Seen from this perspective, the election of Donald Trump is neither the result of Trump's own genius nor dumb luck but rather reflects a unique articulation of the presidency to the nation. In the next section, I identify factors that contributed to the articulation of Trump in relation to the presidency. I note how Trump's deviation from traditional and widely accepted standards for presidential behavior reasserted the presidency as a site of privilege. In doing so, it articulated authoritarianism as a backlash to the Democratic party's articulation of the presidency to pluralist democracy.

Articulating the Presidency

From the moment Donald Trump publicly announced his candidacy for president in June 2015, his campaign was anything but conventional. His blunt language stoked xenophobia from the outset when he complained that the United States had become "a dumping ground for everybody's problems," citing Mexico supposedly sending "drugs," "crime," and "rapists" into the nation via illegal immigration.[43] Throughout the campaign, Trump, his advisors, and his spokespeople seemed to break rules and long established norms. The big surprise throughout the campaign, though, was not just what Trump himself said but also its level of acceptance among certain segments of the American electorate. Early polls in the Republican primaries showed Trump with a lead, and despite claims that his polls would eventually decline, he managed to hold that lead throughout the primaries with very few bumps in the road.[44] Those who flocked to Trump did so despite, or possibly because of his constant violation of rules and traditions of the presidency.[45] He exhibited a brash, often impulsive, public persona. He insulted John McCain for being captured in Vietnam. He mocked *New York Times* reporter Serge Kovaleski's disability.[46] He impulsively tweeted his opinions with little concern for decorum, grammar, or spelling. He was explicitly endorsed by multiple white supremacist groups, which would be a deal breaker for virtually any other candidate.[47] He often spread information that was not only false but easily disprovable. He said and did things that would get any other politician in trouble, yet with one notable exception toward the end of the campaign, he never apologized. In the primary, his poll numbers never suffered enough to threaten his candidacy. In the general election, although he consistently trailed Hillary Clinton in opinion polls and did lose the popular vote of the general election by 2,864,974 votes,[48] Trump managed to secure enough electoral votes in the right states to win the White House, despite the Clinton campaign's persistent claims that Trump's multiple decorum violations made him unfit for the office.

While the presidency is, as Karlyn Kohrs Campbell and Kathleen Hall Jamieson have noted, "an amalgam of roles and practices shaped by what presidents have done,"[49] Trump's campaign and presidency appear shaped largely by what presidents have not done. The distance between Trump's behavior and presidential behavior has all but defined Trump's political persona. It is tempting to suggest that Trump's deviations from a more traditional form of presidential ethos undermine the presidency as an institution, but I contend they actually constitute a new articulation of the presidency to the nation. This articulation influences the parameters of what may be considered "presidential" by attaching new behaviors to a presidential subject. When CNN host Jake Tapper asked Trump campaign manager and counselor Kellyanne Conway after the election whether Trump's tweets constituted presidential behavior, she responded "Well, he's the president-elect. So that's presidential behavior, yes."[50] The question for scholars is how Trump's non-traditional persona rhetorically constitutes the presidency.

Answering this question requires an examination of the ways that Trump's presidential persona relates to recent and longstanding interpretations of the presidency. Trump's three biggest deviations were authoritarian tendencies, personal attacks on opponents, and the repetition of blatant falsehoods. Throughout the campaign and during his presidency, Trump has shown little interest in the constitutional function of the presidency or in working with Congress. Much of his rhetoric focused on broad, sweeping actions that would "Make America Great Again." His acceptance speech at the Republican National Convention, for instance, painted the United States as a chaotic, dangerous land in need of a savior. Trump posited himself as that savior, saying, "when I take the oath of office next year, I will restore law and order to our country."[51] Rather than emphasize a collective approach to the problems facing the country, Trump suggested, "I alone can fix it."[52] Such rhetoric cast the president as a monarch rather than an executive in a divided government. Trump's expression of the presidency during the campaign assumed little to no resistance from other agents: the other branches of the federal government, state governments, national news media, or the citizenry at large. Such an approach differs from other candidates' promises because it assumed not that Trump's plans are superior to the status quo—a claim that Trump would need to support with evidence—but that his ideas were so great that they would simply happen. Indeed, Trump's ethos has been central to his administration, a perspective that has been criticized for its similarity to other autocratic regimes.[53] The Trump campaign's reliance on personality rather than evidence allowed Trump both to advance vague policies and contradict himself, which undermined independent scrutiny.

Additionally, Trump's personal attacks on people who either challenged him or refused to support his assertions reflected a lack of the respect that is often associated with the presidency. In addition to referring to opponents and critics with such epithets as "losers," Trump encouraged supporters at his rallies to assault protestors.[54] Trump has also repeatedly told lies about the legitimacy of the popular vote count, the murder rate in the United States, the vetting process for refugees seeking entry into the US, and even the size of the crowds attending his inauguration.[55] The administration continued to assert these claims as fact, even after they had been debunked.

To understand the effect these moves had on the presidency, we must examine the central qualities of the presidency. Officially, it is the highest civilian office in the United States and the single most powerful position in the United States government. Beyond the official capacity, however, it confers more than influence and control. For all the official and institutional formality of the office, the presidency has a certain cultural cachet as well. The American presidency is, as Mary Stuckey rightly notes, "a site of political, social, and economic privilege."[56] Stuckey explains that because the presidency has been associated with "upper class, straight, white male expectations and practices,"[57] both the occupiers of the office and the actions of individual presidents have tended to reflect the perspective of the nation's more privileged citizens. The institutional privilege often found in the presidency merges with the social privilege of the occupiers of the office to produce presidential subjects that embody privilege par excellence. That perspective often emerges in both the rhetoric and the personae of individual presidents as they navigate the office and perform its various duties.

The one notable, if limited exception to this trend is President Barack Obama. President Obama's presence in the most privileged job in the federal government altered the perception of who could be president by being the nation's first non-white male to occupy the office. Additionally, Obama's rhetoric and actions reflected a different perspective than that of previous presidents. In 2009, he intervened in the controversy surrounding the arrest of the African-American Harvard Professor Henry Louis Gates outside his own home. The incident sparked national attention, and it led to the famous "beer summit" where Obama, Vice President Joe Biden, Gates, and arresting officer James Crowley met to discuss the incident and attempt to reach an understanding. Obama's comments gave Gates the benefit of the doubt rather than the arresting officer, a dramatic shift from previous administrations that tended to side with law enforcement in similar matters.[58] In response to the killing of Trayvon Martin, Obama spoke at length about the black experience in the United States. He said, "when Trayvon Martin was first shot I said that this could have been my son. ... Trayvon Martin could have been me 35 years ago."[59] His remarks were the first of their kind because an African-American president not only spoke of his own personal experiences with racism but also connected them to the African-American community's reaction to the Trayvon Martin shooting and other killings of unarmed black citizens. This moment and others like it—his eulogy for the victims of the mass murder at Emmanuel A.M.E Church in Charleston, SC, for instance—showed Obama enacting and bearing witness to the black experience in the United States, which departed from some of the privilege associated with the presidency. Even though the Obama administration challenged traditional expectations for the presidency as a site of privilege, it did so within the broad, structural parameters of the office and kept a commitment to democracy as a form of government. In fact, Obama's presidency underscored a commitment to pluralist democracy.

Hillary Clinton's 2016 presidential campaign continued the Obama administration's emphasis on inclusive diversity. Clinton was the first female presidential nominee of a major political party, and her approach to the presidency married traditionalism with the unprecedented nature of her candidacy. Her background as law professor, lawyer, first lady of Arkansas, first lady of the United States, Senator from New York, and Secretary of State prepared her for the presidency in a traditional way, even though Clinton herself was an unconventional candidate of her own. Embodying traditional norms, she embraced pluralist democracy, employing the slogan "Stronger Together." Her acceptance speech at the Democratic National Convention emphasized this theme while advocating standard Democratic policies: affordable college tuition, gun control, raising taxes on the wealthy and Wall Street firms, and the protection of "civil rights, human rights and voting rights … women's rights and workers' rights … LGBT rights and the rights of people with disabilities."[60] Taken together, Clinton and Obama signified the Democratic party's articulation of the presidency as first and foremost pluralist, inclusive, and tolerant. Their articulation remained within the confines of traditional presidential norms of decorum, respect, maturity, and an embrace of the institutional principles that comprise the presidency.

In contrast, the Trump campaign violated norms for the presidency practically daily. Trump was the least qualified major party nominee in recent memory. He had no experience in government whatsoever. Before the 2016 election, Trump had been a businessman, real estate mogul, and reality television star. Trump was a celebrity candidate, not unlike other celebrities that run for office. Trump's lack of qualifications, his unpresidential behavior, and his tendency to act and govern more like an authoritarian strongman than a president committed to democracy were notable in their own right. What made them more than idiosyncrasies was that the campaign developed a substantial, devoted following. In fact, Trump's behavior was attractive to many Americans, and the attraction enhanced his cult of personality. The popularity of his actions within the Republican party rearticulated traditional lines of privilege to the presidency by suggesting that qualifications, separation of powers, transparency, and respect for the rule of law were less important in the 2016 presidential election than imposing racial, sexual, gender, and class privilege back onto the nation through the highest office in the land. The Trump campaign's perpetual assertion of obviously false statements—what Kellyanne Conway called "alternative facts"—showed a connection between presidential behavior and an imposition of social privilege.[61] All politicians lie to a certain extent, but the boldness of the Trump campaign's falsehoods and "bullshit"[62] coupled with their steadfast adherence to those lies even in the face of clear evidence to the contrary constituted more than an attempt to avoid admitting uncomfortable facts. They asserted a kind of control over human perception of events and ideas; they constituted a world that treated Trump as the arbiter of knowledge, which solidified the connection between Trump and authoritarianism.[63]

The continued assertion of empirically false statements also mirrors actions that impose social privilege by asserting dominance over the information upon which a society operates. One subtle, yet powerful move of privilege involves both an imposition of perspectives that benefit the privileged and the dismissal of those that do not.[64] Stories from the perspective of the oppressed—lynchings, widespread discrimination, police brutality, disenfranchisement, sexual assault, etc.—often face massive inertia to reach a large audience, whereas stories of the powerful can spread with relative ease. Control over the narrative of history is directly associated with privilege. During the 2016 election, news organizations pushed back against Trump and his surrogates for their constant falsehoods, but those responses had limited effect partially because the campaign and the administration continued to make false claims.

Despite resistance from much of the national news media and the American public, the Trump campaign's authoritarian imposition of privilege was not a deal breaker for many voters. He also found support for his tendencies from government officials like Maine Governor Paul LePage, who expressed the sentiment perfectly: "we need a Donald Trump to show some authoritarian power in our country and bring back the rule of law."[65] LePage suggested that President Obama had been tyrannical, undermining the rule of law, and that Trump was just the sort of person to bring it back to the United States. Le Page's comments and the rise of white supremacist groups in support of Trump reflect white resistance to President Obama.[66] Slate columnist Jamelle Bouie argued that President Obama's comments on the incident where Henry Louis Gates was arrested outside his house initiated white America's disillusionment with the nation's first African-American president.[67] White citizens' approval for Obama declined in the aftermath of the incident and never recovered throughout the remainder of his presidency.[68] Obama's comments on the Trayvon Martin killing had a similar effect on white attitudes toward him. White citizens' views of President Obama were their most negative when Obama discussed racism, and that resistance translated into a broader resistance to Obama's presidency.[69] LePage's statement also reveals a larger perspective rooted in a distrust of democracy. From this perspective, the flaw of democracy, borne out by both Obama and Clinton, is that it gives the wrong kinds of people—minorities, women, LGBTQ people, refugees, immigrants, Muslims, etc.—too much political influence.

Trump signified a reaction to Obama's and Clinton's articulation of the presidency as linked with pluralist democracy by reconnecting authoritarianism and privilege to the presidency. The clearest line of privilege articulated in the election of Donald Trump was whiteness. On election night, Van Jones called the election of Donald Trump "a whitelash against a changing country ... against a black president."[70] Michael Eric Dyson argued similarly that Trump's victory "was all about whiteness."[71] This "whitelash" resembles what Carol Anderson calls white rage, a reaction by white Americans to actions and trends they see as threatening to the viability of white supremacy.[72] Anderson argues that "black advancement" is a central "trigger for white rage."[73] In the wake of eight years of a black president, which many Americans saw as "the ultimate affront,"[74] Trump signified both an impulse to restore white supremacy to the presidency, and the clearest path to this goal.

Male privilege also appeared in the election. Trump's opponent, Hillary Clinton, would have been the first female president of the United States. His misogyny and predation were publicly known throughout the campaign with both the accusation of sexual assault by multiple women and the October 2016 release of a video tape on which Trump admitted to sexual assault. Though the Trump campaign's and its supporters' virulent, sexist attacks on Clinton were unsightly, they did not cost Trump the election. Instead, his victory reasserted traditional lines of privilege as dominance; Trump's supporters either endorsed Trump's offensive acts or tolerated them. The election, then, addressed the "flaw" in pluralist democracy by returning a white man with authoritarian tendencies to the highest office in the land.

Forces of white supremacy, gendered lines of power, and American conservatism aligned to rearticulate the presidency to authoritarianism in the election of Donald Trump. Although authoritarianism runs counter to democracy, it aligns with privilege. In the wake of Obama's actions and Clinton's positions, which associated democracy with support for oppressed people, the election of Donald Trump reasserted dominance from the rich, white men. Trump's violations of presidential norms established new connections between the presidency and privilege. That the Trump campaign could repeatedly bend and break rules in the campaign with impunity not only asserted a kind of dominance in favor of Trump but also reflected a central tenet of privilege: the privileged can make, break, and remake the rules at their discretion. The spike in hate crimes after the 2016 election testifies to this relationship as Trump's election appears to have emboldened many of his supporters to express publicly (if anonymously) their disdain for the very people for whom Obama and Clinton advocated.[75] That some Trump supporters were willing to risk breaking the law to express their hatred shows, at minimum, a lack of respect for the Other that both mirrors authoritarian regimes and exemplifies privilege.

Trump reworked cultural figurations of the presidency by embodying a backlash—in both substance and tone—to Obama's and Clinton's embrace of pluralist democracy. The backlash made Trump's personal and political stances viable in relation to the presidency. While some previous presidents have had tendencies toward authoritarianism, Trump's leadership style, personal ethos as a businessman and reality television star, praise for dictators and strongmen around the globe, and emphasis on his own infallibility suggest a total embrace of authoritarianism as an ethos of the presidency. Rearticulating the presidency to an intensified authoritarianism reasserted the presidency as a site of privilege.

One early implication of Trump is that such a radical shift in the presidency does not necessarily correlate to a similar shift in the entire American government. Like all articulations, the Trump presidency is neither stable nor static. Both the individual presidential subject and the presidency as an institution are in process; the modes of their existence are subject to shifts in forces and discourses. Trump's authoritarianism leaves a mark on the presidency, but that mark only makes sense in relation to the rest of the nation. The first four months of the Trump administration have seen consistently low approval ratings,[76] massive protests around the world,[77] battles with the news media over the administration's frequent falsehoods,[78] judicial injunctions against some of Trump's executive orders,[79] the resignation of National Security Advisor Michael Flynn,[80] the firing of FBI Director James Comey for suspicious reasons,[81] and multiple investigations into possible ties between the Trump campaign and Russian interference in the 2016 election, one of which is led by special counsel Robert Mueller.[82] Such resistance and disarray so early in a new president's term is unprecedented in American politics, and it complicates the authoritarianism in Trump as a presidential subject.

Trump reconfigured representations of the presidency in the wake of Obama by re-establishing the presidency as a site of privilege. His authoritarian moves reasserted traditional lines of power, substituting the cooperation and compromise typically found in democracy with bullying and dominance often found in autocratic regimes. Such moves, however, existed in relation to the democratic structure that undergirds the entire United States government. Much of Trump's authoritarianism has been enabled by Republicans in Congress, yet even that support does not ensure that this articulation of the presidency to privilege will calcify. The articulation of the presidency to privilege alters power relations between the federal government and the citizenry, yet it implicates both the presidency itself and the national response to it. The multiple challenges and setbacks that Trump has endured during his first few months in office reflect responses to this sudden and radical shift. The pushback from multiple agents in various places signifies the contingency of the presidency. It is notable that numerous stories emerged within the first month suggesting crisis in the Trump administration, another unprecedented development so soon into a new presidential term.[83] While the presidency has traditionally been a site of governmental leadership, Trump's authoritarianism has shifted the political terrain by giving multiple agents—both within and beyond the state apparatus—motivation to resist it. Certainly, resistance to a presidential agenda is not new, but the level of resistance coupled with the variety of resisters sets both the authoritarian tendencies and the privilege of Trump as presidential subject in sharp relief against the democratic traditions of the United States.

Conclusion

The election of Donald Trump articulated the presidency with authoritarianism, deviating radically from its recent pluralist democratic articulations. The support that this articulation received among substantial pockets of the electorate indicates a tolerance among many American citizens for a more authoritarian presidential subject in defense of "political, social, and economic privilege."[84] That the rise of racist hate groups, misogyny, and bullying in American political life on behalf of Trump did not prevent many undecided voters from voting for Trump suggests a commitment, on some level, to the preservation of white male supremacy.

The instability of the presidential subject means that it must be articulated out of the presidency as an institution, the national ethos, global and national events, the individual occupying the office, and other parts of the government. Each articulation exists in relation to these other factors, and it produces responses from them as well. Given the ways that Trump as a presidential subject reconfigured the cultural representations of the presidency, we can identify a few implications of this articulation. First, articulations of the presidency are as unstable as presidential subjects are. Articulations are made from a plethora of factors and can be unmade, remade, or adjusted as shifts in any of the above factors alter the presidential subject. The protests, judicial rulings, investigations, negative press coverage of the Trump administration, and satirical portrayals of Trump around the world are as vital to the construction of the presidential subject as words from Trump himself are.[85] Second, Trump obliterates any notion that presidential subjects are stable or static. Even if the Trump administration does follow some broad policy parameters, they must be constantly asserted rather than assumed. Importantly, though, we must not presume that this issue is unique to Trump. All presidential subjects are constructed and negotiated from forces, discourses, conditions, and events that make their subjectivity intelligible. Third, the authoritarianism of the Trump administration is, in part, an assertion of privilege. I say in part because this articulation is simply one of many. Each construction of the presidential subject arises out of multiple articulations, some aligned with the presidency and some not. The Trump administration may not be an explicit attempt to resurrect Nazi Germany or institute ethnic cleansing, but the Trump administration's authoritarian tendencies fit quite well with traditional lines of privilege. The election of

Trump shows that when privilege is threatened, the privileged often assert their dominance with overwhelming force. They fight to restore what they believe to be the proper social order by any means necessary. Finally, the backlash that produced Trump has also contributed to another recent political development called "anti-anti-Trumpism," in which conservative support of Trump takes the form of a backlash against moderate and liberal opposition to Trump.[86] Many of Trump's supporters defend Trump from a position of hostility to the left rather than on the merits of his actions.[87] The rise of anti-anti-Trumpism in the United States echoes the backlash that Trump signified in relation to the pluralist democracy of the Democratic party.

The 2016 election and initial stages of the Trump administration suggest that the trend toward authoritarianism in the federal government presents a unique rhetorical challenge for Americans. As of now, millions of Americans resist the shift to authoritarianism. How opposition forces—the Democratic party, governmental agencies at state and federal levels, citizens in protest—respond to Trump will say a lot about how the state and the nation contend with the most radical articulation of the presidency in decades. The silver lining in the Trump administration, though, is its instability. The radical contingency of the presidency opens space for resistance to authoritarian tendencies in a presidential subject, and embracing that contingency provides a way forward in extremely challenging times.

Notes

1. Daniel Politi at *Slate* has a weekly column devoted to chronicling the ongoing developments in the Trump administration at http://www.slate.com/articles/news_and_politics/this_week_in_trump.html (last accessed May 25, 2017).
2. Ruth Ben-Ghiat, "An American Authoritarian," *The Atlantic*, August 10, 2016, http://www.theatlantic.com/politics/archive/2016/08/american-authoritarianism-under-donald-trump/495263/; Rod Nordland, "Authoritarian Leaders Greet Trump as One of Their Own," *The New York Times*, February 1, 2017, https://www.nytimes.com/2017/02/01/world/asia/donald-trump-vladimir-putin-rodrigo-duterte-kim-jong-un.html; Brian Stelter, "Is Trump's Behavior Authoritarian? Columnists Are Asking the Question," *CNN*, January 30, 2017, http://money.cnn.com/2017/01/30/media/authoritarianism-media-donald-trump/index.html.
3. Robinson Meyer, "Donald Trump Is the First Demagogue of the Anthropocene," *The Atlantic*, October 19, 2016, http://www.theatlantic.com/science/archive/2016/10/trump-the-first-demagogue-of-the-anthropocene/504134/; Michael Signer, "The Electoral College Was Created to Stop Demagogues Like Trump," *Time*, November 17, 2016, http://time.com/4575119/electoral-college-demagogues/; Stephen Stromberg, "In His Acceptance Speech, Trump Displays His Demagoguery," *The Washington Post*,

July 22, 2016, https://www.washingtonpost.com/blogs/post-partisan/wp/2016/07/22/in-his-acceptance-speech-trump-displays-his-demagoguery/?utm_term=.21bbfc57523f.

4. In a tweet as president-elect, Trump denounced China's act of taking an American drone as "unpresidented." Critics seized on the typo as a kind of Freudian slip that revealed the radical difference between Trump's behavior and that expected of American presidents. See Adam Gabbatt, "'Unpresidented': Donald Trump Invents the Guardian's Word of the Year," *The Guardian*, December 19, 2016, sec. US news, https://www.theguardian.com/us-news/2016/dec/19/unpresidented-trump-word-definition; Lisa Suhay, "History Proves That Donald Trump's 'Unpresidential' Behavior Is Not a Roadblock to the White House," *Business Insider*, August 10, 2015, http://www.businessinsider.com/trump-unpresidential-behavior-2015-8; The *Times* Editorial Board, "Donald Trump's List of Presidential Shortcomings Seems Bottomless. What Do We Do Now?," *Los Angeles Times*, January 20, 2017, http://www.latimes.com/opinion/editorials/la-ed-trump-inauguration-20170119-story.html; The *Times* Editorial Board, "Trump's Long-Awaited News Conference Was Spectacularly Unpresidential," *Los Angeles Times*, January 12, 2017, http://www.latimes.com/opinion/editorials/la-ed-trump-press-20170112-story.html.

5. Mary Stuckey argues that the presidency is a site of privilege, not simply because of the power invested in the office but also because of its association with privilege along the lines of race, gender, and class. See Mary E. Stuckey, "Rethinking the Rhetorical Presidency and Presidential Rhetoric," *Review of Communication* 10, no. 1 (2010): 38–52, doi:10.1080/15358590903248744.

6. David A. Graham, "'Alternative Facts': The Needless Lies of the Trump Administration," *The Atlantic*, January 22, 2017, https://www.theatlantic.com/politics/archive/2017/01/the-pointless-needless-lies-of-the-trump-administration/514061/.

7. Jane C. Timm, "141 Stances on 23 Issues Donald Trump Took during His White House Bid," *NBC News*, November 28, 2016, http://www.nbcnews.com/politics/2016-election/full-list-donald-trump-s-rapidly-changing-policy-positions-n547801.

8. Emily Schultheis, "Donald Trump, Mexican President Discuss Border Wall at Meeting in Mexico City," *CBS News*, August 31, 2016, http://www.cbsnews.com/news/donald-trump-mexican-president-discuss-border-wall-at-meeting-in-mexico-city/.

9. Nick Gass, "Rick Perry: Trump's Mexico Wall Will Be a 'Digital Wall,'" *POLITICO*, July 11, 2016, http://politi.co/29JlkFA; Olivia Beavers, "GOP Senator: Trump's Wall a 'metaphor' for Securing Border," Text, *TheHill*, (April 6, 2017), http://thehill.com/homenews/senate/327555-gop-sen-trumps-wall-a-metaphor-for-securing-border; Charlie May, "Is Donald Trump's Wall a Physical Wall or Just a Metaphor? The Republican Debate Rages on," *Salon*, April 7, 2017, https://www.mediamatters.org/embed/static/clips/2016/12/08/51436/cnn-nd-20161208-steveking.

10. Clare Malone, "Trump Dropped His Demand To Fund The Wall — That's Smart Politics," *FiveThirtyEight*, April 26, 2017, https://fivethirtyeight.com/features/trump-dropped-his-demand-to-fund-the-wall-thats-smart-politics/.

11. Reed Abelson, "Donald Trump Says He May Keep Parts of Obama Health Care Act," *The New York Times*, November 11, 2016, sec. Business Day, https://www.nytimes.com/2016/11/12/business/insurers-unprepared-for-obamacare-repeal.html.

12. Donald Trump, Twitter Post, May 7, 2015, 11:38a.m., http://twitter.com/realDonald Trump.

13. Sarah Kliff, "The Obamacare Repeal Bill the House Just Passed, Explained," *Vox*, May 3, 2017, https://www.vox.com/policy-and-politics/2017/5/3/15531494/american-health-care-act-explained.

14. "Trump's Letter Firing FBI Director James Comey," *CNN*, accessed May 31, 2017, http://www.cnn.com/2017/05/09/politics/fbi-james-comey-fired-letter/index.html.

15. Tim Hains, "President Trump's Full Interview with Lester Holt: Firing of James Comey," May 11, 2017, http://www.realclearpolitics.com/video/2017/05/11/president_trumps_full_interview_with_lester_holt.html.

16. Donald Trump, Twitter Post, May 28, 2017, 8:33a.m., http://twitter.com/realDonaldTrump

17. Rebecca Savransky, "Trump Retweets Report Based on Anonymous Source after Blasting Anonymous Sources," *The Hill*, May 30, 2017, http://thehill.com/homenews/administration/335598-trump-retweets-story-based-on-anonymous-source-after-blasting.

18. Donald Trump, Twitter Post, August 6, 2012, 4:23p.m., http://twitter.com/realDonald Trump

19. Greg Miller and Greg Jaffe, "Trump Revealed Highly Classified Information to Russian Foreign Minister and Ambassador," *Washington Post*, May 15, 2017, https://www.washingtonpost.com/world/national-security/trump-revealed-highly-classified-information-to-russian-foreign-minister-and-ambassador/2017/05/15/530c172a-3960-11e7-9e48-c4f199710b69_story.html; "Trump Tells Duterte of Two U.S. Nuclear Subs in Korean Waters: NYT," *Reuters*, May 24, 2017, http://www.reuters.com/article/us-northkorea-missiles-submarines-idUSKBN18K15Y.

20. Donald Trump, Twitter Post, May 21, 2016, 6:56a.m., http://twitter.com/realDonaldTrump
Donald Trump, Twitter Post, October 23, 2014, 11:54p.m., http://twitter.com/realDonald Trump
Donald Trump, Twitter Post, October 14, 2014, 3:35p.m., http://twitter.com/realDonald Trump
Donald Trump, Twitter Post, October 13, 2014, 8:03p.m., http://twitter.com/real DonaldTrump
Richard Feloni, "Trump Played Golf 19 Times in His First 100 Days—Here's Why American Presidents Have Been Historically Obsessed with the Game," *Business Insider*, April 30, 2017, http://www.businessinsider.com/why-american-presidents-play-so-much-golf-2017-4.

21. Dan Merica, "Trump on Pace to Surpass 8 Years of Obama's Travel Spending in 1 Year," *CNN*, April 11, 2017, http://www.cnn.com/2017/04/10/politics/donald-trump-obama-travel-costs/index.html.

22. Ashley Kilough, "Trump: 'You Can Get the Baby out of Here,'" *CNN*, August 3, 2016, http://www.cnn.com/2016/08/02/politics/donald-trump-ashburn-virginia-crying-baby/index.html.

23. Aaron Blake, "Trump's Old Tweets Are Becoming a Minefield of Hypocrisy," *Washington Post*, April 18, 2017, https://www.washingtonpost.com/news/the-fix/wp/2017/04/18/trumps-old-tweets-are-quickly-becoming-a-minefield-of-hypocrisy/; Alexi McCammond, "8 Most Hypocritical Things Donald Trump Has Said or Done Since the

Election," *Cosmopolitan*, March 2, 2017, http://www.cosmopolitan.com/politics/a9084563/donald-trump-hypocrisy/.

24. May Bulman, "President Donald Trump Approval Rating," *The Independent*, April 21, 2017, http://www.independent.co.uk/news/world/americas/donald-trump-dangerous-mental-illness-yale-psychiatrist-conference-us-president-unfit-james-gartner-a7694316.html.

25. Matthew Yglesias, "The Bullshitter-in-Chief," *Vox*, May 30, 2017, https://www.vox.com/policy-and-politics/2017/5/30/15631710/trump-bullshit.

26. Salena Zito, "Taking Trump Seriously, Not Literally," *The Atlantic*, September 23, 2016, http://www.theatlantic.com/politics/archive/2016/09/trump-makes-his-case-in-pittsburgh/501335/.

27. Noah Berlatsky, "Peter Thiel Wants America to Take Trump Seriously, but Not Literally. That's Dangerous," *Quartz*, November 1, 2016, https://qz.com/824650/peter-thiel-wants-america-to-take-donald-trump-seriously-but-not-literally/; Jamelle Bouie, "OK, Now Can We Start Taking Donald Trump Literally?," *Slate*, January 25, 2017, http://www.slate.com/articles/news_and_politics/politics/2017/01/now_can_we_start_taking_donald_trump_literally.html.

28. Barbara Biesecker, "Rethinking the Rhetorical Situation from within the Thematic of Différance," *Philosophy and Rhetoric* 22, no. 2 (1989): 110–130; Ronald Walter Greene, "Another Materialist Rhetoric," *Critical Studies in Mass Communication* 15, no. 1 (1998): 21–40; Bradford Vivian, "The Threshold of the Self," *Philosophy & Rhetoric* 33, no. 4 (October 2000): 303–318; Kevin Michael DeLuca, "Articulation Theory: A Discursive Grounding for Rhetorical Practice," *Philosophy & Rhetoric* 32, no. 4 (October 1999): 334–348.

29. Denise M. Bostdorff, *The Presidency and the Rhetoric of Foreign Crisis* (Columbia, SC: University of South Carolina Press, 1994); Jason A. Edwards, "The Good Citizen: Presidential Rhetoric, Immigrants, and Naturalization Ceremonies," *American Communication Journal* 16, no. 2 (Fall 2014): 43–51; Amos Kiewe, *The Modern Presidency and Crisis Rhetoric*, Praeger Series in Political Communication (Westport, Conn.: Praeger, 1994); Rebecca A. Kuehl, "The Rhetorical Presidency and 'Accountability' in Education Reform: Comparing the Presidential Rhetoric of Ronald Reagan and George W. Bush," *Southern Communication Journal* 77, no. 4 (2012): 329–348, doi:10.1080/1041794X.2012.678926; John Murphy, "'Our Mission and Our Moment': George W. Bush and September 11th," *Rhetoric and Public Affairs* 6, no. 4 (2003): 607–632; Mary E. Stuckey, *The President as Interpreter-in-Chief* (Chatham, NJ: Chatham House Publishers, 1991); Jeffrey Tulis, "Revising the Rhetorical Presidency," in *Beyond the Rhetorical Presidency*, ed. Martin J. Medhurst, Presidential Rhetoric Series: No. 1 (College Station: Texas A&M University Press, 1996), 3–14; David Zarefsky, "Presidential Rhetoric and the Power of Definition," *Presidential Studies Quarterly* 34, no. 3 (2004): 607–619, doi:10.1111/j.1741-5705.2004.00214.x.

30. Biesecker, "Rethinking the Rhetorical Situation."

31. DeLuca, "Articulation Theory," 340.

32. Yglesias, "Bullshitter."

33. Don J. Waisanen and Amy B. Becker, "The Problem with Being Joe Biden: Political Comedy and Circulating Personae," *Critical Studies in Media Communication* 32, no. 4 (2015): 256–271, doi:10.1080/15295036.2015.1057516.

34. Stephen Heidt, "The Presidency as Pastiche: Atomization, Circulation, and Rhetorical Instability," *Rhetoric & Public Affairs* 15, no. 4 (2012): 623–633.

35. Biesecker, "Rethinking the Rhetorical Situation."

36. Ernesto Laclau and Chantal Mouffe, *Hegemony and Socialist Strategy: Towards a Radical Democratic Politics*, 2nd ed (London: Verso, 2001).

37. Davi Johnson, "Mapping the Meme: A Geographical Approach to Materialist Rhetorical Criticism," *Communication & Critical/Cultural Studies* 4, no. 1 (March 2007): 27–50, doi:10.1080/14791420601138286.

38. Murray J. Edelman, *Constructing the Political Spectacle* (Chicago: University of Chicago Press, 1988), 9.

39. DeLuca, "Articulation Theory."

40. Jennifer Daryl Slack, "Articulation," in *Communication as: Perspectives on Theory*, ed. Gregory J. Shepherd, Jeffrey St. John, and Theodore G. Striphas (Thousand Oaks, Calif: Sage Publications, 2006), 223–231.

41. Anne Norton, *Republic of Signs: Liberal Theory and American Popular Culture* (Chicago: University of Chicago Press, 1993), 91.

42. Slack, "Articulation."

43. Donald Trump, "Here's Donald Trump's Presidential Announcement Speech," *Time*, June 16, 2015, http://time.com/3923128/donald-trump-announcement-speech/.

44. Phillip Bump, "Donald Trump Led the Polls for 107 Straight Days. Until Today.," *Washington Post*, November 4, 2015, https://www.washingtonpost.com/news/the-fix/wp/2015/11/04/after-100-plus-days-donald-trump-falls-from-the-polling-average-lead/; Nate Silver, "Dear Media, Stop Freaking Out About Donald Trump's Polls," *FiveThirtyEight*, November 23, 2015, http://fivethirtyeight.com/features/dear-media-stop-freaking-out-about-donald-trumps-polls/.

45. Clare Foran, "The Optimism and Anxiety of Trump Voters," *The Atlantic*, January 20, 2017, https://www.theatlantic.com/politics/archive/2017/01/trump-inauguration-popularity-voters-approval/513602/; Anthony Zurcher, "Election 2016: Trump Voters on Why They Backed Him," *BBC News*, November 9, 2016, sec. US Election 2016, http://www.bbc.com/news/election-us-2016-36253275.

46. Callum Borchers, "Meryl Streep Was Right. Donald Trump Did Mock a Disabled Reporter," January 9, 2017, http://www.washingtonpost.com/video/entertainment/meryl-streeps-golden-globes-speech-annotated/2017/01/09/5218fd98-d645-11e6-a0e6-d502d6751bc8_video.html.

47. Peter Holley, "KKK's Official Newspaper Supports Donald Trump for President," *Washington Post*, November 2, 2016, https://www.washingtonpost.com/news/post-politics/wp/2016/11/01/the-kkks-official-newspaper-has-endorsed-donald-trump-for-president/; Peter Holley, "Top Nazi Leader: Trump Will Be a 'Real Opportunity' for White Nationalists," *Washington Post*, August 7, 2016, https://www.washingtonpost.com/news/post-nation/wp/2016/08/07/top-nazi-leader-trump-will-be-a-real-opportunity-for-white-nationalists/; and Sarah Posner and David Neiwert, "Meet the Horde of Neo-Nazis, Klansmen, and Other Extremist Leaders Endorsing Donald Trump," *Mother Jones*, September 21, 2016, http://www.motherjones.com/politics/2016/09/trump-supporters-neo-nazis-white-nationalists-kkk-militias-racism-hate.

48. David Wasserman, "2016 National Popular Vote Tracker (Final)," *The Cook Political Report*, January 2, 2017, http://cookpolitical.com/story/10174.

49. Karlyn Kohrs Campbell and Kathleen Hall Jamieson, *Presidents Creating the Presidency: Deeds Done in Words*, 2nd edition (Chicago: University Of Chicago Press, 2008), 2.

50. Justin Baragona, "Kellyanne Conway Loses It When Pushed by Jake Tapper Over Trump's Lack of 'Presidential Behavior,'" *Mediaite*, December 4, 2016, http://www.mediaite.com/online/kellyanne-conway-loses-it-when-pushed-by-jake-tapper-over-trumps-lack-of-presidential-behavior/.

51. Donald Trump, "Full Text: Donald Trump 2016 RNC Draft Speech Transcript," *POLITICO*, July 21, 2016, http://politi.co/2a30O4N.

52. Ibid.

53. Ben-Ghiat, "An American Authoritarian"; Jeet Heer, "Donald Trump Is Becoming an Authoritarian Leader Before Our Very Eyes," *New Republic*, January 23, 2017, https://newrepublic.com/article/140040/donald-trump-becoming-authoritarian-leader-eyes; Casey Michel, "Spreading Lies Is a Classic Authoritarian Power Move. Don't Let Trump Get Away with It," *Quartz*, February 10, 2017, https://qz.com/907097/spreading-lies-is-a-classic-authoritarian-power-move-dont-let-trump-get-away-with-it/; Nordland, "Authoritarian Leaders Greet Trump as One of Their Own." *New York Times*, Feb. 1, 2017.

54. Jeremy Diamond, "Donald Trump on Protester: 'I'd like to Punch Him in the Face'," *CNN*, February 23, 2016, http://www.cnn.com/2016/02/23/politics/donald-trump-nevada-rally-punch/index.html; Tina Nguyen, "Trump's Violent Campaign Rallies Come Back to Haunt Him," *Vanity Fair*, May 2, 2017, http://www.vanityfair.com/news/2017/05/donald-trump-campaign-rally-lawsuits-incitement.

55. Igor Bobic, "The First 100 Lies: The Trump Team's Flurry Of Falsehoods," *Huffington Post*, February 26, 2017, sec. Politics, http://www.huffingtonpost.com/entry/donald-trump-administration-lies-100_us_58ac7a0fe4b02a1e7dac3ca6.

56. Stuckey, "Rethinking Presidential Rhetoric," 39.

57. Ibid.

58. Jamelle Bouie, "The Professor, the Cop, and the President," *Slate*, September 21, 2016, http://www.slate.com/articles/news_and_politics/the_next_20/2016/09/the_henry_louis_gates_beer_summit_and_racial_division_in_america.html.

59. Barack Obama, "Remarks by the President on Trayvon Martin," *Obamawhitehouse.archives.gov*, July 19, 2013, https://obamawhitehouse.archives.gov/the-press-office/2013/07/19/remarks-president-trayvon-martin.

60. Hillary Clinton, "Full Text: Hillary Clinton's DNC Speech," *POLITICO*, July 28, 2016, http://politi.co/2arPHST.

61. Alexandra Jaffe, "Kellyanne Conway: WH Spokesman 'Gave Alternative Facts' on Inauguration Crowd," *NBC News*, January 23, 2017, http://www.nbcnews.com/politics/politics-news/wh-spokesman-gave-alternative-facts-inauguration-crowd-n710466.

62. Yglesias, "Bullshitter."

63. Heer, "Trump Is Becoming Authoritarian"; Greg Sargent, "GOP Voters Know Trump is Telling Them the Truth, and the Media Is Lying to Them," *The Washington Post*, February 22, 2017, https://www.washingtonpost.com/blogs/plum-line/wp/2017/02/22/gop-voters-know-trump-is-telling-them-the-truth-and-the-media-is-lying-to-them/.

64. See Peggy McIntosh, "White Privilege and Male Privilege: A Personal Account of Coming to See Correspondences Through Work in Women's Studies," in *Race, Class and Gender: An Anthology*, ed. Margaret Andersen and Patricia H. Collins (Belmont, CA: Wadsworth, 1988), 94–105.

65. Derek Hawkins, "'We Need a Donald Trump to Show Some Authoritarian Power,' Says Maine Governor," *Washington Post*, October 12, 2016, https://www.washingtonpost.com/news/morning-mix/wp/2016/10/12/were-slipping-into-anarchy-maine-governor-calls-on-trump-to-show-authoritarian-power/.

66. Peter Holley and Sarah Larimer, "How America's Dying White Supremacist Movement Is Seizing on Donald Trump's Appeal," *Washington Post*, February 29, 2016, https://www.washingtonpost.com/news/morning-mix/wp/2015/12/21/how-donald-trump-is-breathing-life-into-americas-dying-white-supremacist-movement/; Evan Osnos, "The Fearful and the Frustrated: Donald Trump's Nationalist Coalition Takes Shape—For Now," *The New Yorker*, August 31, 2015, http://www.newyorker.com/magazine/2015/08/31/the-fearful-and-the-frustrated; Sarah Posner and David Neiwert, "How Trump Took Hate Groups Mainstream," *Mother Jones*, October 14, 2016, http://www.motherjones.com/politics/2016/10/donald-trump-hate-groups-neo-nazi-white-supremacist-racism.

67. Bouie, "The Professor, the Cop, and the President."

68. Ibid.

69. Ibid.

70. Josiah Ryan, "'This Was a Whitelash': Van Jones' Take on the Election Results," *CNN*, November 9, 2016, http://www.cnn.com/2016/11/09/politics/van-jones-results-disappointment-cnntv/index.html.

71. Michael Eric Dyson, *Tears We Cannot Stop: A Sermon to White America* (New York: St. Martin's Press, 2017), 219.

72. Carol Anderson, *White Rage: The Unspoken Truth of Our Racial Divide* (New York, NY: Bloomsbury, 2016).

73. Ibid., 3.

74. Ibid., 5.

75. Carter Evans, "Hate, Harassment Incidents Spike since Trump Election," November 19, 2016, http://www.cbsnews.com/news/hate-harassment-incidents-spike-since-donald-trump-election/; Alexis Okeowo, "Hate on the Rise After Trump's Election," *The New Yorker*, November 17, 2016, http://www.newyorker.com/news/news-desk/hate-on-the-rise-after-trumps-election.

76. Steven Shepard, "Poll: Trump Approval Rating Hits New Low," *POLITICO*, May 17, 2017, http://politi.co/2qvs8hv, FiveThirtyEight has aggregated and weighted many of the approval rating polls, showing, as of June 1, 2017, an approval rating below 40%.

77. Anemona Hartocollis and Yamiche Alcindor, "Women's March Highlights as Huge Crowds Protest Trump: 'We're Not Going Away'," *The New York Times*, January 21, 2017, https://www.nytimes.com/2017/01/21/us/womens-march.html.

78. Kyle Balluck and Mallory Shellbourne, "Trump Rails against 'Fake News Media,' Leaks from Intelligence Community," *The Hill*, February 15, 2017, http://thehill.com/homenews/administration/319597-trump-fake-news-media-is-going-crazy-with-conspiracy-theories-and.

79. Colin Dwyer, "Court Denies DOJ Request For Stay; Trump Immigration Order Remains Suspended," *NPR.org*, February 4, 2017, http://www.npr.org/sections/thet-wo-way/2017/02/04/513415447/airlines-again-board-travelers-barred-by-travel-or-der-as-trump-vows-to-fight; Adam Liptak, "Appeals Court Will Not Reinstate Trump's Revised Travel Ban," *The New York Times*, May 25, 2017, sec. Politics, https://www.nytimes.com/2017/05/25/us/politics/trump-travel-ban-blocked.html; Ilya Solin, "Federal Court Rules against Trump's Executive Order Targeting Sanctuary Cities," *Washington Post*, April 25, 2017, https://www.washingtonpost.com/news/volokh-conspiracy/wp/2017/04/25/federal-court-rules-against-trumps-executive-order-targeting-sanctuary-cities/.

80. Maggie Haberman et al., "Michael Flynn Resigns as National Security Adviser," *The New York Times*, February 13, 2017, https://www.nytimes.com/2017/02/13/us/politics/don-ald-trump-national-security-adviser-michael-flynn.html.

81. Michael D. Shear and Matt Apuzzo, "F.B.I. Director James Comey is Fired by Trump," *The New York Times*, May 9, 2017, sec. Politics, https://www.nytimes.com/2017/05/09/us/politics/james-comey-fired-fbi.html.

82. Kevin Uhrmacher and Kim Soffen, "A Guide to the Five Major Investigations of the Trump Campaign's Possible Ties to Russia," *Washington Post*, Updated June 17, 2017, https://www.washingtonpost.com/graphics/national/trump-russia-investigations/.

83. Stephen Collinson, Sara Murray, and Elizabeth Landers, "For Trump, Chaotic White House Becomes the Norm," *CNN*, February 16, 2017, http://www.cnn.com/2017/02/16/politics/donald-trump-power-white-house/index.html; Michael D. Shear, "'Unbeliev-able Turmoil': Trump's First Month Leaves Washington Reeling," *The New York Times*, February 14, 2017, https://www.nytimes.com/2017/02/14/us/politics/trump-white-house.html.

84. Stuckey, "Rethinking Presidential Rhetoric," 39.

85. Ronald Brownstein, "The Formidable Checks and Balances Imposing on President Trump," *The Atlantic*, February 16, 2017, https://www.theatlantic.com/politics/archive/2017/02/trump-constraints-opposition/516825/?utm_source=twb; Heidt, "The Presidency as Pastiche"; Waisanen and Becker, "The Problem with Being Joe Biden."

86. Charles J. Sykes, "If Liberals Hate Him, Then Trump Must be Doing Something Right," *The New York Times*, May 12, 2017, sec. Opinion, https://www.nytimes.com/2017/05/12/opinion/sunday/if-liberals-hate-him-then-trump-must-be-doing-something-right.html.

87. Jonathan V. Last, "Anti-Anti-Trumpism Lives!," *Weekly Standard*, June 2, 2017, 07:45a.m., http://www.weeklystandard.com/anti-anti-trumpism-lives/article/2008320.

CHAPTER EIGHT

Trump, Twitter, and the Microdiatribe

The Short Circuits of Networked Presidential Public Address

STEPHEN J. HEIDT AND DAMIEN SMITH PFISTER

Refiguring the contours of presidential public address is one of the unintended consequence of Donald J. Trump's campaign and the early months of his presidency. Although all candidates and all presidents since Bill Clinton—the first candidate to have a website—have used internetworked media to publicize their agendas, raise money, get out the vote, connect with citizens, and otherwise stimulate public deliberation, Donald Trump's love affair with Twitter marks a departure from previous, more formal, presidential uses of digital media.[1] Where prior scholarship addressed the integration of presidential speech and digital presentations,[2] scholars of presidential rhetoric are now faced with the challenge of taking Trump's tweets seriously as a primary mode of public address. Given the changing media ecology, Twitter and analogous genres of internetworked rhetoric are henceforth likely to be permanent fixtures in presidential rhetoric. Even if Twitter falls into disuse, the "basic architecture" of microblogging "prevails across internetworked media genres."[3] While presidents may use alternative and evolving genres in the future, digital communication is likely to retain the affordances of addressivity to others, capacity of response, and ease of re-circulation.

The challenge of accounting for new modes of presidential public address is particularly acute in the context of Trump's use of Twitter. Unlike most politicians, Trump sends most of his tweets himself, many of his tweets violate the conventional norms of decorum that have historically governed presidential rhetoric, and he routinely propagates questionable if not entirely false information.[4] Presidents have traditionally distanced themselves from petty partisan attacks, instead relying on surrogates to say nasty things about their opponents.[5] Unlike his predecessors, Trump's vituperative use of Twitter combined with his reliance on "alternative facts" has led critics to wonder if the dignity of the office is being threatened, raising serious questions about the future of presidential deliberations on issues of public import.[6] Further, Trump's use of Twitter establishes a faster and more direct connection between the president and his base, while supplanting more traditional modes of address, like press conferences or televised addresses.

While tempted to write off Trump and his use of Twitter as an outlier—and, indeed, future politicians may well look at his Twittering as an object lesson in how not to use this novel genre of presidential rhetoric—we contend this case holds important lessons for scholarship on public address. The presidency is a self-referential institution. Future presidents will likely replicate his use of Twitter, if not his rhetorical style. Moreover, given the rise of right-wing populism across the globe since the Great Recession of 2008, Trump's use of Twitter may well be a harbinger of things to come. In either event, Trump's use of Twitter demonstrates that stirring populist energies through new digital technologies displaces formal mechanisms of deliberation; these mechanisms are premised on traditional modes of public address that invest the president with interrogative dynamics that encourage public deliberation.[7]

To make sense of presidential rhetoric dispensed 280 characters at a time,[8] we make three moves in this chapter. First, we argue Trump's use of Twitter challenges the conventional constitution and operation of publics by creating short circuits of communication. While Twitter may well play an important role in the informal networked public sphere, Trump's use of the microblogging platform poses challenges to conventional routines of democratic deliberation.[9] Second, we identify and explore the form this rhetoric takes—what we call the "microdiatribe"—that channels affective energies of outrage. While Trump's tweets congealed a populist outsider persona that facilitated his electoral victories, his microdiatribes issued through Twitter have thwarted his attempts to govern. By examining the short circuits produced by Trump tweets in two cases marking the transition from candidate Trump to President Trump, we demonstrate the limitations of presidential Twitter and the institutional power the presidency retains over a president. Rather than a global critique of Twitter or presidential tweeting, our critique focuses on the particularities of Trump's rhetorical messaging as it interacts with the broader affordances and cultures of a complex internetworked media ecology.

Short Circuits of Deliberation

Although the peculiarities of Trump's penchant for Twitter could be dismissed as epiphenomenon, drawing critical attention that might be better focused on structural issues like sexism, racism, and authoritarianism, the public negotiation of those issues cannot occur outside of this historical moment's dominant genre. Indeed, Trump's use of Twitter as a key mode of public address provides an opportunity to explore some fundamental transformations in the constitution and operation of publics. In making this observation, we follow up on Ronald Greene's claim that "the increasing speed demanded of new technologies circulating public discourse suggests the beginnings of a qualitative break with the forms of punctuality associated with the modern idea of a public. The modern forms of print and television, with their monthly, weekly, and daily news cycles and serialization are beginning to give way to an instantaneous and continuous 24/7/365 circulation of discourse."[10] This chapter focuses on how communication in "the network society disrupts the preferred temporality of rhetorical deliberation."[11]

Deliberation is a slow and layered process, especially when it becomes enshrined in governmental institutions. In the context of the United States' government, this intentional sluggishness is systematized through the committee structure of Congress and the agencies of the federal government, the system of checks and balances among the three branches of government, and a national press still largely committed to the daily, weekly, and monthly publication of formal communication from the president's office. Where Obama was often accused of being too deliberative, leveraging the republic's dense advisory infrastructure to a fault, Trump is attacked for moving too quickly and without the merest hint of public deliberation or even warning. Trump's Executive Order halting immigration from seven Muslim majority countries, which was immediately stayed by court order, is a good example of fast policy implementation without appropriate legal vetting.

The advent of the networked public sphere complicates the routinized processes of deliberation, as Greene intimates, by providing new pathways for the energies of civic culture to flow. Indeed, we suggest that Donald Trump is a conductor of rhetorical energy capable of canalizing publics' energies through his continuous and expressive use of Twitter: each tweet creates a communicative circuit, released into an extant rhetorical ecology with the effect of energizing and/or enervating publics.[12] Trump's tweets are rapidly networked into the communicative grid: retweeted by supporters and lambasted by critics; scrolled on cable news tickers and seeded into social media newsfeeds; interrogated by pundits and explicated by surrogates. These pops of energy power the networked public sphere until the next tweet, which does the same until the next tweet—in a cycle that seems to ever-accelerate.[13]

To make sense of how Trump's tweets conduct rhetorical energy, we turn to Bernard Stiegler's distinction between short circuits and long circuits. For Stiegler, the combination of profit-driven media companies, a rampant consumer economy, and digital media technology produce short circuits of communication that frustrate the creativity necessary for a meaningful individual life. Stiegler's insight can be scaled up to democratic politics: there, too, creativity is necessary for the deliberation that enables a meaningful democratic public life. Attention is at the core of Stiegler's distinction: a short circuit is a fleeting experience that minimally alters one's being; it passes into and out of consciousness—the individual experience of attention—without stimulating deeper engagement.[14] The throwaway culture of consumerism is Stiegler's exemplar of the short circuit: doing a little retail therapy may make one feel better momentarily, but elides the structural issues that produce the need to feel better in the first place, which reproduces the need for another retail fix.[15] In contrast to the consumer economy, philosophy is the exemplar of the long circuit. To think philosophically requires one to engage with the history of philosophy, to attend to an issue from many different, perhaps contradictory perspectives, to allow oneself to be shaped by philosophical inquiry even as one endeavors to shape it. So too with democratic public life: short term, feel-good activity often comes at the expense of the difficult process of thinking creatively about our collective future.

The distinction between a short circuit and a long circuit can be appreciated through a few examples of digital practices. The glance at a mobile phone is a classic example of a short circuit—quickly trying to acquire information like a sports score or text message. The scroll, as through one's news feed, is very often an engagement with short circuits. Reading the title of a headline—but not the article itself—and then sharing it on social media is a short circuit. Indeed, the whole fake news phenomenon from the election of 2016 is a result of short circuits: people passing around rumor with the feel of truthiness until a story just becomes part of the enthymematic backdrop of a particular social network. Trump's use of Twitter instead of press conferences is another example of a short circuit. Instead of an extended back and forth with critical journalists, capable of asking follow-up questions and working with an expectation that he ought to answer them, Twitter offers Trump the patina of public engagement without the responsibilities that inhere in democratic accountability.

These examples evidence the difference between long and short circuits (a difference of gradations rather than a sharp binary). A long circuit engages what Stiegler calls both the synchronic and the diachronic, whereas the short circuit privileges the synchronic. The long circuit reaches back into history to contextualize the present; the short circuit pays attention only to the current moment. It is thus notable that Twitter co-founder Jack Dorsey emphasized the now as the essential horizon of Twitter: "I don't go back in time [to read old tweets]. You're kind of as good as your last update. That's what you're currently thinking or doing, or your current approach towards life ... It's only relevant in the now."[16]

A long circuit creates conditions for individuation and creativity; a short circuit creates conditions for standardization and banality. As Stiegler notes, the contemporary culture industries hope "to achieve gigantic economies of scale, and, therefore, through appropriated technologies, to control and homogenize behavior."[17] Culture industries want to create short circuits because short circuits activate immediate drives and simple affects that find temporary satisfaction through the buying of commercial goods. This kind of standardization of banality is at odds with the openness to experience that individuation—and, one might say, argumentation and democratic deliberation—requires. Given Stiegler's connection between individuation and creativity, individuation might be thought of a process of rhetorical invention.[18] Inventive speech is so central to democratic public life because it generates and sustains long circuits of communication across culture and across generations. There is a rich intertextual legacy surrounding the history of public address—amplified within the context of the presidency—that offers insight into culture and sources of wisdom to guide us in making sound judgments. Eloquent speech enriches public discourse by transforming not just topics of public discourse but the discoursers themselves; any serious study of the complicated history of public address imparts an appreciation for the interplay of rhetoric and culture and transforms the student —it individuates.[19] Plain speech, by contrast, lends itself to short circuitry.

A short circuit of communication is a burst of rhetorical energy that dissipates almost as soon as it emerges; it is so simple that it doesn't need to do much else. It comes, it goes, minimally altering its environment. It is banal, uninventive, worth registering but not enfolding too deeply into one's subjectivity. A long circuit of communication is a burst of rhetorical energy that junctions with other rhetorical energies, bouncing along different routes which transform it and the larger communicative ecology—the people, places, and things that constitute our everyday lives. A long circuit is energized by invention, and so draws in participation from many diverse perspectives to power our civic culture.

We suggest long and short should be seen as heuristics, not absolutes. There is an obvious threshold problem that muddies the distinction, and in practice the long and the short can blur. One can be on social media for a long time and not make a long circuit; one can start in a short circuit mode but end up in a long one; and shortness is not necessarily a sign of a short-circuit—a short aphorism could create a long circuit over a lifetime of contemplation. We are not developing a global critique of terse messaging, nor are we aiming to indict Twitter *writ large*. Instead, we are marrying an emphasis on form demanded by a theory of short circuits while accounting for the textuality of Trump's tweets to consider how Trump's use of Twitter as a genre of presidential rhetoric shapes large patterns of public deliberation.

This synthetic approach departs from an effort to understand Trump's tweets in terms of either form or content. Brian Ott, for example, argues from a media ecology perspective that Twitter's form emphasizes simplicity, impulsivity, and incivility; thus "Twitter ultimately trains us to devalue others, thereby, cultivating mean and malicious discourse."[20] Alternatively, George Lakoff seeks a generic diagnosis of Trump's approach to public address through Twitter.[21] Lakoff argues the content of Trump's tweets can be taxonomized as either preemptive framing, deflection, diversion, or trial balloons.[22] These analyses suggest the way short circuits of communication erode the long, slow, layered contemplation necessary for democratic deliberation; yet, neither account for how the form and content of Trump's tweeting are mutually implicative. We contend that the genre of Twitter affords a specific form—what we call the microdiatribe—that aids Trump in producing short circuits of rhetorical energy.

Trump, Twitter, and the Microdiatribe

Early theorists of the 'digital citizenship' thesis spoke to "the potential the internet" offers to improve civic discourse by connecting citizens across physical space, improve civic education and knowledge, and enable a rhetorical forum that "better incorporates the political, ethical, cultural and aesthetic qualities of a wide variety of forms of engagement, including provocation, passion and intensive (digital) civic participation."[23] These theorists evoked an optimism premised on the prospect of deep and wide connectivity offered by the medium of an internetworked media ecology. Connectivity, they argued, lent force to civic engagement because it enabled diverse and dispersed groups to share information, form collective responses to political challenges, and interact with if not directly address political actors.[24] Yet, as actual practices of digital citizenship have unfolded, the provocation, passion, and intensity of participation in the maturing networked public sphere sparked "vitriolic or aggressive expression and exchange."[25] Trolling, flaming, and other kinds of abuse are motivated by the absence of social sanction enabled by many kinds of computer-mediated communication.[26]

Although much popular and scholarly analysis of vitriolic communication judges it detrimental to democratic politics, vitriolic speech "allow[s] space for the flow of passion and contested interaction among adversaries."[27] This mode of contestation, we contend, played an outsized role in the 2016 presidential campaign and continues to govern Donald Trump's presidential discourse.[28] Specifically, Trump's use of Twitter addressed one of the challenges for any insurgent candidate in getting and maintaining the attention of an electorate. While third party candidates have sought to win the presidency, the structure of presidential elections—including the financial needs of campaigns, the tradition of two dominant parties, and the challenge of even getting on the ballot in all 50 states—incentivize the rise of party insiders.[29] Perhaps having learned from the failure of prior insurgent candidates, Trump's adoption of the Republican Party offered his candidacy the opportunity to capture the benefits of both the insurgent and the institutionalized.[30] But, in a crowded field of 18 candidates with virtually identical policy platforms, that is—NoBama—Trump faced the challenge of distinguishing his candidacy from the field.

In one of the great ironies of contemporary political rhetoric, Trump drew on a rhetorical form that Theodore Otto Windt, Jr., called the "last resort for protest," the diatribe.[31] Generally associated with resistance from the margins, the diatribe is a style of communication in which "logic is inverted; assumptions are reversed; the unexpected is not unusual."[32] Practitioners of the diatribe disdain "customs regardless of the disguises they wear: laws, civil authority, political institutions, and social mores."[33] For a specific audience of Trump supporters and voters, purportedly fed up with "politics as usual," Trump's campaign rhetoric fell in line with this intellectual tradition of delegitimizing convention (despite the fact that Trump's vision for the United States merely replaces one set of social mores with another, which marks a departure from the classical diatribe). By rarely invoking democratic ideals like freedom, liberty, rights, and the public, candidate Trump's unconventional communication signaled his distance from the rhetorical order of democracies and the politics-as-usual ethos of the Republican Party.[34]

While the diatribes typified by Diogenes might be suitable to Twitter's compressed word play, Windt's analysis of contemporary diatribes points to more extended riffs delivered before a live audience. That is, they are oral. By contrast, many of Trump's tweets are better conceived of as microdiatribes. Microblogging yields the microdiatribe.[35] Etymologically, *micro-* is derived from the Greek *mikros*, meaning "small, little, petty, trivial, slight;" thus registering both the truncated form of Trump's microdiatribes but also the small-mindedness of many of his tweets. The condensed version of Trump's microdiatribes have effects analogous to those of the classical diatribe of Diogenes. First among these is creating shock, which "gathers an audience when orthodox speeches will not."[36] Second, both Diogenes and Trump adopt an abrasive approach: "the style, marked by obscenity and slang, was far from dignified."[37] Quite often, (micro)diatribes are marked by appeals that "shock, criticize, and deride a public figure." For Diogenes, this included Athenian politicians and intellectuals; for Trump, the public figures deserving derision included rival candidates and media critics.[38] Gaining attention through shock helps explain how Trump elevated his candidacy above the rest of the GOP field. Third, this rhetorical shock doctrine congeals audiences to actuate a secondary effect: rearranging perspectives. As Windt notes, "the diatribe is intended both to satirize fundamental values and expectations by dramatizing the chasm that exists between ideals and practices, between language and actions, between illusions and actualities."[39] Unlike resistant diatribes, which seek to disrupt civic culture in order to critique its excesses or outrages, Trump's diatribic form sought to cultivate an *ethos* around the figure of the outsider, able and willing to violate the norms of speech, in order to reassert a nostalgic conservative politics.

Windt notes "the major weakness of the diatribe is that it is limited in effectiveness. Once attention has been gained and criticism voiced, the diatribe diminishes in usefulness. People demand serious remedies, seriously treated. Moral dramaturgy must give way to conventional rhetorical forms."[40] Or, in more contemporary parlance, one cannot govern through affect alone. The first months of Trump's administration suggest that one can campaign with short circuits, but a president must govern within long ones. Ironically, winning the election produced its own exigence. No longer a protest candidate, and having no actual plans to guide his governing strategy, Trump's short circuit assertions were enfolded into the long circuits of policy enactment. Yet, instead of engaging in the rhetorical work of making long circuits that foster democratic deliberation, Trump recommitted to the short circuits of communication fostered by his use of Twitter.

Take, for example, this tweet on November 10, 2016: "Just had a very open and successful presidential election. Now professional protesters, incited by the media, are protesting. Very unfair!" The tweet exemplifies how Trump uses Twitter and serves as a useful exemplar of the networked nature of Trump's digital communication. First, he asserts the election had no irregularities. This statement establishes a line that divides his potential audiences, represents an either/or fulcrum that animates much of Trump's rhetoric. In spite of significant irregularities on election day, FBI Director Comey's highly prejudicial and unprecedented statement about Hillary Clinton's emails, news reports relating to possible links between Trump's campaign and Vladimir Putin and the Russian government, among other entanglements, Trump's tweet dismisses all possible concerns to assert an essential fairness of the process and outcome.

Then, pointing to protests, Trump dismisses the protesters as paid by fake grassroots groups and scapegoats "the media" as the culprit, building the case that "special interests" are out to destroy him. Finally, the "very unfair" line suggests that Trump is the victim. In a simple sense, this tweet follows the contours of conservative victimage rhetoric by suggesting the cause of national disunity and instability as inspired and led by outside forces, while positioning Trump as the party suffering the most.[41] This tweet hews closely to what we've described as a microdiatribe: it is unconventional, borderline illogical, ridiculous, vitriolic, and appears intended to energize the base and shock the opposition with its sheer mendacity.

With 71,413 retweets and 234,155 likes, the tweet did not stand out as exceptionally important or significant. Its circulation and recirculation did not make this one of Trump's most liked or talked about tweets. But it did generate significant blowback both on Twitter and in the press and demonstrates how Trump's rhetorical energy set off a back and forth cycle by detractors and supporters. First, a significant number of retweets were oppositional. Many were accompanied by the hastag "#shegotmorevotes" or "#theloserwon." Those retweets also added information to recontextualize Trump's original claim. For example, one oppositional commenter tweeted, "That time in 2012 when you said we should march to protest election outcome and abolish electoral college." As a conductor of the energies of public life, Trump's tweet was absorbed into an oppositional "long circuit" by circulating his original claim of victimage to demonstrate his hypocritical and inconsistent stance toward the Electoral College. These tweets further a broad discourse looking to portray Trump as a hypocrite willing to say anything to win the presidency.

Alternatively, Trump supporters responded to the opposition. For example, one Trump supporter responded, "Are you #Hillary #CryBabies #BasementDwellers #Gullibles that weak? Oh GOD!" Another replied, "prayers for you in this. Evil is chasing you on a constant … You will not break. God will guide." And a third, "LOOK & WEEP LITTLE ONE THIS MAN @realDonaldTrump AND I DO MEAN MAN IS OUR PRESIDENT BY POPULAR AND ELECTORAL VOTES USA USA." These tweets are just a few examples of a broader network of retweets that both belittled the opposition and extended gendered tropes about Trump's victory. This ecology of tweets also demonstrates the way Trump's micro-diatribes attract and capture diverse audiences. In producing small bursts of rhetorical energy, these tweets reaffirm the affects (in support of and in opposition to) produced by his tweets while also reflecting how Trump continuously creates new short circuits for those affects. In a moment when candidate Trump would normally have been shifting to president Trump, these tweets also reflect how the microdiatribic form fails to create conditions for effective governance and sets the stage for endemic conflict between Trump and the press after the inauguration.

In short, Trump uses Twitter to conduct populist energies of outrage, an affect that circulates quickly and burns brightly in a campaign but flickers more wanly when governing.[42] The affective charge created by outrage is often treated as more authentic speech—straight from Trump's heart and mouth –building upon each other to produce an echo chamber of outrage and applause. Recall the anonymous participant of Frank Luntz's focus group responding to Trump's first address to a joint session of Congress, for example. Noting that Trump appeared presidential, the participant then said, "I'm going to look for him on Twitter tomorrow and see what he really thinks."[43] The combination of the rhetorical velocity of Trump's tweets with the inevitable cycles of interpretation of the outlandish, offensive, vague, or threatening message of his tweets appears part of what presidential historian Douglas Brinkley calls the Administration's shock and awe strategy: "every day there's a new, radical initiative, and it doesn't give journalists or the public a chance to get a grip on what just happened."[44] Furthermore, Trump's regular tweeting enhances the "symbiotic relationship" already established between Twitter and television, playing right into the conflictual orientation of television by providing new news for the 24/7 cable television news programs to scrutinize.[45] Trump's tweets feed into the bias of television for short circuits of communication: they appear first on the scrolling ticker, are then reported as a consequential presidential communique, and are then often interpreted by two bickering partisans.

Another example after Trump's inauguration underlines this point. After Trump read a poorly sourced *Breitbart* story about Obama wiretapping his campaign, he sent a series of tweets that captivated the political press. The three most significant tweets read as follows: T 6:35 AM, 4 March 2017: "Terrible! Just found out that Obama had my 'wires tapped' in Trump Tower just before the victory. Nothing found. This is McCarthyism!". T 6:49 AM, 4 March 2017: "Is it legal for a sitting President to be 'wire tapping' a race for president prior to an election? Turned down by court earlier. A NEW LOW!". And finally, at 7:02 AM, 4 March 2017: "How low has President Obama gone to tapp [sic] my phones during the very sacred election process. This is Nixon/Watergate. Bad (or sick) guy!".[46] By implicating Obama in a series of microdiatribic tweets, Trump reasserted an essential antagonism against politics itself that his rhetoric embraced from the start of the campaign. The micro-level analysis of Trump's tweets reflects a president committed to address the public in ways that encourages short, energetic bursts of outrage and little more.

To some extent, Trump's audiences responded as expected. The tweet storm achieved what is for Trump a fairly normal level of political engagement. The first tweet received 145,155 likes, 51,878 retweets, and approximately 49,000 replies;[47] the second received125,063 likes, 36, 735 retweets, and approximately 31,000 replies;[48] and the third received 164,442 likes, 53,275 retweets, and approximately 105,000 replies.[49] The majority of the responses were negative. The lines of opposition generally formed around fact checking his claim, linking Trump and these tweets to the Russia controversy, raising questions about Trump's mental health, and circulating memes poking fun of Trump's comments. For example, as @hankgreen and others pointed out, "presidents can't order wire taps."[50] Other oppositional responses focused on the unsubstantiated nature of the claim, terming it a conspiracy theory. Those who connected the tweets to Russia implied, as @Stepleton6 put it, "all Americans do support getting to bottom of Russia's influence in elections and in WH."[51] Finally, one tweeter expressed buyer's remorse, stating, "after voting for you and supporting you, I realize now I made a huge mistake. Your [sic] not a little egotistical, your just NUTS."[52] These tweets were coupled with a number of humorous memes. Varying from the president in House of Cards throwing away his phone (and implying that Trump should do the same) to pictures of Trump as a babe in Putin's arms, these memes poked fun at the president's ignorance and depicted him as a puppet controlled by others.

This network of tweets responding to Trump's initial utterances provoked an additional round of tweets in support of the president. These supporting tweets focused on defending Trump's notion (@2Alpha "Potential Obama Wiretapping is 'Soviet-level Wrongdoing'"[53]) and on defending the president from insinuations about Russia's influence (@WJFinlay "every shred of 'Russia hax' evidence has been pathetic. Fake News!"[54]). As these snippets suggest, the entire ecosystem of tweets related to Trump's allegations constituted a classic short circuit of communication—assertions traded back and forth with little inventive work to transcend or navigate differences of opinion.

This case shows how Trump was still in the short circuit mode of the campaign, while the institutional press committed to covering the president was enfolding his tweets into longer circuits of inquiry. After the controversy's initial energy dispersed, White House Press Secretary Sean Spicer backed off of Trump's claims. In doing so, he exposed the power of the long circuitry produced by the tweet. The comments came in a press briefing and, in parsing the words of Trump's tweet, Spicer noted that many news organizations had reported something similar, specifically citing Fox News, the New York Times, and the BBC. Claiming the press "widely reported," surveillance activities during the 2016 election, Spicer broadened Trump's definition of the word "wiretapping" to imply any form of surveillance.[55] While Spicer's comments stretch definitional gymnastics to absurdity, two factors demonstrate how this tweet energized a long circuit of communication.

First, the forum of a press conference is inherently connected to deliberative practice. While adversarial and, as one scholar put it, "not a cooperative effort at achieving understanding among parties deliberating over the common good," the press conference is a forum for "transparency and accountability," both of which are vital to public deliberation.[56] Second, journalists who attend press conferences incorporate the press secretary's answers in news stories that directly deliberate on presidential controversies. In this instance, the movement from tweet to reporting to press conference to more reporting led to significant, if varied, deliberation on: the source of Trump's "knowledge," the implications for the intelligence and law enforcement communities, the role of the president in making public such allegations, what his claims implied, Obama's response to the tweets, and serious and humorous takes on Trump's mental composition.[57]

Through the analysis of these two brief examples, we show how diverse audiences that respond to and recirculate Trump's tweets reproduce short circuits rather than the long circuits of individuation necessary for democratic deliberation. We suggest analyzing the audiences with a higher level of scrutiny yields different forms of networked circuitry overlaid simultaneously and with differential implications. As president, Trump's commitment to micro-diatribic tweets matters in ways that prior studies of the so-called digital presidency could not anticipate.[58] On the one hand, Trump's use of Twitter differs significantly from prior presidential use of the medium. Where Obama used Twitter to supplement prior or ongoing statements, to deliberate on policy, to educate his supporters, and to fundraise or otherwise link supporters to his campaign, Trump uses Twitter to make declarations, antagonize, and self-aggrandize. Twitter offers Trump the opportunity to emit rapid-fire staccato pulses of self-promotional, non-deliberative rhetorical energy, directed to specifically invigorate short circuits of communication for his partisan supporters. We conclude this section by parsing this claim on the micro-level of Trump's tweets themselves, the meso-level of press reception and engagement with Trump's tweets, and the macro-level of institutional deliberation.

At the micro-level of Trump's tweets, the 140-character constraint is conducive to a rhetorical culture that privileges the short circuit. This is, of course, potentially a critique of Twitter itself—the technical affordances of the genre do not incline it toward sustained, iterating, evidenced argument. Yet many Twitter users find ways of expanding their observations through linking practices, serialized tweets, and extended back and forth conversations. These ways of making long circuits, however, are not Trump's *modus operandi* when it comes to Twitter. Rather, the assertion, the quip, and the exclamation of feeling (SAD!) dominate. The lack of comparative thinking evidenced in Trump's tweets—metaphors, analogies, contrastive ideas—limits the length of circuit that can be produced. We can imagine presidential microblogging could play a valuable role in contemporary political communication, but not if it comes at the expense of other modes that are embedded in a stronger culture of deliberation and if it is used primarily to issue microdiatribes that shock but have limited value in forging the common ground necessary for governing.

At the meso-level, this critique of Trump's tweets as short circuits must be nested within the political economy of the press and the agonistic culture of the internet. Put simply, every Trump tweet sets off a cycle of interpretation and criticism—other Twitterers, bloggers, journalists, press organizations—get into the act of figuring out what Trump means. As Representative Bill Foster (D-IL) recently said, we've become "reduced to listening to the tweets from the president as sort of the bird entrails of the 21st century."[59] This high technocultural drama makes for good television (and, indeed, the obsession by the televisual press with Trump's spectacular antics as a campaigner, which translated into free publicity, is often credited for his election).[60] Trump's rapid-fire tweets and the press response to them are a limit case of what Jodi Dean calls communicative capitalism, a cultural formation that commodifies communication itself with deleterious effect:

> today, the circulation of content in the dense, intensive networks of global communications relieves top-level actors (corporate, institutional and governmental) from the obligation to respond. Rather than responding to messages sent by activists and critics, they counter with their own contributions to the circulating flow of communications, hoping that sufficient volume (whether in terms of number of contributions or the spectacular nature of a contribution) will give their contributions dominance or stickiness. Instead of engaged debates, instead of contestations employing common terms, points of reference or demarcated frontiers, we confront a multiplication of … assertions so extensive that it hinders the formation of strong counterhegemonies.[61]

Dean, writing a full decade before Trump's election and well before Twitter, might as well be writing about Trump's use of Twitter. Quantitatively and qualitatively, both the number of tweets and the spectacular nature of them, Trump's use of Twitter adds to the quickening flow of communication commodities. This rhetorical velocity, intensified because of the speed with which terse messages can be circulated and critiqued through Twitter, risks the development of what Dean calls counterhegemonies and, ultimately, a kind of critical exhaustion that may weaken citizens' deliberative energies.[62] Although resistance to Trump appeared strong in the early days of his administration (i.e. the Women's March on Washington and protests in airports against the travel ban on Muslims from seven countries), only time will tell if the various protests falling under the generic label of #resistance can sustain networking their energies against Trump's agenda.

Simultaneously, Trump's presidential tweets have received a significantly different response from the political press. Instead of fact-checking or policing Trump's rhetoric, as one might expect, the campaign press treated Trump as an insurgent reality star, a made-for-profit respite in an otherwise grueling campaign. In Tim Wu's view, press attention to Trump's tweets bears responsibility for "the Trump circus ... [and] has more of the nation paying more attention to the president than at any time in decades, and maybe since Roosevelt himself."[63] While Wu is pessimistic about the press's ability to perform its typical role of investigating the president and informing the public, we suggest that press response to Trump's tweets shifted once he became president. The press now treat Trump's tweets as if they were official forms of presidential communication. Constituted to engage in deliberation as a matter of course, we argue the political press is an audience that recirculates Trump's tweets and, in doing so, attempts to create long circuits of communication that can lead to engaged and meaningful forms of deliberation. Deeply rooted in deliberation, press discussion of Trump's policies has taken an institutional form, even though the interlocutors proposing policy are recklessly ignorant or outright duplicitous about their intentions.

At the macro-level, Trump's tweets might be seen as short circuiting the deliberative infrastructure of the United States. Here, the colloquial use of short circuit as blowing a fuse or circuit breaker is an apt evolution of Stiegler's circuit analogy that nonetheless retains its heuristic value, for a blown circuit can never become a long circuit. A short circuit in this sense refers to situations in which there is low impedance for the electrical current; such a situation can increase voltage in a hazardous way. Without a fuse or circuit breaker to interrupt the flow of the current, excessive voltage could cause fire or explosion. Ideally, electrical circuits stabilize the voltage through resistors built into the circuit. Analogically, Trump's use of Twitter at the expense of conventional deliberative channels risks excessive voltage—serial microdiatribes that flow through networks of outrage in unpredictable and dangerous ways that circumvent the dampening effects of the U.S. system of deliberation.[64] Without this deliberative insulation, explosions of populist violence—like the discharge of a gun in the Washington, D.C. pizzeria Comet Ping Pong, rumored to be the center of a child sex ring run by Hillary Clinton during the 2016 campaign, or, more seriously, the shooting of two Indian nationals (one of whom died) in a Kansas bar in February 2017, not to mention the uptick in harassment against Muslims, people perceived to be immigrants (legal or illegal)—is inevitable.

Analyzing Presidential Rhetoric in a Digital Media Ecology

Trump's reliance on Twitter as a primary mode of public address is the linchpin of a broader tendency to erode the resistance provided by layers of democratic deliberation. Put simply, Trump doesn't need the traditional broadcast press to circulate his communication. While this has been a possibility for at least a couple of decades, Trump is the first president to take full advantage of the shifting landscape of publicity. Indeed, as one astute observer of the Trump administration states, "they believe they have shifted the paradigm of media coverage, replacing the traditional media with their own."[65] Following a decades-long assault on the purportedly (and perpetually disproven) liberal bias of the "mainstream media,"[66] conservatives have cobbled together their own media ecosystem of Fox News, conservative talk radio, a red blogosphere, and now a direct conduit to the president through Twitter. Trump's criticisms of the traditional institutional press from the campaign, where he regularly assaulted their perceived unfairness to him, his rhetoric, and his supporters, intensified in his first months in office. He and his spokespeople have co-opted the "fake news" trope that circulated as an explanation for how citizens were duped into voting for Trump by using the term to refer to any news that is not a glowing endorsement of the administration. On February 17, 2017, he reiterated his critique of the media by tweeting "The FAKE NEWS media (failing @nytimes, @NBCNews, @ABC, @CBS, @CNN) is not my enemy, it is the enemy of the American People!" Trump (probably unknowingly) echoes fascist rhetoric with this tweet: the Nazis were famous for asserting that media outlets unsupportive of Nazi goals were the "lügenpresse" (lying press) and characterizing the press as the "enemy of the people" was invoked by Hitler and Stalin.[67] The senior advisor to Donald Trump, Steve Bannon, is on record as saying that "the media should shut its mouth." For Bannon, the mainstream media are part of the establishment that he wants to destroy in a Leninist spirit.[68] As part of this assault on the press, Press Secretary Sean Spicer banned reporters from certain outlets, like CNN, the *New York Times*, Politico, and Buzzfeed, from an informal briefing on February 24, 2017.[69] Press outlets in the avowedly pro-Trump media circle were selected instead. Over the course of the first five months of the presidency, these trends have continued, with reporters prohibited from recording briefings or arbitrarily blacked out entirely.[70]

Journalists and columnists have expressed fear that Trump's use of Twitter to circulate outrageous claims will distract the public from the issues that truly matter. Lakoff, for example, routinely worries that Trump's tweets serve as "distraction[s]." For example, Lakoff argued Trump's tweets about Obama ordering surveillance of his campaign shifted journalistic attention from Trump's policy agenda into a faux scandal.[71] These concerns reflect the nature of short circuits of communication. At base, these public commenters worry about the public's lack of attention and inability to deliberate on issues of national concern. These commenters' disquiet stems from a concern that Trump's tweets will divert journalists and consumers of journalism from issues that really matter to the superfluous mix of conspiracy theory and victimage, thus undermining the possibility of deliberation on more important policy developments.

Our reading of Trump's use of Twitter, however, points to something different. As we have suggested in this chapter, as president, Trump's attempt to produce short circuits of communication increasingly fail to achieve desirable outcomes. One of the reasons for this is that the role of the journalist shifted after the election. As Nate Silver noted, journalists are increasingly specific and persistent, making "it more difficult to avoid sustained coverage of a single issue." In Silver's terms, the "stakes" are greater and "the media's incentives" have shifted in ways that reduce the prospect of distraction.[72] Our premise suggests the institution of the presidency is the gravitational force that raises the stakes. We contend that the presidency retains power over "secondary interest groups particularly attuned to presidential rhetoric,"[73] an observation that helps clarify the stakes and incentives faced by journalists during the Trump presidency. Seen from this vantage point, the combination of institutional layers of deliberation in the U.S. government (the Congress, agencies, the national security and intelligence apparatus) with the informal networks of deliberation constituted by the traditional press and newer internetworked intermediaries with a symbiotic relationship with the press (bloggers, vloggers, citizen Twitterers) insulates civic culture against the rhetorical surges that we now associate with Trump's use of Twitter.

At best, we see the strategy of marginalizing the press as how the Trump Administration envisions assembling a conservative governing coalition in the short term: demonize press critics and flood supporters with selective (mis)information. The microdiatribe is a key rhetorical form in this process, as it whips up enthusiasm among the conservative base and encourages over-reaction from the liberal base. At worst, this parallel conservative media ecosystem continues to be powered by short circuits of communication, by networks of outrage that burn bright and quick, by a desire to see some vague "system" come crashing down, by extremists that have outsized rhetorical cache in these almost hermetically sealed echo chambers where truthiness and alternative facts reign. In this scenario, the capacity of the United States' deliberative infrastructure slowly rusts, electrifying fascist impulses for an active segment of the population that embraces nostalgia, ethnonationalism, and militarism.

There is nothing unusual about a president attempting to change the conversation when things aren't going their way. But there is something unique about the form and speed with which Trump orchestrates such conversational maneuvers. While we remain unconvinced that Trump's presidential Twitter and short circuits of communication fully undermine deliberative practices, we are concerned that media organizations invested in the need to respond with a similar form and speed is at odds with creating longer circuits of deliberation. That is, rather than fear the chimera of distraction, perhaps the real danger is that the speed of the medium incentivizes publics to divest themselves of the role of monitoring and contesting the presidency and instead place a fuller faith in the supervisory possibilities of investigatory journalism.

Conclusion

Trump's use of Twitter has deeply impacted American political culture. As Will Bunch wrote, his tweets "have flooded the system and short-circuited the ability of our institutions such as the media, Congress and the courts to process it all in real time."[74] In our estimation, two reasons account for this short-circuiting of democratic processes. First, Trump's tweets make real the notion of "interruption." It is literally impossible to follow politics and not anticipate the likelihood that the president will use Twitter in a way that disrupts or interrupts the normal routines of the day. Given the state of US relations with Russia, North Korea, and Iran and the president's penchant for 280 character policymaking, presidential twitter has induced the nation into a semi-permanent fugue state of expecting the worst while grasping at institutional barriers for salvation. Second, each tweet is absurd and ridiculous and unable to withstand minimal scrutiny. But, like much of the microblogging genre, the addressivity of the Trump era is defined by affect, not logic, consistency, or evidence. His tweets represent his truths and, as such, they make an immediate impact. By the time fact-checking journalists muster the energy to respond, there's another tweet and another affective burst of inanity.

It remains to be seen, however, if the complex social media ecosystem that powered Trump to the presidency and serves as his preferred mechanism for reaching supporters will continue in the post-Trump era. Typically, subsequent aspirants mimic presidential innovations and the promise of the new strategy.[75] One only has to recall the rush by both parties to copy Obama's web strategy after his '08 victory to hypothesize that web savvy operatives in the Democratic Party are already at work to copy the essential components of Trump's social media strategy to produce a similarly situated imprint for the next Democratic candidate.

There are reasons to doubt the prospects for those efforts, however. Trump seems to be the ultimate exception to the rule. What we have identified in this essay—Trump's ability to fire off rapid bursts of charged political energy—are likely difficult to recreate because Trump's rhetoric reflects a political grammar unique to Trump. Violating the norms of presidential discourse is ingrained in his public persona and it is hard to see another candidate with an equal facility for managing a hyperengaged public. Mimicking a generic speech form—like the State of the Union—is a comparatively simple task. One merely examines the archive of prior speeches, identifies the form, and adapts the form to fit the president's ideological orientation. Mirroring a political grammar premised on racialized, gendered, religious, and national antagonisms, however, is a rather more difficult task and one that is antithetical to Democrats.

Rather than mirroring Trump's political grammar, future candidates will likely draw lessons from his melding of form and content to manage controversies that surround his presidency. As we have noted, Trump's use of Twitter embodies both speed and directness—it grants the appearance of addressivity while enacting an instantaneous form of public address. The appearance of addressivity affords the president the political cover to rely on Twitter when managing scandal. It seems likely that future presidents will mark the ways resorting to Twitter enables the president to retain tighter control over the message while avoiding the dynamism made possible by interaction with journalists. For this reason alone, Trump's presidency may signal a shift in presidential address away from more traditional forms of address—rallies, campus visits, and interviews with major news outlets—toward digital genres and forms (YouTube addresses, live streaming events, Twitter, Instagram, Reddit AMAs (Ask Me Anything) and others).

Presidential participation in these new genres and forms currently outstrips scholarly study of them. Scholars ought to navigate the polarities of seeing these new genres as a mere reformatting of old genres like the press conference or stump speech; similarly, scholars must avoid seeing these new genres as entirely new and unprecedented. We urge scholars to look beyond the ways presidents use Twitter and other forms of social media to circulate information about their agenda, to publicize events, pressure for votes, point to polling, etc. Instead, scholars of presidential rhetoric ought to see how these older genres are hybridized, with communicative affordances enabled by digital technologies changing the way in which the newer genres meet the civic needs of contemporary democracies. The study of a highly digital form of presidential address should recognize that genres of digitality hold the potential to deepen or curtail democratic culture, processes of deliberation, and the formation and maintenance of the presidential persona not only because of the content of the message, but because of the form in which the message appears.

Notes

1. Jennifer Stromer-Galley, *Presidential Campaigning in the Internet Age* (Oxford: Oxford University Press, 2014); Daniel Kreiss, *Taking Our Country Back: The Crafting of Networked Politics from Howard Dean to Barack Obama* (Oxford: Oxford University Press, 2012).
2. J. Kurr, "Going Digital: Rhetorical Strategies in the Enhanced State of the Union," in Anne Teresa Demo (ed), *Rhetoric Across Borders* (Anderson, SC: Parlor Press, 2015), 146.
3. Damien Smith Pfister, *Networked Media, Networked Rhetorics: Attention and Deliberation in the Early Blogosphere* (University Park, PA: The Pennsylvania State University Press, 2014), 5.
4. Some reporting indicates Dan Scavino, White House social media director, now writes some of Trump's tweets, either as drafts for the president or in published form. Our point remains, however, that authoring tweets represents a seismic shift away from writing speeches, requiring significantly less knowledge about issues, rhetoric, and decorum. See: Robert Draper, "The Man Behind the President's Tweets," *The New York Times* (April 16, 2018), https://www.nytimes.com/2018/04/16/magazine/dan-scavino-the-secretary-of-offense.html
5. For example, Franklin Delano Roosevelt did not commonly name his political opponents when going on the offensive; Mary E. Stuckey, *The Good Neighbor: Franklin D. Roosevelt and the Rhetoric of American Power* (East Lansing: Michigan State University Press, 2013), 134. Dwight D. Eisenhower stayed "above the fray" while deploying surrogates to go after the Democrats; Richard V. Damms, *The Eisenhower Presidency, 1953–1961* (New York: Routledge, 2014), 6. Richard Nixon employed Spiro Agnew to do his "dirty work." See: Yanek Mieczkowski, *The Routledge Historical Atlas of Presidential Elections* (New York: Routledge, 2001), 123. More recently, Barack Obama never attacked a political opponent with anything more than gentle attempts at humor. Obama's extended joke at the 2016 White House Correspondents' Dinner about his long form birth certificate is about as far as he went in ridiculing a political opponent; Joseph D. Lyons, "Obama's 'The Lion King' Birther Video Will Go Down As The Funniest Moment Of His Presidency," *Bustle* (April 28, 2016), https://www.bustle.com/articles/156927-obamas-the-lion-king-birther-video-will-go-down-as-the-funniest-moment-of-his-presidency
6. See, for example, Gracy Olmstead, "Trump's Twitter Presidency Is The One We All Deserve," *The Federalist* (June 8, 2017), http://thefederalist.com/2017/06/08/trumps-twitter-presidency-one-deserve/
7. Roderick P. Hart & Joshua M. Scacco, "Rhetorical Negotiation and the Presidential Press Conference," in Roderick P. Hart (ed.), *Communication and Language Analysis in the Public Sphere* (Hershey, PA: IGI Global, 2014), 59–80.
8. Twitter increased the character limit from 140 to 280 on November 7, 2017. The tweets referenced in this chapter all appeared prior to this change.
9. Presidential rhetoric, of course, exists for purposes other than fostering deliberation. Our intent here, however, is to highlight this particular feature of Trump's use of Twitter. It is likely that his use of Twitter violates other generic forms, frustrating both analysts and his communication staff.

10. Ronald Greene, "Rhetorical Pedagogy as a Postal System: Circulating Subjects through Michael Warner's 'Publics and Counterpublics,'" *Quarterly Journal of Speech* 88, no. 4 (2002): 437.

11. Greene, "Rhetorical Pedagogy as a Postal System," 438.

12. The presidency has an outsized capacity in this regard. On the connection between rhetoric and energy, see George A. Kennedy, "A Hoot in the Dark: The Evolution of General Rhetoric," *Philosophy & Rhetoric* 25, no. 1 (1992): 1–21; Debra Hawhee, "Toward a Bestial Rhetoric," *Philosophy & Rhetoric* 44, no. 1 (2011): 81–87; Carolyn Miller, "What Can Automation Tell Us About Agency?," *Rhetoric Society Quarterly* 37, no. 2 (2002): 137–157. In connecting rhetorical energies with the genre or Twitter, we are not trying to replicate the errors of what Brenton Malin calls "media physicalism," a media theory that presumes that media transmit certain emotions that can be detected through physiological measurement (which is then policed by social convention). See his *Feeling Mediated: A History of Media Technology and Emotion in America* (New York: NYU Press, 2014). Rather, we are arguing that we might see *networks* of communication as essentially reliant upon rhetorical energy for their formation and sustenance.

13. Editorial, "For Better of Worse, The Trump Twitter Presidency," *Chicago Tribune,* Jan. 6, 2017, http://www.chicagotribune.com/news/opinion/editorials/ct-trump-twitter-president-gm-ethics-house-edit-0106-jm-20170105-story.html

14. Our use of individuation here sublimates Stiegler's articulation of the role that the libidinal economy plays in individuation. Nonetheless, the term, especially as it is linked to rhetorical invention and implicated in the broader consumerist political economy, is useful in differentiating short and long circuits. See Bernard Stiegler, *The Re-enchantment of the World: The Value of Spirit against Industrial Populism* (London: Bloomsbury, 2014), 33–37 for a lucid discussion of individuation. See also Jon Carter's unpacking of the term in the context of memes in "Enchanting Memes: Memetic Politics in the Face of Technocratic Control." PhD diss., University of Nebraska-Lincoln, 2016.

15. As Martin Crowley suggests, "The proliferating differences of commercial product offer nothing but the same, short-term rhythm; repeated encounters with the same aesthetic object can, on the contrary, let us experience something different each time. And the long circuit of these encounters, reconnecting with and differing from the collective milieu, can sustain our existence;" in "The Artist and the Amateur, from Misery to Invention," *Stiegler and Technics*, 127.

16. David Sarno, "Jack Dorsey on the Twitter Ecosystem, Journalism and How to Reduce Reply Spam. Part II. *Los Angeles Times Technology Blog*, February 19, 2009, http://latimesblogs.latimes.com/ technology/2009/02/jack-dorsey-on.html.

17. Bernard Stiegler, *The Decadence of Industrial Democracies*, trans. Daniel Ross and Suzanne Arnold (Cambridge: Polity Press, 2011), 110.

18. Bernard Stiegler, *What Makes Life Worth Living: On Pharmacology*, trans. Daniel Ross (Cambridge: Polity Press, 2013), 30.

19. Stiegler, *What Makes Life Worth Living*, 62–4.

20. Brian Ott, "The Age of Twitter: Donald J. Trump and the Politics of Debasement," *Critical Studies in Media Communication*, 34, no. 1, (2017): 59–68. Ott notes that not all Twitter discourse falls into this category, yet, he lays blame for the debasement of public discourse on the genre's formal elements.

21. See "A Taxonomy of Tweets," *On the Media* (January 13, 2017), http://www.wnyc.org/story/taxonomy-trump-tweets/

22. George Lakoff, "Trump's Twitter Distraction," (Marcy 7, 2017), https://georgelakoff.com/2017/03/07/trumps-twitter-distraction/

23. Anthony McCosker and Amelia Johns, "Contested Publics: Racist Rants, Bystander Action and Social Media Acts of Citizenship," *Media International Australia* 151 (May 2014): 6672.

24. W. Lance Bennett & Alexandra Segerberg, *The Logic of Connective Action: Digital Media and the Personalization of Contentious Politics* (New York: Cambridge University Press, 2013).

25. McCosker and Johns, "Contested Publics," 68.

26. Emma A. Jane, "Flaming? What Flaming? The Pitfalls and Potentials of Researching Online Hostility," *Ethics and Information Technology* 17, no. 1 (2015): 65–87.

27. Anthony McCosker, "Trolling as Provocation: YouTube's Agonistic Publics," *Convergence: The International Journal of Research into New Media Technologies* 20, no. 2 (2014): 201–217.

28. We do not believe it appropriate to refer to Trump's mode of address as "trolling," as the term implies a dark sort of digital game and elides the seriousness with which we must take Trump's discourse. See: Whitney Phillips, "Donald Trump Is Not a Troll," *Slate* (June 23, 2016), http://www.slate.com/articles/technology/future_tense/2016/06/the_problems_with_calling_donald_trump_a_troll.html?wpsrc=sh_all_dt_tw_ru

29. See: Emily Cadei, "Why Third-Party Candidates Are Doomed—At Least This Year," *Newsweek* (June 1, 2016), http://www.newsweek.com/third-party-candidate-2016-465342

30. See Ryan Neville-Shepard's chapter in this volume.

31. Theodore Otto Windt, Jr., "The Diatribe: Last Resort for Protest," *Quarterly Journal of Speech* 58, no. 1 (1972): 1–14; see also R. L. Ivie, Enabling Democratic Dissent. *Quarterly Journal of Speech* 101, no. 1 (2015): 46–59.

32. Windt, "The Diatribe," 7.

33. Windt, "The Diatribe," 4.

34. David Beaver and Jason Stanley, "Unlike All Previous Presidents, Trump Almost Never Mentions Democratic Ideals," *Washington Post*, February 7, 2017, https://www.washingtonpost.com/news/monkey-cage/wp/2017/02/07/unlike-all-previous-u-s-presidents-trump-almost-never-mentions-democratic-ideals/?utm_term=.c1c2092dc0f8. Perhaps Trump's appointment of former Breitbart News editor Steve Bannon, a self-proclaimed Leninist who wants to "destroy the state," as a senior advisor best signals just how unconventional the Trump Administration has positioned itself as being. Ronald Radosh, "Steve Bannon, Trump's Top Guy, Told Me He Was a 'Leninist' Who Wants to 'Destroy the State,'" *The Daily Beast*, August 22, 2016, http://www.thedailybeast.com/articles/2016/08/22/steve-bannon-trump-s-top-guy-told-me-he-was-a-leninist.html.

35. See Damien Smith Pfister, "Ambient Intimacy in Salam Pax's *Where is Raed?*," in *Networked Media, Networked Rhetorics* (University Park, PA: Pennsylvania State University, 2014), 89–133 for an account of the diatribe in the context of blogging.

36. Windt, "The Diatribe," 8.

37. Windt, "The Diatribe," 8.

38. Roderick P. Hart and E. Johanna Hartelius, "The Political Sins of Jon Stewart," *Critical Studies in Media Communication* 24, no. 3 (2007): 264.

39. Windt, "The Diatribe," 8.

40. Windt, "The Diatribe," 9.

41. See: Paul E. Johnson, "Imagining American Democracy: The Rhetoric of New Conservative Populism." PhD (Doctor of Philosophy) thesis, University of Iowa, 2013; and, Caitlin Duffy, "Vilifying Obamacare: Conservative Tropes of Victimage in the 2009 Healthcare Debates." MA (Master of Arts) thesis, Wake Forest University Graduate School of Arts and Sciences, 2013.

42. Manuel Castells, *Networks of Outrage and Hope* (Cambridge: Polity Press, 2012). Trump's use of Twitter is a case study of conservative affective publics; see Zizi Papacharissi, *Affective Publics: Sentiment, Technology, and Politics* (Oxford: Oxford University Press, 2015).

43. Marykate Jasper, "This Focus-Group Prophet Predicted Trump's Twitter Meltdown After Watching the 'Presidential' Joint Address," *The Mary Sue* (March 4, 2017), http://www.themarysue.com/focus-group-predict-trump-twitter-meltdown/

44. Lisa Tolin, "President Trump and the 'Shock and Awe' Doctrine," *NBC News*, February 1, 2017, http://www.nbcnews.com/news/us-news/president-trump-shock-awe-doctrine-n714766.

45. Brouder & Brookey, 2015, p. 46; M. Brouder, & R. A. Brookey "Twitter and Television: Broadcast Ratings in the Web 2.0 Era," in J. V. Pavlik (Ed.), *Digital technology and the future of broadcasting: Global perspectives* (New York: Routledge, 2015), 45–59.

46. Tweets embedded in this story: Jeremy Diamond, "Spicer: Trump Didn't Mean Wiretapping when He Tweeted about Wiretapping," *CNN* (March 14, 2017), http://www.cnn.com/2017/03/13/politics/sean-spicer-donald-trump-wiretapping/

47. https://twitter.com/realDonaldTrump/status/837989835818287106

48. https://twitter.com/realDonaldTrump/status/837993273679560704

49. https://twitter.com/realDonaldTrump/status/837996746236182529

50. https://twitter.com/hankgreen/status/838053406057050112

51. https://twitter.com/Stepleton6/status/838066185010753536

52. https://twitter.com/MikeWalters19/status/838170752897679363. Grammar unchanged.

53. https://twitter.com/2Alpha/status/838235868703952896

54. https://twitter.com/WJFinlay/status/838111174923255808

55. Jeremy Diamond, "Spicer: Trump Didn't Mean Wiretapping when He Tweeted about Wiretapping," *CNN* (March 14, 2017), http://www.cnn.com/2017/03/13/politics/sean-spicer-donald-trump-wiretapping/

56. Jeffrey Edward Green, *The Eyes of the People: Democracy in an Age of Spectatorship* (New York: Oxford University Press, 2010), 196.

57. See: Jeremy Diamond, Jeff Zeleny, and Shimon Prokupecz, "Trump's Baseless Wiretap Claim," *CNN* (March 5, 2017), http://www.cnn.com/2017/03/04/politics/trump-obama-wiretap-tweet/; Peter Alexander, Kristin Donnelly, and Ali Vitali, "Source: Obama 'Rolled His Eyes' at Unsubstantiated Trump Wiretapping Claims," *NBC News* (March 9, 2017), http://www.nbcnews.com/politics/white-house/source-obama-rolled-his-eyes-unsubstantiated-trump-wiretapping-claims-n730721; and, David Remnick and Evan Osnos, "What to Make of Donald Trump's Early-Morning Wiretap Tweets," *The New Yorker* (March 4, 2017), http://www.newyorker.com/news/news-desk/what-to-make-of-donald-trumps-early-morning-wiretap-tweets

58. See: J. Kurr, "Going Digital: Rhetorical Strategies in the Enhanced State of the Union," in *Rhetoric Across Borders*, ed. Anne T. Demo (Anderson: SC, Parlor Press 2015), 146-158.

59. Rep. Bill Foster, http://www.sciencefriday.com/segments/theres-a-science-advocate-in-the-house-of-representatives/

60. Victor Pickard, "Media Failures in the Age of Trump," *The Political Economy of Communication* 4, no. 2 (2016): 118-122, http://polecom.org/index.php/polecom/article/viewFile/74/264; Darren Samuelsohn, "Trump's Twitter Army," *Politico* (June 15, 2016), http://www.politico.com/story/2016/06/trumps-twitter-army-224345; and, Thomas E. Patterson, "Pre-Primary News Coverage of the 2016 Presidential Race: Trump's Rise, Sanders' Emergence, Clinton's Struggle," (June 13, 2016), https://shorensteincenter.org/pre-primary-news-coverage-2016-trump-clinton-sanders/

61. Jodi Dean, "Communicative Capitalism: Circulation and the Foreclosure of Politics," *Cultural Politics* 1, no. 1 (2005), 51-74.

62. While not entirely pessimistic about the possibility that Trump's tweets can also connect to long circuits of communication and thus strengthen resistant energies, such possibilities remain outside the scope of the present inquiry.

63. Tim Wu, "How Donald Trump Wins by Losing," *New York Times* (March 3, 2017), https://mobile.nytimes.com/2017/03/03/opinion/sunday/how-donald-trump-wins-by-losing.html?smid=fb-share&_r=0&referer=http%3A%2F%2Fm.facebook.com%2F

64. One only has to ponder the logic that led a Trump supporter to storm a D.C. pizzeria to recognize the potential for overloads to end in tragedy. See: Faiz Siddiqui and Susan Svriuga, "N.C. Man Told Police He Went to D.C. Pizzeria with Gun to Investigate Conspiracy Theory," *Washington Post* (December 5, 2016), https://www.washingtonpost.com/news/local/wp/2016/12/04/d-c-police-respond-to-report-of-a-man-with-a-gun-at-comet-ping-pong-restaurant/?utm_term=.d3d660b6c0ec

65. Charles Sykes, "Why Nobody Cares the President Is Lying, *The New York Times*, February 4, 2017, https://www.nytimes.com/2017/02/04/opinion/sunday/why-nobody-cares-the-president-is-lying.html?_r=0.

66. Robert McChesney, *The Problem of the Media* (New York: Monthly Review Press, 2004).

67. Veronika Bondarenko, "Trump's new *favorite phrase*—'Enemy of the People,'—Has a Very Ugly History," *Business Insider*, February 28, 2017, http://www.businessinsider.com/history-of-president-trumps-phrase-an-enemy-of-the-people-2017-2

68. John Cassidy, "Steve Bannon's War on the Press," *The New Yorker*, January 27, 2017, http://www.newyorker.com/news/john-cassidy/steve-bannons-war-on-the-press

69. Paul Farhi, "CNN, New York Times, Other Media Barred from White House Briefing," *The Washington Post*, February 24, 2017, https://www.washingtonpost.com/lifestyle/style/cnn-new-york-times-other-media-barred-from-white-house-briefing/2017/02/24/4c22f542-fad5-11e6-be05-1a3817ac21a5_story.html

70. See: Julie Hirschfeld Davis, "Trump Bars U.S. Press, but Not Russia's, at Meeting With Russian Officials," *New York Times* (May 10, 2017), https://www.nytimes.com/2017/05/10/us/politics/trump-russia-meeting-american-reporters-blocked.html; and, Scott Bixby, "President Trump's White House Media Blackout Has Reporters Talking Mutiny," *The Daily Beast* (June 19, 2017), http://www.thedailybeast.com/president-trumps-white-house-media-blackout-has-reporters-talking-mutiny

71. George Lakoff, "Trump's Twitter Distraction," (Marcy 7, 2017), https://georgelakoff. com/2017/03/07/trumps-twitter-distraction/. See also: Paul Farhi, "Were Trump's 'Hamilton' Tweets 'Weapons of Mass Distraction'?" *Washington Post* (November 21, 2016), https://www.washingtonpost.com/lifestyle/style/were-trumps-hamilton-tweets-weapons-of-mass-distraction/2016/11/21/4367dfda-af8a-11e6-8616-52b15787add0_story. html?utm_term=.3a33ba7c42d1; Richard Wolffe, "Out of Control? Or is Trump's Tweeting Designed to Distract?" *The Guardian* (March 4, 2017), https://www.theguardian.com/us-news/2017/mar/04/donald-trump-tweeting-designed-to-distract-russia-obama

72. Nate Silver, "What Makes A Trump Story Stick: Specificity—and a lot of Persistence," *FiveThirtyEight* (February 15, 2017), https://fivethirtyeight.com/features/what-makes-a-trump-story-stick/

73. Stephen J. Heidt, "Presidency as Pastiche: Atomization, Circulation, and Rhetorical Instability", *Rhetoric & Public Affairs* 15, no. 4 (2012): 630.

74. Will Bunch, "The Week Trump Went Full Dictator and No One Tried to Stop Him," *The Inquirer, Daily News, philly.com* (June 3, 2018), http://www.philly.com/philly/columnists/will_bunch/trump-is-becoming-a-dictator-pardons-lies-obstruction-of-justice-20180603.html

75. Bethany Anne Conway, Kate Kenski, and Di Wang, "Twitter Use by Presidential Primary Candidates During the 2012 Campaign," *American Behavioral Scientist* 57, no. 11 (2013): 1596-1610.

CHAPTER NINE

Pioneers, Prophets, and Profligates

George W. Bush's Presidential Interaction with Science

LEAH CECCARELLI

The "March for Science" in Washington D.C., and over 150 other cities in April 2017 was organized by scientists and their allies to protest against "the mischaracterization of science" by Donald Trump's presidential administration.[1] They had reason to be concerned. Before he was elected, Trump publicly identified climate change as a Chinese hoax, and linked vaccines to autism, despite the overwhelming scientific consensus that climate change is real and vaccines do not cause autism.[2] Vice President Mike Pence is a believer in intelligent design creationism and has said it should be taught alongside evolution in public schools, to the consternation of the vast majority of American scientists.[3] Mick Mulvaney, Trump's pick for budget director, questioned the fully established link between Zika virus and microcephaly and said he wondered whether "we really need government-funded research at all," an alarming question for scientists who rely on federal research grants, especially considering Mulvaney's role in setting funding priorities for the new administration.[4]

When Michael Lubell, Director of Public Affairs for the American Physical Society, stated immediately after the election that "Trump will be the first antiscience president we have ever had," he expressed the anxiety that many scientists felt at the time.[5] However, while the prospect of a post-truth presidency in an era of alternative facts sent chills down the spines of scientists and friends of science alike, Lubell was wrong; this is not the first time a presidential administration has been "anti-science." The same charge was leveled against President George W. Bush. Since scrutiny of a precursor can sometimes help us build knowledge about the more developed stage of something, examination of the 43rd president's troubling interactions with science can prepare us for future efforts to understand the 45th president's charged relations with science. As this chapter will demonstrate, the anti-science rhetoric adopted by George W. Bush broke new ground in American presidential public address, preparing the way for the arguably even more anti-science presidency of Donald Trump. A study of the way in which a long-standing American presidential tradition that celebrated science and its practitioners was transformed into a rhetoric of skepticism and even antagonism toward science and scientists can help us identify the starting point for a subsequent presidency that seems to even more enthusiastically embrace the "death of expertise."[6]

In February 2004, the Union of Concerned Scientists released a report that detailed the many ways in which the authority of science in federal policymaking had reached what they saw as a historical nadir during George W. Bush's first term of office. They concluded that "the scope and scale of the manipulation, suppression, and misrepresentation of science by the Bush administration is unprecedented."[7] An accompanying statement condemned the administration for undermining the scientific advisory system. Signed by more than 15,000 scientists over the course of the president's second term of office, the statement called on the U.S. government to restore scientific integrity to federal policy making.[8] As one of the scientists responsible for these documents put it, the administration was exhibiting a dangerously "cavalier attitude towards science."[9]

Journalist Ron Suskind confirmed the existence of such an attitude when he reported that a senior adviser to President George W. Bush told him that those who valued empiricism were living in what the administration dismissively labeled "the reality-based community." People who "believe that solutions emerge from your judicious study of discernible reality" are living in the past, according to the White House insider.

> That's not the way the world really works anymore. We're an empire now, and when we act, we create our own reality. And while you're studying that reality—judiciously, as you will—we'll act again, creating other new realities, which you can study too, and that's how things will sort out. We're history's actors ... and you, all of you, will be left to just study what we do.[10]

Historian David Greenberg maintains that this braggadocio perfectly encapsulates President Bush's contempt for scientific expertise, an attitude that was

> one of the more significant and all-encompassing features of his administration. ... As never before, administration officials and their allies in politics and the news media

openly disregarded the empirically grounded evidence, open-minded inquiry, and expert authority that had long underpinned governmental policymaking.[11]

Observers of George W. Bush's presidency perceived this "assault on reason" as a significant break from tradition.[12] So it came to pass that Bush was cast as the first anti-science president of the nation.

The denigration of scientific authority as a ground for decision-making by the Bush administration has been thoroughly documented, so there is no need to belabor the point.[13] What has not yet been documented, though, is the degree to which that anti-science attitude was present in the administration's public address. There are at least two reasons we might expect disregard for scientific expertise to be less evident in Bush's speeches than in his ideological and patronage-driven committee appointments and policy decisions. First, the cognitive authority of science in Western culture remained strong when Bush took office. Not long before Bush became president, sociologist of science Thomas Gieryn claimed that in the public eye, science "stands metonymically for credibility, for legitimate knowledge, for reliable and useful predictions, for a trustable reality: it commands assent in public debate."[14] This authoritative ethos is why Bush administration officials were loath to dismiss science in their public pronouncements, forcing them to make their Machiavellian sneers about the earnest research efforts of the "reality-based community" only in backstage, off-the-record remarks. In *public* discourse, an alignment with the authority of science, with what "the research says" about an issue, is the sort of appeal that Americans still expected to hear from their opinion leaders when Bush took office.[15] Second, the cultural authority of science has long carried a special weight in American presidential discourse. As I have established elsewhere, almost every American president since Calvin Coolidge gave speeches in which they invested American scientists with a nationalistic American spirit, attributing the greatness of the nation at least partially to the brilliance and dedication of its researchers who conquer new knowledge territory to lead us forward toward a brighter future.[16] In light of this patriotic performative tradition that conventionally praised scientists as carriers of American greatness, George W. Bush's presidential rhetoric was unlikely to suddenly and radically veer from the norm by adopting an explicitly anti-science posture. A rhetorical transformation of the ethos of the scientist in American presidential rhetoric, from hero to fool to enemy, had to be carefully cultivated. As will become clear, a number of George W. Bush's speeches were designed to subtly effect that transition.

Because of the cognitive and cultural authority of science in American presidential rhetoric prior to his presidency, the signs of George W. Bush's adversarial relationship with science in his public speeches could not be too obvious. A focused rhetorical reading can identify less obvious signs of such an attitude, though, revealing the subtle moves that prepared the soil for the more explicit attacks on science to follow in a subsequent Republican administration that made its dismissive and antagonistic orientation toward science so overt that it sparked a protest from scientists not at the end of its term, but at the beginning. In this chapter, I look at how scientists are treated in George W. Bush's public address to illuminate an antecedent to a later, even more antagonistic and dangerous interaction between the American presidency and science.

In the interest of understanding how a presidential administration hostile to the authority of science rhetorically constructs the persona of the scientist in its public pronouncements, I have examined a number of speeches delivered by George W. Bush during his two terms of office, with a focus on speeches that are about science or that involve science-related policy issues. A rhetorical reading of these texts reveals that the 43rd President of the United States charted a complicated view of the authority of science in his public address. Sometimes he enacted the conventional presidential performative tradition, celebrating scientists as the embodiment of America's pioneering spirit; however, he offered a twist on this tradition by describing them also as prophets. At other times, he characterized scientists as plagued with uncertainty while engaged in debate and supposition over complex matters; he thus called the authority of science into question. And at yet other times, he identified scientists as immoral agents who must be constrained from taking America down a dark and dangerous path. Mapping the ethos of scientists as represented in George W. Bush's presidential speeches, assessing those portrayals, and contrasting them with how other recent presidents have depicted scientists in similar speeches, I outline the rhetorical contours of the fraught relationship between Bush and the scientific community as it appears in his public address. His rhetorical transformation of scientists from pioneers to false prophets and profligates set the stage for the next Republican administration's broad dismissal of expertise and commitment to severely reducing federal funding for scientific research.[17]

Scientists as Pioneers and Prophets

The most positive treatment of the ethos of scientists in Bush's public address is found in epideictic speeches that he delivered to audiences made up primarily of scientists. The occasion of the awarding of the National Medals of Science and Technology is a recurring opportunity for presidents to praise scientists as the embodiment of American values, and George W. Bush performed this ritual with the same frequency as other recent presidents.[18] Significantly, in fulfilling this ceremonial role, he evoked a familiar pioneer ethos for scientists that aligned them with American values and attributed the nation's endless economic growth to their efforts. For example, in 2005, he gave a speech celebrating the frontier spirit of scientists, noting especially their courage and fortitude.

> Over the centuries, the same passion for discovery that drove Lewis and Clark to the Pacific has also led bold Americans to master the miracle of flight, to conquer dread diseases, and explore the frontiers of space ... I am proud to recognize a diverse and deserving group of American citizens, what we call pioneers.[19]

Twelve years before, Bill Clinton identified the scientists he feted in the same way, as "the dreamers, the pioneers, the risk takers ... the new scouts in our timeless urge for adventure."[20] George H. W. Bush offered the same description of the Medals of Science and Technology winners he honored. They are "pioneers" who are carrying out "a pioneering heritage"; these "trailblazers of today" are "our true pioneers," embodying the values of devotion in the face of danger and perseverance in the face of adversity and pain.[21] All three presidents drew explicitly on Vannevar Bush's argument that America's investment in these modern pioneers supports the exploration and development of an endless frontier of science that promises everlasting economic returns to the nation.[22] It is not at all surprising to hear this kind of rhetoric used by Americans to describe scientists; in fact, there are so many examples of it that one could write a whole book on the subject.[23]

What *is* unusual about George W. Bush's characterization of scientists in his National Medals of Science and Technology speeches is that in four of the six speeches he gave on these occasions, he suggested that scientists were not only pioneers, but prophets as well. The most striking example was in his first such speech in 2002: "Our honorees are the prophets of a better age, seeing the future before a lot of folks don't see the present."[24] The flub at the end of this sentence is an authentic Bushism, awkward and confused. But the "prophets of a better age" phrase at the beginning of the sentence has an unexpected touch of eloquence to it. Scientists are being depicted as having the ability to communicate with the divine to foresee the future. In addition, they are either doing so in an era that is better than the one in which the old prophets lived, or they are prophesizing a better age to come.[25] Both interpretations mark them as improvements in some way upon the prophets of old. Although Bush did not use the specific term "prophets" again in later Medals of Science and Technology speeches, he did call scientists "some of the most gifted and visionary men and women in America," or used some variation of that phrase, in three of the other speeches he gave on these occasions.[26] As far as I can tell, no other president has used the words "prophets" or "gifted and visionary" to describe scientists in these speeches. The only one who came close is

George H. W. Bush, who once described the scientists he was honoring as having "persistent and, at times, clairvoyant determination."[27] But the connotative chasm between a clairvoyant and a prophet points to what is unique about the younger Bush's characterization of scientists. It is bound up with his religious worldview.[28]

The metaphor identifying scientists with prophets may be atypical in these speeches, but it is not a novel idea. The rhetoric of science literature has long recognized a pseudo-religious ethos lurking in public communication about science.[29] But it does seem to be an odd way of talking about scientists if you are a deeply religious person and you are waging a Republican war on science. Those who have a cavalier or dismissive attitude toward prophets do so at their own peril. Equating scientists with prophets and then ignoring their advice would seem to be setting the stage for tragedy. But surely Bush was not using this analogy to prophesize his own tragic downfall.

The puzzle of this language choice becomes even deeper as we examine the characterizations of scientists that George W. Bush offers in his other speeches. As rhetoric of science scholar Lynda Walsh explains in her book *Scientists as Prophets*, the prophetic ethos is embraced by scientists and their supporters in the public sphere because it "manufactures political certainty in times of crisis."[30] But as I will show in the next section of this chapter, the 43rd president's characterization of scientists in speeches about climate change did just the opposite—he portrayed scientists in a way that manufactured *uncertainty* in the public sphere. And as I will also show in the third section of this chapter, George W. Bush's treatment of scientists in speeches about stem cell research and human cloning depicted them as anything but "prophets of a better age"; instead, they were represented as so lacking in the visionary insight of religious inspiration that they will drag the nation headlong to a dystopian future if not restrained from doing so. The apparent conflict between the prophet persona George W. Bush creates for scientists in his epideictic speeches and the befuddled or morally deficient personae he creates for them in his policy speeches raises a question about how his public rhetoric of science coheres across his public address. It is a puzzle that can be resolved with a new understanding of the role of the scientist-as-prophet metaphor in his speeches.

Scientists as Uncertain

A review of George W. Bush's speeches on climate change reveals the first clear presence of an anti-science attitude in his public address, even as the speeches are designed to offer plausible deniability that he is trying to weaken the authority of science. For example, in his first major presidential speech on global climate change, on the eve of a trip to Europe where he was going to have to defend his recent decision to reject the Kyoto treaty on carbon emissions, Bush began by admitting that "we know the surface of the Earth is warming" and "the National Academy of Sciences indicates that the increase is due in large part to human activity."[31] Rather than the speech of someone who denies the scientific consensus on climate change, this opening appears to introduce a leader who is listening to his science advisors.

However, these concessions are immediately followed by a lengthy discussion of "what is not known on the science of climate change." Scientists are described as "offering a wide spectrum of views," and offering "many theories and suppositions." An anaphora repeating the phrase "we do not know" sets out three things the National Academy of Sciences cannot say about climate change, including the degree to which warming is a result of natural fluctuations rather than human activity, and the amount as well as the speed of change. This passage ends with the reminder that "no one can say with any certainty" what level of warming is dangerous, a statement that is repeated later in the speech. In addition, the word "scientific" only appears in the speech as an adjective before the word "uncertainties." If one were to sketch an image of what scientists are from how they are portrayed in this speech, it would be a gaggle of people plagued by doubt and failures of knowledge.

At the same time, the speech was designed so that George W. Bush could deny that he was trying to undermine the credibility of science. After all, his initial concession that global warming is real, and that greenhouse gases have something to do with it, aligned him with the consensus of the scientific community. Also, it would be hard to pin an anti-science charge on someone who ended his speech with a pledge to invest in science. Here was a president promising to support science, literally, with federal dollars. Indeed, newspapers reported on the speech with dueling headlines. Some led with a claim that Bush acknowledged the connection between man-made emissions and global warming, and insisted that he was vowing to fight the environmental catastrophe by committing more funding to scientific research.[32] Others framed the speech as being about the president's doubts regarding the cause and significance of global warming; such reports critiqued the airing of that doubt and the call for more research, calling it a delaying strategy.[33] The fact that both readings could be supported by the text suggests that at least for the former group, Bush might have successfully masked the fact that he was seeking to undermine the authority of science to justify a wait and see attitude, even while exposing audiences to a narrative that cast scientists as hopelessly uncertain.

The claim that Bush's emphasis on scientific uncertainty was a rhetorical strategy to delay policy action is supported by the observation that his treatment of science in this speech neatly fits the advice that political consultant Frank Luntz was giving to Republicans around that time. Luntz argued that Republican politicians should take advantage of the voters' belief "that there is no consensus about global warming within the scientific community," even though there really was. By continuing "to make the lack of scientific certainty a primary issue in the debate," and thus exploiting this "window of opportunity to challenge the science," Republicans could delay regulatory action on carbon emissions.[34] Bush's first major presidential speech on global climate change could have served as a model for how to apply Luntz's advice.

Later speeches on climate change by George W. Bush built upon this portrayal of science as untrustworthy. For example, in a February 2002 speech, Bush claimed that the administration's approach to climate change will harness "the creativity of entrepreneurs, and draw upon the best scientific research." One wonders why scientific research needs to be qualified as "best" (implying a "worst" science to avoid), while entrepreneurs are not so qualified. Apparently, the fact that the entrepreneurs are best goes without saying. The term "sound science" also appears in this speech, twice, to again imply a dissociation between best and worst science. The speech goes on to stress "scientific uncertainties," and science is described as both "complex" and lacking in definitive answers.[35]

As a point of contrast, consider a speech given by President George H. W. Bush ten years earlier, when he was about to depart for a United Nations Conference on Environment and Development and was similarly expected to defend his decision to not support an international environmental treaty. The speech given by the elder Bush did not portray science as uncertain or potentially untrustworthy. Although both presidents believed that environmentalist concerns should not outweigh economic considerations, the first President Bush did not destabilize the science to tip the scales between the two. In his speech, the modifier "sound" is connected only to action, not to science (implying that some *actions* might be unsound, but not the science used to support them). The only modifier that appears before the word "science" is "U.S.," and what follows is the phrase "the most advanced in the world."[36] As with his son's later presidential epideictic speeches about scientists, science was celebrated as a national treasure rather than undermined as uncertain or unreliable.

Returning to the puzzle I introduced earlier, we might now have an explanation for why George W. Bush's National Medals of Science and Technology speeches identified scientists as not only pioneers but also as prophets. The term "false pioneer" does not have an obvious referent, but the term "false prophet" does. It is at least possible that George W. Bush identified scientists as prophets so that he could imply a dissociation between sound science that receives an award from the president and unsound science that offers false prophesies, say, about the dire consequence of global warming. The true prophet is a visionary who is certain about what God has revealed; uncertainty in a prophet or disputes among prophets are signs that we are in the presence of false prophesy. If scientists are identified with prophets, then uncertainty and dispute among scientists suggests that we are in the presence of unsound science, a false prophesy that should not be used to guide policy decisions. In other words, the scientist-as-prophet metaphor rhetorically creates a space for audiences to demarcate sound science from unsound science; the scientist-as-pioneer metaphor does not.

Of course, another way of thinking about a false prophet is to see him or her as being in league with the devil. This alternative was suggested in George W. Bush's speeches on stem cell research and human cloning.

Scientist as Immoral

The president's nationally televised August 2001 speech about stem cell research used what rhetorician of science John Lynch describes as a Manichean idiom, setting science against morality.[37] This was most clearly established in a part of the speech where Bush voiced the arguments of both sides of the issue, pitting a "researcher" against a religiously-minded "ethicist."[38] While the structure of this *dissoi logoi* section of the speech might suggest balance to some, since it offers equally earnest arguments from both sides, the fact that each imagined exchange ends with the voice of the ethicist suggests that Bush was not trying to evenly build up the legitimacy of both sides.[39] Instead, this appears to be a prolepsis to explain why the president opposes this research. For our purposes, it is important to note that the arguments on the ethicist's side are both ad hominem attacks on scientists. In these exchanges, scientists were judged to be making "a callous attempt at rationalization" and as wanting to unjustly begin "experimenting on" a living being or "exploiting it as a natural resource." Scientists thus came out of the debate having been branded with the unsavory character traits of being uncaring and selfish.

In the next section of the speech, Bush further established the questionable character of scientists when he argued that modern scientific discoveries "lay vast ethical minefields." This metaphor aligned the actions of scientists with the deliberate placement of hidden and deadly explosives.[40] The speech then suggests that "the genius of science" is responsible for dragging us into a dystopian science fiction future.

> We have arrived at that brave new world that seemed so distant in 1932, when Aldous Huxley wrote about human beings created in test tubes in what he called a "hatchery."

In recent weeks, we learned that scientists have created human embryos in test tubes solely to experiment on them.

These actions of scientists are troubling, but even worse activities are being contemplated, according to Bush.

Scientists have already cloned a sheep. Researchers are telling us the next step could be to clone human beings to create individual designer stem cells, essentially to grow another you, to be available in case you need another heart or lung or liver.

This incrementum of moral transgressions reached a climax when the president concluded that most Americans "recoil at the idea of growing human beings for spare body parts or creating life for our convenience." Scientists though, apparently do not recoil at this idea. They are presented as attempting to do those very things. They belong to "a culture that devalues life," according to Bush, a culture that made him worry. So he decided to set out a policy that would keep them from "crossing a fundamental moral line." Scientists might have "intellect" and "capabilities," but they need the "heart" and "conscience" of religiously-oriented ethicists to restrain them.

One might wonder how this characterization of the terrible and awesome power of scientists who have made science fiction nightmares into a reality meshes with the uncertain, unknowledgeable scientists of Bush's climate change speeches. But it turns out that the two characterizations are not entirely incompatible. The word "scientists" appears several times in this first stem cell speech as the subject of a sentence. In most cases, it is attached to the word "believe" or some variation of that word (such as "feel") as scientists are portrayed as offering predictions about the promise of stem cell research. Early in the speech, Bush made it clear that scientists "admit they are not yet certain," and late in the speech, he reminded the audience that "eight years ago, scientists believed fetal tissue research offered great hope for cures and treatments, yet the progress to date has not lived up to its initial expectations." There is some room here for the image of the scientist as an incompetent false prophet, even as the image of the scientist as an immoral actor with fierce intellect and capabilities dominates the rest of the speech to fashion the frightful prophet of a worse age.

The fact that many people interpreted the speech as walking an even-handed middle line between scientists and their critics is evidence once again of the administration's ability to offer plausible deniability that they were adopting an anti-science stance.[41] As I discuss elsewhere, the stylistic form of the speech helps to create this illusion, with its pattern of equal time devoted to each side and its pleasantly balanced phrasing suggesting that its policy proposal is a fair response to both those who favor the research and those who oppose it.[42] Also, his promise to vigorously fund a narrow strip of this research that he considered morally acceptable made it seem as if he were supporting science materially, with an infusion of financial resources. But his very characterization of the debate as a conflict between scientists and ethicists, and the characterization of scientists within that debate as immoral agents seeking to create and use living beings for their own convenience, suggests that the speech was, on a deeper level, another part of the Bush administration's war on science. As insider David Frum put it, the speech was a rhetorical "masterstroke," presenting the president's "not at all middle-of-the-road position" in a way that "not only protected but actually expanded his image as a moderate."[43]

Depictions of scientists as immoral were also offered in a speech that George W. Bush gave the next year on human cloning. "Human cloning has moved from science fiction into science," he announced. He told the audience of this speech about scientists who produced "embryonic human clones for research purposes," who combined "human DNA and rabbit eggs," and who "announced plans to produce cloned children, despite the fact that laboratory cloning of animals has led to spontaneous abortions and terrible, terrible abnormalities." This litany of moral crimes committed by scientists paints them as frightening characters. "Science now presses forward the issue of human cloning," according to Bush, but since the president is guided by human conscience, he would press back. "Allowing cloning would be taking a significant step toward a society in which human beings are grown for spare body parts and children are engineered to custom specifications, and that's not acceptable." Scientists must be restrained. So human cloning must be banned. Once again, the scientists in this speech are dangerously lacking in compassion; they are the sort of people who see children as "products to be designed and manufactured," rather than "gifts to be loved and protected."[44] In contrast, the president, who is a moral and religious man, stands against them.

That this is not the only way for a president to take a stand against cloning is demonstrated by looking again at the public address of another recent president making a similar argument. In early 1998, President Bill Clinton banned the use of federal funds for human cloning and called on Congress to adopt a ban on human cloning itself. But in the speeches he gave explaining his position, he did not pit scientists against religiously-oriented ethicists or represent himself as constraining a dangerously immoral scientific community. Instead, he characterized the scientists and moral leaders as united. As he put it in his 1998 State of the Union Address, "we must ratify the ethical consensus of the scientific and religious communities and ban the cloning of human beings."[45] That scientific and religious communities could be united against particular kinds of research is unimaginable in the younger Bush's speeches, but perfectly natural in Clinton's.

In a weekly radio address, Clinton set out the problem by indicating the moral transgression of "a member of the scientific community"—not of scientists in general, but of a single scientist. Clinton then assured his audience that "there is virtually unanimous consensus in the scientific and medical communities that attempting to use these cloning techniques to actually clone a human being is untested and unsafe and morally unacceptable." Evidently, scientists in Clinton's world can engage in both scientific and moral reasoning, and come to a reasonable moral conclusion. Clinton's policy was presented as something that the scientific community was itself seeking, a way to restrain rogue scientists who "ignore the consensus of their colleagues and proceed without regard for our common values."[46] The scientific community and the government were thus characterized as sharing the same principles and seeking the same end.

Another speech that Clinton gave the following month to the American Association for the Advancement of Science took the issue even further. After repeating the point from his radio address about the scientific community recognizing cloning as morally unacceptable, he made an argument that explicitly countered the image of scientists as mad geniuses who will be responsible for a dystopic future. Introducing an optimistic depiction of the future written by Benjamin Franklin, Clinton said that it was much preferable to contemporary dystopic movies in which we see "a world where science has run amok or where the community and government have withered away." Clinton insisted that neither he nor the scientists in his audience "believe that's what it's going to be like." Rather than use a frightening image of the future to argue for restraints on science, he insisted to scientists themselves that "we need never run away from the dangers of our work run amok … we must never for a moment be afraid of the future."[47] This identification strategy, using the words "we" and "our," unites the president and scientists, rather than creating an antagonistic relationship between them. Both are portrayed as having an optimistic belief in the future of science, and both act in a morally responsible way.

Conclusion

Much still remains to be studied regarding the epistemic and cultural authority of science in George W. Bush's public address. For example, how did he negotiate the competing interests of his two base constituencies, the theoconservatives who distrusted science for religious reasons and the economic conservatives who looked to science for investment opportunities and technological solutions? Were the figures of the prophet and the pioneer meant to reach out to each of these constituencies in turn? Did the president's portrayal of climate scientists as uncertain and unknowledgeable, or stem cell scientists as morally-challenged prophets of a worse age, have an effect on how Americans came to think about scientists? After the Union of Concerned Scientists published their statement, were presidential speeches written to better conceal the administration's anti-science stance?

Those are all questions for another time. For now, we can draw a few preliminary conclusions about the way George W. Bush portrayed scientists in his public address. Although he embraced the conventional treatment of scientists as American pioneers who carry the national character traits of courage and determination, he also depicted them as lacking another American character trait, namely, a religiously-inspired morality. Although he portrayed scientists as uncertain and lacking in knowledge, he also portrayed them as the most gifted and visionary men and women in America, and as both intelligent and competent. That these characterizations are not all compatible with each other is proof that the persona of the scientist in George W. Bush's speeches morphed to fit the need of each situation. When the subject was the greatness of American heroes, scientists were pioneers and prophets who embodied all that is good about the nation. When the subject was inconvenient science that indicated the need for costly restraints on energy consumption, scientists were portrayed as uncertain. And when the subject was promising new science that compromised the president's pro-life position, scientists were portrayed as immoral and in need of restraint. In the latter two cases, a carefully balanced rhetorical style and the promise to fund science allowed the president to claim that he was a friend to science, not an adversary trying to undermine its authority. But his characterization of scientists in those speeches belied this claim, and the fact that his treatment of scientists changed so radically from one situation to another aligns with the claim of the Union of Concerned Scientists that the Bush administration manipulated, suppressed, and misrepresented science to suit its political needs.

The fact that other presidents were able to make some of the same arguments against international environmental regulations that would harm the U.S. economy and against human cloning, *without attacking science*, suggests that the George W. Bush administration's efforts to undermine the authority of science were not politically necessary. Instead, they likely reflected an attitude that the president and many other contemporary Americans have, an attitude that is skeptical or downright dismissive of science. Alternatively, they reflected a calculated political strategy that he adopted to align with the common sense of his Middle American base against the egghead experts who were voicing inconvenient truths and challenging his suitability for the office of the presidency.[48] Looking for signs of both the attitude and the strategy, and their concealment in American presidential address, could help those of us in the "reality-based community" expose, and insofar as we can, begin working to counter such efforts. In light of the Trump administration's subsequent adoption of some of the same attitudes and strategies, to respond to a parallel situation, we should look to see if scientists end up being characterized in Trump's presidential speeches as not only pioneers, but also false prophets and profligates in need of constraint, or if other personae emerge in this new presidency's charged interactions with science. If the Bush administration set the stage for an anti-science American presidency, what narratives does the Trump administration play out on that stage, and what new characters does he introduce to challenge the authority of science? In the 21st century American presidency, there's been a break in how Republican administrations portray science and relate to the authority of scientific expertise. Understanding the rhetorical dynamics of that break might help those of us who march with science plan effective counter-narratives and counter-characterizations in the years to come.

Notes

1. "March for Science," https://www.marchforscience.com/, accessed 28 February 2017; Lindzi Wessel, "Updated: Which Science Groups Have Endorsed the March for Science?," *Science*, 28 February 2017, http://www.sciencemag.org/news/2017/02/will-they-or-won-t-they-what-science-groups-are-saying-about-joining-march-science.

2. Donald J. Trump, Twitter post, 6 November 2012, 11:15 a.m., https://twitter.com/realdonaldtrump/status/265895292191248385?lang=en; Donald J. Trump, Twitter post, 28 March 2014, 5:35 a.m., https://twitter.com/realDonaldTrump/status/449525268529815552. See also Christopher A. Sanford and Paul S. Pottinger, "Trump's Reckless Linkage of Vaccines and Autism," *The Seattle Times*, 2 January 2017; and Edward Wong, "Trump Has Called Climate Change a Chinese Hoax. Beijing Says It Is Anything But," *New York Times*, 18 November 2016.

3. Shaena Montanari, "VP-Elect Mike Pence Does Not Accept Evolution: Here's Why That Matters," *Forbes*, 10 November 2016; Alex Kasprak, "Does Mike Pence Believe in Evolution?," *Snopes*, 13 November 2016, http://www.snopes.com/2016/11/13/mike-pence-evolution/.

4. Alex Kasprak, "Appropriation Negation," *Snopes*, 20 December 2016, http://www.snopes.com/trumps-budget-director-pick-asked-really-need-government-funded-research/.

5. Jeff Tollefson, Lauren Morello, and Sara Reardon, "Donald Trump's US Election Win Stuns Scientists," *Nature News*, 9 November 2016.

6. Tom Nichols, *The Death of Expertise: The Campaign against Established Knowledge and Why It Matters* (New York: Oxford University Press, 2017).

7. Union of Concerned Scientists, *Scientific Integrity in Policymaking: An Investigation into the Bush Administration's Misuse of Science* (Cambridge, MA: Union of Concerned Scientists, February 2004), 1–2.

8. Union of Concerned Scientists, "2004 Scientist Statement on Restoring Scientific Integrity to Federal Policy Making," http://www.ucsusa.org/scientific_integrity/abuses_of_science/scientists-sign-on-statement.html.

9. Kurt Gottfried, quoted in James Glanz, "Scientists Say Administration Distorts Facts: Accusations Include Suppressing Reports and Stacking Committees," New York Times, 19 February 2004, A18.

10. Ron Suskind, "Without a Doubt," New York Times Magazine, October 17, 2004, p. 51. It is widely acknowledged that the senior advisor in question was Karl Rove. See David Greenberg, "Creating Their Own Reality: The Bush Administration and Expertise in a Polarized Age," in The Presidency of George W. Bush: A First Historical Assessment, ed. Julian E. Zelizer (Princeton, NJ: Princeton University Press, 2010), 199–226; and Mark Danner, "Words in a Time of War: On Rhetoric, Truth, and Power," in What Orwell Didn't Know: Propaganda and the New Face of American Politics, ed. András Szántó (New York: PublicAffairs, 2007), 16–36.

11. Greenberg, "Creating," 200.

12. Al Gore, The Assault on Reason (New York: Penguin Press, 2007).

13. In addition to the February 2004 report of the Union of Concerned Scientists and the Greenberg essay cited above, see Union of Concerned Scientists, Scientific Integrity in Policy Making: Further Investigation of the Bush Administration's Misuse of Science (Cambridge, MA: Union of Concerned Scientists, July 2004); and Chris Mooney, The Republican War on Science (New York: Basic Books, 2005).

14. Thomas F. Gieryn, Cultural Boundaries of Science: Credibility on the Line (Chicago: University of Chicago Press, 1999), 1.

15. Robert Asen, Deb Gurke, Ryan Solomon, Pamela Conners and Elsa Gumm, "'The Research Says': Definitions and Uses of a Key Policy Term in Federal Law and Local School Board Deliberations," Argumentation and Advocacy 47, no. 4 (2011): 195–213.

16. Leah Ceccarelli, On the Frontier of Science: An American Rhetoric of Exploration and Exploitation (East Lansing: Michigan State University Press, 2013), 111–121.

17. At the time this chapter was being written, President Trump's 2018 budget request had just been released with deep cuts to federal funding of basic scientific research; see "Science Gets Little Love in Trump Spending Plan: 2018 Proposal Calls for Deep Cuts at Research Agencies, But Congress Will Need to Agree," Science 356, no. 6340 (26 May 2017): 795.

18. However, one sign of his uncomfortable relationship with science is that outside of the National Medals of Science and Technology ceremonies, he chose not to give many speeches to scientists. Presidents George H. W. Bush, Bill Clinton, and Barack Obama all gave speeches before the National Academy of Sciences (the latter two giving two speeches each to this advisory body), and both the elder Bush and Bill Clinton gave speeches before the American Association for the Advancement of Science. George W. Bush never spoke to either group.

19. George W. Bush, "Remarks on Presenting the National Medals of Science and Technology," March 14, 2005, online by Gerhard Peters and John T. Woolley, The American Presidency Project, http://www.presidency.ucsb.edu/ws/?pid=73682.

20. William J. Clinton, "Remarks on Presenting the National Medals of Science and Technology," September 30, 1993, online by Gerhard Peters and John T. Woolley, The American Presidency Project, http://www.presidency.ucsb.edu/ws/?pid=47137.

21. George H. W. Bush, "Remarks at the Presentation Ceremony for the National Medals of Science and Technology," October 18, 1989, online by Gerhard Peters and John T. Woolley, *The American Presidency Project*, http://www.presidency.ucsb.edu/ws/?pid=17667.

22. George H. W. Bush, "Remarks at the Presentation Ceremony for the National Medals of Science and Technology," November 13, 1990, online by Gerhard Peters and John T. Woolley, *The American Presidency Project*, http://www.presidency.ucsb.edu/ws/?pid=19028; William J. Clinton, "Remarks on Presenting the National Medals of Science and Technology," April 27, 1999, online by Gerhard Peters and John T. Woolley, *The American Presidency Project*, http://www.presidency.ucsb.edu/ws/?pid=57470; George W. Bush, "Remarks on Presenting the National Medals of Science and Technology," June 12, 2002, online by Gerhard Peters and John T. Woolley, *The American Presidency Project*, http://www.presidency.ucsb.edu/ws/?pid=65017. For Vannevar Bush's argument, see, *Science: The Endless Frontier* (Washington, D.C.: United States Government Printing Office, 1945).

23. Ceccarelli, *On the Frontier of Science.*

24. G. W. Bush, "Remarks," June 12, 2002

25. A Google search turns up a possible origin for this phrase. In 1843, Orestes Augustus Brownson identified scholars as "prophets of a better age" in "The Scholar's Mission: An Oration Pronounced Before the Gamma Sigma Society, of Dartmouth College, Hanover, N.H., July 27, 1843," in *The Works of Orestes A. Brownson: Literary Criticisms*, edited by Henry F. Brownson (Detroit: Thorndike Nourse, 1885), 83. There is also an entry in the memoir of Margaret Fuller dated October 1842 that uses the phrase "prophet of a better age" to eulogize the Unitarian preacher, Dr. William Ellery Channing, *Memoirs of Margaret Fuller Ossoli, Volume 2* (Boston: Phillips, Sampson & Co., 1852), 70.

26. George W. Bush: "Remarks on Presenting the National Medals of Science and Technology," November 6, 2003, online by Gerhard Peters and John T. Woolley, *The American Presidency Project*, http://www.presidency.ucsb.edu/ws/?pid=64596; see also George W. Bush: "Remarks on Presenting the National Medals of Science and Technology," February 13, 2006, online by Gerhard Peters and John T. Woolley, *The American Presidency Project*, http://www.presidency.ucsb.edu/ws/?pid=65320; George W. Bush: "Remarks on Presenting the 2007 National Medals of Science and Technology and Innovation," September 29, 2008, online by Gerhard Peters and John T. Woolley, *The American Presidency Project*, http://www.presidency.ucsb.edu/ws/?pid=84484.

27. George H. W. Bush, "Remarks at the Presentation Ceremony for the National Medal of Science and the National Medal of Technology," June 23, 1992, online by Gerhard Peters and John T. Woolley, *The American Presidency Project*, http://www.presidency.ucsb.edu/ws/?pid=21132.

28. For studies of the influence of religion on George W. Bush's rhetoric, see Martin J. Medhurst, "George W. Bush, Public Faith, and the Culture War over Same-Sex Marriage," in *The Prospect of Presidential Rhetoric*, eds. James Arnt Aune and Martin J. Medhurst (Texas: Texas A&M University Press, 2008), 209-237; Robert E. Denton, Jr., "George W. Bush and Religion: Faith, Policy, and Rhetoric," in *The George W. Bush Presidency: A Rhetorical Perspective*, ed. Robert E. Denton Jr. (Lanham, MD: Lexington Books, 2012), 157-172.

29. See Thomas M. Lessl's oeuvre, beginning with "Science and the Sacred Cosmos: The Ideological Rhetoric of Carl Sagan," *Quarterly Journal of Speech* 71, no. 2 (1985): 175-187.

30. Lynda Walsh, *Scientists as Prophets: A Rhetorical Genealogy* (New York: Oxford University Press, 2013), ix.

31. George W. Bush, "Remarks on Global Climate Change," June 11, 2001, online by Gerhard Peters and John T. Woolley, *The American Presidency Project*, http://www.presidency.ucsb.edu/ws/?pid=45985.

32. David L. Green, "Bush Vows to Fight Global Warming," *Baltimore Sun*, June 12, 2001, 1A; Ann McFeatters, "Bush Admits Big U.S. Role in Global Heat," *Pittsburgh Post-Gazette*, June 12, 2001, A3; John J. Fialka, "Bush Says Global-Warming Pact is Flawed," *Wall Street Journal*, June 12, 2001, A2.

33. Mike Allen and Eric Pianin, "Bush Voices Doubt on Global Warming Causes," *Washington Post*, June 12, 2001, A1; Andrew Revkin, "Warming Threat Requires Action Now, Scientists Say," *New York Times*, June 12, 2001, A12.

34. Frank Luntz, "The Environment: A Cleaner, Safer, Healthier America," The Luntz Research Companies—Straight Talk, n.d., http://www.ewg.org/files/LuntzResearch_environment.pdf. Elsewhere, I have established that this memo was likely written between November 2001 and November 2002, so I am not claiming that it was the cause of the strategy in this speech. I am only suggesting that it was the same strategy. See Leah Ceccarelli, "Manufactured Scientific Controversy: Science, Rhetoric, and Public Debate," *Rhetoric & Public Affairs* 14, no. 2 (2011): 195–128.

35. George W. Bush, "Remarks Announcing the Clear Skies and Global Climate Change Initiatives in Silver Spring, Maryland," February 14, 2002, online by Gerhard Peters and John T. Woolley, *The American Presidency Project*. http://www.presidency.ucsb.edu/ws/?pid=73200.

36. George H. W. Bush, "Remarks on Departure for the United Nations Conference on Environment and Development," June 11, 1992, online by Gerhard Peters and John T. Woolley, *The American Presidency Project*, http://www.presidency.ucsb.edu/ws/?pid=21070.

37. John Lynch, *What Are Stem Cells? Definitions at the Intersection of Science and Politics* (Tuscaloosa: University of Alabama Press, 2011), 124, 144.

38. George W. Bush, "Address to the Nation on Stem Cell Research," August 9, 2001, online by Gerhard Peters and John T. Woolley, *The American Presidency Project*, http://www.presidency.ucsb.edu/ws/?pid=63209. All further quotations in this paragraph and the next two come from this speech.

39. Also note that after the first exchange, he adopted the language used by the ethicist (embryo) rather than the language used by the researcher (pre-embryo), suggesting that he had been persuaded by the ethicist's argument.

40. In the summer of 2001, people in America were just becoming aware of the horrors of unexploded mines in former war zones. In that context, the land mine metaphor might have connotatively aligned scientists with the gruesome deaths of innocent children. See Ceccarelli, *On the Frontier of Science*, 125.

41. See, for example, "Principled Balance," *Atlantic Journal and Constitution*, August 13, 2001, A8; "Splitting the Embryo," *Wall Street Journal*, August 13, 2001, A12; Richard Lacayo, "How Bush Got There," *Time*, August 12, 2001, http://content.time.com/time/magazine/article/0,9171,170839,00.html.

42. Ceccarelli, *On the Frontier of Science*, 127–133.

43. David Frum, *The Right Man: The Surprise Presidency of George W. Bush* (New York: Random House, 2003), 110.

44. George W. Bush, "Remarks on Human Cloning Prohibition Legislation," April 10, 2002, online by Gerhard Peters and John T. Woolley, *The American Presidency Project*, http://www.presidency.ucsb.edu/ws/?pid=65029.

45. William J. Clinton, "Address Before a Joint Session of the Congress on the State of the Union," January 27, 1998, online by Gerhard Peters and John T. Woolley, *The American Presidency Project*, http://www.presidency.ucsb.edu/ws/?pid=56280.

46. William J. Clinton, "The President's Radio Address," January 10, 1998, online by Gerhard Peters and John T. Woolley, *The American Presidency Project*, http://www.presidency.ucsb.edu/ws/?pid=55669.

47. William J. Clinton, "Remarks to the American Association for the Advancement of Science in Philadelphia, Pennsylvania," February 13, 1998, online by Gerhard Peters and John T. Woolley, *The American Presidency Project*, http://www.presidency.ucsb.edu/ws/?pid=55474.

48. John Murphy's response to my presentation of a previous version of this essay at the 2014 Public Address conference clarified how Bush's attacks on the authority of science utilized a "conservative, plain folks style" that made him the voice of "real Americans"; this voice of "common sense" connected the Republican president to his Middle American base, in what "has been the most electorally effective language of contemporary conservatism." Given the subsequent rhetorical style of President Trump, whose common sense anti-intellectualism appeals to the "forgotten men and women" of the American heartland, Murphy's point seems especially insightful.

CHAPTER TEN

Negotiating the Limits of a Multiparty Democracy

Michelle Bachelet's Rhetoric of Commitment

BELINDA A. STILLION SOUTHARD

Days before Chilean citizens cast their final vote in the 2013 presidential election, candidate Michelle Bachelet addressed more than twenty-five thousand supporters in anticipation of her re-election.[1] Putting forth a vision of her presidency, she said, "You know me, I don't make promises, I make commitments." She added, to build the nation "you need the commitment of each of us. Are we ready? Are we committed?"[2] And commit she did. After taking the oath in 2014, Bachelet manufactured the passage of a bill that significantly increased taxes on corporations, bankrolling massive education reform. This is notable because in Chilé, the president's ability to effect policy change is particularly constrained. In a multiparty democracy, the president is the leader of the coalition of parties that they represent. In short, since Chilé became a democracy in 1990, policy changes have been the result of consensus politics. In 2005, Chilé's constitution was amended to place greater limits on presidential power to rid its vestiges of dictatorial politics and to curb the increasingly exclusionary processes of consensus politics, especially those of Bachelet's coalition, *Concertación*. The same year, Chileans elected Bachelet president, hoping she would make good on her promises to include disenfranchised groups in policymaking processes. She left her term a remarkably popular yet fairly ineffective president. Barred from consecutive terms by a new constitutional amendment, she returned four years later, in 2013, with her sights set on a second presidential term.

Bachelet's rhetorical situation demanded that she reckon with the ineffectiveness of her first term, the constraints of the presidency, the need to negotiate the tensions between the strength of consensus politics and her desire for a people's government, and the reality that government agencies design and implement most change. In light of those constraints, Bachelet deployed a rhetoric of commitment to position herself as an agent of change, but one whose agency is bound by committed relationships between and among her, the people, her government, and her policy agenda. Bachelet generated the perception that she is a committed and effective leader, but strategically distributed the work of political change across state and civilian actors, linking policy outcomes to collective, rather than individual, action.

The motivation for this study goes beyond its appeal of its subject matter: the first woman president of Chilé, one democratically elected (the most difficult way for a woman to come to office), and one who survived political persecution. Examining Bachelet's rhetoric helps rhetorical scholars of the presidency understand how presidents negotiate the constraints of a multiparty democracy, a young constitution, and their previous political performance. To the point, Bachelet's rhetoric provides a case study for how presidents can simultaneously center and decenter themselves as agents of inevitable change. Specifically, she constructed herself as committed to the Chilean people, who in turn, must commit to her. She positioned Chilean voters as committed actors, whose votes commit them to Chilé, situating the people as committed authors of the nation's policy agenda. She posited the State as a committed agent who must implement the people's policy agenda. And last, she argued that her government program contracted the people and the State to carry out change.

To make this case, it's necessary to explain why and how to study the rhetoric of non-US presidents. Rhetorical critics must navigate language barriers, availability of and accessibility to archives, and the ethics of translation. Following a discussion of method, a sketch of Bachelet's life and context sets up her rhetorical situation as one in which a rhetoric of commitment offered her strategic solutions. Then, an analysis of campaign, victory, and policy texts reveals that she defined commitment as constitutive of a relationship between and among multiple actors—relationships that ensured the fulfillment of her promises.

Why Study Non-U.S. Presidential Rhetoric?

Studying Bachelet's rhetoric allows scholars of presidential rhetoric to expand upon their assumptions of what constitutes executive leadership and to understand how presidents can negotiate competing demands of coalitional politics and democratic practice. Bachelet's rhetoric represents at least two understudied content areas: non-U.S. presidential rhetoric and women's presidential rhetoric. With a few exceptions, our field's robust studies of presidential rhetoric center on U.S. discourse.[3] This is understandable and even expected as we seek to understand our nation's political philosophies, commitments, and failures. On a more practical note, many non-U.S. and women presidents do not deliver speeches in English, which presents an obstacle I will address later in the chapter. Most studies of non-U.S. and women presidents come from scholars of political science, comparative politics, and feminist politics. Rhetoricians are well positioned to augment these studies by examining how the rhetoric of non-U.S. and women presidents can shape national and global politics and negotiate different political realities.

Additionally, an increasingly transnational world compels scholars to resist viewing discourses through nationalist lenses. As national boundaries become increasingly flexible and porous, so too are the rhetorics that have sustained and fortified those boundaries.[4] Moreover, as scholars of nationalism and citizenship concur, the nation can no longer be considered an isomorphic unit of power.[5] Presidents and presidential rhetoric are not bound by national contexts. Studying non-U.S. presidents sheds light into how the U.S. president's rhetorical context is shaped by factors abroad, can add to understandings to the inevitable diplomatic interactions of presidents, and can point to the universal power of rhetorical strategies of invention. Yet, I argue that studies of the presidency, like nationalism and citizenship, cannot and should not solely focus on the president of the United States. No doubt, non-U.S. political and presidential discourses have received scholarly attention, as have the ways in which globalism and transnationalism have challenged the U.S. presidency.[6] But most studies examine these discourses in relationship to U.S. institutions and discourses. An examination of Bachelet's rhetoric prods us to ask if it is enough to study non-U.S. presidents without seeking or yielding contributions to what we know about the U.S. presidency.

Next, as scholars committed to making sense of our immediate and enduring contexts, we must pay attention to the direct, democratic election of women presidents. Currently, this is an overlooked global phenomenon.[7] Today, twenty women serve as the elected presidents or prime ministers of their nations.[8] Since 1953, forty-three women across thirty-four nations have served as president on either an interim or a full-term basis.[9] Longitudinal studies show that many women assumed national leadership positions through familial association or appointment by parties in power. More recently, however, women lead as the result of direct democratic election—the most difficult way for a woman to come to office.[10] While this case study does not overtly attend to the gendered contexts or contours of her rhetoric, it does shed light on how Bachelet's gendered identity shaped her governing goals, strategies, and rhetoric of commitment.

To point, women who are elected president typically do so within extraordinary rhetorical situations. Political scientists attribute the recent uptick in the direct democratic election of women presidents to "unusual times."[11] These unusual times often create political openings and opportunities for women previously unavailable to them. These times include an antiestablishment climate, as in the case of Michelle Bachelet's 2005 and 2013 elections in Chilé; party turmoil and unification, as in the case of Angela Merkel's 2005 and 2013 elections in Germany; and post-conflict nation-building, as in the case of Ellen Johnson Sirleaf's 2005 and 2011 elections in Liberia. People perceive these women as symbols of national change and assurances that the nation will transition from unusual to usual times. Moreover, these presidents are often expected to effect positive change for women and minority groups since, typically, large constituents of women elect women presidents to secure freedom from cultures of male domination.[12]

More than telling us more about presidencies in understudied contexts, this case study can also help scholars of presidential rhetoric understand how a president of a multiparty democracy negotiates the demands for efficient governing and for deeper democratic practice. While democratically-elected presidents have always had to negotiate the realities of legislative and executive politics and the ideals of an engaged, participatory citizenry, presidents of coalitional governments face a particularly acute version of this tension. The parties that make up a coalition typically align for electoral power, to secure seats within legislative bodies. However, parties do not necessarily have to align in terms of their policy agenda. But, as Eduardo Alemán and Sebastián M. Saiegh argue, "in multiparty presidential systems[,] stable legislative coalitions play a vital role in providing effective government."[13] As leaders of their coalition, presidents are often engaged in consensus-building among party and coalition leaders. Often this "cross-party communication" enables "informal negotiations" among political elites, which limits if not excludes citizen engagement in policymaking.[14] This was the case in Chilé. In 2005, Bachelet was elected as an outsider to these elite circles who promised to democratize policymaking. By 2013, the *Concertación* had dissolved, positioning Bachelet as a president who must negotiate the exigencies of heightened demands for citizen engagement and the breakdown of consensus within her coalition.

How to Study Non-US Presidential Rhetoric

Analyzing the rhetoric of non-US presidents presents some methodological and practical challenges. In short, scholars must authenticate texts prior to analyzing them.[15] Robert N. Gaines calls for rhetorical studies scholars to select and justify a "composition-text" as "a concrete exemplar of the text that may serve as the basis for a refined text suited to scholarly purposes."[16] It is incumbent upon scholars to recognize that no version or translation of a text is complete, true, or absolute (translation, as one scholar put it, is "an infinite task"), and so they must do their best to immerse readers into the rhetorical contexts of speakers and texts and to acknowledge the limits and losses of translated material.[17] Gaines argues, "Text authentication is a critical endeavor," and selections of composition-texts is "based on the authenticator's judgment of what constitutes an appropriate text to examine."[18] Because these "judgments may be open to question," he says, "Every selection of a composition-text must be based on a rationale."[19] When analyzing speeches delivered in English or speeches already translated into English, for example, scholars must cite the sources of their texts and acknowledge the risks in trusting a particular source and text. It might very well be the case that a presidential speech found on a president's web site is an edited and/or translated version that a president's administration intends for the public to consume, rather than a transcription of the president's exact words when delivered in real time. If the scholar's goal is to better understand how a president and/or their administration wanted the public to perceive the president, then perhaps the version on the web site is a more ideal composition-text than the one transcribed from a recording of its delivery.

When analyzing speeches not delivered in English, scholars have a few options. If the scholar speaks and reads the language fluently, then scholars may provide their own translations. This was the case in a recently published article on Angela Merkel's rhetoric.[20] Editors and readers are asked to trust the translations. If this is an accepted practice, then we can hope that scholars fluent in the languages of presidents will conduct more analyses.

What to do if scholars do not speak, read, or write in the language of our subjects? Attending to the ethics of translation is paramount. As Sandra Bermann reminds us,

> [L]anguage remains radically contingent upon specific local histories and contexts. Cultural practices produce and sustain—and are in turn sustained by—the lexicon and syntax of a given language. Highly particularized cultural markers must therefore be taken into account in any linguistic interpretations.[21]

It follows then, that scholars of interpretation and translation warn sharply against the exclusive use of automatic online translation mechanisms (i.e., Google Translate). Their translations are often so literal that they lose internal context and coherence.

Next, a scholar can seek out and hire a translator with whom they can work closely, as I did. Ideally, a translator is a native speaker of the language and/or scholar or student of translation (my translator was both). Scholars and translators can engage in an ongoing dialogue about the project's goals, the translator's findings, cultural and rhetorical inflections, and so on. One potential limit to through this process is that it may produce a composition-text that bears the imprint of a scholar's intent. Consciously or unconsciously, the translator may bend to the will of the project. However, if we acknowledge this risk, we can appreciate the translated text as one generated to be as coherent and culturally sensitive as possible.

Finally, these translation processes present cost and time constraints. Paying for translators may be prohibitive to many scholars, especially in a climate of shrinking budgets. Many research grants won't even accept proposals to cover translation costs. Securing money and engaging in the translation processes also take time. If a scholar works within the constraints of the proverbial tenure clock, for example, then pursuing a project that requires translated texts may be less than ideal.

Bachelet's Life and Context

Bachelet lived under Augusto Pinochet's dictatorship during the first couple decades of her adult life. In 1973, Pinochet overthrew Chilé's socialist government and replaced civilian rule with a military junta. Pinochet's dictatorship was marked by massive human rights violations, with which Bachelet was quite familiar. Her father worked under President Salvador Allende, Pinochet's predecessor, and was kidnapped and tortured for months until he died of cardiac arrest. Two years later, Bachelet and her mother were blindfolded, kidnapped, and taken to detention centers, where they were subject to interrogation, torture, and rape.[22] Eventually, Bachelet was granted exile to Australia. Shortly thereafter, she moved to Germany where she completed a medical degree.

In 1979, Bachelet was able to return to Chilé. Her medical credentials were denied, prompting her to repeat her medical studies. Over the next decade, she worked for multiple children's hospitals and organizations, focused especially on helping children orphaned by Pinochet's junta. Simultaneously, Pinochet's Constitution, passed in 1980 via plebiscite, facilitated incremental shifts away from dictatorial rule toward the restoration of democracy. Losing re-election in 1987, Pinochet stepped down, which created an opening for the election of Chilé's first democratic president since the coup.[23] While Chilé's government slowly worked to restore democratic practices and the inclusion of those who suffered under Pinochet's rule, a large portion of Chileans remained loyal to Pinochet. Amidst these political tensions, Bachelet worked for the Ministry of Health and then studied civil-military relations and military strategy in the United States and in Chilé, earning her a position in Chilé's Ministry of Defense.[24]

In 2000, President Ricardo Lagos appointed her Minister of Health. She was soon recognized for dramatically increasing access to Chilé's public health system and for making the morning-after pill widely available.[25] In 2002, Lagos appointed her as Minister of National Defense, the first woman to serve the post—a post thought to be key to her presidential bid. She is credited with bringing Chilé into regional and international political relations, reconciling relationships with former Pinochet junta members, and for leading a rescue mission after a flood in Santiago. Regarding the mission, many argue that images of her donning camouflage and khaki clothing, riding in a tank, and walking through muddied landscape solidified the perception of her as a strong national leader.[26]

In 2005, during her first presidential campaign, Bachelet ran on her credentials as a former Minister of Health and Minister of Defense.[27] She also argued that because of her experiences as a tortured woman and as a single working mother, she was intimately familiar with the needs of the Chilean people, especially women and the poor. In interviews, she recalled how she tended to the wounds of brutalized women in her cell.[28] She attributed these experiences to motivating her to become a pediatrician and to care for orphaned children.[29] She also drew upon her experiences as a struggling mother of three children to identify with women and the working classes.[30] Many argued that this helped curb criticism of her as an agnostic in a Catholic nation and a single woman with children from two different fathers, one of whom she never married.[31] Bachelet's popularity is also attributed to a political climate in which Chileans had grown wary of a *Concertación* elite. Bachelet positioned herself as "an 'outsider' and an anti-establishment leader" who was "invested more in the nation than in petty party concerns, and willing to promote a more horizontal way of doing politics."[32] This "horizontal way" meant the inclusion of citizens' voices in the formation of public policy.

Upon winning her first presidential election, she needed to lead a multi-party representative democracy only fifteen years out from a brutal dictatorship. Moreover, she was elected the same year Chilé's constitution was amended to purge the remaining measures that ensured the inclusion of Pinochet's party members. By 2005, Bachelet's *Concertación* coalition, had gained enough Senate seats to control the Senate altogether, effectively replacing the former Pinochet Senate seats. In order to keep *Concertación* from becoming an authoritarian block in legislative politics, the 2005 constitutional amendments placed a one-term limit on the presidency and repealed provisions that gave lifetime Senate seats to former presidents, as well as the power of the majority party to appoint senators and control the appointments of Supreme Court justices, military commanders, and

Constitutional Tribunal.[33] Bachelet championed these reforms as necessary steps toward deepening Chilé's democracy.

Bachelet needed to negotiate these new limits on government power, her position as an outsider, the leader of an institutionally elite coalition, and she needed to make good on her promise to make Chilé a participatory democracy.[34] Regarding the latter, she appointed equal numbers of men and women to her cabinet ministry posts.[35] She required ministries and public services to create "special commissions," mechanisms by which citizens were included in the "formulation, execution and evaluation" of public policies. Moreover, she pushed for the formation of civil society organizations to work with ministries on policy formation.[36] Bachelet's rhetorical leadership has been described as "transformative," one that stressed participation and citizen engagement.[37]

Within the first year of her presidency, however, she learned that policy change came slow and her promises to effect quick change fell under scrutiny. Pressure to keep promises to reform pension and to make education affordable compelled her to replace some new female ministers with more experienced, male ones. Gregory Weeks and Silvia Borzutzky argue that the "special commissions," consisting of large, diverse groups of citizens, resulted in very few legislative changes.[38] They observe that she gradually left her ministers responsible for policy change while she performed duties as a head of state more so than a head of government.[39]

Nonetheless, she left her first presidential term with an 84 percent approval rating.[40] Many argue that Bachelet led the people as a feminine and motherly figure who worked to restore the health of the nation and deepen its dedication to an inclusive democracy.[41] This may explain why her critics assailed her leadership as a *cariñocracia* or "love-ocracy, in which she led with affection for the people more so than with a commitment to social justice."[42] This may also explain why her approval rating was so high and why the approval of the Chilean government was abysmal, hovering somewhere between 30–38 percent.[43] Aldo C. Vacs argues that this disparity is owed to Bachelet's conflicting efforts to create "a more efficient *concertacionista* (institutional-administration) direction," which relies upon consensus among political elites, and "a more effective *gobierno ciudadano* (popular participation) approach."[44] Due to the constitutional limit of one presidential term, Bachelet could not run for re-election immediately. Because of the increasingly negative perception of *Concertación* and political gridlock, the coalition lost the next presidential election.

Bachelet left Chilé to serve as the first Executive Director of United Nations Women. In the meantime, Chilé's president, Sebastián Piñera, earned a reputation for ignoring the heightened demands of the people. In April 2013, amidst rumors of her return to run for the presidency, Bachelet resigned from UN Women.[45]

Later that year, she won the presidential election with a narrower margin than her first. Her win is attributed to her promise to end education for profit, motivating students to vote in Chilé's first election with voluntary voting.

Bachelet's Rhetoric of Commitment

Selection and Translation of Texts

I examine public addresses and documents dated between October and December 2013, just before and after her second presidential election. These texts include a campaign speech, her victory speech, and two documents that outline her policy agenda and program for her presidency.[46] This collection of texts is the result of practical and critical concerns. Motivated to study the rhetoric of women presidents, I applied for and received seed grant money from my academic department. Because Bachelet's speeches are not posted in English, I sought out and hired a translator. Owing to time and cost constraints, I selected ten texts for translation.

I was struck by Bachelet's victory speech, in which she employed anaphora, beginning multiple, successive sentences with the same statement, "I commit."[47] A search for more uses of the verb, "to commit," and the noun, "commitment," suggested their significance to Bachelet's rhetorical leadership, in both frequency and intensity. This prompted a return to the archive of Bachelet's speeches delivered toward the end of her second presidential campaign and in her formal policy proposals (in Spanish), resulting in a new selection of texts to be translated for analysis.

The campaign and victory speeches were translated in full and in the policy documents, Bachelet's "Government Program" and "50 Commitments for the First 100 Days of Office," paragraphs were translated if they contained the noun, "commitment" (*compromiso*) or any verbal conjugation of "to commit" (*compromete*); or verbal conjugations such as "I commit" or "we commit" (e.g., *me comprometo, nos comprometemos*), "I am committed," "I should commit," and "I have committed" (e.g., *estoy comprometido, debo comprometerme, se han comprometido*). Of particular interest was the title of the "50 Commitments" ("50 *Compromisos*") document. In the document, she frequently refers to the measures ("*medidas*") she committed to making. Unlike the document's title, its .pdf title is "50medidasMB," which suggests that "measures" and "commitments" are similar if not synonymous concepts in the textual context of laying out policy proposals. The analysis, then, explores how Bachelet deployed a rhetoric of commitment. In brief, how and to what effect did Bachelet commit to commitments?

Analysis: Committed to the Commitments of the People and the State

In light of Bachelet's context, a rhetoric of commitment was expedient. During her first presidency, she was not nearly as effective an administrator as she promised to be. While she is credited with reforming tax codes and pension laws, she is noted for ignoring the groundswell of student protests. Her successor failed to adequately respond to protests, so when she ran in 2013, Bachelet fashioned a campaign that vowed to make education affordable. In short, she capitalized on "commitment" as two things: as a relationship between two actors and a relationship that ensures success. These rhetorical functions are similar to those Lyndon B. Johnson employed in his "We Shall Overcome" address. Garth E. Pauley argues that Johnson's use of the "American promise" invoked two meanings of "promise" as:

> [R]eferring to the nation's vow and its potential. Both senses of the word imply a story. Though making a vow is a stand-alone act, it beckons further action: The vow must be kept or broken. Having potential is a state of being but also signals future action: The potential must be fulfilled or neglected.[48]

To be sure, "commitment" refers to a vow or promise, which also implies future action. So how is a rhetoric of commitment different from a rhetoric of promise? To Bachelet, a commitment requires shared if not compulsory action. When Bachelet discusses commitments to things and actions, she conscripts at least two actors into a committed relationship. Her rhetoric of commitment constitutes multiple and often interrelated relationships between and among herself, the Chilean people, state agencies, and her policy agenda. To Bachelet, these relationships ensure the fulfillment of commitments, uphold her dedication to inclusion, and attend to the constraints of her power.

While Bachelet did not shy away from asserting, "I commit" in the present tense, she invoked commitment as shared tasks that enlisted two dedicated actors. One of her key strategies, for example, was to position Chileans as already engaged actors whose previous and ongoing commitment compelled Bachelet to commit. The shift in agency justified her second mandate as originating not from personal ambition but rather as a response to popular incitement. In other words, Bachelet's statement, "I commit," can be read as her *response to* popular pressure, as an acceptance of the burden of leadership, and as her willingness to lead pre-existing social and political movements for policy change. This rhetoric construed a committed relationship between the people and the state, insofar as the commitment of the people necessitated the resources and energies of her state actors and agencies. Finally, she framed her policy documents as contracts—or commitments—that tethered the state and Chilean people to the policy's implementation. Altogether, these strategies constructed her as an active change agent whose devotion compelled and supported the commitments of Chileans, the state, and policy. These strategies also helped create the perception that, despite the administrative constraints on her power, she could lead by consensus, include Chileans in governance, and successfully implement her proposed changes.

To begin, Bachelet contrasted "commitments" to "promises," which positioned her as an agent of change whose commitment enlisted the Chilean people as participants in that change. As mentioned before, one of Bachelet's campaign speeches boldly proclaimed: "You know me, I don't make promises, I make commitments."[49] To Bachelet, promises and commitments were different things. She continued: "We don't have magic recipes! But you know that, together, we will be able to keep these commitments. This task is not only for one president. It is also not for a party or a group of parties, nor for a political sector. It is a task for an entire nation."[50] Within this textual context, "promises" are aligned with "magic recipes," or perhaps, quick fixes. "Commitments," then, can be inferred to mean something more substantive, such as a complex set of "tasks" that are time-consuming and require a pragmatic approach to complete. This passage is also illustrative of how Bachelet's rhetoric of commitment positioned herself as a leader of substantive change while it also decentered herself as an agent that completed these tasks. They were to be shared among party members, coalitions, and the people.

Bachelet's rhetoric of commitment also constituted a relationship between herself and Chileans as fellow citizens dedicated to change.[51] Bachelet employed anaphora to craft a rhetoric of unity, a rhetoric that de-emphasized her role as a leader and emphasized her part in fulfilling a common destiny shared by all Chileans. The repetition of "I commit," however, was preceded by the repetition of "It's time." To Bachelet, it was time to "fight inequality together," to "believe in us again," to believe "that happiness of a nation is shared," "to look at each other without fear, mistrust, or exclusion," "to believe in our neighbor, in our ally, in those who are different from us," "to commit to this common destiny."[52] She punctuated the end of these sentences with: "I commit." In the successive sentences, she said, "I commit to" complete "the tasks we have given ourselves," "think about diversity," and "cultivate good politics."[53] Through two anaphoric passages, Bachelet constructed an urgency that necessitated the dedication of "us," the nation, neighbors, allies, and "those who are different." Likewise, her discourse of unity stressed the "shared" work of "us" and "each other," not the work of a leader hungry for power. Her deft transition to "I commit" not only positioned her as a bold leader willing to govern at a crucial moment in time, but it also positioned her as a fellow citizen committed to the work. She simultaneously modeled for her audience what it looked and sounded like to commit to change and positioned herself as a fellow citizen who happened to be in the position to facilitate collective change. Thus, her rhetoric of commitment asked the people to see her commitment to the work of change as the embodiment of a task shared by all.

Throughout her campaign and victory speeches, Bachelet's rhetoric of commitment allowed her to do what most presidents need to do after a democratic election: unite a divided nation.[54] In her case, she framed all voters—her supporters and detractors—as engaged actors, whose votes evidenced a committed relationship to Chilé. In her campaign speech, she addressed the task of constructing a nation. She said, "It needs the commitment of each and every one of us. Are we ready? Are we committed?"[55] Her successful campaign, then, became evidence that symbolically, the Chilean people answered, "yes, we are committed." She said of those who supported her: "with their vote and their commitment [they] have demonstrated that they believe in me as much as I believe in them!"[56] Addressing all voters, including those who did not support her, she said: "You have made a commitment with Chile's destiny."[57] Because she positioned all Chileans as committed—to her and/or to Chilé's destiny—she motivated them to continue their work toward the realization of "a Chilé that is truly for all."[58] Nearing the conclusion of her speech, she said, "I also ask you to commit. With your contribution, your voice, and with your work."[59] Her speech had already positioned Chileans as committed actors, so if Chileans rejected her request for continued action, then they would transgress their dedication to realizing Chilé's destiny.

Bachelet also constituted a committed relationship between Chileans and her policy agenda that would ensure the implementation of her policy proposals. One of her policy documents, "50 Commitments for the First 100 Days in Office," begins with a brief letter by Bachelet addressed to "Dear Friends," to whom she directly commits to implementing the proposed measures. She said, "My commitment was to listen to the people, and allow that the guidelines of our program would result from collective work, from dialogue with citizens who represent the richness and diversity of Chilé today."[60] The result of "this common deliberation," she said, are the "50 urgent measures that I commit to implement."[61] To Bachelet, the measures are representative of "the first step of a broader project": "to build" "a more diverse, participatory, and democratic country." Here, Bachelet began to decenter herself as an actor of change. She did not own the project; it is "*a* project."[62] Immediately following, she again employed anaphora, leading successive statements with "A country," putting forward an ideal or vision of a fully realized participatory democracy. She described "A country" "with quality education," better "health services," "safer neighborhoods," with "fairer labor relations," and, among other things, a place "where difference is valued."[63] As she concluded the letter, she argued that realizing this "dream" necessitated "the commitment of all."[64] In sum, the logic of Bachelet's message to Chileans goes: you helped generate these measures, as a responsive leader, I commit to implementing them, but if you want to become a better country, you must stay committed to implementing the policies. Bachelet claimed that she fulfilled her vow to listen, and although she committed to implementing these measures in her first 100 days in office, she constructed an ideal Chilé that she alone cannot create. By the end of the letter, it is the people, not her, who "own" the challenge of creating this ideal Chilé.

In Bachelet's other policy document, her "Government Program, 2014–2018," she posited a committed relationship between state agencies and policy change. She released the 198-page document during her 2013 campaign and it is currently posted to the president's web site. The program commits her administration and state agencies to nationalist values and to actions and/or policies that uphold those values. In a context of surging student protests and growing apathy, the program made commitments to human rights and to the inclusion of the disenfranchised. Her program, for example, makes an "unavoidable commitment to human rights," and an "unconditional commitment" to the eradication of discrimination.[65] Other state commitments were "to ensure that everyone is important" and "to lay the grounds for a society that respects difference."[66] To substantiate these policy goals, Bachelet's program compelled the state to serve specific segments of society and to carry out measures. This committed relationship between the state and policy positioned the Chilean people as the recipients of the relationship's positive outcomes. Regarding the most vulnerable populations in Chilé, the program says:

> The State will strive to commit to implement all the appropriate legislative, administrative, social, and educational measures that will protect boys and girls against any form of prejudice, mental or physical abuse, carelessness or negligence, ill-treatment, exploitation, or sexual abuse. We require the prohibition of child labor and any type of physical or psychological violence towards boys or girls.[67]

Likewise, her program said that the state should be or is dedicated "to educate our citizens" on "pet ownership," "to provide" regional government with autonomy, to maintain "the gas emission commitment" of 2009, and "to define the extent of" protections for fishermen.[68] Thus, when it came to allocating resources to more specific things or groups, particularly things that necessitate administrative action, Bachelet minimized the agency of the people and rather, constructed them as beneficiaries of the relationship between state agencies and policy goals. These seemingly contradictory constructions of the people expose how Bachelet arranged multiple actors to construct a series of committed relationships. To spotlight the agency of two committed actors such as the state and policy, she mitigated the agency of others, such as the people. Although these maneuverings might limit the extent to which the people participated in policy change, the committed relationship between the state and policy change potentially allowed more disempowered citizens to reap the benefits of human rights legislation. If the state and policy sought to "ensure that everyone is important," then perhaps their efforts enabled disempowered citizens to participate as actors in other committed relationships.

Likewise, Bachelet constructed a committed relationship between her policy documents and herself as an actor dedicated to the values that undergirding the policy documents. In this arrangement, she spotlights the agency of policy and her work ethic, downplaying the agency of her political influence as well as the people. In light of the 2005 amendments to the Constitution and a multi-party government that requires consensus for legislative action, the president cannot singularly implement any one measure. In light of these limitations, Bachelet's rhetoric of commitment allowed her to assert agency as an actor faithful to human rights, especially to the most vulnerable populations. She said:

> I reaffirm my commitment to push forward, without rest or fear, the task of making Chile a modern country, less unequal, that expands its growth capacity with better education for boys and girls, with better health for all, fairer and transparent in its relationships, more secure, and with a strong democracy.[69]

Invoking her life-long work for the rights of women and children, Bachelet positioned herself as an actor who will fearlessly work for social change. However, note that she does not explicitly commit to "better education" and "better health." Rather, she commits to *"push forward* ... the task of making Chile a modern country."[70] Thus, Bachelet's rhetoric of commitment allowed her to position herself as an actor who supports the process of fulfilling democratic values, a primarily legislative and bureaucratic process. Like the relationship between state agencies and policy, the people are recipients of this committed relationship's efforts. Yet Bachelet's goal is for this relationship to empower Chilean citizens to be part of "a strong democracy," one that relies on the active engagement of the people.

To point, Bachelet constructed a committed relationship between her Government Program and Chilean citizens. While she said her program "commits my future government to a great challenge," she also argued that it "commits us to complete tasks that we can currently carry out."[71] In this case, Bachelet humanized the process of fulfilling policy change, deemphasizing the bureaucratic aspect of policy change. For example, she said, "This program forces us to elevate the value of public service and forces us to commit the best [people] we have."[72] If we chain out Bachelet's logic, then we see how the program and by extension, the 50 Commitments, galvanize people into action. To Bachelet, the people demonstrated their commitment to her and/or to Chilé; she vowed to making Chilé better, as all Chileans should; after all, they designed the 50 commitments and are already engaged; her state agencies will implement these commitments (with her unfailing support) that seek to empower the people to better contribute to the country; and finally, her program contracts the state and the people to complete this work, ensuring its fulfillment.

As mentioned before, "commitments" and "measures" are closely aligned, if not synonymous, terms, especially in the context of the "50 Commitments" document. If we also consider her Government Program's policies as measures, then we can see how Bachelet's rhetoric conflates commitment as a vow and commitment as the manifestation of that vow. Bachelet exploits the polysemy of "commitment" as something to be done and as the done thing. She positioned herself as a leader who makes bold commitments to act upon the things to which she—and the people—are already dedicated. The people authorized her leadership and they authored her policy agenda, which functioned as evidence of her commitment to the people and the people's commitment to policy change. In short, she already fulfilled her commitments to which she commits. From then on, the people and the state need to put in the work. This logic worked to simultaneously position her as an active, committed leader, while it also deemphasized herself as *the* primary change agent, a particularly deft rhetorical move in the context of a coalitional government, societal demands for greater inclusion, and a second presidential term.

Conclusion: The Potential and Limits of a Rhetoric of Commitment

By spring 2015, Bachelet's approval rating had dropped to 15 percent, the lowest rating of any Chilean president. Owing to a financial scandal involving her son and daughter-in-law, her rating implied that Bachelet had transgressed her claims to inclusion, openness, and dialogue.[73] However, in December 2015, Bachelet's Ministry of Education successfully pushed an education reform bill through its Congress, making tuition partially free for some students, for the following year.[74] In the fall of that year, Bachelet announced a pared down reform agenda referred to as "realism without renouncement," suggesting that a rhetoric of commitment needed to bend to the realities of legislative and administrative processes.[75]

While Bachelet's rhetorical situation is unique, insofar as she ran for and secured a second non-consecutive presidential term, her case allows scholars of presidential rhetoric to better understand how a president of a multiparty democracy negotiates the demands for efficient governing and for deeper democratic practice. In a multiparty democracy that governs by coalitional consensus, a president's ability to effect legislative change is particularly constrained. A rhetoric of commitment enables presidents to position themselves as actors of change in relationship to their constituents and the state. It allows them to posit positive change as the outcome of multiple committed and interrelated relationships. Some spotlighted and some decentered Bachelet's agency and the agency of the people, exposing Bachelet's maneuvering of actors at work to empower others to better fulfill their commitments in other relationships. These relationships commit her to the people, the people to her, her and the people to Chilé, the people to writing policy, the state to policy change, her to supporting the state and policy change, and finally, the people to greater social change.

Ideally, this chapter models one way to analyze the rhetoric of non-U.S. presidents whose speech texts aren't already translated or cannot be translated by the scholar. Beyond negotiating the ethics of translation and arriving at composition-texts to analyze, scholars must be willing to immerse themselves in the study of a nation's government, political and social history, and a president's relationship (historic and current) to its constitution and its people. Often, scholars of the U.S. presidency are able to assume that readers have some level of familiarity with these aspects in a U.S. context. Thus, the burden to contextualize non-U.S. presidential rhetoric is greater and to be sure, a scholar's attempt can never offer a full account of a nation's social, political, economic, and cultural contexts.

To scholars interested in the rhetoric of women presidents, or the ways in which women in national politics negotiate their gendered constraints, Bachelet's case study spotlights the potential and pitfalls of crafting a more inclusive mode of governance based on gender identity. Bachelet argued that her unique experiences as a woman shaped her will to include the participation of citizens in policy formation and governance. Throughout her first presidential term, however, this approach stymied legislative action that necessitated consensus. When running for her second term, Bachelet needed to communicate her ongoing commitment to the disenfranchised with whom she claimed to identify, and to communicate her plan to legislate efficiently. In sum, Bachelet's case is not unlike other women presidents elected as symbols of challenges to patriarchal vestiges of the past. They are confronted with the often-contradictory tasks of serving the excluded populations they claim to represent, and to do so within the structures and norms steeped in long histories of nationalism and patriarchy. For Bachelet, a rhetoric of commitment allowed her to position herself as one of many devoted actors to change, providing her a buffer from criticisms of elitism and inefficiency.

Notes

1. Chilé holds binomial elections, so unless a candidate wins an absolute majority in a first round of voting, the candidates with the first- and second-most votes are subject to a run-off election.
2. Michelle Bachelet, November 14, 2013, 3, 5. All speeches are found at: Michelle Bachelet's official website at http://michellebachelet.cl/. Bachelet's speeches are posted in Spanish.

The English translations of her speeches were conducted by Marcela Reales Visbal, a PhD candidate in the Department of Romance Languages, with an emphasis on Spanish Translation, at the University of Georgia. Translations are also cross-checked with widely available translation tools, including Google Translate and Linguee (http://www.linguee.es/espanol-ingles).

3. Regarding non-US women's discourse, see Lisa M. Corrigan, "After the Revolution: Cuban Women's Healing Practices and Knowledge Spaces," *Advances in the History of Rhetoric* 11/12 (2008): 103131; Lisa M. Corrigan, "Writing Resistance and Heroism: Guerrilla Strategies from Castro's Gulag," *Communication Quarterly* 59, no. 1 (2011): 6181; Ellen W. Gorsevski, "Wangari Maathai's Emplaced Rhetoric: Greening Global Peacebuilding," *Environmental Communication* 6, no. 3 (2012): 290–307; Cheryl Jorgensen-Earp, *"The Transfiguring Sword": The Just War of the Women's Social and Political Union* (Tuscaloosa: University of Alabama Press, 1997); Russell Kirkscey, "Accommodating Traditional African Values in Globalization: Narrative as Argument in Wangari Maathai's Nobel Prize Lecture," *Women & Language* 30, no. 2 (2007): 12–17; Mariko Izumi, "Asian-Japanese: State Apology, National *Ethos*, and the 'Comfort Women' Reparations Debate in Japan," *Communication Studies* 62, no. 5 (2011): 473–490; Valerie Palmer-Mehta, "Theorizing the Role of Courage in Resistance: A Feminist Rhetorical Analysis of Aung San Suu Kyi's 'Freedom from Fear' Speech," *Communication, Culture, & Critique* 5, no. 3 (2012): 313–332; Valerie Palmer-Mehta, "Aung San Suu Kyi and the Rhetoric of Social Protest in Burma," *Women's Studies in Communication* 32, no. 2 (2009): 151–179; Mary Cecilia Monedas, "Neglected Texts of Olympe de Gouges, Pamphleteer of the French Revolution of 1789," *Advances in the History of Rhetoric* 1, no. 1 (1996): 43–54; Regarding non-US presidential rhetoric, see, for example, William L. Benoit and Andrew A. Klyukovski, "A Functional Analysis of 2004 Ukrainian Presidential Debates," *Argumentation* 20, no. 2 (2006): 209225; Maria Cheng, "Constructing a New Political Spectacle: Tactics of Chen Shui-bian's 2000 and 2004 Inaugural Speeches," *Discourse & Society* 17, no. 5 (2006): 583–608; René Agustín De los Santos, "'A Nation of Institutions and Laws': Plutarco Elias Calles and the Presidential Rhetoric of the Mexican Revolution," *Advances in the History of Rhetoric* 11/12 (2008): 263–94; Sangchul Lee and Karlyn Kohrs Campbell, "Korean President Roh Tae-Woo's 1988 Inaugural Address: Campaigning for Investiture," *Quarterly Journal of Speech* 80 (1994): 37–52; Wei-Chun Wen, William L. Benoit, and Tzu-Hsiang Yu, "A Functional Analysis of the 2000 Taiwanese and US Presidential Spots," *Asian Journal of Communication* 14, no. 2 (2004): 140–155.

4. Elora Halim Chowdhury, *Transnationalism Reversed: Women Organizing against Gendered Violence in Bangladesh* (Albany: SUNY, 2011), 6–7; Rebecca Dingo, *Networking Arguments: Rhetoric, Transnational Feminism, and Public Policy Writing* (Pittsburgh, PA: University of Pittsburgh Press, 2012).

5. Aiwha Ong, *Flexible Citizenship: The Cultural Logics of Transnationality* (Durham, NC: Duke University Press, 1999); Ingo Pies and Peter Koslowski, eds., *Corporate Citizenship and New Governance: The Political Role of Corporations* (London: Springer Press, 2011); Luis Cabrera, *The Practice of Global Citizenship* (Cambridge, UK: Cambridge University Press, 2010).

6. See, for example: Rebecca Dingo and J. Blake Scott, eds., *The Megarhetorics of Global Development* (Pittsburgh: University of Pittsburgh Press, 2012); Jason A. Edwards, *Navigating*

the Post-Cold War World: President Clinton's Foreign Policy Rhetoric (Lanham, MD: Lexington, 2008).

7. Of particular importance to rhetoricians is Rebecca S. Richards's essay, "Cyborgs on the World Stage: Hillary Clinton and the Rhetorical Performances of Iron Ladies," *Feminist Formations*, 23, no. 1 (2001): 1–24. Richards discusses a number of woman heads of state and their "Iron Lady" performances through the media. Other studies examine public opinion and media coverage of women presidents. See, for example, Sebastián Valenzuela and Teresa Correa, "Press Coverage and Public Opinion on Women Candidates," *International Communication Gazette*, 71, no. 3 (2009): 203–223; Jemima Asabea Anderson, Grace Diabah, and Patience Afrakoma hMensa, "Powerful Women in Powerless Language: Media Misrepresentation of African Women in Politics (the case of Liberia)," *Journal of Pragmatics* 43, no. 10 (2011): 2509–2518; Gwynn Thomas, "Michelle Bachelet's Liderazgo Femenino (Feminine Leadership): Redefining Political Leadership in Chile's 2005 Presidential Campaign," *International Feminist Journal of Politics* 13, no. 1 (2011): 63–82.

8. This number does not include women were appointed by the party in power to prime minister positions, women who succeeded a predecessor that resigned or was impeached, or women who took office after a coup. See "Female World Leaders Currently in Power," at http://www.filibustercartoons.com/charts_rest_female-leaders.php. Accessed February 27, 2017.

9. Ibid.

10. Farida Jalalzai, "Women Leaders: Past and Present," *Women and Politics* 26, no. 3/4 (2004): 85–108.

11. Farida Jalalzai, "Women Rule: Shattering the Executive Glass Ceiling," *Politics & Gender* 4, no. 2 (2008): 205–231.

12. Ibid.

13. Eduardo Alemán and Sebastián M. Saiegh, "Legislative Preferences, Political Parties, and Coalition Unity in Chile," *Comparative Politics* 39, no. 3 (April 2007): 253–272.

14. Lise Rakner and Vicky Randall, "Institutional Perspectives," in *Politics in the Developing World, 4th edition*, eds. Peter Burnell, Lise Rakner, and Vicky Randall (Oxford: Oxford University Press, 2014), 44–57.

15. Robert N. Gaines details the importance, theory, and method of text authentication for public address scholars. See Robert N. Gaines, "The Processes and Challenges of Textual Authentication," in *The Handbook of Rhetoric and Public Address*, eds. Shawn J. Parry-Giles and J. Michael Hogan (Malden, MA: Wiley-Blackwell, 2010), 133–156.

16. Ibid., 142.

17. Sandra Bermann, "Introduction," in *Nation, Language, and the Ethics of Translation*, eds. Sandra Bermann and Michael Wood (Princeton, NJ: Princeton University Press, 2005), 4.

18. Gaines, "The Processes and Challenges," 142.

19. Ibid.

20. Kristina Horn Sheeler and Karrin Vasby Anderson. "Gender, Rhetoric, and International Political Systems: Angela Merkel's Negotiation of Proportional Representation and Party Politics." *Communication Quarterly* 62, no. 4 (2014): 474–495. Sheeler translated Merkel's speeches.

21. Bermann, "Introduction," 4.
22. Gwynn Thomas and Melinda Adams, "Breaking the Final Glass Ceiling: The Influence of Gender in the Elections of Ellen Johnson-Sirleaf and Michelle Bachelet," *Journal of Women, Politics & Policy* 31, no. 2 (2010): 105-131.
23. Gregory B. Weeks and Silvia Borzutzky, "Introduction," in *The Bachelet Government: Conflict and Consensus in Post-Pinochet Chile*, eds. Silvia Borzutzky and Gregory B. Weeks (Gainesville: University of Florida Press, 2010), 1-3.
24. Thomas and Adams, "Breaking the Final Glass Ceiling," 119.
25. Susan Franceschet, "Gender Policy in the Bachelet Administration," in *The Bachelet Government*, 173.
26. Thomas and Adams, "Breaking the Final Glass Ceiling," 120.
27. Ibid., 119.
28. Gayle Tzemach Lemmon, "Michelle Bachelet Has a Mission," *Newsweek*, Sept. 19, 2011, vol. 158, no. 12, 7-8.
29. A. Daniels, "From Torture Victim to President," *The Progressive* 70, no. 3 (2006): 30-32.
30. Thomas and Adams, "Breaking the Final Glass Ceiling," 123.
31. Ibid., 115.
32. Marcela Ríos Tobar, United Nations Development Program, Santiago, Chile, "Seizing a Window of Opportunity: The Election of President Bachelet in Chile," *Politics & Gender* 4, no. 3 (2008): 509–519.
33. J. Esteban Montes and Tomás Vial, "The Role of Constitution-Building Processes in Democratization—Case Study: Chile," *International IDEA: Democracy Building and Conflict Management*, 2005, 23.
34. Gregory Weeks and Silvia Borzutzy, "Michelle Bachelet's Government: The Paradoxes of a Chilean President," *Journal of Politics in Latin America* 4, no. 3 (2012): 97-121.
35. Jennifer Ross, "Michelle Bachelet," *International Journal* 61, no. 3 (2006): 724-733.
36. Weeks and Borzutzy, "Michelle Bachelet's Government," 106-107.
37. Thomas and Adams, "Breaking the Final Glass Ceiling," 123. See also Emily A. Haddad and William E. Schweinle, "The Feminine Political Persona: Queen Victoria, Ellen Johnson Sirleaf, and Michelle Bachelet," in *Women and Management: Global Issues and Promising Solutions*, ed. Michele A. Paludi (Santa Barbara, CA: Praeger, 2013), 309-322; Thomas, "Bachelet's Liderazgo Femenino."
38. Weeks and Borzutzy, "Michelle Bachelet's Government," 106-108.
39. Ibid., 116.
40. Ibid., 112; "Bachelet is Back," *The Economist*, April 6, 2013.
41. Thomas and Adams, "Breaking the Final Glass Ceiling."
42. Linda S. Stevenson, "The Bachelet Effect on Gender-Equity Policies," *Latin American Perspectives* 39, no. 4 (2012): 129-144; Weeks and Borzutzky, "Michelle Bachelet's Government," 114.
43. Weeks and Borzutkzy, "Michelle Bachelet's Government," 112; "Bachelet is Back," *The Economist*, April 6, 2013.
44. Aldo C. Vacs, "Paved with Good Intentions: The Bachelet Administration and the Decline of Consensus," in *The Bachelet Government*, 217.
45. "Bachelet is Back."

46. "50 Commitments for the First 100 days in Office," October 2013, accessed Feb. 22, 2017, http://michellebachelet.cl/pdf/50medidasMB.pdf; "Government Program," October 2013, accessed Feb. 22, 2017, http://michellebachelet.cl/programa; "Thousands of Chileans," *Michelle Bachelet*, Nov. 14, 2013, accessed May 2013, http://michellebachelet.cl/; "Michelle Bachelet, We Will Go to the Government to Serve," *Michelle Bachelet*, December 15, 2013, accessed May 2013, http://michellebachelet.cl/. .

47. My thanks to Stephen Heidt for the accurate translation and for prompting an investigation into the ethics of translation.

48. Garth E. Pauley, "Lyndon B. Johnson, 'We Shall Overcome,' (15 March 1965)," *Voices of Democracy* 3 (2008): 17–33.

49. Bachelet, "Thousands of Chileans," 5.

50. Ibid.

51. Bachelet, "We Will Go," 4.

52. Ibid.

53. Ibid., 4–5.

54. This is an essential task of inaugural addresses, in particular. See: Karlyn Kohrs Campbell and Kathleen Hall Jamieson, *Presidents Creating the Presidency: Deeds Done in Words* (Chicago: University of Chicago Press, 2008), 29–56.

55. Bachelet, "Thousands of Chileans," 6.

56. Ibid.

57. Bachelet, "We Will Go," 2.

58. Ibid., 5.

59. Ibid.

60. Bachelet, "50 Commitments," 3.

61. Ibid.

62. Emphasis mine.

63. Bachelet, "50 Commitments," 3.

64. Ibid.

65. Bachelet, "Government Program," 182, 186.

66. Ibid., 7, 186.

67. Ibid., 31.

68. Ibid., 122, 122, 114, 127, 68.

69. Ibid., 34.

70. Emphasis mine.

71. Bachelet, "Government Program," 7.

72. Ibid., 6.

73. Roland Benedikter, Katja Siepmann, and Miguel Zlosilo, "Chile: The Midlife Crisis of Michelle Bachelet's Second Term. Are Bachelet's 'Policies that Change Cultures' Reaching Their Premature End?" *Council on Hemispheric Affairs*, May 24, 2016, accessed February 27, 2017, http://www.coha.org/chile-the-midlife-crisis-of-michelle-bachelets-second-term-are-bachelets-policies-that-change-cultures-reaching-their-premature-end/

74. "Chilean Students March as Education Reform Passed," *telesur*, Dec. 23, 2015, accessed February 27, 2017, http://www.telesurtv.net/english/news/Chilean-Students-March-Against-Education-Reform-20151222-0019.html

75. Benedikter et al., "Chile."

Reading the Presidency through Interruptions

CHAPTER ELEVEN

The Debt Ceiling Debacle

Presidentialism as Cruel Optimism

PAUL JOHNSON

Few concepts have more traction in our present political moment than polarization. In 2014 the Pew Research center dedicated an entire year of special reports to the phenomenon of polarization, with a report noting that, "nearly all of the traditional gaps between Republicans and Democrats have widened." News reports have amplified other studies of division as synecdochal for America, like Bill Bishop's *The Big Sort*, which argues that like-minded Americans are now clustering more and more not only in ideas but also in their decisions about where to live and work.[1] Since 2012, interest in the book has peaked twice, once in mid-January 2016 when it became clear that Donald Trump was a viable candidate for the Republican presidential nomination, and then later in November, 2016, when he won the election.[2] On November 4 of the same year, *The New York Times* cited Bishop in a large report on the divide between "red and blue America," focusing on the rise of "landslide counties" in which one political party's hold is so strong that the dominant party does not have to worry about campaigning to win.[3] In a 2015 report on the "No Labels" political movement, *The Atlantic's* Rebecca Nelson noted the centrist group's difficulty "in the age of Donald Trump and Bernie Sanders, of Fox News and MSNBC, of total partisan warfare at all levels of government," making clear the group is "out of step" with the zeitgeist of U.S. politics.[4] The influential work of Hetherington and Weiler ascribes the increasing intensity of division to the ideology of authoritarianism, which they find is what has "come to divide Republicans from Democrats."[5]

Polarization also dominates talks about America's legislative fortunes, ranging from the willingness of conservative news media like *The Wall Street Journal* to note the historically salient partisanship attached to congressional appointment hearings during Barack Obama's presidency to Steve Benen's observation that Senate Democrats had to invoke cloture—the procedure required to end a filibuster—more times in 2009 and 2010 than the "sum total of instances from 1919 through 1982."[6]

There are many potential causes of polarization. In this essay, I suggest another, less discussed input: the ideology of presidentialism. Presidentialism offers a unitary vision of the nation's chief executive, which attempts to compensate for the heterogeneity, division, and exclusion that doggedly inhere in the construction of American national identity. Instead of offering a messy and uncomfortable vision of democracy in which disagreement persists as an unsublimated element of politics, presidentialism pushes away confrontations and disagreements by offering up a single body to testify to the nation's composition. Per Dana Nelson, "The discomfiting actuality of fraternal *disagreement*—a discomfort that always threatens but is entirely fundamental to the possibilities for deliberative democratic self-governance—seemingly disappears in the representatively singular body of the president" (emphasis original).[7] The presidency and its real and fictional inhabitants are imaginative resources for subjects who might renew their faith in democracy—or recoil at the configuration of the polity in a given moment—by reducing their idea of the nation into a single figure. Particularly because the tension between the ideals of "inclusive liberalism and a more cautious republicanism" is irresolvable and lies at the heart of American identity, the presidency must not only mediate modest disagreements but also cover over constitutive differences.[8]

Presidentialism's capacity to gesture at unity may offer a snapshot of the nation, but not without costs. There are at least two issues. First, too often the desire for reduction of complexity attendant to presidentialism qualitatively worsens deliberation by narrowing the criteria for judging a presidency, routing "emergent radical democratic energies" away from tough, substantive policy deliberations into repressed "structures of practical, political, and affective containment," as in media speculation about a president's character or soul.[9] Second, the presidency carries the accumulated expectations and associations of more than two hundred years of history and discourse. The cultural imagination surrounding the presidency remains very narrow; the American "understanding of power—what it means, how it is exercised, how it is understood—has been inflected by upper class, straight, white male expectations and practices."[10] Investments in the presidency not only impoverish the scope of questions to be asked about what the president is doing, then, but also create a self-fulfilling prophecy crafting expectations for candidates and office holders as white, heterosexual men.

It is not surprising that the Obama presidency and its aftermath have been characterized by significant upheaval and vitriol, if not an outright political realignment, suggesting the need for textured readings of political controversies. A non-white president ran into sedimented, conservative expectations regarding the office. Rather than disrupting the ideology of presidentialism, however, for many Americans the Obama presidency facilitated their disidentification with him, rather than the office itself. The uncanny "strange familiarity" Flores and Sims claim resonant across the Obama presidency appears as an effect of the racial difference and implicit threat to whiteness embodied in Obama's blackening of the White House. The continued insistence by many partisans that Obama be "named in the threatening but seemingly race-neutral language of politics—socialism and communism" some twenty-odd years after the end of the Cold War indexed not just white supremacy, but also an investment in the presidency.[11] Its occupant had to be understood as somehow fundamentally "un-American" in order to prevent a reckoning with what reducing the United States into a non-white body would mean for imagining the nation. Flores and Sims' study illuminates an important method for reading the presidency: examining controversies during the Obama administration as indexes of a broader demand that the occupant of the White House be otherwise. It is this approach that I wish to take up in this chapter.

Perhaps no controversy better emblematizes the deep, even nihilistic discord of the Obama administration's time in office than the 2011 congressional struggle to raise the debt ceiling. A bit of arcane legerdemain dating back to the First and Second World Wars, the debt ceiling refers to the amount of monetary obligations that the United States government commits to repaying. Rather than automatically assuming such obligations will be paid, each year the Congress must act to raise the debt ceiling in order to approve the continued honoring of the nation's debt obligations. Previously, debates about raising the limit had been the subject of partisan sniping and bickering but under Obama it became something more, described by former Bush administration officials as "catastrophic."[12] The 2011 legislative debacle can be distinguished from past skirmishes over the debt ceiling by the occupant in the White House.

In this chapter, I draw on Lauren Berlant's work on "cruel optimism" as a way of explaining the debt ceiling crisis. Cruel optimism names a relationship between a subject and object which organizes one's world in such a way that "something you desire is actually an obstacle to your flourishing … when the object that draws your attachment actively impedes the aim that brought you to it initially." Not all "kinds of optimistic relation are … inherently cruel" but where there is a repetitive attachment to an object that enervates rather than empowers, a subject's investment in the world as they imagine it becomes cruel: the very thing which the object is thought to promise the subject never arrives by virtue of the forward-looking nature of the interest in the object.[13] Presidentialism, I argue, is a variety of cruel optimism, precisely because the kind of flourishing that subjects demand—namely a sense of political existence that carries with it the substantive possibility of realizing a vision of the good life—is undermined by the tendency of presidentialism to configure politics in ways that "voter/citizen judgment is truncated, limited to simple assessments of character and fitness for office."[14] In turn, such narrow assessment criteria depoliticize deliberation, such that circulating political discourses about the presidency focus on presidential character and ethics rather than policy goals. Presidentialism helps to explain how Tea Party head William Temple could claim that agreeing to meet debt obligations would constitute a GOP "cave to Obama": the economic consequences of a dangerous game of chicken over the national debt take a back seat to a demand that legislative policy decisions instead serve as singular referenda on the Obama presidency.[15] Playing legislative hardball to the point of threatening an existential economic collapse suggests a need to investigate the investments of the involved agents and go beyond readings geared to think about politics as an exercise in straightforward, calculative rationality. Psychoanalysis, precisely because it is capable of describing the way in which actors become invested in their own traumas and sufferings, is an appropriate lens for reading this controversy.

I proceed in three steps. First, I discuss presidentialism as an ideology, outline some of its more nefarious effects on the polity, and explain the intensity of American investment in it. Second, I rehearse Berlant's work on cruel optimism to describe presidentialism, while reviewing psychoanalytic and semiotic work on the presidency to argue for thinking about the presidency as object. Third, I briefly read a few discourses involved in the debt ceiling stand-off, to demonstrate that the clash itself was as much about investment in the office of the presidency as a set of policy goals related to austerity and budgetary concerns. I conclude by discussing what it means to take presidentialism as an object of critique.

Presidentialism's Effects and Appeal

The presidency occupies an outsized role in both the American political imagination and our discursive, governing infrastructures. Presidentialism organizes the American political imagination around a single, unitary figure, producing a conservative understanding of politics that not only encourages the accumulation of symbolic and political authority in the office of the chief executive, but also matriculates culturally regressive expectations back and forth between culture and politics. This process solidifies a conservative dialectic in which rhetorical performances "confirm" that certain narrow understandings of what it means to be the president—and what the responsibilities and obligations of the office are—reflect an underlying, objective reality rather than the arrangement of one set of possibilities and expectations that might be otherwise. Vanessa Beasley characterizes this ballooning sense of the presidency as a colossus striding the polity as a "rapid expansion" of the presidency's centrality "almost to the point of inevitability—that is, the feeling that both presidential rhetoric and executive power are expanding in ways that will not and/or cannot be self-limiting."[16] While Beasley is interested in the convergence between the idea of the rhetorical presidency and unitary executive theory, her observations bear on presidentialism as well, for it is this "gravitational symbolic and institutional place that the presidency assumes" to which Dana Nelson refers.[17] Indeed, unitary executive theory might not apply only to studies of agency rulemaking, but to discourses which give the executive an outsized role in shaping our public life.

A guiding assumption of both popular and political culture is that "the president ... 'stands for' U.S. democracy, and in particular its national unity."[18] But it is important to remember that claims of unity are not factual claims. Such claims may be attractive for a number of reasons, not the least of which that the heterogeneity of America and its alternatingly textured yet blood soaked founding narratives make answering the question, "Who are we?" quite difficult.[19] Critics of presidentialism argue that both explicit and tacit investments in the presidency—whether in the form of ham fisted assertions that conflate electoral results with universal consensus, or in the more measured cultural and political discourses that analyze and discuss the office and its real or fictional inhabitants almost *ad infinitum*—confuse the representational function of the presidency for some kind of substantive political content. Reflecting on the depoliticizing effects of this desire for "spiritualized, virtual wholeness," Nelson suggests that the vision of presidentialism "offers unity and harmony as its goal" in ways that organize political expectations around a search for consensus and agreement rather than other substantive goals.[20] If a nation cannot agree on what the character of the United States really is, we at least agree that, to some extent, the presidency represents it. Presidentialism works to place the "to some extent" in this phrase under erasure, simultaneously taking up the appeal of a single office that can claim to represent the nation while disavowing that, in any account of nation, there will be significant disagreement and discord.

Rhetorical scholars have explicitly and implicitly taken up presidentialism, noting the ways the presidency structures the national imaginary, while questioning civic investments in the office. Trevor Parry-Giles and Shawn Parry-Giles invoke presidentiality to describe texts that try to define "the national community by offering a vision of this central office in the U.S. political system".[21] Taking as their point of departure the television show *The West Wing*, they note that presidentiality manifests in the form of a romantic attachment to the office, one marked by a measure of postmodern cynicism. That allows it to nod to "a more progressive, community-based notion of inclusivity" by positioning the president and their office as inclusive and reflexive. But the show is "ultimately contained and controlled by" the "conventional discourse of presidential politics" like "intellectualism, militarism, masculinity, and whiteness" and whose markers are often confused with the characteristics of desirable presidential leadership. The accumulated ideas of a "real president," while accommodating some progress, nevertheless anchor the social imagination of the nation through the presidency.[22]

Trevor Parry-Giles' work on the television program *24* further details how culture shapes and narrows the range of acceptable "presidential" behaviors and identities. Arguing that the show reflects broadly held cultural expectations about the office, Parry-Giles notes that while the show makes space to judge presidents, it also limits the scope of these judgments to referenda on either their character or very narrow political questions. Hence, the fictional David Palmer is noble while Charles Logan's president is venal.[23] The show does not raise broader, complicated questions about executive authority in times of crisis or the rhetorical construction of crisis. Decisions are not evaluated on their ethical or moral consequences, but instead upon whether or not they are made resolutely, and characteristics like rationality and gravitas function to define what it means to be a "good president." There are real life analogs: take presidential candidate John Kerry's 2004 procedural explanation of an early vote for, and a later vote against, appropriations for the Iraq War. This incident became part of a referendum on his indecisiveness as a leader, rather than an opportunity for discussion the fraught and perilous decision to go to—and continue—war. Presidentiality tacitly cedes the "power and authority for governmental and political action" to "the nation's chief executive" making him not only a representative of the *vox populi* but also submitting their agency to the president's decisions, especially in the foreign policy arena.[24]

In this light, Nelson's warnings about the fantasy of wholeness and unity at the heart of presidentialism relate directly to the work of presidential rhetoricians. Parry-Giles, citing Nelson's work, concurs that the tendency to figure presidential leadership as a matter of masculine decisiveness and a willingness to go to war expresses the tacit assumed relationship between the imagined ideal of a strong president and the appeal of their reductive wholeness as national representative. This imagined ideal reflects what Shane Phelan calls the idea of nation as a "phallic body politic," a pre-ordained national community unencumbered by internal differences and clearly established and separated against an outside world which has no purchase in the body politic.[25] The president serves this phallic function, configuring politics as a kind of theatrical mirror in which the public looks for signs of its own image (or signs of an image of white masculinity which is con-flated with the "true" American identity), rather than participating as one kind of stakeholders among many, including other branches of the government, and subsections of the population.

As King and Beasley argue, presidentialism is mimetic to the extent that cultural discourses overwhelmingly envision the presidency as white, male and heterosexual and, historically, we have seen only one departure from that script and disavowed others. But "mimetic similitude" should not be taken to reflect that there is a true reality of the presidency beyond the one that has simply been performed repeatedly over time.[26] If presidentialism is not wholly mimetic then it is a more fraught resource for identification. Reconfigurations of the political in ways that cannot wholly affirm or confirm the feedback loop of presidentialist aspirations constitute moments of presenting these assumptions with their own hollow authority instead of interruptions of mimetic functions. If presidentialism exacerbates rather than resolves cognitive dissonance about the representational failure of liberal democracy, the constant returns to the presidency as a national church or source of divine sovereignty might be an "exhausting repetition of the politically depressed position" that invests in its own powerlessness even as it ges-tures at a civic function of commonality.[27] In short: presidentialists might be forced to confront a reality wildly at odds with their expectations. Scholars of presidential rhetoric can profit from taking this possibility seriously.

The Obama presidency may have reconfigured American national identity, but did not disrupt presidentialism. Stuckey's observations about the legacy of white supremacy in terms of imagining the presidency bear repeating here: ideals about the "true" characteristics of a president are inseparable from both the his-tory of who has occupied the office and cultural expectations for what a president is "supposed" to look like. The racial threat of the Obama presidency has been well documented and discussed and much of this discussion has assumed, quite rightly, that the presidency is a central tool for imagining American political life.[28] It is not clear Obama's presidency disrupted white ideals of presidential character: Birtherism, cries of socialism, and repeated insistences that Obama was some-how un-American separated the occupant from the office. Individuals remain very invested in the presidency, even when it is occupied by someone who might threaten to disrupt their identification with the office.

Three factors seem crucial in intensifying the hold of presidentialism on American politics. First the increased prevalence of hostility towards the idea of government itself, thematizable through Michel Foucault's work on what he calls "state-phobia." In this construction, subjects constitute themselves as naturally and originarily economic, and thus opposed as a matter of principle to state authority. To the state-phobic, there is a kindship, a sort of genetic continuity or evolutionary implication between different forms of the state, with the administrative state, the welfare state, the bureaucratic state, the fascist state, and the totalitarian state all being, in no matter which of the various analyses, the successive branches of one and the same great tree of state control in its continuous and unified expansion.[29]

State-phobia is not a singularly partisan affect, and cannot be differentiated strictly on the basis of party affiliation. Even if it is more clearly a constitutively central discourse on the right, shifts in welfare policy in the 1990s, show that "state phobia has migrated from the fringe … to the mainstream to infect socialism and social democracy, such as under President Clinton."[30] The persistent life of tropes about "death panels" during and after the debate over the Affordable Care Act cannot be disarticulated from a fear of government as administrator of life and death. And, state-phobia ran through discourse of the Tea Party.[31] Liberal politicians may invoke the state with considerably less sinister associations than conservative politicians, but the state is still often a figure of last resort, called upon during exceptional circumstances—like the 2008 financial crisis—as a stopgap measure rather than an equal participant in public life.[32] State-phobia is also an unequally distributed fear. Some parts of the government, like the military, consistently poll as fairly trustworthy while public trust in Congress has declined over the last decade.[33] Relative to these numbers, the trust in the presidency remains somewhat stable.[34] Meanwhile, generic trust in government to handle domestic and foreign problems hovers at a much lower baseline today than it did 15 years ago.[35] State-phobia is a prevalent affect, even if its felt differentially in relation to particular parts of government.

A second factor in increased reliance on the presidency as a symbolic source of a comfort is the crisis in publicness and an exacerbated awareness about problems of social mobility and growth. The 2008 financial crisis contributed to this, but there are other factors as well. Berlant identifies a general trend since the 1980s, in which the recession of 2008 appears as a clarifying moment representative of "decades of class bifurcation, downward mobility, and environmental, political, and social brittleness that have increased … the probability that structural contingency will create manifest crisis situations in ordinary existence for more kinds of people."[36] Elizabeth Anker concurs, pointing to the same declines in upward mobility and widening of various gaps in employment, education and resources as the causes of what she calls "felt powerlessness," the idea that individuals make sense of themselves through starting from the point of their own lack of agency.[37] Moreover, even the more materially well-off may consider themselves victims, as in the case of Tea Partiers, many of whom were privileged members of society who nevertheless imagined themselves to be victims of tyranny.

A third, related cause, has been more persistent over time. American democracy is built on a tension between its commitments to an individualist, capitalist culture, "the shared philosophical idea of Lockean individualism" which challenges the idea of equality underwriting our political imagination. Because our national imaginary is invested in "the possibility of a united, interdependent citizenry," this unity and its component demand for abstract, theoretical equality runs into the rough road of "a capitalistic system that is guaranteed to produce inequality of results."[38] Beasley notes that this relationship is paradoxical because American culture oscillates between celebrating the individual and the community. The ideology of individualism, she contends, represents a threat to "the potential for American political community." Historically, presidents are understood to manage this, both straightforwardly as in Stuckey's arguments but also more generally, in the way presidentialism functions as an ideology. The presidency reassures citizens that there is a body politic, drawing attention to its unifying function as a way to help think through the paradoxical tensions of liberal individualism as a productive resource rather than an existential threat to the polity. Thus, racial disruption of the presidency offers, "An increased awareness of difference seems to frighten Americans who perceive the gains of others as impediments to their own achievements."[39] An understanding about gains as being zero-sum is, of course, not limited just to economics. This particular rationality underwrites, in Beasley's observation, skepticism "towards laws protecting minorities from discrimination" among other initiatives.[40] So too it underwrites the presidency's raced-ness, itself a rhetorical supposition with no backing.

The first two conditions suggest a polity facing what Jurgen Habermas calls a "legitimation crisis," a situation or circumstance in which government "lags behind programmatic demands *that it has placed on itself*. The penalty for this failure is withdrawal of legitimation" (emphasis original).[41] These are endemic in "liberal capitalist societies" to the extent that "temporarily unresolved steering problems, which the process of economic growth produces at more or less regular intervals, *as such* endanger social integration."[42] I want to be clear here that the legitimation crisis to which I am referring is probably one mostly experienced by white men. Historically, the presidency has often reflected their preferences, enabling some of the polity to sidestep the more difficult questions on offer by prevalent inequality and structural exclusion. In fact, America has long been in a legitimation crisis for some: for other populations, especially those less historically marginal, it has become easier and easier to think about rising levels of distrust in governance.

Here, then, the Obama presidency poses an interesting question: with presidentialism a resource for making sense of their relationship to politics, a non-white president could have undermined presidentialism itself by rendering the office as an unappealing resource for national imagination. Instead, however, the Obama presidency became a permanent object of interest and concern for many, trickling up and down into the legislative battles of the era. Psychoanalytic theory helps explain why a non-white president did not result in mass disidentification with the office.

Cruel Optimism and the Presidency

Psychoanalysis reminds us that subjects often have to make sense of their worlds and their selves through the taking of objects. Without objects, subjects become trapped in narcissistic feedback loops of their own (literally) making, in the sense that they cannot differentiate between themselves and their environment. Object theorists like D. W. Winnicott emphasize that the orientation to the world through objects is crucial for understanding subjects: precisely because society is so much bigger than any individual, taking objects is a means for a subject "to deal with a lack of immediate satisfaction" in order to understand that political existence is a "compromise between spontaneity (total satisfaction) and restraint (frustration)."[43] If presidentialism names an ideology through which subjects come to make sense of their political community and national identity, then the presidency functions as the object that establishes what Winnicott would call a "*facilitating environment*" (emphasis original).[44] That is to say, it enables the work of world making so that subjects might make sense of themselves in relationship to a broader community.

It thus makes sense that Parry-Giles and Parry-Giles describe the attachment to the presidency as a romantic one, bearing directly on Berlant's description of taking objects to make a world as a process of finding "cushions for enjoyment."[45] The presidency is not only an object that enables subjects to make sense of themselves and their world but for the reasons enumerated in the previous section, it is a particularly central one. Other elements of the government are either too heterogeneous or not to be trusted. In the abstract, the idea of the state is connected with ideas of violence and threats to freedom, with both actual and felt powerlessness are evidence of a widespread investment in what Anker identifies as the cult of the heroic individual.[46] In fact, the typical characteristics of the president as represented in culture—masculine, decisive, and charismatic—link to these fantasies about the individual in America, which Anker notes are tied in to the American ideals of the "normal and rational individual: unencumbered, masculine, almost omnipotent."[47] If individuals cannot be masters of their universe owing to the actual or felt powerlessness described by Anker, then their attachments to the presidency facilitate an investment in imagining otherwise.

Ultimately, Obama's presidency is a case of cruel optimism owing to the three conditions that imperil American democracy: the expansion of state-phobia, the declining capacity of the polity to partially satisfy its population's demands for the good life, and the historically present—but now more salient—problem of tension between liberalism and republicanism. Skeptical of the government, feeling increasingly marginalized, and less capable of squaring the circle between individual and community, Berlant notes that the attachment to politics "may be a relation of cruel optimism, when, despite an awareness that the normative political sphere appears as a shrunken, broken, or distance place of activity among elites, members of the body politic return periodically to its recommitment ceremonies and scenes."[48] The central role of the presidency—not only in public discourse but also in public culture and also, yes, in academic scholarship about our political world—functions as a cruel optimism because it reduces the complexity of the political world to a drama about identification with a persona. Doing so figures politics as a romance not about judging claims by utilizing our "skills for adjudicating incommensurate visions of the better good life" but is instead about "the demand for affective attunement."[49] If a citizenry demands from politics that it confirm their expectations of leadership—but these leadership expectations themselves are depoliticizing and result in worsened governance and stratified resource distributions—then the cruelty of this optimism is placed in sharp relief. The demand for decisive and familiar representation of the totality of the nation impedes producing an idea of democracy, which is itself contestable and therefore more open to debating about different versions of the good life.

Implicit in the application of cruel optimism to the presidency is an understanding that the president already functions as an object in psychoanalytic theory, an observation which holds significant potential for presidential rhetoricians. Diane Rubenstein charts a path through three accounts of the presidency before settling on an object theory and the work of Jean Baudrillard.[50] The first "representational" phase is encapsulated by Michael Rogin's *Ronald Reagan the Movie and Other Episodes in Political Demonology*. Drawing on Reagan's cinematic history and his transition from actor to politician, Rogin deftly points out the way in which Reagan's "lost" cinematic self is made whole through Reagan's political persona.[51] Denied charismatic leading man roles where he would be a phallic man of action—Reagan's characters were often disabled and unlucky in love—his political career represents his fully realized public self. Thus, for Rogin, Reagan's televisual appearance at the 1984 Republican National Convention, while still recovering from John Hinckley's assassination attempt, constitutes a circuit of desire between leader and public that offers escape from "public and private anxieties by allowing you to watch Big Brother."[52] Reagan's public was aware of its exteriority to the political but mostly as a function of their shared exteriority to it with Reagan, who was himself not political, the paradoxical source of his political success.

Rubenstein offers a friendly amendment—she agrees substantively with the importance of Reagan in enabling a crucial mapping of the American political imaginary—but rejects the argument that Reagan ever became "whole" as a mechanism for presidential identification. Rather, the well-worn bromides about Reagan such as, "He's playing the role of his life: himself!" were not specific to Reagan but indexed the capitalist intensifications of the 1980s. Rubenstein argues that the "real Reagan" lived not in the unity between the Reagan of Hollywood and the Reagan of politics, but in the insistence by so many that what mattered was that there had been a split between the two. In fact, to see the two as separate rather than as part of the same whole was the mistake of many of Reagan's opponents who failed to understand his appeal as he swept the ideology of the New Right into office.[53]

The second presidentialism is the semiotic approach represented by Anne Norton's *Republic of Signs*. Norton's work troubles the liberal idea of the unified self. As she remarks, "convinced, in theory, that the unity of the self is necessary to happiness and perhaps to sanity, we experience" the fragmented condition of living in a community whose existence denies the unity of our selfhood as a "deconstructive enterprise" which is "not only ... a source of anxiety but also as an act of authority and a source of pleasure."[54] Here the tension between self and society foregrounds how anxieties about selfhood are evidence of the ascendance of liberal ideology. Pure individuation, after all, is not a society except perhaps in the eyes of the worst Randian fantasies. Norton's second important point is a critique of representation. She identifies the way in which the president and the office collapse in on themselves, such that "the signifier and the signified are finally inseparable in the sign. Their interdependence is entailed in the concept of representation. When we recognize that the office is distinct from its occupant ... We fail to remember that the form a representation takes affects its meaning and significance."[55] Attempts to the separate the presidency and president vainly strive to find some vanishing mediator, when in fact it is the constitutive inseparability of the two to which the critic reacts. Here, too, is the issue with the mimetic thesis: it imagines some kind of clean separation between politics and culture when the two are mutually implicated in a single whole.

Acknowledging the importance of both of these arguments, Rubenstein nevertheless goes beyond them, arguing that Norton's focus on the function of political representation as compensatory for loss is problematic. By virtue of her "reliance on Barthesian myth," Norton relies on a depth hermeneutic which presumes that there is something which the president's gestures towards unity covers up, or hides.[56] But if the presidency is a commodity—and therefore an exchanged object whose value is in the exchange itself rather than an object whose exchange is covering up some other "reality"—then critics must attend to the presidency differentially.[57] Civic investment in the presidency does not produce some "not seeing" of reality but instead civic investment in the presidency is, by itself, the reality of the presidency. On this reading, the significance of the presidency is not that it provides a certain stylized access to a national imaginary, but the president *is* the national imaginary.[58] Reagan did not, despite Rogin's protestations, play himself. Reagan simply was.

Rubenstein insists that the presidency is not an object that enables subjects access to a greater whole of the nation. It also doesn't secure consent to one version of a national imaginary. Instead, the presidency is the object through which the public comes to an understanding of who they are, not in reference to some greater horizon or imagination. This function is not outside politics, for Rubenstein, but correlates with the intensifications of capitalism seen since the middle of the twentieth century.[59] With society increasingly seen, however incorrectly, as a drama of an individual against the system, the presidency increasingly presents a drama of an individual struggling against a system. The change in the function of the presidency parallels the shift in the presumed function of signification from referential to self-referential to functional in, of, and for-itself. Where in Saussure's schema it is well known that signs never referred to objects, Rubenstein's point is that capitalism has undermined and ultimately destroyed the broader, social investment in a referential logic that characterized the relationship of a polity's population and the national imaginary itself. She chalks this up to intensities of mediation, an increasingly significant phenomenon.[60]

The ideology of presidentialism invests subjects in fantasies of the good life.[61] Bollas discusses "transitional objects," objects that allow subjects to play with their "own omnipotence" while also mitigating loss.[62] Extending Winnicott, Bollas emphasizes that the loss being discussed is one's self: since one's identity is made through participation in a political community, one's "previous" self is often remade or lost in the process of being and living with others. However, where there is a lack of a "facilitating environment," when there is no context that enables the subject to make sense of themselves over and against other objects, the risk is "ego collapse" which may "precipitate psychic pain."[63] Where the pendulum between liberalism and republicanism becomes stuck on the liberal side of the equation, we risk inhabiting a polity trapped in a permanent ego crisis. This is the kind of situation that Anker describes as that of the American subject confronted with "their presumed capacity under reigning norms of liberal individualism to be self-reliant and sovereign over their own bodies."[64] Or, in other words, when liberal democracy is premised on a productive tension between self and society but the latter constantly works to undo the former, there is a national ego crisis in which the subject is certain of their own existence by unable to confirm it through the taking of an object.

The president is a transitional object in that it affords a pathway for civic participation in politics. Rather than participating in a broader imaginary that corresponds to the life of the public as might be rehearsed amongst scholars who study certain specific and contingent imaginary notions of the public sphere, however, the idea of the president as a transitional object relates to the investments in the presidency as such. "Transitional phenomena allow for the pursuit of happiness" not in the sense that they may put the subject on that path to receiving satisfaction but because they give satisfaction by themselves. Hence, the description of the relation between civic subject and president as "*operational* as well as *representational* form of knowledge"[65]insofar as the presidency does not stand in for politics but is politics. If the chief executive were one object upon many through which subjects might imagine themselves as political or public this could be a good outcome. However, intensifications of late capitalism are −or have already—eradicated other anchors. The president is a transitional object that absorbs considerable energy in terms of enabling subjects' civic existence, but it struggles to discharge this energy because into what it transitions is unclear. Whatever feigned universality there was to the idea of the good life is in crisis, many governmental organs of public life are objects of skepticism owing to state-phobia, and the more trusted institutions, like the military, have their own authority that might also threaten the subject's felt autonomy. The presidency, then, offers up one kind of public, but a narrow one, whose limitations threatens the health of the polity. In demonstration, in the next section I make sense of the intensity of the debt ceiling fight by reading it through the theory of presidency as object.

The Debt Ceiling Fight

During the midst of a contentious presidency, the debt ceiling fight stood out for the threat it posed to economic stability. *USA Today* observed that "Even the suggestion of failure to raise the ceiling could send markets into a free-fall. And the government can't just quit borrowing overnight without causing a calamity" while on *Good Morning America* George Stephanopoulos interviewed Jake Tapper about what they described as the "financial Armageddon" that would take place should U.S. credit become a shaky bet.[66] The Bipartisan Policy Center noted that if the Congress refused to raise the debt ceiling "the Treasury Department would not be able to pay all its bills and would to implement an immediate 44 percent cut in federal spending" which would prove disastrous.[67] A former John McCain economic adviser called the macroeconomic impact "staggering."[68] Even if the government simply shifted priorities and agreed to prioritize paying some services and not others, it would result in a "cut of 44% from $3.4 trillion" in federal spending, which would constitute an economic disaster.[69]

Moreover, one cannot simply write off the GOP position as a negotiating posture. During the debt ceiling crisis, the Obama administration repeatedly came to the GOP offering significant cuts to popular entitlement programs. The White House offered to raise the retirement age for Medicare.[70] The administration put Social Security cuts on the table.[71] While there is no doubt that some of the offers were part of Obama administration optics, the proposal to couple these cuts with a commitment on the part of congressional Republicans to let the George W. Bush-era tax cuts for the rich expire suggested seriousness about tackling the deficit.

Conservative demands and statements during the debate do not make much sense when read in terms of policy goals, but cohere as what Christian Lundberg calls "demand politics."[72] While I do not have space for an exhaustive account, the debt ceiling crisis suggests a devil-may-care attitude towards the debt ceiling, framed around a refusal to approve an increase unless the Congress agrees to enact massive cuts in government spending. Given that no debt ceiling raise had ever before brought the United States so close to calamity, the theory of president-as-transitional object offers a persuasive explanation of some of the GOP's cavalier attitude, with the traumatic rehearsal of Obama's occupancy of the office joining with the threatened economic apocalypse of a default. Losing the presidency meant losing the nation, in a very real, existential sense, to the point of a traumatic return via a coincidence between symbolic and real apocalypse.

Moreover, the debt ceiling fight came not long after the government's successful mission to kill Osama bin Laden and Obama's release of the long form birth certificate, both of which dampened concern about Obama's otherness. While such beliefs were not held by a plurality of the GOP—though as late as 2015, 30% of all Americans and 43% of Republicans still thought so—it helps to explain why those conservatives who were more well off materially (and therefore plausibly had more access to the good life) might nevertheless react with horror to Obama either on the basis of his race or seeming foreignness.[73] If the president is unfamiliar, then the presidency—and the nation it represents—must cease to exist. The rehearsal of the threat of destruction became a way to play with, even imagine, the destruction of America as a way of managing the destabilization of fantasies of whiteness in the presidency.

By early May, William Temple, head of the 2011 Tea Party convention, reminded John Boehner and other Republicans whose demands came first, stating "We're telling Boehner and all of the House Republicans, they came into office with Tea Party help. We now expect them to keep their promises and hold the ceiling on the national debt ... The Tea Party will not be in a very forgiving mood this fall ... if House freshmen and others elected by the Tea Party cave to Obama."[74] Temple's statement figures politics as a zero-sum battle between Obama and the Tea Party. Concessions on a debt deal constitute a broken promise. The only exception to the covenant is "the group could go along with small increase in the debt ceiling, but only if Republicans were able to win a major policy battle such as a repeal of health care." More than just a stretch, the structure of the American political system and its checks and balances made this demand functionally impossible. Obama was still president, the major health care reform - known colloquially as "Obamacare"—represents Obama's signature legislative achievement, and the president can veto any legislation that does not have 67 votes in the Senate.

This demand is compensatory to the presidency's capacity to gesture at wholeness in a way the legislature cannot.[75] If the presidency is the political, *qua* Rubenstein, then the impossible demand that the legislature somehow defeat or negate the president further demonstrates how the presidency remains a shared transitional object. But, the structure of the Tea Party demand leaves nowhere to transition to since the presidency, and therefore America, is lost. Temple's statement continues in ways that reflect this, as he mocks John Boehner's emotionalism as inappropriate for the warfare that is politics: "'I wish our tearful House Speaker would just show some compassion for American taxpayers and our children, but he and Mr. Ryan have already surrendered to President Obama,'" Temple said. "It's a cowardly act of treason against coming generations, and we may be able to give Boehner something to really cry about in 2012."[76] The language of treason and surrender suggests the ways the attachment to the presidency constitute their own, internal idea of nation.[77]

The impossible demand for popular sovereignty in Temple's statement constitutes one repetition of the general post-2008 right-wing turn to a popular politics, one in which the demand that reality be otherwise blends the structure and content of the demand into one inseparable, cathected whole. The rehearsal of the structure of the demand between political system and subject is energized by the positionality of the subject. While discussing leftist anti-globalization movements, Lundberg's analysis obtains for this movement as well because it invests in "taking an addressee (such as the state) that it assumes represents the totality of the political field" when in fact the political field could be understood more broadly.[78] When the presidency is politics and the demand and cause cannot be disarticulated from one another, politics becomes a negative feedback loop of confirming one public's idea of the world over and against that of another.

The fantasy of wholeness intrinsic to presidentialism is significant, especially placed along the latent racial definitions of the presidency operative in American politics. Presidentialism's cruel optimism operates at the level of imagining that the function of the presidency is universal. Thus, the investment in the absolute belief that the presidency will mirror the national population manifests as a forceful desire to defeat or otherwise drive a non-white male president from office as crucial to sustain the presidency's mimetic relationship to white America. Yet presidentialism also means that the division between the office and the office holder is exposed as a political and rhetorical construction. Obama's occupation of the office meant admitting in some way that he was the president, even if he was ultimately to be opposed. Even the far-right organization Freedom Works could not help but imitate Obama in its response to the debt crisis, constituting a panel of citizens "Modeled on President Obama's National Debate Commission, the Tea Party Debt Commission will consist of 18 members."[79] With no other national imaginary, the Tea Party sought to mirror the administration to prove its demands mattered and were intelligible within the system.

With the presidency as an intense cathected object, accumulated rhetorical opposition to Obama could either be adjusted or renounced. The fight over the debt ceiling constituted a substitutive repetition of a demand that reminded conservatives that their investment in the presidency was cruel, precisely to the extent that the occupant of the presidency posed a threat to their sedimented, accumulated ideas of a president's nature. Obama presented them with a crisis of political belonging: if presidentialism is a way to make sense of political community, but the president is not what you think a president should be, then conservative identity engages a kind of sublime/uncanny/dangerous moment in which the subject is threatened with becoming unmoored, and thus has to produce demands which iterate the structure of politics that they assume. However, as Lundberg suggests, this form of demand politics traps the subject in a kind of repetitive feedback loop in which their demands that things become otherwise can never be satisfied. This trap partly explains the intensity and regularity of political gridlock during the Obama era: appointment filibusters, low levels of legislative activity, the insistence that a terrorist attack (Benghazi) was a scandal, and of course the debt ceiling fight itself.

Conclusion

This study allows for two conclusions, one about the maintenance and intensification of polarization and division and a second regarding scholarship about the presidency. First, presidentialism contributes to the polarization and division which are increasingly central to scholarly analyses of politics by creating conditions under which a shared site for political contestation becomes another intensified node for producing existentially divisive political discourse. The presidency is one of a number of institutions of public life. Such institutions offer pathways for discursive engagement and ways for citizens to refigure themselves. The shared investment in the office serves as a kind of binding agent that brings otherwise differentially constituted subjects together. In this respect, the presidency is a resource for the practice of what Chantal Mouffe calls agonistic politics, a mode of political disagreement which configures the exchange of ideas as an exercise of tension-ridden interaction in which differences themselves are expressed through the conduct of politics. In contrast with agonism, antagonism is mode of political exchange in which the aim of political exchange is not the reconfiguration of attitudes—or at least a willingness to admit that democratic life is constituted through living with and among differences—but instead an enterprise in which political exchanges become matters of one interlocutor annihilating and destroying the other.[80] With other potential shared gathering places imperiled by a combination of heterogeneity and public distrust (like Congress), straightforwardly anti-democratic by their nature (the Supreme Court), or characterized by a more fractured character (like a civil society marked by rampant consumerism and individualism), the presidency has served as an object through which debate and deliberation might proceed agonistically. However, if the presidency is an increasingly lonely organizing point for the imagination of politics, presidentialism encourages a cruel optimism about the office itself by elevating its role as an index for analyzing and judging society, when in fact the presidency—and its occupant at a given moment—are both compromise formations whose essence is not reducible to how they are understood or iterated at a given moment. The public's increasing reliance on the presidency as the only reliable shared point for making sense of society shifts arguments about the president to the antagonistic form and makes the presidency an even more deeply charged node. To disagree with the assessment of the presidency is to inhabit what might be an entirely different nation, one structured by what is nominally the same organizing point but different in every way, as subjects are disposed antagonistically towards the orientation of differentially positioned interlocutors. Without the presidency, there is increasingly nowhere else to go.

A second conclusion recognizes the amount of scholarship dedicated understanding presidential rhetoric equally reflects a disciplinary investment in presidentialism. This conclusion, gestured at by Stuckey's admonition that rhetorical scholars "do not do nearly enough work that analyzes the connections between the exercise of presidential power and the exercise of presidential rhetoric," revolves around collocating presidentialism and the study of presidential rhetoric and understanding that it is not only the case that cultural examinations of the presidency should be undertaken.[81] There may be a parallel between what Beasley identifies as, "the dramatic increase in presidential power over executive branch-level agencies" and the continued investment by rhetoricians in studies of presidential rhetoric. At the level of object and text selection, critics are reaffirming the legitimacy of the gravitational pull of the office of the presidency while knowing that there are other ways of thinking with and engaging about politics.[82] What would it mean to think about the ratios and relationships between studies of the presidency and other objects in rhetorical studies, and how should scholars who study politics and the presidency think about orienting themselves and their work with the threat of presidentialism apparent? As Wanzer-Serrano observes, there are at least two ways to deal with the problems of an increasingly fractured world, one which involves insisting that there is actually still some kind of whole there, or another which involves being "reflexive about the place" from which we speak.[83] Right now, it seems, "place" is constituted through the organization of our rhetorical and critical imaginations about the presidency, as if such a figure could constitute an entirely accurate snapshot of the nation in a moment. Things could be otherwise, however.

Notes

1. Bill Bishop, *The Big Sort: Why the Clustering of Like-Minded America Is Tearing Us Apart* (New York: Houghton Mifflin, 2008).
2. Measured by Google Trends.
3. Gregor Aisch, Adam Pearce, and Karen Yourish, "How Large is the Divide Between Red and Blue America?," *The New York Times*, November 4, 2016. Online at https://www.nytimes.com/interactive/2016/11/04/us/politics/growing-divide-between-red-and-blue-america.html?_r=0.
4. Rebecca Nelson, "The War on Partisanship," *The Atlantic*, October 13, 2015. Online at https://www.theatlantic.com/politics/archive/2015/10/the-war-on-partisanship/451461/
5. Marc Hetherington and Jonathan Weiler, *Authoritarianism and Polarization in American Politics* (New York: Cambridge University Press, 2009), 32.
6. Rebecca Balhaus, "Do Obama Nominees Face Stiffer Senate Opposition?," *The Wall Street Journal*, November 21, 2013. Online at https://blogs.wsj.com/washwire/2013/11/21/do-obama-nominees-face-stiffer-senate-opposition/; and Steve Benen, "Unprecedented Obstruction and False Equivalencies," *Washington Monthly*, December 8, 2011. Online at http://washingtonmonthly.com/2011/12/08/unprecedented-obstruction-and-false-equivalencies/.
7. Dana Nelson, *Bad for Democracy: How the Presidency Undermines the Power of the People* (Minneapolis: Minnesota University Press, 2008), 223.
8. Mary Stuckey, *Defining Americans: The Presidency and National Identity* (Lawrence: University of Kansas Press, 2004), 13.
9. Dana Nelson, "Representative/Democracy: The Political Work of Countersymbolic Representation," in *Materializing Democracy: Toward a Revitalized Cultural Politics*, eds. Russ Castronovo and Dana Nelson (Durham: Duke University Press, 2002), 218–247.
10. Mary Stuckey, "Rethinking the Rhetorical Presidency and Presidential Rhetoric," *Review of Communication* 10, no. 1 (2010): 38–52.
11. Lisa Flores and Christy-Dale Sims, "The Zero-Sum Game of Race and the Familiar Strangeness of President Obama," *Southern Communication Journal* 81, no. 4 (2016): 206–222.

12. John Ydstie, "Failure to Hike Debt Limit Would Have Consequences," *National Public Radio*, April 12, 2011. Online at http://www.npr.org/2011/04/12/135336968/failure-to-hike-debt-limit-would-have-consequences.

13. Lauren Berlant, *Cruel Optimism*, (Durham: Duke University Press, 2011), 1.

14. Trevor Parry-Giles, "Presidentialism, Political Fiction, and the Complex Presidencies of Fox's *24*," *Presidential Studies Quarterly* 44, no. 2 (2014): 204–223.

15. Wes Barrett, "Tea Party Slams Boehner and Ryan on Debt Ceiling," *Fox News*, May 9, 2011. Online at http://www.foxnews.com/politics/2011/05/09/tea-party-slams-boehner-and-ryan-on-debt-ceiling.html.

16. Vanessa Beasley, "The Rhetorical Presidency Meets the Unitary Executive: Implications for Presidential Rhetoric on Public Policy," *Rhetoric & Public Affairs* 13, no. 1 (2010): 12.

17. Nelson, *Bad for Democracy*, 18.

18. Nelson, *Representative/Democracy*, 219.

19. Stuckey, *Defining*, 13.

20. Nelson, *Representative/Democracy*, 219.

21. Trevor Parry-Giles and Shawn Parry-Giles, "*The West Wing's* Prime-Time Presidentiality: Mimesis and Catharsis in a Postmodern Romance," *Quarterly Journal of Speech* 88, no. 2 (2002): 209–227.

22. Parry-Giles and Parry Giles, "Romance," 210.

23. Parry-Giles, "Presidentialism," 213; 216.

24. Parry-Giles, "Presidentialism," 221.

25. Shane Phelan, *Sexual Strangers: Gays, Lesbians, and Dilemmas of Citizenship* (Philadelphia: Temple University Press, 2001), 55.

26. Claire Sisco King and Vanessa Beasley, "Running on Screen While Black: Representations of Black Presidential Candidates in U.S. Film and Television," *Quarterly Journal of Speech* 103, no. 1–2 (2017): 117–125.

27. Berlant, *Cruel Optimism*, 227.

28. See Ta-Nehisi Coates, "Fear of a Black President," *The Atlantic*, September, 2012. Online at http://www.theatlantic.com/magazine/archive/2012/09/fear-of-a-black-president/309064/; Vincent Pham, "Our Foreign President Barack Obama: The Racial Logics of Birther Discourses," *Journal of International and Intercultural Communication* 8, no. 2, (2015); and Eric Watts, "Postracial Fantasies, Blackness, and Zombies," *Communication and Critical/Cultural Studies* 14, no. 4 (2017), DOI: https://doi.org/10.1080/14791420.2017.1338742.

29. Michel Foucault, *The Birth of Biopolitics: Lectures at the College de France, 1978–1979* (London: Palgrave-MacMillan, 2008): 187.

30. Mitchell Dean and Kaspar Villadsen, *State Phobia and Civil Society: The Political Legacy of Michel Foucault*, (Palo Alta: Stanford University Press, 2016): 18.

31. Benjamin Anderson, "Affect and Biopower: Towards a Politics of Life," *Transactions of the Institute of British Geographers* 37, no. 1 (2012): 28–43.

32. Joshua Hanan and Catherine Chaput, "Stating the Exception: Rhetoric and Neoliberal Governance During the Creation and Passage of the Emergency Economic Stabilization Act of 2008," *Argumentation and Advocacy* 50, no. 1 (2012): 18–33.

33. "Military and National Defense," *Gallup*, 2016. Available online: http://www.gallup.com/poll/1666/military-national-defense.aspx; and "Congress and the Public," *Gallup*, 2016. Available online: http://www.gallup.com/poll/1600/congress-public.aspx.

34. "Presidential Approval Ratings—Gallup Historical Statistics and Trends," *Gallup*, 2017. Available online: http://www.gallup.com/poll/116677/presidential-approval-ratings-gallup-historical-statistics-trends.aspx.

35. "Trust in Government" *Gallup*, 2016. Available online: http://www.gallup.com/poll/5392/trust-government.aspx

36. Berlant, *Cruel Optimism*, 11.

37. Elisabeth Anker, *Orgies of Feeling: Melodrama and the Politics of Freedom* (Durham: Duke University Press, 2014), 14.

38. Vanessa Beasley, *You, the People: American National Identity in Presidential Rhetoric* (College Station: Texas A&M University Press, 2004), 38.

39. Beasley, *You*, 39.

40. Ibid.

41. Jürgen Habermas, *Legitimation Crisis* (Cambridge: Polity Press, 1992), 69.

42. Habermas, *Legitimation*, 25.

43. D. W. Winnicott, *The Child, the Family, and the Outside World* (Reading, MA: Perseus Publishing, 1964): 10.

44. Winnicott, *Family*, 19.

45. Parry-Giles and Parry-Giles, "Romance," 210, and Berlant, *Cruel Optimism*, 3.

46. Anker, *Orgies*, 107.

47. Anker, *Orgies*, 170.

48. Berlant, *Cruel Optimism*, 227.

49. Berlant, *Cruel Optimism*, 228.

50. Diane Rubenstein, *This Is Not a President: Sense, Nonsense, and the American Political Imaginary* (New York: New York University Press, 2008).

51. Michael Rogin, *Ronald Reagan, The Movie: And Other Episodes in Political Demonology* (Berkeley: University of California Press): 38–40.

52. Rogin, *Reagan*, 42.

53. Rubenstein, *President*, 28.

54. Anne Norton, *Republic of Signs: Liberal Theory and American Popular Culture* (Chicago, University of Chicago, 1993): 3.

55. Norton, *Signs*, 93.

56. Rubenstein, *President*, 39.

57. Rubenstein, *President*, 39–40.

58. Rubenstein, *President*, 42.

59. Rubenstein, *President*, 14, 26.

60. Rubenstein, *President*, 14.

61. For disciplinary examples of similar reading strategies of the presidency, see Atilla Hallsby, "Imagine There's No President: The Rhetorical Secret and the Exposure of Valerie Plame," *Quarterly Journal of Speech* 101, no. 2 (2015): 354–378, and Calum Matheson, "'What Does Obama Want of Me?' Anxiety and Jade Helm 15," *Quarterly Journal of Speech* 102, no. 2 (2016): 133–149.

62. Christopher Bollas, *The Shadow of the Object: Psychoanalysis of the Unthought Known* (New York: Columbia University Press, 1989), 15.

63. Bollas, *Shadow*, 15.

64. Anker, *Orgies*, 12.

65. Rubenstein, *President*, 6, 8.
66. "Our View: Debt Limit Fights Risks a Dangerous Game of Chicken," *USA Today*, April 27, 2011. Online at http://usatoday30.usatoday.com/news/opinion/editorials/2011-04-27-debt-limit-fight-dangerous-game_n.htm, and George Stephanopoulos, "Preventing 'Financial Armageddon,'" *Good Morning America*, April 11, 2011. Accessed via EBSCO.
67. Erik Wasson, "Report: Treasury Must Cut Spending 44 Percent in Default," *The Hill*, June 28, 2011. Accessed online: http://thehill.com/policy/finance/168803-independent-report-outlines-huge-cut-in-spending-if-debt-ceiling-breached.
68. Brian Beutler, "Top Economist: Even Brief Default Will Cause New Recession and Blow Recovery 'Out of the Water,'" *Talking Points Memo*, June 28, 2011. Accessed online: http://talkingpointsmemo.com/dc/top-economist-even-brief-default-will-cause-new-recession-and-blow-recovery-out-of-the-water?ref=fpa.
69. David Frum, "How to Make 2011 a Repeat of 1931," *Frum Forum*, July 12, 2011. Accessed online: http://www.frumforum.com/how-to-make-2011-feel-like-1931/.
70. Sam Stein, "Obama Offered to Raise Medicare Eligibility Age as Part of Grand Debt Deal," *The Huffington Post*, July 11, 2011. Accessed online: http://www.huffingtonpost.com/2011/07/11/obama-medicare-eligibility-age_n_894833.html.
71. Lori Montgomery, "In Debt Talks, Obama Offers Social Security Cuts," *The Washington Post*, July 6, 2011. Accessed online: https://www.washingtonpost.com/business/economy/in-debt-talks-obama-offers-social-security-cuts/2011/07/06/gIQA2sFO1H_story.html?utm_term=.325b3482663a.
72. Christian Lundberg, "On Being Bound to Equivalential Chains," *Cultural Studies* 26, no. 2-3, (2012): 299–318.
73. Sarah Bailey, "A Startling Number of Americans Still Believe President Obama is a Muslim," *The Washington Post*, September 14, 2015. Accessed online: https://www.washingtonpost.com/news/acts-of-faith/wp/2015/09/14/a-startling-number-of-americans-still-believe-president-obama-is-a-muslim/?utm_term=.4a713282b1e9.
74. Barrett, "Tea Party."
75. Norton, *Signs*, 121.
76. Barrett, "Tea Party."
77. Temple's statement also allows the critic to flesh out further the meaning of Tea Party slogans like "Take Our Country Back" and their investment in objects like the Gadsden flag.
78. Lundberg, "Equivalential," 314.
79. Dean Clancy, "FreedomWorks Announces 'The Tea Party Debt Commission,'" *FreedomWorks*, June 27, 2011. Accessed online: http://www.freedomworks.org/content/freedomworks-announces-tea-party-debt-commission.
80. Chantal Mouffe, *The Democratic Paradox* (London: Verso, 2000), 102–103.
81. Stuckey, "Rethinking," 49.
82. Beasley, "Unitary," 31.
83. Darrel A. Wanzer, "Delinking Rhetoric, or Revisiting McGee's Fragmentation Thesis through Decoloniality," *Rhetoric & Public Affairs*, 15, no. 4 (2012): 647–657.

CHAPTER TWELVE

The Discursive Antecedents to Richard Nixon's War on Drugs

JOEL M. LEMUEL

The "War on Drugs" (WOD) may be the most controversial and compelling Oval Office initiative in the post-World War II (WWII) era.[1] From the time Richard Nixon announced a "total war against public enemy number one" to the present, presidents have attempted to influence the direction of narcotic policy by modifying understandings of the essential nature of drug addiction.[2] Democratic presidents foreground rehabilitation as the primary strategy for intervention and tend to frame addiction as a disease, arising from biological adaptions to chronic drug use, and over which addicts have no choice or control. In contrast, Republican presidents prioritize criminal justice strategies and generally frame drug abuse as an irresponsible and immoral act for which addicts are rightly held responsible and judged accordingly.[3] Public address scholars and historians contend the war metaphor, popularized by Nixon in the early 1970s, facilitated the marginalization of treatment and rehabilitation interventions and the overdetermination of punitive criminal justice strategies.[4] And with President Trump's claim that "we're becoming a drug-infested nation," there is a real possibility that the WOD will restart in earnest.[5]

The dearth of evidence supporting the bellicose perspective of narcotic control invites speculation about the original purpose of the WOD: "[Was] it a genuine public health crusade or … a ploy to undermine Nixon's political opposition—meaning, black people and critics of the Vietnam War?"[6] Historical speculation about this question rose when Nixon's former domestic policy chief

John Ehrlichman claimed the WOD was a means to "disrupt" black and hippie communities.[7] I suggest, however, such a formulation overestimates the president's ability to shape the rhetorical constructions that make their way into their public statements. It also underestimates the symbolic and material connections between criminal justice strategies and public health approaches.

I contend a thorough understanding of Nixon's drug policy rhetoric is impossible to grasp without contextualizing the former within a broader network of motives, emerging gradually during the 19th and 20th centuries, which transformed addiction from a private affliction to a problem that threatens the entire community. Specifically, the motives driving advocates to action in juridical (criminal justice agents), medical (mental health practitioners/public health officials), forensic (criminologists/geographers), and scientific (epidemiologists) discourse communities intersected in the conceptualization of heroin addiction as "social contagion."

The term "contagion" refers to communication processes that are literally or figuratively pathological. A literal contagion transmits disease through close contact between organisms, while a figurative contagion constitutes a pathological form of crowd behavior resulting in the rapid diffusion of a harmful theory or practice.[8] This semantic ambiguity makes social contagion rhetoric a useful quilting point for tying together medico-scientific discourse about biological pathogens that infect and destroy the tissues of the human body and juridico-forensic discourse about the social pathologies that disable the rational and moral faculties of the human mind. In this chapter, I show how the contagion metaphor laid the foundation for new patterns of exchange that all but determined the way Nixon framed the drug problem. Toward that end, I extend genealogical analysis to the presidency itself, tracing the discursive fragments that constituted Nixon's definitional approach to drug addiction.

The Postmodern Turn in Presidential Address

The postmodern turn in public address interrogates the process by which presidential address, conceived as a complex yet comprehensible whole, is subsequently fragmented into easily digestible sound bites and re-circulated in public discourse.[9] Postmodern approaches represent a significant departure from the conventional theorization of rhetorical effect in public address. Humanistic scholars have traditionally deduced the effects of presidential discourse by tracing the diffusion of terms and topics—which have their origin in the president's speeches, press conferences, and messages to Congress—in public culture.[10] But contemporary scholars, concerned linear diffusion may not be the most appropriate model for explaining presidential persuasion in network society, seek to understand "how questions of circulation impel and impede our work as rhetorical critics and theorists."[11] On the other hand, this recent body of work is fundamentally similar to conventional public address scholarship in that it stops short of conceptualizing presidential address as fragmentary shards awaiting criticism.[12] On the contrary, proponents of the postmodern turn insist "[t]here is an order to things, a governing logic that" moves from the presupposed center of power (i.e., the presidency) to presumably less powerful advocates located in the extremities of society.[13]

The tendency to theorize presidential address as a coherent text awaiting fragmentation and dissemination is owed to our discipline's humanistic orientation. Public address scholars treat the presidency as a particular arena for studying the principles and practices of rhetoric—the human capacity to see what is most likely to be persuasive to a given audience on a given occasion.[14] Once we accept the instability of the text and the demise of the author, what is the rationale for studying presidential address?[15] In my view, anxieties about the eventual dissolution of public address as an object of inquiry are overblown. After all, the best work on the presidency tells us something about the institution, and the institutional perspective implies a preoccupation with quasi-stable, recurring patterns of behavior that transcend the motives of individual rhetors because they mediate the rules that govern social activity.[16] Said differently, the concern with informal social control through institutions constitutes an affinity between rhetorical scholars who study presidential address and poststructuralists who interrogate the organized practices (mentalities, rationalities, and techniques) through which subjects are governed.[17] This chapter pilots a mode of genealogical analysis that enables public address scholars to understand the dense textuality of presidential discourse as a product of historical phenomena.

The WOD is widely regarded as one of the most successful, enduring examples of the use of presidential definition to delineate a domestic issue.[18] While the president exerts tremendous influence on our national definitions, I argue his ability to construct persuasive definitional arguments hinges on the extent to which discourse communities external to the office have successfully asserted authority over the issue in question. Discourse communities may capture social problems on a provisional basis by developing (1) a truth discourse capable of explaining the phenomena and (2) modes of intervention that can ameliorate negative consequences.[19] The former constitutes episteme—a corpus of knowledge bound by abstract, immutable, and universal laws. The latter consists of technes, which evolve from humanity's imperfect attempts to imitate nature. Technes resemble episteme in their reliance on general principles about human nature, but they differ in that their intent is making and/or doing as opposed to disinterested understanding.[20] In the context of drug addiction, forensic discourse from (A) criminology (the science of crime) and (B) epidemiology (the science of disease) produce and maintain a regime of truth that underwrites state of the art practice as it pertains to (C) criminal justice and (D) medicine. I draw traces of this discourse from a range of primary and secondary sources. Primary sources include research articles, manuscripts published in peer-reviewed journals, books written for lay audiences, official reports, and congressional testimony and floor debates. Secondary sources include book and law reviews, press narratives, and institutional biographies. I use this material to explain how the mesh between juridico-forensic and medico-scientific discourse conditioned the exercise of presidential power as it pertained to the problem of addiction between 1967 and 1974.

Addiction in Forensic Discourse (1910s–1960s)

During the early stages of the 20th century, pioneering criminologists urged their colleagues to take up the problem of social deviance with the ultimate goal of reducing criminal behavior, including drug abuse, to a relatively small number of principles or laws, testing these principles through prediction, and ultimately affording techniques of control.[21] If successful, criminology and closely aligned disciplines might achieve a comparable level of status as modern medicine had during its "golden age." Despite this somewhat competitive dynamic, criminology drew inventional resources from medicine in its quest to explain the causes of crime. Cesare Lombroso, the father of the field, predicted this trend when he asserted crime, like disease, stemmed from natural causes, and so, "the remedial treatment [of crime] must be specifically adapted to that cause."[22]

The addiction studies that emerged from criminology traced the spread of heroin abuse in Chicago, St. Louis, and the District of Columbia—three densely populated urban areas with relatively large African American populations.[23] Social scientists tracked the natural history of heroin epidemics in these areas with statistical methods borrowed from economic geography, a subfield of the discipline of geography concerned with the location, distribution, and spatial organization of economic activity.[24] Statistics on addiction patterns were developed from official records furnished by police departments, drug courts, hospitals, and social service agencies. The data were used to produce maps illustrating the spatial distribution of addictive behavior throughout the urban landscape. The geographic approach revealed the diffusion of heroin was confined to a small number of low-income black neighborhoods. Robins and Murphy claimed police records were appropriate indicators of drug abuse because "no heroin addict fails to come to police attention."[25] Nevertheless, it is reasonable to assume the high rate of heroin addiction observed in black communities was partially an artifact of using police records to measure the variable of interest.[26] The influence of conscious and unconscious racism, combined with the disproportionate police presence in these areas, made it harder for black addicts to stay out of trouble than their white counterparts.

Techniques from geography could describe the pattern of heroin addiction, but criminologists ultimately sought to explain the underlying causal processes that give rise to crime. Statistics about the mobility and migration patterns of drug addicts provided a factual foundation from which sociological explanations of addictive motivation were abstracted. Most studies integrated two complimentary sociological frameworks. The first of these, *the ecological approach*, tested for correlations between environmental variables (e.g., economic conditions, urbanization, immigration processes) and the concentration of drug abuse within specific geographical units. The results of ecological studies generally supported the conclusion that black youths who experimented with heroin were responding "naturally" to disorganized environmental conditions.[27]

Since ecological studies only examined macro-level variables, however, they could not "provide a theoretical mechanism for the translation of environmental factors into individual motivations."[28] Scientists filled this knowledge gap using a *socio-linguistic* framework.[29] This approach conceptualized drug abuse as behavior "learned in interaction with other persons in a process of communication." From this perspective, addiction included, not only techniques for acquiring and using drugs, but also "the specific direction of motives, drives, rationalizations, and attitudes" regarding the act. To shed light on the subject, criminologists used ethnography and other qualitative methods to examine interpersonal communication occurring in intimate group settings (e.g., family, school, and peer groups) where young people were socialized to accept or reject criminal values and behavior.[30]

Kobrin and Firestone's study examining the heroin epidemic that ravaged Chicago in the aftermath of the WWII exemplifies the socio-linguistic approach.[31] After their ecological analysis revealed the epidemic was confined to a relatively small number of poor black neighborhoods,[32] the authors conducted interviews with paid informants to discover what features of their cultural environment contributed to this finding. Their interpretation of the data suggested these communities were dominated by a "street corner society," which incentivized "behavior which [was] generally inconsistent with the norms of conventional society, and often openly hostile to many of its expectations."[33] Experimentation with heroin, then, provided black adolescents with the means to express their rejection of conventional social norms. Heroin abuse snowballed, they reasoned, because "the urban adolescent is [known to be] exceptionally vulnerable to epidemics of bizarre and unconventional behavior." After noting that contagions of novel behavior among young people are normally brief and inconsequential, the authors concluded such epidemics "seem to spread more rapidly, go farther, and remain unchecked for longer periods" in those segments of urban society dominated by street corner culture.[34]

The socio-linguistic explanation provided by Kobrin and Firestone illustrates how social scientists produced implicit models of addictive pathology that could be used to rationalize specific modes of intervention.[35] While the authors acknowledged prolonged opiate use produced physical dependency, they concluded cultural factors (i.e., the internalization of street corner culture) laid at the root of the heroin epidemic. In similar fashion, Robins and Murphy concluded "the problem of drug addiction is not simply one of physical dependence on heroin per se but is rather the general readiness of the addict to use drugs that alter mood or level of consciousness."[36] Said differently, the most important factors contributing to addiction—having an absent father, dropping out of high school, and a history of delinquent behavior—were unrelated to the narcotics. As a general rule, the types of interventions indicated by social scientific addiction research involved the restoration of civic institutions (e.g., the family, the school, and the church) responsible for exercising the legitimate forces of social control in people's lives.[37] For this reason, forensic discourse furnished rhetorical resources for juridical discourse communities who agreed social disorder was the root cause of the heroin epidemic.

Addiction in Juridical Discourse (1880s–1960s)

Drug addiction was not politicized in America until the turn of the 20th century. The shift in public sentiment was related to changing perceptions of who drug addicts were, how they acquired their habits, and how they behaved under the influence of drugs. The moral panic concerning drug addiction facilitated the passage of the Harrison Narcotic Act of 1914, a bill that required anyone who sold or distributed narcotics to register with the government and to pay a small tax. The bill essentially outlawed the possession of narcotics, except in cases where a registered physician had prescribed the drugs in good faith. The enactment of this legislation marked the point at which forensic discourse successfully captured the problem of drug abuse.[38]

However, the Harrison Act did not specify whether it was legal for physicians to maintain patients in a comfortable state of addiction by prescribing narcotics on an indefinite basis. This "medical loophole" generated contestations over the legality of so-called drug maintenance therapy. Prohibition agents from the Treasury Department's Federal Bureau of Narcotics took a negative view and aggressively prosecuted doctors and pharmacists who gave opiates to addicts. The Bureau and other law enforcement agencies would sometimes resort to coercion and intimidation in the fight against maintenance therapy.[39] But the naked application of state power was at best a temporary solution. In order for juridical discourse communities to consolidate their authority over the problem of drug abuse, they needed to rationalize criminal justice strategies using terms and topics drawn from epistemic discourse.

Anti-drug crusaders routinely engaged medical authorities in public-moral argument over the desirability and efficacy of maintenance therapy. The Bureau's response to the interim report of the American Bar Association and American Medical Association (ABA-AMA) Joint Committee on Narcotics and Drugs provides useful insight into 20th century juridical discourse.[40] The report, which carried the prestige of two of the country's most power and established institutions, reflected dissatisfaction with the operation of existing drug laws and embraced the view that addiction should be considered a medical problem. While the final version of the report remained agnostic on the question of maintenance therapy, the interim version unequivocally supported the practice. The Bureau's commissioner, Harry Anslinger, organized his own committee composed of distinguished addiction experts to rebut the report's conclusions.[41]

The core of the juridical rationale against maintenance therapy was an argument from definition. That is, anti-maintenance advocates identified addiction as a moral pathology caused by self-abusive indulgence. For example, the Deputy Chief of the Los Angeles Police Department explicitly and aggressively framed addiction through a moral lens:

> The cause of narcotic addiction is so well established that it did not deserve more thorough investigation in the report. The report, however, fails to mention that addiction is a "permissive disease"; that the sufferers, except for those few who acquire the disease through medical treatment, and the insignificant number who acquire the disease under conditions amounting to fraudulent overtures, *become narcotics addicts by self-administration; i. e., with and by their own permission.* Therefore, narcotic addiction (particularly after an addict has once undergone a "cure") may be considered as a self-induced or, more pointedly, a "disease" resulting from self-abusive indulgence. In this sense, it is not a true disease such as tuberculosis or diphtheria nor may those who become self-infected be considered unfortunate victims of a disease of contemporary society acquired innocently in the course of normal, moral pursuit of life.[42]

The author refuted the case for medical intervention by distinguishing the social causes of addiction from the biological causes of legitimate diseases, and by highlighting the addict's own complicity in his affliction. The debilitating withdrawal symptoms a drug addict experienced did not require any sort of medical intervention. Indeed, the more painful his withdrawal, the less likely the addict would fall back into depravity. Just as 20th century criminologists attributed heroin epidemics to the influence of "street corner society," juridical discourse framed addiction as a visible symptom of a more serious social contagion—a widespread anti-establishment attitude. According to one self-proclaimed "narcotics expert" from the Los Angeles College of Medical Evangelists, commitment to temperance and virtue was the only cure available for the "youthful vipers whose disrespect for authority, parental, religious, governmental or otherwise, [was] responsible for a wave of juvenile delinquency unparalleled in the history of our Nation."[43]

Juridical discourse framed drug addicts as moral lepers who needed to be identified and isolated before they could spread their affliction. Maintenance therapy would only make the problem worse because it is impossible to reeducate the young, rebellious drug addict on how to live a virtuous life, while supplying him with the implement of his transgression on an indefinite basis. Additionally, this discourse warned that clinics delivering this supposed treatment would hasten the spread of contagion by encouraging the infected to congregate with other high-risk individuals. The ABA-AMA committee's apparent disregard of "the contagion element" perturbed the LAPD deputy chief:

> The report recommends the establishment of an "out-patient clinic" where the "carriers" of the disease may obtain the "virus" which will be carried away to be used to "infect" another "uninfected" person, who will become "infected"; [sic] who in turn will present himself at the "clinic" to obtain more "virus" to "infect" another, ad infinitum.[44]

The contagion frame bolstered the position of juridical advocates because it shifted the locus of discussion away from the health of the individual addict to the security of the American public. Consider the observation, from the aforementioned narcotics expert, that physicians "would not hesitate to ask for police enforcement of laws protecting the country if an epidemic of bubonic plague developed and endangered the general population, even though the plague victims were sick individuals."[45] The logical extension of the juridical rationale is civil commitment, a legal process through which an individual with a severe mental disorder is court-ordered into treatment in a psychiatric hospital or in the community. Confining drug addicts made it impossible for them to spread the vice. Involuntary confinement became more prominent in juridical discourse when a spate of state court rulings in the 1960s transformed the framework for civil commitment from a "needs-based" model—derived from the authority of the "Parens patriae,"[46] —to a "dangerousness" model—rooted in the state's police power.[47]

The contagion metaphor is a heuristic device that is most effective when the agent of disease transmission is readily apparent. As it turns out, anti-drug crusaders and criminologists generally seemed to agree that racial minorities, especially blacks, constituted the source of the infection. One of ABA-AMA committee's strongest arguments was the well-known fact that the rate of addiction was higher in the U.S. than in Britain, even though maintenance therapy was perfectly legal in the latter. Juridical advocates refuted this argument by constructing enthymemes that leveraged racist tropes about black culture. One commentator found it "utterly unbelievable" that the committee failed to evaluate "the disparity in the ethnological components of the two nations." In his view, the rate of addiction in the U.S. was higher than the rates in England and Wales because the ratio of "Caucasians" to "Noncaucasians" in the States was less favorable.[48] Such racism is generally consistent with a broader trend in juridical discourse in which violent crime sprees supposedly committed by black men and poor immigrants were used to rationalize the use of penal sanctions and/or compulsory rehabilitation.[49]

While other discourses existed concurrently, juridical perspectives dominated policy debates about the problem of drug abuse until the late 1950s and early 1960s. In the end, juridical discourse communities were not ultimately successful in their attempt to demonize the maintenance therapy proponents, but their arguments helped to foreground the public health aspects and the racial dimensions of the drug problem. This was a significant victory in itself that paved the way for closer collaboration between medical and juridical interventions in the late 1960s and early 1970s.

Addiction in Medical Discourse (1880s–1960s)

One of the earliest formal elaborations of the disease model of addiction appeared in *An Essay, Medical, Philosophical, and Chemical, on Drunkenness and Its Effects on the Human Body*.[50] This treatise, written by a physician practicing in the late 18th and early 19th centuries, defined the habit of drunkenness as "a disease of the mind." Parsons and moralists had failed to solve the social problem presented by alcohol addiction, the author claimed, because they lacked expert knowledge about the biological and psychological consequences of chronic drunkenness. Although details varied between different doctors, 19th century medical discourse generally framed drug addiction as a clinical issue.[51] By the middle of the 20th century, however, the problem of drug abuse had been transformed into a public health issue.[52]

The field of public health consists of organized community efforts for maintaining, protecting, and improving the health of the population. In an article written about the medical significance of the "mental hygiene movement," the director of the National Institute of Mental Health (NIMH), explained the relationship between public health practice and clinical medicine: "To the arts of the medical practitioner, public health adds those of the research worker, the laboratory technicians, the educator, the nurse, and many others whose skills can be massed in an integrated attack on the disease." The author articulated clinical psychiatry and public health as complementary strategies for achieving a common goal. Mental disorders became public health issues "when sick individuals become a source of danger or contagion." In such cases, "individual efforts cannot cope with the disease unaided" and "economic dependencies or other social problems created by the illness become a community burden."[53] The specter of contagion, then, necessitates an all-out offensive that integrates environmental sanitation, infectious disease control, personal hygiene education programs, early diagnosis and preventative treatments, and the development of social machinery that maintains a standard of living adequate for the maintenance of mental health.[54]

By framing addiction as a threat to public health, medico-scientific authorities secured public investments, furnishing them with the money, manpower, and human subjects needed to evolve therapeutic practice. Public support for medical discourse found its clearest embodiment in the Federal Narcotic Farm—a government-funded prison, rehabilitative center, and research center that operated in Lexington, Kentucky between 1935 and 1974. The Farm housed the Addiction Research Center (ARC), the only organization in the world where the potential for addiction was assessed in human beings. The doctors and scientists who worked there "saw themselves as protectors of public health," and worked to develop a permanent cure for the condition.[55] As it turns out, both of the dominant therapeutic strategies for opiate addiction developed out of ARC research.

Therapeutic Communities: The Spiritual Path to Recovery

Therapeutic communities (TC) are drug free residences in which people in recovery from substance abuse disorders help each other to understand and change their behaviors. TCs bridge the individualistic approach of modern behavioral therapies with principles from mutual aid societies designed to help addicts stay sober and help other addicts achieve sobriety. The oldest and most influential of these societies, Alcoholics Anonymous (AA), pioneered the "Twelve Step" program of spiritual and character development—a set of guiding principles outlining a course of action for recovering from various types of addiction. While slight variation exist between different groups, the process generally requires patients to admit they cannot control their addiction, to recognize a higher power through which they may gain strength, to work with sponsors as they examine past transgressions and make amends, to learn how to live clean lives with a new moral code, and to help others who suffer from the same affliction.[56] Mutual aid societies for opiate addiction evolved from the efforts of patients at the Narcotics Farm who adapted AA's twelve-step principles to treat their own afflictions. Between the late 1940s and the mid-1950s, what started off as a small self-help group for opiate addicts within the Lexington facility spiraled into a quasi-movement of isolated groups lacking connection through a common service structure.[57]

Synanon, which pioneered the TC paradigm, evolved from mutual aid societies that sprung up on the west coast in the early 1960s. Synanon differed from earlier twelve-step groups in two significant ways. First, members forged their identities and internal relationships, not on the shared history of substance abuse (i.e., a person's drug of choice) but on the shared process of addiction per se. The universal conception of addiction made TCs a viable treatment modality, not just for alcoholics, but also for all types of addiction.[58] Synanon also deviated from twelve-step traditions because it dispensed with rules that barred members from directly discussing the content shared during meetings. Proponents claimed difficult, direct, and highly personal conversations were an essential component of the therapeutic process:

> To effectuate treatment, one must first remove the encapsulating shell. Then, once exposed to the light of reality, powerless to isolate himself without his fortress prison, he is in a position to be taught how to grow up. For the primary addict, also called the "street" addict, a full-time institutional therapeutic environment must be utilized to enable the individual to grow up and develop emotionally, sexually, vocationally and educationally. This is no small undertaking, but nothing less will suffice.[59]

The affinity between spiritual approach to recovery and the juridical perspective on rehabilitation is obvious. It should come as no surprise, then, that federal and state civil commitment programs for drug offenders routinely incorporated TC as one of their primary treatment modalities.[60]

Methadone Maintenance Therapy: The Pharmacological Path to Recovery

Methadone is a long-acting synthetic opiate agonist developed by German scientists before the start of the Second World War. After the war, research conducted at the Farm demonstrated methadone could be used to effectively withdraw heroin addicts.[61] The goal was to completely detoxify addicts by prescribing descending doses of methadone. While methadone proved to be excellent withdrawal agent, studies revealed about 90% of the patients treated relapsed after leaving the Farm.[62] This failure prompted advocates in the medical community to agitate for the establishment of outpatient clinics that would proscribe opiate agonists to patients to maintain their addiction in a community setting.[63]

A book entitled, *Drug Addiction: A Medical Problem* typifies public advocacy from the medical community during this period.[64] Written by Lawrence Kolb, one of the nation's foremost experts on the science of narcotic addiction, the purpose of the book was to persuade an audience consisting of doctors, scientists, and policy-makers to support a legal regime that would permit physicians to administer opiates or like-acting synthetics to patients on an indefinite basis. In order to achieve this goal, the author tried to change the institutional context used to evaluate drug policy. To this end, he delivered a scathing critique of "propaganda" disseminated by law-enforcement officials who ignored or were not acquainted with the wealth of scientific information on addiction written by medical specialists and pharmacologists. Arguments of this sort likely resonated with the anti-authority ethos of the era.

Furthermore, the author paired explicit authority appeals with a highly technical, inductive style of reasoning in which the selective inclusion of empirical evidence created the perception of objectivity. Consider Kolb's rebuttal of the claim that drug addiction causes violent crime, a common justification for the zero tolerance approach. Juridical discourse suggested the typical addict, because he lacks the motivation and discipline required for gainful employment, eventually resorts to criminal behavior to support his habit. To refute this argument, the author foregrounded his first-hand experiences treating and observing patients "who worked regularly for years despite their use of as much as 40 grains of morphine daily."[65] Moreover, these experiences convinced him that regular opiate use made it possible for some addicts to improve their social relations to such an extent that it carried over into work, offsetting the adverse effects on their efficiency. This inductive style served to distinguish medical discourse on addiction from the largely deductive style employed by juridical discourse communities who opposed maintenance strategies.

The concept of legal opiate maintenance was gaining steam within the medical community, but the debate was far from settled. Definitive research was still needed to answer critics who believed it was morally reprehensible for doctors to disguise indulgence as treatment. The Health Research Council of New York City, which was searching for a way to control the heroin epidemic raging through the city, funded the earliest maintenance research. A small group of male heroin addicts voluntarily enrolled in a pilot study conducted at the Rockefeller Research Institute.[66] Having determined short-acting narcotics made poor substitutes for heroin, the researchers experimented with long-term maintenance using methadone. The relatively long half-life (24–36 hours) of this particular agonist, combined with the ability to administer the drug orally, indicated MMT might be somewhat effective. The early returns were promising. Patients were no longer preoccupied with drugs and many began making plans for the future. Most importantly, they reported a reduced craving for drugs. Researchers speculated the methadone created a "blockade effect" against the analgesic effects of heroin, morphine, and other narcotics.[67]

The results from pilot research on MMT in the mid-1960s led to the creation of community mental health clinics (CMHCs) in the New York area to provide outpatient MMT to heroin addicts.[68] Medical authorities used the relative successes of outpatient MMT to argue the CMHCs model was a better strategy for reducing drug-related crime than civil commitment. Still, MMT faced resistance from juridical discourse that framed addiction through the lens of morality.[69]

Addiction in Scientific Discourse (1960s–1970s)

The scientific study of factors contributing to the incidence and distribution of drug addiction in different populations was late in coming. The psychiatric epidemiology was generally hampered by the embryonic state of scientific knowledge regarding the internal processes of the mind and/or brain, and specifically impeded by the absence of tools for assessing and treating the condition with technological precision. But the development of modern toxicological assessments during the 1960s and 1970s created opportunities for discursive exchange between epidemiologists and criminologists interested in the natural history of heroin epidemics. The circulation of terms, topics, and techniques found its expression in a series of scientific papers examining the prevalence of heroin abuse in the D.C. Department of Corrections (DCDC) between 1969 and 1973.[70] In one such study, an epidemiologist and his team set out to define the modern heroin epidemic and its relationship to crime. Urinary analyses conducted over a 30-day period revealed 44 percent of the men entering the D.C jail in August 1969 tested positive for heroin.[71] "Even more importantly, a one-page questionnaire that the new jail inmates filled out asked them, 'What year did you first use heroin'?" The combination of objective toxicological assessment and self-report data allowed researchers to "literally correlate the rising rates of the initiation of heroin use to the rising rate of crime." The results of the study raised the question: "What [could be done] about the city's heroin problem?"[72]

A growing body of independent epidemiological evaluations indicated community-based maintenance clinics were effective weapons in the fight against the New York City heroin epidemic.[73] Epidemiologists utilized studies documenting the link between the rise of heroin addiction and the D.C. crime wave to secure approval and resources for a pilot MMT program within the DCDC system. The spiral of positive momentum eventually manifested in the creation of a citywide outpatient MMT initiative called the Narcotic Treatment Association (NTA).

Between 1970 and 1973, the NTA treated 15,000 out of 20,000 probable addicts and dramatically changed the dynamics of heroin use in the city.[74]

Epidemiological interventions like the NTA resulted from the intermingling of juridical, forensic, and scientific discourse in a "contagious disease framework," which "shift[s] emphasis from the psychological characteristics of 'diseased' individuals to the specific mechanisms of disease spread," and thus rationalizes the coercion of actively diseases individuals who refuse to seek treatment voluntarily.[75] Medical authorities who favored the CMHC model pushed back against the scientific perspective on drug addiction. According to the researchers who pioneered MMT, integration of maintenance therapy within the criminal justice system altered the essential nature of the practice: "The climate which is created by forcing a man into treatment is antithetical to rehabilitation." CMHC proponents believed the voluntary association between doctor and patient was an indispensible element of the therapeutic process. Moreover, they argued the large and spontaneous demand for voluntary treatment belied the assumption, implicit in a contagious disease framework, that drug addicts must be compelled to seek treatment.[76] Nevertheless, the circulation of juridical, forensic, and scientific discourse in the specter of social contagion produced positive momentum that overwhelmed objections from medical discourse communities.

Addiction in the Rhetoric of the Nixon Administration

Six months into his presidency, Richard Nixon delivered a special message to Congress on the subject of narcotics in which he argued "drug abuse [had] grown from essentially a local police problem into a serious national threat to the personal health and safety of millions of Americans." The grave nature of the threat justified the passage of legislation that would "allow quicker control of dangerous drugs before their misuse and abuse reached epidemic proportions."[77] Just three months later, the president signed into law, the Comprehensive Drug Abuse Prevention Act (CDAPA), a bill that essentially combined the totality of federal drug law into a single statute, and thus provided cover for the expansion of controversial "no-knock" warrants. Criminal sanctions were tied to an elaborate schedule of drug-classifications with scheduling decisions determined, not by medical authorities, but by the nation's chief law enforcement officer. The CDAPA represented a call to arms against a growing contagion, with a declaration of war soon to follow. On June 17, 1971 the president appeared at a nationally televised press conference and beseeched Congress for authority and funds to wage "a new, all-out offensive against [America's] public enemy number one".[78] Although the tone of the administration's drug policy rhetoric remained more or less consistent, the content of the message had shifted dramatically.

The president was forced to admit the CDAPA over privileged law enforcement strategies and, for that reason, would not be enough to stem the tide of addiction. The reason was simple. The trade of illicit narcotics, like any business, was governed by the rules of supply and demand; the law enforcement provisions of the CDAPA were effective in reducing the supply of narcotics, but they were not designed to curb the demand for drugs. "We must rehabilitate the drug user," he argued, "if we are to eliminate drug abuse and all the antisocial activities that stem from drug abuse".[79] The complimentary relationship posited between criminal justice approaches and treatment strategies was mirrored in the president's decision to address the nation flanked by "Bud" Krogh and Dr. Jerome Jaffe. The former was the White House deputy for domestic affairs responsible for lowering crime in D.C., the latter an addiction specialist who Nixon tapped to lead the Special Action Office of Drug Abuse Prevention (SAODAP), a new agency housed within the Executive Office of the President that would become the central authority responsible for overseeing all major federal drug abuse prevention, education, treatment, rehabilitation, training, and research programs. The president portrayed the administration's embrace of rehabilitation as a pragmatic pivot from his original strategy, but genealogical analysis reveals the administration's drug policy was all but determined by the intermingling of juridico-forensic and medico-scientific discourse from the very beginning.

Addiction as a Symptom of Civil Disorder: Echoes of Juridico-Forensic Discourse in Nixon's Campaign Rhetoric

In many ways, Richard Nixon's campaign rhetoric echoed 20th century juridical discourse about America's growing drug problem. He secured the presidency by positioning himself as an authoritative leader who could extinguish the blazing inferno of urban anarchy that engulfed the nation in the summer of 1967. His public statements framed the outbreak of urban riots as "the most virulent symptoms" of a grave sickness.[80] He attributed varied manifestations of civil disorder such as the trafficking of illicit drugs, the volume of teen-age arrests, the scale of anti-war protest, the public antipathy toward police, and the growth of white-collar crime to the same cause— a decline in respect for public authority and the rule of law. America was well on its way to becoming a "lawless society," Nixon argued, because a widespread permissive sentiment had undermined her natural immunity to social disorder. Too many Americans excused widespread delinquency because they either disagreed with certain aspects of the prevailing social order or they sympathized with past grievances of lawbreakers. The beneficiaries of this permissive attitude notably included those who defied the law in pursuit of civil rights during the 1960s:

> [T]o the professor objecting to de facto segregation, it may be crystal clear where civil disobedience may begin and where it must end. But the boundaries have become fluid to his students and other listeners. Today in the urban slums, the limits of responsible action are all but invisible.

The civil rights movement had successfully framed racial disorder as the inevitable consequence of minority disenfranchisement. But Nixon argued the rise of urban anarchy was a foreseeable outcome wrought by the architects of civil disobedience. In doing so, his rhetoric shifted the locus of conversation from social reform to punishment. He claimed criminal justices strategies were the fastest and most effective way to control the spread of lawlessness. Increasing the quality and quantity of police in urban ghettos would bring "the physical presence of the law into those communities where the writ of authority has ceased to run" and thus root out the underlying infection.[81] This tough-on-crime message resonated with the so-called "great silent majority" of disaffected white middle-class voters who resented what they perceived as irrational protest of and profound disrespect for American institutions.[82]

Nixon's campaign rhetoric also bears a striking similarity to forensic explanations of the heroin epidemic in that each stream of discourse naturalized structural racism through definitional argument. While Nixon paid lip service to the presence of "racial animosities—and agonies," he did not accept the historical grievances of African Americans as a legitimate excuse for delinquency. His rationale for criminal justice strategies appeared as a deductive argument extending logically from his definition of a healthy society: "In a civilized nation no man can excuse his crime against the person or property of another by claiming that he, too, has been a victim of injustice. To tolerate that is to invite anarchy."[83] Likewise, criminologists studying the natural history of heroin epidemics in black communities designed research protocols that could not account for the influence of minority disenfranchisement on addiction patterns. For example, quantitative studies mapped the diffusion of heroin abuse by substituting evidence of crime (i.e., arrest records) for the incidence of addictive behavior. Such an approach made it extremely difficult for researchers to account for the moderating effect of racist police practices. Moreover, qualitative studies exploring the motives driving adolescent drug abuse defined "street corner culture" as a value system characterized by non-utilitarianism, malice, and negativism.

The logical consequence of this move is to paint certain anti-social behaviors (e.g., getting high) as rejections of conventional liberal values (social harmony) rather than expressions of frustration with unconsummated liberal ideals (social justice).

Addiction as a Public Health Problem: Echoes of Medico-Scientific Discourse in President Nixon's Drug Policy Rhetoric

Between 1969 and 1973, the Nixon administration marshaled a range of government resources, through the Law Enforcement Assistance Administration and the Office of Drug Abuse Law Enforcement, in "a concentrated assault on the street level heroin pusher."[84] From a medico-scientific perspective, these criminal justice interventions became perfect compliments to contagious disease control. That is, the police took on the function of epidemiologic field teams that contained new outbreaks by identifying actively sick and other high-risk individuals and funneling them into treatment programs. Under Jaffe's leadership, the SAODAP used federal resources to increase treatment by contracting with and letting grants to state governments and other local providers.[85] The period between 1971 and 1973 saw a massive expansion in the total number, geographical distribution, and funding of outpatient treatment services delivered through CMHCs and private facilities and in-patient rehabilitation in state hospitals and correctional facilities via civil commitment frameworks.[86] While most historical accounts of the agency's legacy focus on its support for methadone programs, the SODAPA also increased investments in non-methadone treatments such as the TC approach. According to Jaffe, "[the agency] was trying to show ... there wasn't any single best road to recovery from addiction, but that many treatments could work well and synergistically together."[87] For some addicts, recovery involved maintaining their addiction indefinitely under the watchful eye of the federal government. For others, rehabilitation involved spiritual redemption through confrontation, confession and, ultimately, conversion to a better way of life.

The mutually constitutive relationship between rehabilitation and compulsion is evident in the way Nixon discussed allegations of widespread heroin abuse among military personnel stationed in Vietnam. By the early 1970s, drug abuse had become a powerful yet convenient explanation of the failing war effort, especially among its most ardent supporters. This sentiment gained steam with the publication of "The World Heroin Problem," an inflammatory report claiming some 10 to 15 percent of the servicemen stationed in Vietnam were addicted to pure heroin. The authors of the report gave the impression that the soldiers ran a greater risk of becoming drug addicts than combat casualties.[88] For the most part, public reaction to the report focused attention on the threat the military heroin epidemic posed, not to war effort, but American society. The fascination with and fear of the trained solider returning to wreak havoc on society has been a persistent theme in postwar literature throughout American history.[89] Disquiet about returning soldiers is usually manifested in news stories placing the particular struggles of this generation in the context of a consistent historical narrative about postwar readjustment difficulties. Since the Vietnam War was conducted against the backdrop of the Civil Rights Movement, anxieties about race riots add novelty to a familiar narrative. Having been previously exposed to narcotics in America's ghettos, black GIs were believed to be even more likely to return from Vietnam as drug-addled junkies looking to support their habits with all manner of criminal activity.[90] Some expressed fear these men would use their training to support radical black nationalist groups in waging civil war against the nation.[91] The federal government had to be held accountable for disciplining and rehabilitating these men, lest they be handed a slip of paper or thrown onto the streets for society to deal with.[92] In order to get the problem under control, the president ordered the immediate establishment of testing procedures and initial rehabilitation efforts to be taken in Vietnam:

> The Department of Defense will provide rehabilitation programs to all servicemen being returned for discharge who want this help, and we will be requesting legislation to permit military services to retain for treatment any individual due for discharge who is a narcotic addict. All of our serviceman must be accorded the *right to rehabilitation*.[93]

Nixon envisioned legislation that not only made rehabilitation a mandatory requirement for discharge, but also gave the SODAPA chief the authority to subsequently refer veteran addicts to mandatory treatment programs housed in Veterans Administration Medical Centers or state psychiatric hospitals. Such rhetoric obviously stretched the term "right," generally understood as a legal entitlement that an one may waive at their discretion, beyond the point of recognition.

Conclusion

This chapter contributes to the study of presidential rhetoric by urging public address scholars to seek different answers to the questions that drive them. Historical evidence suggests President Nixon believed drug use represented an existential threat to American society on par with communism and homosexuality.[94] How then does one explain his administration's substantial investments in medical treatments for drug addiction? Those familiar with Nixon's broader body of work might explain the contradiction as yet another case of "Tricky Dick" saying one thing and doing another.[95] Such an account misses the mark, however, because it focuses on the personal characteristics of the rhetor. We might reach a different conclusion if we focus, not on the Nixon-ness of the rhetoric, but on its antecedents—things that made Nixon's discourse possible.

My genealogical approach to studying presidential address infuses the humanistic enterprise with postmodern sensibilities. Instead of asking how a president achieves their goals through discourse, the genealogical approach investigates the historical process through which words, deeds, and things are packaged in discursive fragments that are networked together and manifested through presidential discourse. Said differently, genealogy inverts the relation of president-message-people in favor of message-people-president. My approach revealed popular accounts that frame Nixon WOD as either a genuine public health crusade or a ploy to undermine anti-war groups and black communities are overly simplistic. In reality, the way the president discussed the problem of heroin abuse was more or less determined by an emergent discursive network that, by the early 1970s, had altered the terms experts used to discuss the problem of addiction. Clinical psychiatrists came to view addiction as a literal contagion (i.e., a permanent metabolic disorder produced by/spread through chronic drug use) while law enforcement communities and criminologists analogized addictive behavior to a figurative contagion (i.e., a mimetic spiral resulting in herd-like behavior). Epidemiologists used terminology that allowed them to oscillate between these perspectives. The result was juridico-forensic and medico-scientific discourse seemed to be mutually reinforcing even when discourse communities posited radically different modes of intervention (e.g., TC via civil commitment and the CMHC model of MMT).

Popular accounts that frame Nixon's drug policy as either a genuine public health crusade or a ploy to undermine anti-war groups and black communities are overly simplistic. Genealogical analysis revealed Nixon's narcotics discourse was more or less determined by an emergent rhetorical network that, by the early 1970s, had altered the terms experts used to discuss the problem of addiction. Clinical psychiatrists came to view addiction as a literal contagion (i.e., a permanent metabolic disorder produced by/spread through chronic drug use) while law enforcement communities and criminologists analogized addictive behavior to a figurative contagion (i.e., a mimetic spiral resulting in herd-like behavior). Epidemiologists used terminology that allowed them to oscillate between these perspectives. The result was juridico-forensic and medico-scientific discourse seemed to be mutually reinforcing even when discourse communities posited radically different modes of intervention (e.g., TC via civil commitment and the CMHC model of MMT).

Notes

1. Andrew B. Whitford and Jeff Yates, *Presidential Rhetoric and the Public Agenda: Constructing the War on Drugs* (Baltimore, MD: Johns Hopkins University Press, 2009).

2. Richard Nixon, "Remarks During a Visit to New York City to Review Drug Abuse Law Enforcement Activities," March 20, 1972, online by Gerhard Peters and John T. Woolley, *The American Presidency Project,* http://www.presidency.ucsb.edu/ws/?pid=3779.

3. James E. Hawdon, "The Role of Presidential Rhetoric in the Creation of a Moral Panic: Reagan, Bush, and the War on Drugs." *Deviant Behavior* 22, no. 5 (2001): 419–445.

4. David F. Musto, *The American Disease: Origins of Narcotic Control* (Oxford University Press, 1999); Edward Jay Epstein, *Agency of Fear: Opiates and Political Power in America* (London: Verso, 1990); William N. Elwood, "Declaring War on the Home Front: Metaphor, Presidents, and the War on Drugs," *Metaphor and Symbolic Activity* 10, no. 2 (1995): 93–114; Thomas J. Johnson, Wayne Wanta, and Timothy Boudreau, "Drug Peddlers: How Four Presidents Attempted to Influence Media and Public Concern on the Drug Issue," *Atlantic Journal of Communication* 12, no. 4 (2004): 177–199; Emily Dufton, "The War on Drugs: How President Nixon Tied Addiction to Crime," *The Atlantic* March 26, 2012.

5. Donald J. Trump: "The President's News Conference," February 16, 2017, online by Gerhard Peters and John T. Woolley, *The American Presidency Project,* http://www.presidency.ucsb.edu/ws/?pid=123364.

6. German Lopez, "Nixon Official: Real Reason for the Drug War Was to Criminalize Black People and Hippies," *Vox,* March, 23, 2016.

7. Quoted in Tom LoBianco, "Report: Aide Says Nixon's War on Drugs Targeted Blacks, Hippies," *CNN,* March 24, 2016.

8. Susan Sontag and Heywood Hale Broun, *Illness as Metaphor* (Center for Cassette Studies, 1977); Oxford English Dictionary, *Concise Oxford English Dictionary* (Oxford: Oxford University Press, 2002); Richard Topol, "Bubbles and Volatility of Stock Prices: Effect of Mimetic Contagion," *The Economic Journal* 101, no. 407 (1991): 786–800.

9. Stephen Heidt, "The Presidency as Pastiche: Atomization, Circulation, and Rhetorical Instability," *Rhetoric & Public Affairs* 15, no. 4 (2012): 623–633; Megan Foley, "Sound Bites: Rethinking the Circulation of Speech from Fragment to Fetish," *Rhetoric & Public Affairs* 15, no. 4 (2012): 613–622.

10. David Zarefsky, "Presidential Rhetoric and the Power of Definition," *Presidential Studies Quarterly* 34, no. 3 (2004): 607–619.

11. Stephen John Hartnett and Jennifer Rose Mercieca, "'A Discovered Dissembler Can Achieve Nothing Great'; Or, Four Theses on the Death of Presidential Rhetoric in an Age of Empire," *Presidential Studies Quarterly* 37, no. 4 (2007): 599–621; Mary E. Stuckey, "On Rhetorical Circulation," *Rhetoric & Public Affairs* 15, no. 4 (2012): 609–612; Joshua M. Scacco and Kevin Coe, "The Ubiquitous Presidency: Toward a New Paradigm for Studying Presidential Communication," *International Journal of Communication* 10 (2016): 2014-2037.

12. Michael Calvin McGee, "Text, Context, and the Fragmentation of Contemporary Culture," *Western Journal of Communication (includes Communication Reports)* 54, no. 3 (1990): 274–289.

13. Stephen Heidt, "The Presidency as Pastiche: Atomization, Circulation, and Rhetorical Instability," Rhetoric and Public Affairs 15, no. 4 (2012): 623-633.

14. Theodore Otto Windt, "Presidential Rhetoric: Definition of a Field of Study," *Presidential Studies Quarterly* 16, no. 1 (1986): 102–116.

15. Jacques Derrida, *Writing and Difference* (New York: University of Chicago Press, 1978); Roland Barthes, "The Death of the Author," in *Image, Music, Text: Essays Selected and Translated by Stephen Heath* (London: Fontana Press, 1977), 142–148.

16. Mary E. Stuckey, "Rethinking the Rhetorical Presidency and Presidential Rhetoric," *Review of Communication* 10, no. 1 (2010): 38–52; Paul J. DiMaggio and Walter W. Powell, "The Iron Cage Revisited: Institutional Isomorphism and Collective Rationality in Organizational Fields," *American Sociological Review* 48, no. 2 (1983): 147–160.

17. Michel Foucault, *Discipline and Punish: The Birth of the Prison* (New York: Random House, 1977); Michel Foucault, "Michel Foucault's Lecture at the College de France on Neo-Liberal Governmentality," *Economy and Society* 30, no. 2 (1979): 190–207; Michel Foucault et al., *The Foucault Effect: Studies in Governmentality* (Chicago: University of Chicago Press, 1991).

18. Elwood, "Declaring War on the Home Front: Metaphor, Presidents, and the War on Drugs."

19. Paul Rabinow and Nikolas Rose, "Biopower Today," *BioSocieties* 1, no. 2 (2006): 195–217.

20. Charles Sears Baldwin, *Ancient Rhetoric and Poetic: Interpreted from Representative Works* (New York: The Macmillan Company, 1924).

21. Joseph Slabey Rouček, *Sociology of Crime* (New York: Philosophical Library, 1961).

22. Cesare Lombroso, *Crime, Its Causes and Remedies*, vol. 3 (Boston: Little, Brown, 1911), vi–vii.

23. Robert L. DuPont and Mark H. Greene, "The Dynamics of a Heroin Addiction Epidemic," *Science* 181, no. 4101 (1973): 716–722; Lee N. Robins and George E. Murphy, "Drug Use in a Normal Population of Young Negro Men," *American Journal of Public Health and the Nations Health* 57, no. 9 (1967): 1580–1596; Patrick H. Hughes and Gail A. Crawford, "The High Drug Use Community: A Natural Laboratory for Epidemiological Experiments in Addiction Control," *American Journal of Public Health* 64, no. 12(Suppl) (1974): 11–15; Solomon Kobrin and Harold Finestone, "Drug Addiction among Young Persons in Chicago," in *Gang Delinquency and Delinquent Subcultures,*ed. James F. Short (New York: Harper & Row, 1968), 110–130; Solomon Kobrin and Harold Finestone, "Opiate Addiction among Adolescent Males in Chicago," in *Papers Delivered at the 48th Annual Meeting*, 1953, 4.

24. Gordon L. Clark, Meric S. Gertler, and Maryann P. Feldman, *The Oxford Handbook of Economic Geography* (Oxford University Press, 2003).

25. Kobrin and Finestone, "Drug Addiction among Young Persons in Chicago," 1586.

26. D. J. Shoemaker, *Theories of Delinquency: An Examination of Explanations of Delinquent Behavior* (Oxford, NY: Oxford University Press, 1984).

27. Clifford Robe Shaw and Henry Donald McKay, "Juvenile Delinquency and Urban Areas," 1942.

28. Shoemaker, *Theories of Delinquency: An Examination of Explanations of Delinquent Behavior*, 132.

29. Kobrin and Finestone, "Drug Addiction among Young Persons in Chicago"; Robins and Murphy, "Drug Use in a Normal Population of Young Negro Men."

30. Alfred R. Lindesmith, "A Sociological Theory of Drug Addiction," *American Journal of Sociology* 43, no. 4 (1938): 593–613; E. H. Sutherland and Donald R. Cressey, *Criminology*, 10th ed. (Philadelphia: JB Lippincott Company, 1978), 80.

31. Kobrin and Finestone, "Drug Addiction among Young Persons in Chicago."
32. The study revealed more than half the city's drug users resided in "only five of the city's 75 community areas (Oakland, Douglas, Near South, Grand Boulevard, and Washington Park)" (p. 116). It should be noted that, contrary to their stated intentions, the authors choose not include any information on the racial composition of these communities. However, historical sources show black residents dominated all five areas from 1947–1953. For more information, see: James R. Grossman, Ann Durkin Keating, and Janice L. Reiff, eds. *The Encyclopedia of Chicago* (Chicago: University of Chicago Press, 2004).
33. Kobrin and Finestone, "Drug Addiction among Young Persons in Chicago," 118.
34. Ibid., 126–127.
35. Kobrin and Finestone, "Drug Addiction among Young Persons in Chicago"; Thaddeus E. Weckowicz, *Models of Mental Illness: Systems and Theories of Abnormal Psychology* (Springfield, IL: C. C. Thomas, 1984).
36. Robins and Murphy, "Drug Use in a Normal Population of Young Negro Men.," 1595.
37. Shoemaker, *Theories of Delinquency: An Examination of Explanations of Delinquent Behavior.*
38. David T. Courtwright, "A Century of American Narcotic Policy," *Treating Drug Problems* 2 (1992): 1–62.
39. Ibid.
40. Drug Addiction, *Crime or Disease? Interim and Final Reports of the Joint Committee of the American Bar Association and the American Medical Association on Narcotic Drugs* (Bloomington: Indiana University Press, 1961).
41. Advisor Committee to the Federal Bureau of Narcotics, "Comments on 'Narcotic Drugs: Interim Report of the Joint Committee of the American Bar Association and the American Medical Association on Narcotic Drugs'" (Federal Bureau of Narotics, July 3, 1958), https://druglibrary.net/special/king/caba/britishsystem.htm; Rufus King, *The Drug Hang-up: America's Fifty-Year Folly* (New York: Norton, 1972).
42. Lynn White, quoted in Advisor Committee to the Federal Bureau of Narcotics, "Comments."
43. Richard Bloomquist, quoted in ibid.
44. Lynn White, quoted in ibid.
45. Richard Bloomquist, quoted in ibid.
46. Latin for "parent of the nation." It's a legal term referring to the public policy power of the state to intervene against an abusive or negligent parent, legal guardian or informal caretaker, and to act as the parent of any child or individual who is in need of protection.
47. Megan Testa and Sara G. West, "Civil Commitment in the United States," *Psychiatry* 7, no. 10 (2010): 30–40.
48. Lynn White, quoted in Advisor Committee to the Federal Bureau of Narcotics, "Comments."
49. Courtwright, "A Century of American Narcotic Policy."
50. Thomas Trotter, *An Essay, Medical, Philosophical, and Chemical on Drunkenness and Its Effects on the Human Body (Psychology Revivals)* (London: Routledge, 2014), https://books.google.com/books?hl=en&lr=&id=y68uAgAAQBAJ&oi=fnd&pg=PP1&dq=An+Essay,+Medical,+Philosophical,+and+Chemical,+on+Drunkenness+and+Its+Effects+on+the+Human+Body+&ots=Wkwad-pqaZ&sig=nPwGwCA-Cu3C-ZjAEzB-GYpbqhE.

51. Gerald N. Grob, *Nineteenth-Century Medical Attitudes toward Alcoholic Addiction: Six Studies, 1814–1867* (New York: Arno Press, 1981); William L. White, "Addiction as a Disease: Birth of a Concept," *Addiction* 51 (2000): 73.

52. B. S. Brown, "Philosophy and Scope of Extended Clinic Activities," in *Perspectives in Community Mental Health*. (Chicago: Aldine Publishing, 1969).

53. R. H. Felix, "Mental Hygiene As Public Health Practice," *American Journal of Orthopsychiatry* 21, no. 4 (1951): 707–708.

54. C. E. A Winslow, "The Untilled Fields of Public Health," *Science* 51, no. 1306 (1920): 23–33.

55. N. D. Campbell, J. P. Olsen, and Luke Walden, *The Narcotic Farm: The Rise and Fall of America's First Prison for Drug Addicts* (New York, NY: Abrams, 2008), 15.

56. Alcoholics Anonymous, *Alcoholics Anonymous: The Story of How Many Thousands of Men and Women Have Recovered from Alcoholism* (Center City, MN: Hazelden Publishing, 2002).

57. W. L. White, "Narcotics Anonymous and the Pharmacotherapeutic Treatment of Opioid Addiction," *To Be Posted at Www.Williamwhitepapers.Com*, 2011.

58. Ibid.

59. David Casriel and David Deitch, *New Success in the Cure of Addicts* (Staten Island: Daytop Village, Inc., 1976), 3.

60. Claire Clark, "'Chemistry Is the New Hope': Therapeutic Communities and Methadone Maintenance, 1965–71," *Social History of Alcohol and Drugs* 26, no. 2 (2012): 192–216.

61. Harris Isbell and Victor H. Vogel, "The Addiction Liability of Methadon (Amidone, Dolophine, 10820) and Its Use in the Treatment of the Morphine Abstinence Syndrome," *American Journal of Psychiatry* 105, no. 12 (1949): 909–914.

62. Vincent P. Dole and Marie E. Nyswander, "Heroin Addiction—a Metabolic Disease," *Archives of Internal Medicine* 120, no. 1 (1967): 19–24.

63. Herman Joseph, Sharon Stancliff, and John Langrod, "Methadone Maintenance Treatment (MMT)," *The Mount Sinai Journal of Medicine*, 67, no. 5-6 (2000), 347-364, https://pdfs.semanticscholar.org/ae14/39e284a4b5fc299306f2a8991b493b36edf4.pdf.

64. Lawrence Kolb, *Drug Addiction: A Medical Problem* (Springfield, IL: Thomas, 1962).

65. Ibid., 11.

66. H. Joseph and P. Appel, "Historical Perspectives and Public Health Issues," *State Methadone Treatment Guidelines. Treatment Improvement Protocol (TIP) Series* 1 (1993): 11–24.

67. Vincent P. Dole, Marie E. Nyswander, and Mary Jeanne Kreek, "Narcotic Blockade," *Archives of Internal Medicine* 118, no. 4 (1966): 304–309.

68. Joseph and Appel, "Historical Perspectives and Public Health Issues."

69. Clark, "'Chemistry Is the New Hope': Therapeutic Communities and Methadone Maintenance, 1965-71."

70. Robert L. DuPont, "Profile of a Heroin-Addiction Epidemic," *New England Journal of Medicine* 285, no. 6 (1971): 320–324; DuPont and Greene, "The Dynamics of a Heroin Addiction Epidemic."

71. DuPont, "Profile of a Heroin-Addiction Epidemic."

72. Quoted in "Conversation with Robert L. DuPont," *Addiction* 100 (2005): 1405.

73. Frances Rowe Gearing and Morton D. Schweitzer, "An Epidemiologic Evaluation of Long-Term Methadone Maintenance Treatment for Heroin Addiction," *American Journal of Epidemiology* 100, no. 2 (1974): 101–112.

74. "Conversation with Robert L. DuPont."
75. Patrick H. Hughes, Noel W. Barker, Gail A. Crawford, and Jerome H. Jaffe, "The Natural History of a Heroin Epidemic," *American Journal of Public Health* 62, no. 7 (1972): 995-1001.
76. Vincent Dole, Treatment and Rehabilitation of Narcotics Addicts, Subcommittee to Amend the Narcotic Rehabilitation Act of 1966 of the Committee on the Judiciary (1971): 390.
77. Richard Nixon, "Special Message to the Congress on Control of Narcotics and Dangerous Drugs." The American Presidency Project, 1969.
78. Richard Nixon, quoted in: Chris Barber. "Public Enemy Number One: A Pragmatic Approach to America's Drug Problem." Richard Nixon Foundation, June 29, 2016. https://www.nixonfoundation.org/2016/06/26404/.
79. Richard Nixon, "Special Message to the Congress on Drug Abuse Prevention and Control." The American Presidency Project, 1971.
80. Richard Nixon, "What Has Happened to America?," *Reader's Digest* 50 (1967).
81. Ibid.
82. Andrew A. King and Floyd Douglas Anderson, "Nixon, Agnew, and the 'Silent Majority': A Case Study in the Rhetoric of Polarization," *Western Speech* 35, no. 4 (1971): 243–255; Matthew D. Lassiter, *The Silent Majority: Suburban Politics in the Sunbelt South* (Princeton, NJ: Princeton University Press, 2013).
83. Richard Nixon, "Special Message to the Congress on Drug Abuse Prevention and Control." The American Presidency Project, 1971.
84. Richard Nixon, "Remarks During a Visit to New York City to Review Drug Abuse Law Enforcement Activities."
85. Nixon, "Drug Abuse Prevention and Control," 1971.
86. G. Larry Mays, "The Special Action Office for Drug Abuse Prevention: Drug Control during the Nixon Administration," *International Journal of Public Administration* 3, no. 3 (1981): 355–371.
87. "Interview with Dr. Jerome Jaffe." FRONTLINE: Drug Wars. Public Broadcasting Service, 1998. https://www.pbs.org/wgbh/pages/frontline/shows/drugs/interviews/jaffe.html.
88. Morgan F. Murphy and Robert H. Steele, The World Heroin Problem: Report of Special Study Mission. US Government Printing Office, 1971.
89. Dane Archer and Rosemary Gartner, "Myth of the Violent Veteran," *Psychology Today*, 1976.
90. Peter Osnos, "Two Veterans Give Details of Drug Use, Attempts to Quit," *The Washington Post*, April 24, 1973.
91. Whitney Young, "When the Negroes in Vietnam Come Home," *Harper's Magazine*, June 1976.
92. William Wyant, "Coming Home With A Habit," *The Nation*, July 5, 1971.
93. Nixon, "Drug Abuse Prevention and Control," 1971, emphasis added.
94. Douglas Brinkley and Luke Nichter, *The Nixon Tapes*, 1971–1972 (Houghton Mifflin Harcourt, 2014).
95. Michael Silverstein, "What Goes around...: Some Shtick from 'Tricky Dick' and the Circulation of US Presidential Image," *Journal of Linguistic Anthropology* 21, no. 1 (2011): 54–77.

CHAPTER THIRTEEN

Home-Making, Nation-Making

American Womanhood in Progressive Era Presidential Rhetoric

LESLIE J. HARRIS

At the risk of stating the obvious, the United States has never had a female president or vice-president. Scholarship on the American presidency has named the president as a national leader, spokesman, and model of Americanness.[1] The president also defines, sometimes implicitly and sometimes explicitly, who is excluded from true Americanness. Yet, women have retained a complex relationship to the presidency, being always both present and absent, necessary and tangential. Not only has a woman never held the role of president, but, for much of American history, womanhood has seemed to exist in a liminal space of Americanness. Until 1920 women were citizens but were not permitted to perform some of the most basic tasks of citizenship. Sometimes even looking for womanhood in American identity can be a baffling enterprise, leading scholarship to focus on *home* and other separate spheres as a way to account for historical and continuing absences of women in civic life. Through a case study rooted in the Progressive Era, I identify a spatial analytic of *home* as way to understand womanhood in U.S. presidential rhetoric. Rather than conceptualizing women as existing in separate spheres, this case study suggests that *home* and *nation* existed in a nested spatial relationship that justified and naturalized the political subjectivities of American women. Thus, I conclude that not only is the presidential body gendered male but that presidential rhetoric also participates in constructing a spatial orientation for citizens—a spatial orientation that is fundamentally gendered and limits mobility of gendered bodies.

Raka Shome insists that "space is not merely a backdrop," but rather, spatial understandings provide a "framework for analyzing the functioning of cultural power and politics."[2] The concept of scale can be an important way of understanding space. Just as the shifting of scales can impose different perspectives on a given cartography, a rhetorical shifting of scale can guide different spatial understanding by folding, networking, nesting, or expanding space. Scale can function as a way of conceptually mapping seemingly disparate spaces. Through a case study of Progressive Era presidential rhetoric, this study tracks a presidential assumption of a nested spatial relationship of different scales of home, specifically the familial and national spaces of home. This nested spatial relationship positions home as a critical foundation of the nation, the president as an authority over the home, and women as maintaining a symbolic role in national identity through association with the home. Presidential rhetoric exalted proper American womanhood while actual women were often considered tangential to national civic life. This analysis demonstrates how presidential rhetoric genders, even when gender may appear to be absent. Nation is not a simple monolithic space; rather presidential rhetoric orders national space in ways that are fundamentally gendered.

The Progressive Era provides a useful case study. In a time before the national adoption of woman's suffrage, women's public visibly was steadily increasing. While the suffrage movement appeared to stagnate during the early years of the era, women were increasingly socially active in issues such as temperance, labor, and education. At the same time, the role of the presidency was beginning to change. As Mary E. Stuckey explains,

> In a time of shifting and uncertain hierarchies and changing institutional arrangements, the presidency began to emerge as a crucial locus for the articulation of the national self. … [As] the economic and political order shifted during the late nineteenth and early twentieth centuries, the presidency began to assume a routine and institutionalized primacy previously lacking.[3]

The Progressive Era set the stage for the public role of womanhood in the American political imaginary that would remain influential for years to come, and the presidency exists as an important site of inquiry into understanding this role.

My argument develops in four stages. I begin by explicating my meaning of home as a way to understand places of belonging, and I situate home as functioning within a *loci* of order. I then contextualize the American Progressive Era as a critical time of political and social development before specifically analyzing the presidential rhetoric during this time period. Within my analyses of presidential rhetoric, I identify home as a national foundation, and I then argue how understanding the role of home can help us understand the political subjectivity of womanhood during this time period. I conclude by arguing that a spatial analytic can be vital to understanding the ways in which presidential rhetoric orders the space of the nation and, in turn, the political subjectivities of those within in nation in ways that are gendered.

Loci of Order and Home

bell hooks describes the creation of a homeplace as having a "radical political dimension."[4] A homeplace can be safe and affirming in the midst of threat and chaos. Similarly, Lisa Flores identifies home as a site of individual and community identity for Chicana feminists who negotiate the complexity of life in a border culture.[5] We also know that the mythology of home often does not match with its reality; home can be a site of violence and oppression just as easily as a site of belonging and safety. Yet, the rhetoric of home as a site of safety and belonging remains powerful, and a spatial analytic can be helpful in finding ways to read understandings of home.

In what Roxanne Mountford has called "rhetorical space" (that is, "the geography of a communicative event"), rhetorical scholars have proven that rhetoric can create spatial meaning, and spaces (such as "home") communicate, constrain, and shape meaning.[6] In conceptualizing space as a critical analytic, not simply a setting or rhetorical resource, we, as critics, can see rhetoric in new ways. In particular, I see the space of home functioning as a *locus* of order in presidential rhetoric. Chaim Perelman and Lucie Olbrechts-Tyteca argue that *loci communes* "serve as the basis for values and hierarchies," forming general premises and, even when merely implied, "play a part in the justification of most of the choices we make."[7] *Loci communes* often emerge as significant when rhetors must defend a value hierarchy.[8] Carol Winkler explains, "Advocates may explicitly articulate their reliance on *loci communes* to justify their new value hierarchies, but more routinely, they simply imply the usages of such commonplaces through the use of antithetical paring."[9] In short, this previous research affirms that *loci* underlie basic value premises and participate in structuring logical possibilities.

Perelman and Olbrechts-Tyteca identify six categories of *loci*, following the analytical systemization of Aristotle but incorporating consideration of context and audience that seemed to gesture toward an approach more indicative of what Michael Leff described as a Latin rhetorical understanding of *loci*.[10] One of those categories that received a fairly small amount of attention is the *loci* of order. Perelman and Olbrechts-Tytecha explain, "*Loci* of order affirm the superiority of that which is earlier over that which is later, sometimes the superiority of the cause, of the principle, sometimes that of the end, of the goal."[11] However, as recent scholarship on spatial rhetoric has shown, temporality is not the only way to impose order. I suggest a friendly augmentation to Perelman and Olbrechts-Tytecha's *loci* of order to include the possibility of spatial order.

This study demonstrates that spatial orientation can function as an organizing logic that guides basic value premises and political subjectivities. When we conceptualize the constructing and organizing of space as a rhetorical process, space can be rhetorically folded, expanded, nested, or networked. Each of these ways of creating and ordering space can entail particular value hierarchies and shape argumentative possibilities.

In this instance, home functions as both a space and an organizing logic. It is a trope that guides understanding of diverse and potentially conflicting sites of belonging. The *loci* of order also function as an organizing mechanism. Through the implicit organization of sites of home into a nested spatial relationship, Progressive Era presidents argue from the premise that home functions as a foundation of nation. This value ordering emerges from spatial ordering (*loci* of order). As a result, the value hierarchies implicit within a separate spheres explanation of women's roles fail to explain the dual presence and absence of women in American political rhetoric. Beginning with home allows us to see that womanhood functions within a broader foundational role.

In order to make sense of women's political subjectivity in the United States, scholarship often draws on the concept of separate spheres.[12] The language of separate spheres was common among Americans throughout much of the nineteenth century, but it is important to recognize that "separate spheres" is a trope that employs spatial language to make sense of social relations. That trope tends to be employed in at least one of three ways, each of which has different implications. First, separate spheres may be used to reflect the material reality of nineteenth and early twentieth century social life, suggesting that women tended to exist in separate social spaces from men. Those different social spaces may have been forced separation based on cultural expectations or spaces for an unique women's culture and community. However, the myriad of ways in which women were in public makes this conclusion problematic.[13] Second, the trope of separate spheres may have been a prescriptive response to social change during the nineteenth and early twentieth centuries. Linda Kerber, for example, suggests, "One plausible way to read nineteenth-century defenses of separate spheres … is to single out the theme of break-down; the noise we hear about separate spheres may be the shattering of an old order and the realignment of its fragments."[14] This theory identifies separate spheres as both an unrealized model and a control mechanism that persists in its appeal for those who call on women to stay in their place. Finally, separate spheres can be used as an analytical frame for rhetorical and historical scholarship to make sense of the time period. I am most interested in challenging this final option because it has limited utility in understand the role of women in public discourse, especially presidential discourse. As an analytical framework, separate spheres naturalizes the social relations scholars are attempting to interrogate. Critical engagement with the *loci* of home reveals a more complicated spatial relationship that helped guide logical possibilities in presidential rhetoric.

Women, the Progressive Era, and Politics

There was no monolithic progressive movement that characterized what is often known as the Progressive Era. Rather, this time period saw the emergence of loosely connected initiatives that ranged from child labor to food safety, and women were politically active in many of these causes. As Mary Ryan explains, "A political formation that looks like a woman's public sphere rose upon the American historical landscape between the 1890s and the 1920s."[15] Women were increasingly organizing as women—using their experiences, roles, identities, and networks to enable social and political change. Although not universally the case, many women organized under the guise of motherhood or a language of home, suggesting an intimate connection between women's role in public life and women's seemingly private identities.[16] As a result, largely middle and upper class women were critical in fomenting political change that included the adoption of mother's pensions, creation of the juvenile court, reform of labor practices, and advances in education.

At the same time, cultural practices of women were beginning to change. Sara Evans argues, "Between 1900 and World War I the old Victorian code which prescribed strict segregation of the sexes in separate spheres crumbled."[17] In what has been commonly called the emergence of the "new woman," by the turn of the century women were increasingly perusing employment, education, and female friendships.[18] Nevertheless, there may have been a disjuncture between cultural performances of womanhood and civic expectations of womanhood, especially among different races and classes of women.

Even while increasing numbers of women were in the workplace, involved in clubs, and engaged in other public activities, the woman's suffrage movement did not make significant progress in the early years of the Progressive Era. Indeed, 1896–1910 came to be known as "the doldrums" because there were no new woman suffrage states during this time period.[19] After the merger of the two national woman suffrage organizations in 1890, the National American Woman Suffrage Association (NAWSA) began a shift toward a state by state strategy which proved to be largely unsuccessful. By 1910 Eleanor Flexner explains that the movement was once again gaining momentum, but there was a "contradictory mixture of awakening, confusion, and continued paralysis."[20] While suffrage remained an important goal, there was little agreement on the best strategy to achieve that goal.

Despite the absence of woman's suffrage on the federal level, prior to 1890 women were active in politics, stumping for candidates, participating in party strategy, and even running for and winning local elective office (especially positions such as school superintendent).[21] However, by the 1890s women were increasingly shut out of mainstream party politics, especially as woman suffrage came to be associated with Populists, and even areas that had partial suffrage saw a backlash against women's political engagement.[22] This shift is evident in the Republican Party platform. In 1892 the platform included:

> We demand that every citizen of the United States shall be allowed to cast one free and unrestricted ballot in all public elections, ... The free and honest popular ballot, the just and equal representation of all the people, as well as their just and equal protection under the laws, are the foundation of our Republican institutions, and the party will never relax its efforts until the integrity of the ballot and the purity of elections shall be fully guaranteed and protected in every State.[23]

While the platform did not explicitly endorse woman suffrage, it did not preclude it, and the statement was vague enough that it may have appeased suffrage advocates. However, after 1892 woman's suffrage was largely absent from the Republic Party platform. Instead, women were praised for their volunteer efforts in the East and West Indies in 1900, and manhood was explicitly exalted in 1908. Further, Wilson did not even mention the issue of woman's suffrage in his 1913 message to Congress, even though suffrage activists had been exerting significant public pressure.[24] Despite women's apparent absence from presidential rhetoric and party platforms 1890–1920, home was apparent in the background of presidential rhetoric.

Home and Presidential Rhetoric

Despite silences and absences in regard to women, presidents often retained an interest in the spaces of home. Indeed, presidents such as Theodore Roosevelt and Woodrow Wilson were explicit in their characterization of the foundational function of home. Roosevelt argued that home was critical to the nation stating, "Successful home-making is but another name for the upbuilding of the nation."[25] Two years later Roosevelt explained, "With a nation as with a man the most important things are those of the household."[26] Both of these statements, casually situated within annual messages to Congress, not only emphasized the significance of a national interest in home, but they also implied a nested spatial relationship.

National home appeared to build up from familial home, situating the American home as both a microcosm of nation and a foundation on which the nation grew.

Wilson, in his justification for World War I, described a similar interrelated spatial relationship between home and nation. Wilson argued, "No man ever saw the people of whom he forms a part. No man ever saw a government. I live in the midst of the Government of the United States, but I never saw the Government of the United States."[27] What we can see, however, is our home, both familial and national; we can see a place, not an idea. For Wilson, nation was an abstract concept, but the idea of nation was visually evident in the space of the home. Throughout his speaking tour of early 1916, Wilson evoked the visual image of the musket or rusted sword displayed in places of honor in American homes. These displays, Wilson insisted, were displays of the spirit of nation within individual homes. He explained that the sacrifices of war were not simply for "hearth and home," rather, "We know that the lads who carried those swords and those muskets loved something more even than they loved peace—that they loved honor and the integrity of the Nation."[28] Within this conceptualization, home and nation were so inextricably connected that the idea of nation existed symbolically within the American home. Wilson's linkage between home and nation was especially critical in the context of World War I because the fighting was in Europe. In the most literal sense, American homes were not at risk, so connecting home and nation helped make the case for war. For Wilson, the familial home was nested within the national home, both spatially and ideologically.

The deep connections between home and nation were certainly evoked in the time leading up to World War I, but that foundational relationship was critical in shaping a broad swath of presidential policy during the Progressive Era. The nested spatial relationship between nation and home was most often evident in terms of national creation and training. Roosevelt in particular framed home as critical to shaping and taming national space. From justifying federal assistance to irrigate Western lands to the land policy of the Hawaiian Islands, Roosevelt maintained a national interest in creating and maintaining home.[29] The right kind of homesteading was thought to enable the building of the right kind of nation.

While home was depicted as a national foundation, the meaning of home was laden with racialized assumptions of what made for a good home and good moral foundation. Slums and tenements, for example, concerned several presidents, particularly the high poverty areas that had emerged in Washington, D.C. However, the slums and tenements were not labeled as "homes." Rather, they were "breeding grounds for vice and disease" or "human pest holes."[30] The terms "slum" and "tenement" were coded ways of referring to communities consisting of racial and ethnic minorities. In speaking of the problem, William Taft, for example, described slum residents as "the very poor […] and the criminal classes."[31] Presidential rhetoric such as this participated in dehumanizing people who lived in conditions of poverty and marked those living in tenements as suspicious and possibly criminal. Within this rhetoric, the defective home functioned as the root of the problem. Taft insisted that "it is of primary importance that these nuclei of disease and suffering and vice should be removed."[32] The fixation on both disease and vice marked the poor as unclean in body and soul that could spread, endangering the nation as a whole. If home building was equated with nation building, tenements were the wrong kind of home and, thus, built the wrong kind of nation.

Home was particularly significant because it was conceptualized as a space of creating nation through a shaping of national spaces and as a site of breeding citizens. Both Roosevelt and Wilson used the term "stock" to depict biological reproduction of citizens. For Roosevelt, "The stocks out of which American citizenship is to be built should be strong and healthy, sound in body, mind, and character."[33] In other words, parents of the nation's future citizens needed to be the right kind of people, and, what is implied in this statement, is that those parents should be white, middle-class, and Protestant. Within this context, the use of "stock," a term of breeding, is significant. By the time of the Progressive Era, an American mythology was developing that exalted the country while denigrating the city as a dangerous space occupied by racial and ethnic minorities.[34] Roosevelt reflected a fairly common concern when he described the nation's cities as "dangerous symptoms in our modern life."[35] Similarly, Wilson argued,

> And as our life has unfolded and accumulated, as the contact of it have become hot, as the populations have assembled in the cities, and the cool spaces of the country have been supplanted by the feverish urban areas, the whole nature of our political questions has been altered.[36]

The fixation on cities reflects not only a concern over proper national homes, but also reinforces a mythology of the country as the site of true Americanness. Thus, conceptualizations of the American population as breeding stock emphasized the need for reproduction in order to grow the nation and highlighted the supposed necessity of white, middle-class Americans to have children, all while drawing on the American mythology of the country.

Roosevelt's language of breeding stock also helps explain his use of the phrase "race suicide" or "race death." For Roosevelt the creating of future citizens was an issue of both "quality" and "quantity." The failure of good men and women to produce children was, according to Roosevelt, "the one sin for which the penalty is national death, race death; a sin for which there is no atonement."[37] Citizens appeared to be hearing Roosevelt's message. In a speech in California Roosevelt recounted,

As I drove through your beautiful streets I passed by one house where there was a large family party assembled, and they had a strip of bunting and printed on it were the words: 'No Race Suicide Here;' and I got up and bowed my acknowledgements and congratulations.[38]

In this anecdote, the president acknowledged a white family for their procreation, much like a president would acknowledge a solder for bravery and sacrifice, reinforcing the national interest in white procreation and, thus, home.

Wilson, on the other hand, appeared to accept that American diversity was both inevitable and occasionally beneficial. In a speech before the Daughters of the American Revolution, Wilson explained,

America has not grown by the mere multiplication of the original stock. It is easy to preserve tradition with continuity of blood; it is easy in a single family to remember the origins of the race the purposes of its organization; but it is not so easy when the race is constantly being renewed and augmented from other sources, from stocks that did not carry or originate the same principles.[39]

Much like Roosevelt, Wilson's use of breeding drew on the mythology of the American country, but it also shaped the logic of the argument. Those familiar with animal breeding would have recognized the value of deliberate renewal and augmentation of breeding stock. Following this logic, deliberate and controlled immigration could be beneficial for the nation, and, for Wilson, the familial home was central to integration of potential immigrants. He continued to explain, "So from generation to generation strangers have had to be indoctrinated with the principles of the American family, and the wonder and beauty of it all has been that the infection has been so generously easy."[40] Within this framework, Americanness can be learned, and home was the site of learning. Proper training could augment the limits to procreation.

Within Progressive Era presidential rhetoric, civic creation (procreation) and training often functioned as two sides of the same coin. Both sides were firmly rooted in home as a foundation of nation and women as responsible for that foundational work. Despite Roosevelt's biological emphasis, he too maintained the importance of training in building national character. For example, during the same tour of California as when he encountered the "No Race Suicide Here" sign, Roosevelt explained to an audience that the nation needs citizens with strong character. He insisted,

In the first place, morality, decency, clean living, […] the qualities that make a man a decent husband, a decent father, and good neighbor, a good man to deal with or work beside; the quality that makes a man a good citizen of the State […]; we need that first as the foundation, and if we have not got that no amount of strength or courage or ability can take its place.[41]

The "fate of the nation depends," according to Roosevelt, on the proper training of children to enter into civic life.[42] Roosevelt's description of training is significant in at least two respects. First, the idea of civic training is ambiguous, but Roosevelt stabilized that meaning by couching it in the home. By locating civic training in the home, Roosevelt reinforced home as a national foundation and implicitly assigned importance to familial roles of training children. Thus, parenting, in general, and mothering, in particular, became understood as civic obligations. A failure of proper mothering was a civic failure, and the nation had an interest in promoting and regulating good mothering.

Additionally, Roosevelt explicitly linked the proper performance of identity in the home, community, and nation. By insisting that the performance of good fatherhood was necessarily connected the performance of good neighbor and national citizen, home and nation were represented as existing in overlapping or connected spaces. For Roosevelt, good citizenship was rooted in the same fundamental characteristics that made someone a good father—"morality, decency, and clean living." As a result, the performance of both good citizenship and good fatherhood were accessible to those willing to accept the roles, and neither required complicated or specialized action. The performance of good citizenship was constructed as a simple extension of other parts of identity, dissolving boundaries between public and private identities. The creation of parenthood as a civic role and establishing the interrelationship of multiple civic roles reinforced the nested spatial relationship of home and nation.

Duties of and to Women

In 1919 Woodrow Wilson said that the "center of the home is the woman."[43] The spatial orientation of centering women's place is critical because it positions women at the root of the nested relationship between familial home and national home. In other words, woman, through her positionality in the home, was considered critical to nation. When homes are not simply places to live but are understood as a national foundation, women's civic duty became indistinguishable from her supposed familial duty. Roosevelt explained:

> Neither man nor woman is really happy or really useful save on condition of doing his or her duty. If the woman shirks her duty as housewife, as home keeper, as the mother whose prime function it is to bear and rear a sufficient number of healthy children,

then she is not entitled to our regard. But if she does her duty she is more entitled to our regard even than the man who does his duty; and the man should show special consideration for her needs.[44]

Roosevelt's language of duty is significant because it posits women's role in the home as a fundamental obligation that extends well beyond desire or talent. Furthermore, Roosevelt positions women's duty as more significant that men's duty, elevating the consequences of shirking that duty.

Although perhaps more profuse in his praise, Harrison expressed a sentiment similar to Roosevelt and Wilson during a monument dedication, which was one of his rare mentions of women in public speech. He declared,

> All honor to the New England mother, the queen of the New England home! There, in those nurseries of virtue and truth, have been found the strongest influences that have molded your people for good and led your sons to honor.[45]

While presidential rhetoric honored men for their bravery in war, public leadership, or industry, women's duty and, thus, honor came from the home. Harrison, Roosevelt, and Wilson not only praised women's roles in the home, but they also reinforced a centering of home in national identity. Establishing home as a national foundation both exalted women as critical to nation but simultaneously limited the possibilities for women to move outside of the space of home.

Presidential rhetoric displayed a national interest in enabling women to fulfil their duty in the home. Roosevelt, for example, repeatedly expressed concern that women working in industry were causing a "change and disturbance in the domestic and social life of the Nation. The decrease in marriage, and especially in the birth rate, has been coincident with it."[46] Roosevelt's statement was predicated on the spatial logic of the home. If women's employment impeded the ability for women to fulfil their primary duties, there was a national interest in regulating women's employment. Similarly, both Harrison and Roosevelt asserted a national interest in regulating marriage. Harrison distinguished between national regulation of "faith or belief" and national regulation of marriage in order to justify continued opposition to Mormon polygamy.[47] In 1901 Roosevelt called on Congress to standardize marriage laws for the Native American population, and by 1906 he called for a constitutional amendment on marriage, arguing,

> At present the wide difference in the law so the different States on this subject result in scandals and abuses; and surely there is nothing so vitally essential to the welfare of the nation, nothing around which the nation should so bend itself to throw every safeguard, as the home life of the average citizen.[48]

Marriage was posited as significant because of the ways it shaped the home and its residents. If motherhood was a civic duty, the state had a national interest in enabling women to properly perform that duty.

Such an observation about motherhood as civic duty is not new. Kerber, for example, coined the term "Republican Motherhood" to explain the expectations of Revolutionary Era women.[49] However, the emphasis of motherhood in Progressive Era presidential rhetoric affirms that the president, as voice and representative of the nation, held fast to traditional conceptions of womanhood despite (or perhaps in reaction to) the emergence of the "new woman" during this time. Furthermore, situating the political subjectivity of womanhood within the larger framework of nested national space may help explain the persistent understandings of women's national duties and well as the national duty to women during this time.

Based on Progressive Era presidential rhetoric, the nation's primary duty to women involved protection. However, that protection tended to be limited to white, middle-class women, which makes sense in the context of home as a foundation for nation. Only women who were building the correct type of foundation were deemed worthy of protection, and those women needed protection from a racialized other. "Negro criminals" and rapists were named by Roosevelt as a specific threat.[50] Taft and Wilson both supported specific federal actions to ameliorate the threat of "white slavery," which was a fear that immigrants, often Eastern European Jews, were trapping middle-class, white women in prostitution.[51] In both of these instances, white women's sexual purity was thought to be endangered by a racialized other. As a result, the failure to protect women from these threats could impede women's abilities to fulfil their maternal duties.

For Roosevelt, women also needed protection from domestic abuse. He argued that the wife-beater necessitated a special type of punishment:

> The wife-beater, for example, is inadequately punished by imprisonment; for imprisonment may often mean nothing to him, while it may cause hunger and want to the wife and children who have been the victims of his brutality. Probably some form of corporal punishment would be the most adequate way of meeting this kind of crime.[52]

Domestic violence, for Roosevelt, violated expectations of women's protection, but it also violated the manly duty that was integral to American citizenship. Roosevelt's purported solution of corporal punishment was not particularly unique, although by the twentieth century, it was a response that many Americans had abandoned as outdated.[53]

The duties to women, however, did not typically include suffrage rights. Progressive Era presidents avoided public speech about women's political rights and, until 1918, no president included suffrage as part of his annual message to

Congress.[54] However, during this time period two presidents spoke before national suffrage meetings, Taft in 1910 and Wilson in 1916. Taft was the first sitting president to speak before the National American Woman's Suffrage Association, and he arrived in the middle of another speech, spoke briefly to welcome the meeting to Washington DC, and left. While the speech included a general statement of support for suffrage, Taft's qualifications of his support were notable and elicited strong reactions from the audience. Taft noted, "The theory that Hottentots or any other uneducated, altogether unintelligent class is fitted for self-government ... is a theory that I wholly dissent from, but this qualification is not applicable here." Further, "The other qualification to which I call your attention is that the class should as a whole care enough to look after its interests, to take part as a whole in the exercises of political power if it is conferred."[55] Although stated in a way that avoids direct confrontation, the qualifications were clearly objectionable to the audience, some of whom began booing and hissing the president.[56] Taken together, the statements intimate a concern that undesirable women would vote, while cultured and desirable women have no interest in voting.

Within a framework of a nested spatial relationship, Taft described a spatial disruption. The label "Hottentot" was typically used to refer to someone from Africa and often implied reference to hypersexualized black women, eluding to the memory of Sarah Baartman, the kidnapped women who was put on display in England in 1810 and commonly called the "Hottentot Venus."[57] The imagery of hypersexualized black womanhood was often circulated under the label of Hottentot, and, as Sander Gilman argues, "The late nineteenth-century perception of the prostitute merged with that of the black ... It is a commonplace that the primitive was associated with unbridled sexuality."[58] Through the use of the word "Hottentot" Taft drew on interrelated assumptions of race, sex, and evolutionary development. Significantly, the Hottentot was both a racial and geographic other, so to label an African American woman "Hottentot" was to remove her Americanness. The threat of empowering the Hottentot or a similar "unintelligent class" was not only about intelligence, but it was most significantly about empowering non-Americans in the American political process.

The hypersexualizing of the Hottentot also belies women's traditional roles within the home, especially as keeper of national morality. If home is built on proper womanhood and nation is built on home, empowering the wrong kind of woman not only destabilizes the American home, but it also threatens to destabilize the nation. Taft's assumption that the right kind of woman would be uninterested in voting was supported, in part, through the contrast with the preceding qualification. If immoral women like Hottentots wanted to vote, naturally good women would be uninterested in voting. The logic meant that these two categories of women could not mix, and any mixing ran the risk of corrupting good women.[59]

Wilson's 1916 speech is equally ambivalent. He was explicit in noting, "It [women's call for suffrage] is because the women have seen visions of duty, and that is something which we not only cannot resist, but, if we be true Americans, we do not wish to resist."[60] By grounding women's motivations in duty to nation, Wilson couched suffrage within women's other duties. Doing so did not necessarily disrupt or replace women's previous duties and, as a result, may have seemed somewhat palatable. Nevertheless, Wilson called on women to exercise patience (a womanly virtue). Through the use of *praeteritio*, he explained,

> It is all very well to run ahead and beckon, but, after all, you have got to wait for the body to follow. I have not come to ask you to be patient, because you have been, but I have come to congratulate you that there was a force behind you that will beyond any peradventure be triumphant, and for which you can afford a little while to wait.[61]

Even while appearing to support suffrage, Wilson evoked spatial dislocation in his imagery of women running ahead and beckoning for the rest of the nation to follow. Indeed, spatial dislocation permeated the short speech. Wilson claimed that because of population movement from the country to the city,

> the whole nature of our political questions has been altered. They have ceased to be legal questions. They have more and more become social questions, questions with regard to the relations of human beings to one another,—not merely their legal relations, but their moral and spiritual relations to one another.[62]

Through this observation, Wilson explicitly connected spatial location to political subjectivity in his imagery of women running ahead and beckoning for the rest of the nation to follow. In doing so, he introduced uncertainty into his already qualified statement of support. Although Wilson suggested the inevitability of woman suffrage, the possibility of suffrage did not disrupt the supposed foundational role of women in the home. Thus, there appeared to be little urgency in shifting the nation's duty to women in order to ensure suffrage.

Although women were largely absent from Progressive Era presidential rhetoric, presidents made occasional statements elucidating the nation's duty to and from women. Through praise, protection, and limitations, women's public identities and civic roles were consistently connected to home and family. These connections are particularly significant when understood through a spatial analytic that positions home as a foundation to nation because nation, then, symbolically rests on the shoulders of women. Presidential rhetoric reaffirmed a national interest in both linking women to the space of the home and establishing women's positionality within that space as so important that women's civic identity and home cannot be safely delinked.

Conclusion: The Presidency and Women's Place

The presidency remains a gendered site of national authority. It is gendered not only through the body that assumes the role of the presidency but also through the ways in which presidential rhetoric configures spatial logics to shape gendered political subjectivities. Thus, it is vital to examine the ways in which presidential rhetoric genders, even when gender may appear to be absent. An analysis of Progressive Era presidential rhetoric reveals an underlying *loci* of order within rhetoric of home. This spatial orientation nests familial home within national home, constructing an intimate interrelation between the two spaces.

The spatial orientation between familial home and national home is significant in at least two respects. First, Progressive Era presidents were talking about womanhood even while women appeared to be absent. Through rhetorically centering women within the home, references to home and things that were thought to occur within the home functioned as ways of referencing womanhood. Uncovering the *loci* of order makes women visible because a discussion of home was necessarily a discussion of womanhood. It is vital to see the ways in which presidential rhetoric was and continues to be gendered, and explicit attention to the *loci* of order can reveal gender even when it appears to be absent by calling attention to spatial ordering implicit within rhetoric.

Second, the spatial logic in presidential rhetoric naturalized a public interest in regulating home and, by extension, womanhood. Because *loci* participate in the construction of value hierarchies, it is not surprising that the *loci* of order both reveals womanhood and ascribes a national value to womanhood. The nested spatial relationship between familial home and national home made womanhood valuable to the extent that it supported familial home and familial home was valuable to the extent that it supported a specific conception of nation. Thus, women may have appeared largely absent in Progressive Era presidential rhetoric, but that same rhetoric constructed women's place as in the home.

There have been significant changes in the United States since the Progressive Era, but presidential rhetoric remains a significant force in shaping national identity and values. Uncovering the spatiality implicit in presidential rhetoric may be a powerful tool for unpacking national identity and values, especially in relationship to political subjectivities. From defending the nation's homeland to debating the composition of American families, presidents have a continuing fixation on home. That fixation on home is not benign. Analysis of Progressive Era presidential rhetoric shows that the ordering of national space, an ordering that may be implicit, has significant implications. National space retains a complex relationship to the spaces within and around it, and analysis of those spatial relationships within presidential rhetoric can reveal the ideological assumptions that shape the way people exist within nation space. Thus, the presidential creation and ordering of nation space is a gendered rhetoric.

Notes

1. Vanessa B. Beasley, "Engendering Democratic Change: How Three U.S. Presidents Discussed Female Suffrage," *Rhetoric & Public Affairs* 5, no. 1 (Spring 2002): 79–103; Leroy G. Dorsey, *We Are All Americans, Pure and Simple: Theodore Roosevelt and the Myth of Americanism* (Tuscaloosa: University Alabama Press, 2007), 4–5; Mary E. Stuckey, "Rethinking the Rhetorical Presidency and Presidential Rhetoric," *Review of Communication* 10, no. 1 (January 2010): 38–52, doi:10.1080/15358590903248744; Mary Stuckey, "Establishing the Rhetorical Presidency through Presidential Rhetoric: Theodore Roosevelt and the Brownsville Raid," *Quarterly Journal of Speech* 92, no. 3 (2006): 287–309; Mary E. Stuckey, "'The Domain of Public Conscience': Woodrow Wilson and the Establishment of a Transcendent Political Order," *Rhetoric & Public Affairs* 6, no. 1 (2003): 1–23.

2. Raka Shome, "Space Matters: The Power and Practice of Space," *Communication Theory* 13, no. 1 (February 1, 2003): 39–56, doi:10.1111/j.1468-2885.2003.tb00281.x.

3. Stuckey, "Establishing the Rhetorical Presidency through Presidential Rhetoric," 304–305. Also see: Peri E. Arnold, *Remaking the Presidency: Roosevelt, Taft, and Wilson, 1901–1916* (Lawrence: University Press of Kansas, 2009)

4. bell hooks, *Yearning: Race, Gender, and Cultural Politics* (Boston, MA: South End Press, 1999), 42.

5. Lisa A. Flores, "Creating Discursive Space through a Rhetoric of Difference: Chicana Feminists Craft a Homeland," *Quarterly Journal of Speech* 82, no. 2 (May 1996): 142–156.

6. Roxanne Mountford, "On Gender and Rhetorical Space," *Rhetoric Society Quarterly* 31, no. 1 (2001): 41–71; Richard Marback, "The Rhetorical Space of Robben Island," *Rhetoric Society Quarterly* 34, no. 2 (2004): 7–27; Valerie Palmer-Mehta, "The Rhetorical Space of the Garden in Shirin Neshat's Women Without Men," *Women's Studies in Communication* 38 (2015): 78–98, doi:10.1080/07491409.2014.989351.

7. Chaim Perelman and Lucie Olbrechts-Tyteca, *The New Rhetoric: A Treatise on Argumentation*, trans. John Wilkinson and Purcell Weaver (Notre Dame, IN: University of Notre Dame Press, 1969), 84.

8. Kathryn M. Olson, "Rethinking Loci Communes and Burkean Transcendence: Rhetorical Leadership While Contesting Change in the Takeover Struggle Between AirTran and Midwest Airlines," *Journal of Business and Technical Communication* 23, no. 1 (January 1, 2009): 28–60, doi:10.1177/1050651908324378.

9. Carol K. Winkler, "The National Counterterrorism Center's Definitional Shift for Counting Terrorism: Use of Loci Communes and Embedded Value Hierarchies," *Argumentation & Advocacy* 45, no. 4 (Spring 2009): 214–227.

10. Michael C. Leff, "The Topics of Argumentative Invention in Latin Rhetorical Theory from Cicero to Boethius," *Rhetorica: A Journal of the History of Rhetoric* 1, no. 1 (1983): 23–44, doi:10.1525/rh.1983.1.1.23; Olson, "Rethinking Loci Communes and Burkean

Transcendence Rhetorical Leadership While Contesting Change in the Takeover Struggle Between AirTran and Midwest Airlines," 40.

11. Perelman and Olbrechts-Tyteca, *The New Rhetoric*, 93.

12. This scholarship often draws from Welter's analysis of "true womanhood," operating from the assumption that privacy and domesticity are feminine domains. I do not intend to suggest that this scholarship is wrong. Rather, I think that scholarship could benefit from explicit interrogation of spatial language in relation to gender. Barbara Welter, "The Cult of True Womanhood: 1820-1860," *American Quarterly* 18, no. 2 (1966): 151–174, doi:10.2307/2711179.

13. Cathy N. Davidson, "Preface: No More Separate Spheres!," *American Literature* 70, no. 3 (1998): 443–463, doi:10.2307/2902705; Julie Roy Jeffrey, "Permeable Boundaries: Abolitionist Women and Separate Spheres," *Journal of the Early Republic* 21, no. 1 (2001): 79–93, doi:10.2307/3125097; Deborah L. Rotman, "Separate Spheres?: Beyond the Dichotomies of Domesticity," *Current Anthropology* 47, no. 4 (2006): 666–674, doi:10.1086/506286.

14. Linda K. Kerber, "Separate Spheres, Female Worlds, Woman's Place: The Rhetoric of Women's History," *The Journal of American History* 75, no. 1 (1988): 9–39, doi:10.2307/1889653.

15. Mary P. Ryan, "The Public and the Private Good: Across the Great Divide in Women's History," *Journal of Women's History* 15, no. 2 (Summer 2003): 10-27.

16. Seth Koven and Sonya Michel, eds., *Mothers of a New World: Maternalist Politics and the Origins of Welfare States* (New York: Routledge, 1993); Linda K. Kerber, Alice Kessler-Harris, and Kathryn Kish Sklar, eds., *U.S. History As Women's History: New Feminist Essays* (Chapel Hill: The University of North Carolina Press, 1995).

17. Sara M. Evans, *Born for Liberty* (Princeton, NJ: Free Press, 1997), 160.

18. Dorothy Schneider and Carl J. Schneider, *American Women in the Progressive Era, 1900-1920* (New York: Facts on File, 1993), 13–18.

19. Eleanor Flexner, *Century of Struggle: The Woman's Rights Movement in the United States* (New York: Atheneum, 1973), 248.

20. Ibid., 263.

21. Rebecca Edwards, *Angels in the Machinery: Gender in American Party Politics from the Civil War to the Progressive Era* (New York: Oxford University Press, 1997), 133.

22. Ibid., 135–36.

23. Republican Party Platforms, "Republican Party Platform of 1892," June 7, 1892, online by Gerhard Peters and John T. Woolley, The American Presidency Project, http://www.presidency.ucsb.edu/ws/?pid=29628.

24. Vanessa B. Beasley, *You, the People: American National Identity in Presidential Rhetoric* (College Station: Texas A&M University Press, 2011), 121, https://muse.jhu.edu/book/135/.

25. Theodore Roosevelt, "First Annual Message," December 3, 1901, online by Gerhard Peters and John T. Woolley, The American Presidency Project, http://www.presidency.ucsb.edu/ws/?pid=29542.

26. Theodore Roosevelt, "Third Annual Message," December 7, 1903, online by Gerhard Peters and John T. Woolley, The American Presidency Project, http://www.presidency.ucsb.edu/ws/?pid=29544.

27. Woodrow Wilson, "Address to an Overflow Meeting at Soldiers' Memorial Hall in Pittsburgh, Pennsylvania," January 29, 1916, online by Gerhard Peters and John T. Woolley, The American Presidency Project, http://www.presidency.ucsb.edu/ws/?pid=117308.

28. Woodrow Wilson, "Address at Memorial Hall in Columbus, Ohio," September 4, 1919, online by Gerhard Peters and John T. Woolley, The American Presidency Project, http://www.presidency.ucsb.edu/ws/?pid=117361.

29. Roosevelt, "First Annual Message."

30. Theodore Roosevelt, "Fourth Annual Message," December 6, 1904, online by Gerhard Peters and John T. Woolley, The American Presidency Project, http://www.presidency.ucsb.edu/ws/?pid=29545; William Howard Taft, "First Annual Message," December 7, 1909, online by Gerhard Peters and John T. Woolley, The American Presidency Project, http://www.presidency.ucsb.edu/ws/index.php?pid=29550.

31. Taft, "First Annual Message."

32. Ibid.

33. Benjamin Harrison, "Second Annual Message," December 1, 1890, online by Gerhard Peters and John T. Woolley, The American Presidency Project, http://www.presidency.ucsb.edu/ws/index.php?pid=29531.

34. Stephen M. Underhill, "Urban Jungle, Ferguson: Rhetorical Homology and Institutional Critique," *Quarterly Journal of Speech* 102, no. 4 (2016): 399, doi:10.1080/00335630.2016.1213413.

35. Roosevelt, "Fourth Annual Message."

36. Woodrow Wilson, "Address at the Suffrage Convention, Atlantic City, New Jersey," 1916, online by Gerhard Peters and John T. Woolley, The American Presidency Project, http://www.presidency.ucsb.edu/ws/?pid=29546.

37. Theodore Roosevelt, "Sixth Annual Message," December 3, 1906, online by Gerhard Peters and John T. Woolley, The American Presidency Project, http://www.presidency.ucsb.edu/ws/?pid=29547.

38. Theodore Roosevelt, "Address at Oakland, California,"May 14, 1903, online by Gerhard Peters and John T. Woolley, The American Presidency Project, http://www.presidency.ucsb.edu/ws/?pid=97736.

39. Woodrow Wilson, "Address to the Daughters of the American Revolution," October 11, 1915, online by Gerhard Peters and John T. Woolley, The American Presidency Project, http://www.presidency.ucsb.edu/ws/?pid=117704.

40. Ibid.

41. Theodore Roosevelt, "Address at Redlands, California," May 7, 1903, online by Gerhard Peters and John T. Woolley, The American Presidency Project, http://www.presidency.ucsb.edu/ws/?pid=97706.

42. Theodore Roosevelt, "Address at Ventura, California," May 9, 1903, online by Gerhard Peters and John T. Woolley, The American Presidency Project, http://www.presidency.ucsb.edu/ws/?pid=97714.

43. Woodrow Wilson, "Address at the Suffrage Convention, Atlantic City, New Jersey," September 8, 1916, online by Gerhard Peters and John T. Woolley, The American Presidency Project, http://www.presidency.ucsb.edu/ws/?pid=65395.

44. Theodore Roosevelt, "Special Message,"February 9, 1909, online by Gerhard Peters and John T. Woolley, The American Presidency Project, http://www.presidency.ucsb.edu/ws/?pid=69656.

45. Benjamin Harrison, "Remarks at an Afternoon Banquet at the Bennington Monument in Bennington, Vermont," August 18, 1890, online by Gerhard Peters and John T. Woolley, The American Presidency Project, http://www.presidency.ucsb.edu/ws/?pid=97736.

46. Harrison, "Second Annual Message."

47. Ibid.

48. Roosevelt, "First Annual Message"; Roosevelt, "Sixth Annual Message."

49. Linda K. Kerber, "The Republican Mother: Women and the Enlightenment-An American Perspective," *American Quarterly* 28, no. 2 (1976): 187–205.

50. Roosevelt, "Sixth Annual Message."

51. Taft, "First Annual Message"; Wilson, "Address at Memorial Hall in Columbus, Ohio."

52. Roosevelt, "Fourth Annual Message."

53. Leslie J. Harris, *State of the Marital Union: Rhetoric, Identity, and Nineteenth Century Marriage Controversies* (Waco, TX: Baylor University Press, 2014), 24.

54. Beasley, *You, the People*, 131.

55. William Howard Taft, "Speech of President William Howard Taft to the National American Convention of 1910," in *History of Woman Suffrage*, ed. Ida Husted Harper, vol. 5 (New York: National American Woman Suffrage Association, 1922), 270–71.

56. "Apologizes for Hisses to Taft," *Chicago Daily Tribune*, April 16, 1910; "Suffragettes Hiss Taft, Their Guest," *New York Times*, April 15, 1910; "Taft Is Hissed by Suffragists," *Washington Post*, April 15, 1910; "Taft Says Hisses Did Not Hurt Him," *Chicago Daily Tribune*, April 16, 1910; "Women Call Taft's Talk on Suffrage 'Unamerican,'" *Chicago Daily Tribune*, April 17, 1910; "Women Hiss Taft; Angry at Speech," *Chicago Daily Tribune*, April 15, 1910; "The President on Woman Suffrage," *Chicago Daily Tribune*, April 16, 1910.

57. Deborah Willis, "Introduction: The Notion of Venus" in *Black Venus 2010: They Called Her "Hottentot,"* ed. Deborah Willis (Philadelphia, PA: Temple University Press, 2010), 4. While the specific memory of Baartman may not have been vivid in the American public imaginary during this time, "Hottentot" was used to reference someone who appeared to be of African dissent. Writing from the time period implied an association with the primitive and hypersexualized body.

58. Sander Gilman, "The Hottentot and the Prostitute: Toward an Iconography of Female Sexuality," in *Black Venus 2010: They Called Her "Hottentot,"* ed. Deborah Willis (Philadelphia, PA: Temple University Press, 2010), 16–18, 23.

59. Catherine H. Palczewski, "The 1919 Prison Special: Constituting White Women's Citizenship," *Quarterly Journal of Speech* 102, no. 2 (2016): 107–132, doi:10.1080/00335630.2016.1154185.

60. Wilson, "Address at the Suffrage Convention, Atlantic City, New Jersey," 1916.

61. Ibid.

62. Ibid.

CHAPTER FOURTEEN

White "Honky" Liberals, Rhetorical Disidentification, and Black Power during the Johnson Administration

LISA CORRIGAN

When scholars talk about the importance of identification as a primary role of presidential rhetoric, they often discuss how presidents use language to unify a country around great themes of American life that mobilize intense feelings of fidelity to the nation.[1] While these studies often focus on inaugural addresses, eulogies, and other moments of national mourning, the politics of identification play perhaps their most important role after presidential assassinations and attempted assassinations. Incoming presidents must furiously reconstitute the nation and the national identity, while building confidence in their own abilities to manage the nation's affairs.[2] Particularly traumatic, John F. Kennedy's assassination elevated Lyndon Johnson to the White House, a moment requiring eulogy, unity, and recognition of the new president. Scholars have studied Johnson's "Let Us Continue" address and remarked on the ways Johnson's rhetorical reconstitution of the nation generated unity by articulating an identificatory discourse that linked his presidency to the people. At the same time, these studies argue Johnson's identificatory discourse facilitated a *blitzkrieg* of domestic legislation in the years that followed.[3]

This study takes a different approach and considers the presidency of Lyndon Johnson as a means for understanding the politics of identification and disidentification that shaped the black freedom struggle. Approaching Johnson's rhetoric from its outside provides a useful approach to the study of how the presidency works within the politics of coalition building. Beginning with Kennedy's assassination in November of 1963 and ending with Johnson's decision not to seek reelection in April 1968, the president attempted various rhetorical strategies designed to rearticulate American liberalism for a mourning country. Johnson's Great Society "drew on the past. The liberal initiatives of the 1960s were descendants of a reform movement that began with Populism and continued through the Progressive Era and the New Deal."[4] Johnson's leadership style favored consensus, which became anathema as the decade wore on and as social movements fragmented consensus about the direction of American policy, both domestic and foreign.

Early in the administration, Johnson capitalized on emerging conditions to push liberal legislation following John Kennedy's assassination. By keeping Robert Kennedy as Attorney General, the president ensured that the "heir of his brother's political legacy" would be closely involved in the Johnson Administration, creating the kind of continuity that presidential identification needs to flourish.[5] Still

> the unusual unity of national mood, the common desire for some renewal of purpose, permitted Johnson, in the first months of his Presidency, to address the general public as one in mind and spirit, as he would a single group—in terms of their ambiguous but shared interests.[6]

This unity created the rhetorical and political space for tremendous consensus building. Johnson's ability to create identification with him as a leader hinged on his ability to parlay consensus building into a coherent agenda by unifying stakeholders into a powerful coalition despite the dynamism and instability that emerge when, say, social movements pressure presidents for outcomes that even the most savvy politician cannot deliver.[7]

The 1964 election marked the end of the initial unity that typified the aftermath of Kennedy's assassination as coalition politics began to fragment the democratic base upon which Johnson had built his mandate. It was only after Johnson propelled the Civil Rights Act of 1964 through Congress, forcing his opponent Barry Goldwater to vote against it, that black Americans became a solid faction of the president's broad political coalition. Nonetheless, the coalitions that supported Johnson helped to build the identificatory practices that messaged the Great Society, at least through the first year and a half of his administration. This period of the Johnson administration (after 1964) merits study because despite successful decisions about messaging civil rights as an ethical imperative for the national body, the politics of disidentification are more prominent as a feature of the coalitions that, by the mid-twentieth century, so clearly had been associated with the Democratic Party. By disidentification, I am indebted to the work of José Esteban Muñoz, who used it in his groundbreaking research on queer identity performance to describe a strategy motivating oppositional social collectivity. "Disidentification is ... descriptive of the survival strategies the minority subject practices in order to negotiate a phobic majoritarian public sphere that continuously elides or punishes the existence of subjects who do not conform to the phantasm of normative citizenship."[8] This process of disidentification characterizes the tactics of civil rights activism after the passage of the Voting Rights Act and is a central feature of the Black Power movement after 1966 as the Johnson Administration's ability to navigate black coalitions began to collapse. Here, I'm particularly interested in the relationship between the rhetoric of liberal triumphalism and racism among liberals and in the American left as the Democratic Party shifted to "law and order" politics after 1966.

Where books about presidential politics seek to center the president in the narrative of coalitional politics, the case of Johnson's civil rights policies is distinct.[9] As historian Julian Zelizer has written, "[w]e need a less Johnson-centric view to understand how this historic burst of liberal legislation happened."[10] This is not to ignore Johnson's extraordinary knowledge of the House and Senate or to minimize his role in advocating the policies that formed his Great Society, but to acknowledge that the political dynamism of these years was a product of popular civil rights activism that also catalyzed the power of the conservative coalition, propelled major legislation in 1964 and 1965 (most notably the Civil Rights Act and the Voting Rights Act), and created pressure for the 1964 elections, giving liberals huge majorities in the House and Senate. To understand the relationship between the Johnson administration and the black freedom struggle is to admit that it changed over time as Johnson became weakened by the decision to expand the war in Vietnam and by his own inability to understand or mitigate the complex factors propelling Black Power.

Particularly in conflating the War on Poverty and the War on Crime, he created conditions where conservatives had "a rare opportunity to attack the Johnson consensus."[11] Johnson's opponents successfully circulated three major arguments that undermined the president's relationships with social movement leaders, particularly those in the black freedom struggle:

> first, that urban rioting and civil disorder grew out of the civil rights movement; second, that the Warren Court favored the rights of criminals over the rights of victims; and third, that the Great Society, in undermining individual initiative and self-reliance, was creating a comity composed of individuals with no self-discipline and a deep-seated sense of entitlement.[12]

These interventions into the public sphere fractured Johnson's ability to create a unified language of identification and help us to understand how assertions of a liberal consensus on civil rights were incomplete assessments of competing frames *within* the Democratic Party. And, these arguments helped to propel Black Power criticisms of Johnson's political limitations.

This chapter charts the role of disidentification as a rhetorical strategy that helped transform White House positions about civil rights activism during the Johnson Administration into a innovative rhetorical space in the Black Power movement. I chart Johnson's hostility to radicalizing black liberation activists and then document how the use of disidentification from whiteness and white liberals emerged as a racialized rhetorical strategy that distanced Black Power leaders from the emergent law and order culture of the Johnson Administration. That movement, I contend, allowed more radical critiques of power, capital, injustice, state violence, and political resistance. Particularly salient was the demonization of President Johnson, which focused disidentification on the effects of new conservatism penetrating the administration. In doing so, Black Power activists unsettled the naturalized symbolism of white liberals' power, shutting down avenues of political affiliation while creating new space for black identification. Harnessing a dystopian imaginary, Black Power rhetors mobilized powerful black images and fantasies with which publics could transgress heavily patrolled social norms, particularly those pertaining to police power. Ultimately, this rhetorical strategy cemented the positionality of Black Power as a movement that would not cooperate with the Johnson White House, magnifying its appeal for urban black citizens and guaranteeing its demise by the FBI. But the disidentification of black activists from white liberals also signaled the limitations of (white) liberals, particularly in the arena of civil rights policy.

LBJ, Identification, and the Black Freedom Struggle

From the beginning of his presidency, Johnson had a complicated relationship with leaders of the black freedom struggle. He was cordial and supportive of Martin Luther King in the days following Kennedy's brutal assassination in Dallas. He also invited prominent leaders from around the country to meet in the White House. Here,

> Johnson acquired information about each of the men with whom he would have to deal—George Meany, Roy Wilkins, Frederick Kappel, Martin Luther King, Henry Ford, and so on. He was interested in their range of skills, and, most importantly, their feelings and attitudes toward him.[13]

Johnson appraised each man and his limits as he accustomed himself to the new office and its responsibilities. But Johnson's moral appeals to white conscience on civil rights were fraught with political risk since the Democratic Party had long relied on blue dogs in the South to carry the presidency.

His presidential victory in 1964 showcased the tremendous power of a man that would eventually walk away from the presidency only four years later. Winning by the largest popular margin in American history, the Johnson administration "saw the legislative realization of many of the noblest aspirations of the liberal spirit in America."[14] And this post-election clout meant that the president would have tremendous discretion to build the kinds of coalitions and identifications that he saw fit, to either satisfy his own personal political agenda or to end political threats.

> The landmark legislation with which the president is associated in the end carries serious political risks as well as potential political gains—a prime reason why the president has been reluctant to push very far in the first place. Unlike legislation that makes universal claims ... legislation that sides with one social group over another runs the risk of establishing controversial presidential identifications.[15]

Johnson understood that his credibility and consensus-building over civil rights was due, at least in part, to the fact that he was a southerner. As Dalleck writes, Johnson attributed his political success to

> his identification as a political moderate, a pragmatic southwesterner capable of good working relationships across the political spectrum. In a time of intense racial and sectional strife, Johnson saw himself as perhaps the only politician who could substantially ease black-white and North-South tensions.[16]

Johnson's "long-standing identification with the crusade for black equality symbolized Johnson's determination to make civil rights a priority of his Administration."[17] This position was especially strident because critics of the administration had seen Kennedy's position of civil rights as half-hearted and inadequate since "Kennedy refused to take on Congress, and particularly its southern power brokers, by asking for a major civil rights law."[18] Johnson's intense identification with civil rights was unique for the political climate in which he lived. In a milieu characterized by the Southern Manifesto, massive resistance, and resurgent Klan activity, his identification with civil rights was notable because he used his southern white masculinity as a vehicle to build identification with civil rights for others whites.

Johnson's embrace of civil rights highlights how identification works as a rhetorical process. Kenneth Burke explains: "[y]ou persuade a man only insofar as you can talk his language by speech, gesture, tonality, order, image, attitude, idea, *identifying* your way with his."[19] Burke offered identification as a key rhetorical term that was less about persuasion and more about how speakers and writers "induce cooperation" in their listeners and readers.[20] Identification is useful as a rhetorical process because it

> permits a rethinking of judgment and the working of rhetorical effect, for he does not posit a transcendent subject as audience member, who would exist prior to and apart from the speech to be judged, but considers audience members to participate in the very discourse by which they would be "persuaded."[21]

Identification is a constitutive process omnipresent in presidential discourse but also in the texts of social movement activists building the platforms of their organizations and the relationship between their organizations and movements with the federal government, who they pressure for political concessions.

Identification is a useful way to understand Johnson, in particular, since he was such an incredible power broker as Senate majority leader and as president. And given the unpopularity of civil rights among southern blue dog democrats, identification is a more precise term to describe the kind of coalition Johnson built against racial discrimination. But liberals advocating for civil rights were not a monolithic group during the period; instead, they were just one voice among many, perhaps more well-positioned than others to force concessions. As Gary Gerstle has argued, liberals supportive of civil rights "were a decided electoral and ideological minority, lacking both the political clout and the moral authority to fashion a broad Democratic consensus on racial matters."[22] But even this analysis doesn't get at the ambivalence even among white civil rights supporters within the Democratic Party. For example, the 1966 gubernatorial elections were a rebuke of Johnson's identificatory potential.

> Three segregationist Democrats—Lester Maddox in Georgia, James Johnson in Arkansas, and George P. Mahoney in Maryland, won their party's gubernatorial nomination. In Alabama, moreover, voters ratified a caretaker administration for Lurleen Wallace, since her husband George, was not permitted to succeed himself. ... What happened in the 1966 gubernatorial race in California, where former movie star Ronald Reagan handily defeated Democratic incumbent Edmund G. Brown, revealed that this conservative insurgency wasn't limited to southern Democrats.[23]

The surge of white backlash in the 1966 gubernatorial races demonstrated how southern and western states saw the executive branch as the primary space to safeguard white privilege and white supremacy. It provided an instantiation of disidentification within the party as southern democrats rebuffed Johnson's civil rights initiatives and it drove the conservatives of the GOP into oppositional political space on the issue of race, which dominated the next two presidential elections. It also widened the space between black freedom advocates in the Johnson White

House as younger, radical activists continued to see tremendous violence across the South against nonviolent civil rights workers. As the violence peaked during the Mississippi Freedom Summer and the nation saw the police repression at Selma, a new slogan, championed by Stokely Carmichael of the Student Nonviolent Coordinating Committee (SNCC), emerged to resist the close relationship between the (Southern Christian Leadership Conference (SCLC), and the Johnson White House.

Fracturing the Coalitions: Black Power and White Liberals

The rise of Black Power in 1966 as the conservative backlash crested also began to prompt a different kind of response to Johnson's coalition-building, particularly in the wake of the assassination of Malcolm X and the riots in Watts. At the Congress on Racial Equality's (CORE) July 1966 convention in Baltimore, Student Nonviolent Coordinating Committee chairman and CORE collaborator Stokely Carmichael spoke as the organization debated whether or not to embrace the Black Power slogan and abandon the liberal reforms that it had championed since CORE's founding in 1942. At the plenary session, Carmichael explained, "We don't need liberals … We need to make integration irrelevant."[24] In seeking to move from integration to justice, Carmichael urged activists to end their collaboration with liberals. While Carmichael's calls for Black Power had inspired tremendous conversation and debate within the movement, he had also participated in the Freedom Rides and in interracial advocacy during Mississippi Freedom Summer, giving his remarks a particular *gravitas*. And ultimately, the intensity of his critiques of white liberals in Baltimore virtually ended white liberal patronage of CORE after a resolution passed denouncing the Vietnam War and as the organization's pledge to uphold nonviolence was tempered by a motion that supported black armed self-defense. By August of 1966, CORE had relocated its headquarters from Chicago to Harlem, signaling a new location for its urban Black Power program, which was significant especially in the wake of Malcolm X's assassination.[25]

For his part, Carmichael had been lecturing and writing on the importance of Black Power in the months following the Meredith March Against Fear after activist James Meredith was shot by a white sniper while attempting a solo walk from Memphis to Jackson. In his essay "What We Want," Carmichael charted a political philosophy of Black Power that emerged from his own experiences organizing for SNCC in the Deep South. Citing the urban ghetto as an untapped location for new agitation and innovation, Carmichael critiqued SNCC's goals and mission, blaming the organization for serving "as a sort of buffer zone" between liberal whites and angry young blacks and for adapting their "tone of voice" "to an audience of liberal whites." He explained:

> For too many years, black Americans marched and had their heads broken and got shot. They were saying to the country, 'Look, you guys are supposed to be nice guys and we are only going to do what we are supposed to do—why do you beat us up, why don't you give us what we ask, why don't you straighten yourselves out?' After years of this, we are at almost the same point—because we demonstrated from a position of weakness.

Carmichael added that black people need to make rhetorical choices that do not reflect what white liberals want to hear about black political needs, saying:

> "[f]or once, black people are going to use the words they want to use—not just the words whites want to hear. And they will do this no matter how often the press tries to stop the use of the slogan by equating it with racism or separatism."[26]

Carmichael contends, "[f]or racism to die, a totally different America must be born," though he also acknowledges that this "is what the white society does not wish to face; this is why that society prefers to talk about integration. But integration speaks not at all to the problem of poverty, only to the problem of blackness."[27] Carmichael's comments speak to the importance of black activists making new, autonomous rhetorical choices in their pursuit of a new strategy to counter white supremacy without the use of white surrogates.

Under Carmichael's leadership, SNCC convened a special meeting in December of 1966 in New York City to consider the new role of Black Power ideology in the organization. At that meeting, the ten-member Central Committee voted to expel all whites from the organization as black leaders interrogated their own traumatic subjectivity in the nation as a whole and in their organizations as microcosms of white supremacy. As this organizational shift emerged, "white liberal" became a dirty term, synonymous with being a sellout and traitor as black activists articulated their feelings of betrayal by white liberals in their organizations and in the federal government. In a 1969 editorial for *The Black Scholar*, CORE leader Floyd McKissick explained that the shift to Black Power was a rejection of the process of seeking white approval. He wrote,

> Disillusioned by the lack of commitment on the part of young white liberals, bewildered by the short-lived idealism of their white counterparts, and angered by the almost unanimous hostility of whites to the initial demands for black power and self-determination—black youth, conditioned all their lives to seek white approval, yet recognizing the inherent worthlessness and even destructiveness of such approval, have subtly compromised their conflicting needs.[28]

As CORE and SNCC embraced Black Power, there was no path forward with whites. Instead, movement leadership affirmed blackness after the expulsion of whiteness. In SNCC's embrace of Black Power, they "stridently demand[ed] black control of the civil rights movement, openly challenging the intentions and abilities of older black leaders, and declaring that no 'honky' (white) was to be trusted." Carmichael, Rap Brown and other black SNCC leaders had "lost faith" in white liberal leaders like the Kennedy brothers and LBJ, "who," in the words of Cooper and Terrill, "appeared all too ready to compromise the interests of blacks and appeared naïve about the seriousness of black problems."[29]

As Black Power advocates were contemplating these major changes in their organizational composition and in their strategic direction, President Johnson complained about the new "extremism" among Black Power advocates, asserting, "we are not interested in Black Power and we're not interested in white power, but we are interested in American democratic power, with a small *d*."[30] For his part, Vice President Hubert Humphrey "considered a respected white liberal" was also critical of Black Power, characterizing it thusly at the fifty-seventh annual NAACP convention: "[r]acism is racism and we must reject calls for racism whether they come from a throat that is white or one that is black."[31] Both Johnson and Humphrey resisted Black Power on the grounds that it was reverse racism and that it was a kind of extremism that threatened the respectability politics of the civil rights movement as well as the civility discourse that was a hallmark of the Democratic Party leadership in both the Kennedy and Johnson administrations.

Even to the left of the administration, though, there were vociferous critiques of Black Power. Robert Kennedy's speechwriter Adam Walinsky famously referred to Black Power's community action organizations as "bitching societies."[32] And Kennedy himself denounced Black Power activists early on, though he came around to thinking that there was room to perhaps work with them in northern cities.[33] Though he received far less criticism from Black Power advocates (perhaps because he was a senator and perhaps because Black Power advocates saw Johnson as the more wily of the two), Jack Newfield wrote in *New York Magazine* in 1968 that members of both the "Old and New Left did not approve of Kennedy's unorthodox mixing of self-help and capitalism with black power."[34] This made Robert Kennedy a more palatable figure for Black Power, as Rep. Adam Clayton Powell noted in his autobiography, writing

> Black Power says don't forget the executive secretary of the NAACP who was murdered in Mississippi. Don't forget the two white boys from Manhattan and a black soul brother who were bulldozed into the earth in Mississippi. Don't forget the assassination of Jack Kennedy. Don't forget the assassination of Bobby Kennedy.[35]

Powell's articulation of Black Power (here, as a strategy of remembrance) links the Kennedy brothers with Medgar Evers and Schwerner, Goodman, and Chaney (the three civil rights workers lynched in Mississippi), suggesting attempts within the movement to link them to a legacy of martyrdom. These articulations also provided a moral grounding for their message as the decade ended with Nixon's presidential victory.

Still, even with Robert Kennedy's attempts during his presidential campaign to engage Black Power ideals on their merits, white reception of Black Power critique was mostly characterized by white backlash. Compounding these characterizations of Black Power from the executive branch was the vitriol from civil rights organizations like the National Association for the Advancement of Colored People. Roy Wilkins was the most vociferous critic, calling Black Power a "reverse Hitler" and a "father of hate" as a way of preserving relationships with white establishment liberals like Johnson and Humphrey.[36] Wilkins also characterized Black Power as "wicked fanaticism" and "in the end only black death."[37] These kinds of statements empowered men like Johnson and Humphrey to push back against Black Power, particularly since their goals did not match up with Black Power demands.

As Devin Fergus has demonstrated, Black Power emerged as a dominant political discourse and young white liberals especially on college campuses and in liberal congregations tried to connect with militants only to be rebuffed with critiques of their solidarity.[38] Additionally, Kevin Boyle has documented white liberal labor's demonization of Black Power and chronicled how the leadership of the United Auto Workers (UAW) suggested "muzzl[ing] this guy [Stokely] Carmichael" as they pushed back against Black Power critiques of segregation in unions.[39] Likewise, Harry Feingold has documented the purge of Jewish civil rights workers as Black Power radicalized the black freedom struggle and as the Johnson administration refused to seat the Mississippi Freedom Democratic Party at the 1968 Democratic National Convention.[40] Beyond movement strategy conflicts between Black Power activists and students, clergy, organized labor, and Jewish organizations regarding nonviolence, housing, education, employment, health care, and political participation were fundamental ideological conflicts about the war in Vietnam, the U.S. embargo of Cuba, the handling of political prisoners, the case of Palestine, South African apartheid, and the assassinations of black political leaders within the U.S.

The publication of the Black Panther's "10-point Program" (1966), the "Black Power" statement by The National Committee of Negro Churchmen (1966), and later, James Foreman's "The Black Manifesto" (1972) followed the purges of SNCC and CORE and echoed much of the critiques of false solidarity leveled at white students, clergy, labor, Jewish organizations, and establishment liberals.

These publications were trenchant critiques of political institutions controlled by whites that benefitted liberals. And, as Black Power took on the separatist overtones popularized by Malcolm X, particularly after the assassination of King in 1968, it became clear that Black Power would have to reject white liberalism because of its increasing dependence on conservative notions of law and order, imperialism, empire, and capital. While the bulk of this chapter discusses how Lyndon Johnson became the major repository for this rhetorical and political conflict, the clash was not confined to the executive branch. In a special section in the *Negro Digest* on the "Meaning of Black Power," Julian Bond wrote of the "white fright" confronting establishment "white liberals" and suggested that they feared retribution after benefitting directly or indirectly from black oppression for 400 years and described white liberals like Vice President Hubert Humphrey as a "victim" of Black Power "panic."[41] These texts demonstrate that Black Power created a different dialectic, one characterized by blanket critiques of whiteness. Black Power advocates implicated even liberals in structural racism by pointing to their failures at solidarity and their investment in preserving particular forms of exclusionary political participation.

These kinds of broad critiques leveled at white liberals led to the purges of sympathetic white liberals from civil rights organizations as Black Power organizations radicalized their political action to survivalist programs, self-defense, and urban political action. As Peter Carroll has documented, the purges meant that Black Power activists could be uncompromising in their critiques of white supremacy and white privilege as new nodes of black consciousness began to question the intentions and strategies of both the civil rights movement and well-meaning whites.[42] King's failure in Cicero, Illinois, in 1966, demonstrated to Black Power leaders the limits of nonviolent organizing, especially in the South, and helped solidify SNCC and CORE against the kind of relationship that King had historically enjoyed with the Johnson White House (at least before his radicalization on the war in Vietnam).[43] Thus did the rousing, if extremely broad, indictments of white liberals by Black Power advocates function as pedagogical tools to teach black Americans how to embrace a racial consciousness that deliberately rejected white norms and framed civil rights as a break from "politics as usual." In the coverage of the era, reporters talked of "white backlash" being the response of white liberals to Black Power. And no wonder: white liberals were struggling with a messiah complex about racial issues; to be told that their missionary work among the poor black folk of the South was contributing to systemic racial inequality was a rude awakening that men like Johnson and Humphrey patently rejected.

This process of dis-identification marked activists' denunciation of the "white liberal" as a potential collaborator in the black freedom struggle, a tremendous departure from the collaborations that defined the early civil rights struggle earlier in the decade. First, Black Power activists worked tirelessly to produce a counter-discourse that reimagined both whiteness and blackness simultaneously through a disavowal or dis-identification of white liberals as audiences for and participants in the black freedom struggle. Second, in charting this rhetorical dis-identification, Black Power activists describe white liberals from a positionality of traumatic subjectivity that acknowledged the betrayal and limited utility of white liberals while using this rupture in relations to build a new black subjectivity. Finally, President Johnson, in particular, became a repository of new vernacular signs about the changing nature of black struggle in the United States. In the Black Power vernacular, "honky" became a particular term of art, and as an anti-white slur, it crystallized how disidentification from whites and whiteness propelled Black Power away from the collaboration with white liberals in the Johnson Administration. "Honky" and other anti-white slurs like, say, "cracker," disrupted and unsettled the naturalized symbolism of white liberals' power by creating rhetorical avenues by which Black Power activists could attack whiteness as the basis of white supremacist violence. Black Power was invested in demonstrating: the limits and disappointments of liberalism as an unrealizable political system that has been explicitly built upon the exclusion of black people; the uselessness of liberals (as inadequate partners in black liberation); the pervasiveness of white violence and the incivility of white culture; the possibilities for new identifications around blackness.

(Dis)identification and Collective Action

Disidentification is a useful way to understand the politics of black freedom in this period because "[d]isidentification can be understood as a way of shuffling back and forth between reception and production."[44] This rhetorical process constitutes and reconstitutes national belonging as the president succeeds and fails in articulating a national policy on civil rights. Butler suggests that the failure of identification with the dominant culture "is itself the point of departure for a more democratizing affirmation of internal difference."[45] Thus does disidentification prefer separatism as the predominant constitutive rhetorical strategy. Black Power activists took the damaging assessments of black culture (particularly black masculinity) and used the fear of black violence as a rhetorical and political resource for a new identity. And while disidentification was certainly a survival strategy as the state continued tremendous violence against black freedom fighters, "Black Power" was a political tool that carved out more space within and outside of the public sphere for radical black intellectuals. As Muñoz explains, disidentificatory practices "circulate in subcultural circuits and strive to envision and activate new social relations" which provide "the blueprint for minoritarian couterpublic spheres."[46] Black Power was just such a counterpublic sphere. There, disidentification emerged as a political challenge to traditional black citizenship as "damaged stereotypes" were "recycled … as powerful and seductive sites of self-creation."[47] While this process is exciting for the individual remaking the self, the "experience of suburban spectatorship" also characterizes disidentification, producing both pleasure and terror, and making disidentification a powerful cross-racial, cross-gender rhetorical form.[48]

While certain forms of disidentification always mark constitutive minoritarian discourses, in the case of the black freedom struggle, it is clear that modes of disidentification changed and shifted over time. Unlike integrationist discourses driven by rhetorical identification with whites that emerged as the primary means of challenging segregation, Black Power discourses disidentified with whiteness. Mark McPhail has mapped this rhetorical landscape, arguing that black rhetors had to overcome the war language used by white segregationists to undermine identificatory practices articulated by civil rights activists. Describing this rhetorical change, McPhail writes that "[e]pistemologically, this marked a tactical shift from emphasizing foundational principles and ideals to invoking and critiquing empirical practices and realities, and a strategic discursive shift assimilationist integration to revolutionary opposition."[49] The Black Power phenomenon was a significant rhetorical departure from the language and strategy of integration and disidentification was a defining rhetorical feature of what I have described elsewhere as "the Black Power vernacular."[50]

Visually, Black Power activists found disidentificatory potential and resonance in the afros, berets, guns, and leather that marked, say, the Black Panther "uniforms," alongside the image of the Black Power fist. These symbols became useful because Black Power activists were quite conscious of the white spectators that were both turned on and freaked out by their ostentatiousness. Black Power activists were unwilling to continue performing a conciliatory blackness. Instead, they said loudly and on camera: "We Want Black Power." The Black Power slogan and its attenuating philosophical and rhetorical iterations marked a profound moment of disidentification with previous styles of accomodationist blackness. In simultaneously embracing the pleasure and terror of blackness in its most powerful and most upsetting posture, Black Power sought to dislodge both urban and suburban spectators and move them into a space where they might question narratives about blackness, whiteness, "crime," "criminals," and "rights." For Black Power, disidentification meant coming to terms with the persistent shaming of blackness. Rhetorically, "Black Power" calls into question the modes by which discourses of state power are produced, circulated, and challenged.

Much of the impetus for Black Power is directed towards the creation of rhetorical identification *among* black people, premised upon a rejection of whites and whiteness through language, posture, style, and art and through an embrace of black pride black judgment, and black political and economic power. Or, in the words of Julius Lester, "Blacks who yell 'Honky' are revolutionizing themselves." As Lester's comment demonstrates, rhetorical confrontation functioned dialectically for Black Power activists.[51] Activists used the confrontational posture to redefine political terms and relationships, to norm black people to different assumptions about themselves and others, and assign blame to white liberals and ineffectual black politicians. Revolutionary language, often borrowed from Third World liberation movements, helped build the ethos and internationalism of Black Power political programs, though the revolutionary posture of Black Power led to early condemnations of the movement as violent and reactionary.

"Black vernacularity" describes a general "repertoire of representation, a politics of being, particular to a racialized, ideologically marginalized constituency."[52] Often, vernacular rhetoric emerges from counter-cultural discourse, where the rhetoric develops "a chain of rhetorical moves … outside of the common cultural storehouse of characterizations and narratives."[53] Moreover,

> vernacular speakers must negotiate dual goals: creating exigency for political action among their vernacular public and appealing to formal political agents and publics included in the policymaking process. This complex negotiation creates constraints for the black vernacular intellectual, who is appealing to black audiences while also attempting to engage white power brokers or at least address them as they eavesdrop on black rhetorical production.[54]

Thus Black Power activists embraced positive strategies of identifying with blackness in a white supremacist state alongside strategies of disidentification that demonstrated how "identity is enacted by minority subjects who must work with/resist the conditions of (im)possibility that dominant culture generates."[55] But even as their innovations in identification were unstable, mobile, oscillating, and multiple, the drive to create coherent identifications drove Black Power activists to simultaneously titillate and menace. The stylistic repertoire of the Black Power vernacular centered primarily in confrontational rhetoric. Confrontational strategies are attractive because there is a "strong sense of success, so strong that it may be a can't-lose strategy," particularly for long-suffering black liberation activists with nothing left to lose.[56]

> Black Power activists articulated this 'nothing left to lose' posture in several ways: they argued that black people are already socially dead and therefore, can't be killed again; they argued that they could be reborn, perhaps as martyrs; they argued that they had

the tenacity for a revolution fight where white conservatives did not; and they argued that black people have a global understanding of oppression and how to collectively destroy it.[57]

Black intellectuals demanded a rhetorical and political posture that took aim at white liberals and liberalism by documenting its limitations, its failures, and its inherent contradictions for black citizens.

In earlier work, I coined the term "Black Power vernacular" to describe this political posture and express the repertoire of signs and symbols that Black Power rhetors mobilized to create black solidarity in the face of symbolic legislative victories that black activists felt had little impact on black lives. As I put it, "rhetorical pugilism" typified this vernacular, simultaneously expressing black pride while extending "anti-white racial slurs" to demonize white liberals.[58] This discourse developed from initial denunciations of "white "honky" liberals and formed the basis of Black Power as it emerged from SNCC and CORE from 1966–1967. In his speech "The Pitfalls of Liberalism," Carmichael explains the gatekeeping function of the white liberal:

> Many people want to know why, out of the entire white segment of society, we want to criticize the liberals. We have to criticize them because they represent the liaison between other groups, between the oppressed and the oppressor. The liberal tries to become an arbitrator, but he is incapable of solving the problems. He promises the oppressor that he can keep the oppressed under control; that he will stop them from becoming illegal (in this case illegal means violent). At the same time, he promises the oppressed that he will be able to alleviate their suffering - in due time. Historically, of course, we know this is impossible, and our era will not escape history.

Carmichael's persistent critiques ushered in a different rhetorical space for black agitation, characterizing white supremacy as a system that has always benefitted white liberals, making it impossible for white liberals to fundamentally undermine it. Carmichael's position was clearly articulated here: "What the liberal really wants is to bring about change which will not in any way endanger his position."[59] Carmichael's rhetorical posture implicated liberals in segregation and anti-black violence and as the decade wore on, this kind of critique frequently circulated.

As his successor at SNCC, H. Rap Brown built on Carmichael's innovation in the Black Power vernacular by using anti-white racial slurs to counter the increasingly hostile political terrain that undermined black equality. In a famous speech in Cambridge, Maryland, Brown shouted:

> Black Power. That's the way to say it. Don't be scared of these Honkies around here. Say Black Power. I come back a few years later and I still find Race Street out there

still dividing the community. That ain't bad because we want to be by ourselves any-way, we don't want to be with no animals. A Honky is an animal. A Cracker is an animal. We don't need to be with him. There is one thing we want to do. We are going to control our community.[60]

Characterizing white people as "honkies," Brown's invective serves to dehumanize white people as a way of pointing to the source of racial inequality and segregation. In Cambridge, Brown berated Johnson for sending "honky, cracker federal troops … to kill black people."[61] Likewise, Brown told the ecstatic crowd,

You better get yourself some guns! … I know who my enemy is, and I know how to kill him. … When I get mad, I'm going out and look for a honky and I'm going to take out 400 years of dues on him.[62]

But Brown was also tremendously critical of President Johnson, calling him a "mad dog" in press releases.[63] In a famous passage in his memoir describing an Oval Office meeting between them, Brown describes him thusly:

Johnson was a big-eared, ugly, red-necked cracker. … And when I was tearing into Johnson's ass, Humphrey, who is supposed to be a "liberal," was getting madder than a pimp with dogshit on his shoe. So I looked at him and knew where he was at. The little red punk.[64]

As a "cracker," "pimp," and "punk," LBJ becomes the darkened other. Brown's invective does the work of undermining Johnson's credibility as civil rights hero and points to the limits of Johnson's ability to really understand black struggle as the civil rights landscape changed after 1965. Black Power activists like Carmichael, Brown and Cleaver unsettled the naturalized symbolism of white liberals' power, shutting down avenues of political affiliation while creating new space for black identification. Harnessing a dystopian imaginary, Black Power rhetors mobilized powerful black images and fantasies with which publics could transgress heavily patrolled social norms. Ultimately, this rhetorical strategy cemented the positionality of Black Power as a movement that could not cooperate with the Johnson White House, magnifying its appeal for urban black citizens and guaranteeing its demise by the FBI. But the disidentification of black activists from white liberals also signaled the limitations of liberalism, particularly in the arena of civil rights policy.

Not surprisingly, disidentificatory identity practices often emerge in black publics when essentialist (and white supremacist) constructions of blackness calcify and ultimately short circuit like they did after Selma. In Muñoz's words, these moments create turmoil where "a representational contract is broken" and the "social order receives a jolt that may reverberate loudly and widely, or in less dramatic, yet locally indispensible ways."[65] As the southern movement became more national, northern, and urban, Black Power emerged as a locus of debate about the constitutive dimensions of identifying with blackness. Working against the erasure of collective identity through routine, mundane legal decisions and local police power, Black Power activists sought to increase the viability of community and solidarity in local institutions like schools, neighborhoods, and civic organizations where political and social identity could be refigured into new models of critical citizenship. In constituting new models of rhetorical belonging, Black Power activists articulated new nationalisms, new political attachments, and new modes of identification that privileged blackness over white ideals of blackness. This was particularly important after Martin Luther King's assassination in Memphis in 1968.

LBJ and Black Power's Disidentification

Among the Black Power activists that used disidentificatory politics to formulate black leadership and political strategy, Rap Brown and Eldridge Cleaver, Minister of Information for the Black Panther Party, were the most contentious. Where Brown undermined Johnson's credibility as a man and as a president with hyperbole and invective, Cleaver used King's death to denounce President Johnson's repression of civil rights efforts, pointing to increased police violence despite the administration's civil rights initiatives. Cleaver's affective hostility reminds the reader that the continued internal repression, harassment, disruption, violence, and assassination that escalated under liberal presidencies spurred the shift from black optimism to pessimism. Cleaver explains:

> The Black Panther Party was born under Johnson. Even Malcolm didn't call for the gun until after Kennedy was killed, which shows how reactionary violence begets reactionary violence, and why we have an internal war on our hands today. ... We asked for our civil and human rights. Instead of getting our rights, we have been killed, jailed, and driven underground, en masse. Now we ask for nothing. Instead, we are moving to take what we want.[66]

Tracing domestic repression of civil rights to Johnson as the catalyst of the BPP's resistance, Cleaver goes on to explain that the Panthers distanced themselves from Johnson, not just because of the lack of support they felt from him after 1965 but also because, in Cleaver's words:

> Both Malcolm and King were killed under Johnson, and Nixon has turned us into a nation of pallbearers and gravediggers. In the almost ten years since the killing of

Kennedy, the official solution to the racial problem has shifted from integration to a policy that approaches apartheid.[67]

Cleaver explains that while JFK and MLK had a symbiotic relationship that helped both men articulate a slow-moving vision of progress, Johnson's America bore nothing in common with the prior administration, especially on civil rights. As Cleaver puts it, "King didn't fit at all into the cracker strategy plotted by Lyndon Johnson. Besides that, LBJ had made it crystal clear that he took a dim view of poor people marching, except off to war."[68] Cleaver's criticisms of the anti-black climate fostered by the Johnson White House demonstrate how hopeless the future felt, especially after King's murder.

In their pioneering work *Black Rage* (1969), Grier and Cobbs wrote:

> For a moment be any black person, anywhere, and you will feel the waves of hopelessness that engulfed black men and women when Martin Luther King was murdered. All black people understood the tide of anarchy that followed his death. It is the transformation of this quantum of grief into aggression of which we now speak. As a sapling bent low stored energy, which will be released in the form of rage—black rage, apocalyptic and final.[69]

In the bitterness and hardness and rage of Black Power commentary following King's death, we see a rhetorical and affective shift that moved black liberation from the "cruel optimism" of nonviolence to unbridled black pessimism about white liberals and the possibility of white consciousness-raising.

In the simplest terms, "cruel optimism" refers to "the condition of maintaining an attachment to a significantly problematic object."[70] It would be difficult to pinpoint a more "significantly problematic object" than nonviolence, especially by 1968. Berlant explains that cruel optimism "explains our sense of *our endurance in the object*."[71] I suggest King's death shook the Black Power movement because they saw themselves in him, even as they sought to define themselves as apart from him. Because cruel optimism is expressed through the fetishizing of an object or ideal, in this case King himself or in his dream for a nonviolent future, the destruction of that thing or ideal is devastating. Berlant explains,

> What's cruel about these attachments ... is that the subjects who have *x* in their lives might not well endure the loss of their object/scene of desire, even though its presence threatens their wellbeing, because whatever the *content* of the attachment is, the continuity of its form provides something of the continuity of the subject's sense of what it means to keep on living on and to look forward to being in the world.[72]

For Berlant, though optimism is a mechanism of mediation that allows humans to process and understand life situations. It becomes cruel when it is linked to institutions that block the realization of the imagined, dreamed of future. King's idea of a nonviolent America is an instance of cruel optimism because it is a dream that could not be realized even under Johnson.

Thus did disidentification become an affective mode that channeled black pessimism, recalibrating black political strategy, black feelings, and black rage through the disavowal of whites, especially after King's assassination. In choosing to invent the Black Power move in the black freedom struggle, activists created an identity that found its voice and its social appeal in vernacular oppositionality. Hyperbole, rhetorical violence, and revolutionary fantasy were all part of the disidentificatory strategies in managing the hyperviolence ascribed to black folks even in the face of the nonviolent southern civil rights organizations like King's SCLC or SNCC.

Since King was a profound object of attachment for many but also a figure provoking affect ranging from extreme ambivalence to hatred, his assassination required rhetorical animation to decide what should come next, for America, for the civil rights movement, for black citizens. The memories of Black Power members reveal deep attachments to King despite the often critical positions that Black Power leaders took against him publicly. Reading the memories of King's assassination by Black Power leaders demonstrates how they were grappling with the loss of their connection to King, evidencing his power to influence them despite their rhetorical aloofness. In Berlant's terminology, leaders like Cleaver are political depressives, who "having adopted a mode that might be called detachment, may not really be detached at all, but navigating an ongoing and sustaining relation to the scene and circuit of optimism and disappointment."[73] It is in the navigation of optimism and pessimism following a public trauma like King's murder that citizens work through what Berlant calls the "infrastructures of belonging" that characterize political life.[74] The structures of belonging to King are keyed to blackness, black masculinity, martyrdom, southern-ness, the Church and an emphasis on *agape*, physical attraction, love, respect, and resistance. In negotiating this web of affect, Cleaver used King's assassination to scapegoat Johnson for failing to protect black intellectuals while simultaneously denouncing nonviolence as a strategy whose time had passed. Robert E. Washington has argued that Cleaver "sounded the death-knell on moral suasion ideology" with the publication of *Soul on Ice*.[75] In Cleaver's words, "The time of the sham is over, and the cheek of the suffering saint must no longer be turned to the brute. The titillation of the guilt complexes of bored white liberals leads to doom."[76] This damning assessment of Cleaver's contributions to the strategies of disidentifying with whites and whiteness suggests that with the death of King, moral suasion no longer had rhetorical power among black activists, particularly given the decline of King's own popularity.

White Backlash and Black Power

White liberals became the terrain of disidentification for Black Power activists and I want to propose that if Black Power was difficult to pin down, as many critics have claimed, one reason was that activists themselves were sorting out what it meant to divest from white liberalism when it had been the primary vernacular of modern day rights campaigns. Black Power was incoherent for *white liberals* who couldn't understand why black activists were so alienated because white liberals thought themselves to be *good* and above reproach. While it would be easy to dismiss criticisms of Johnson and his administration as personal attacks from just one Black Power leader like Carmichael, the radicalization of black freedom activists as the decade wore on led to disidentification across organizations. While Carmichael (in 1966) described the Fair Housing Bill as "a sham," Fannie Lou Hamer wired Johnson to tell him to bring troops home from Vietnam because "where they have no business anyhow, and bring them to Mississippi and Louisiana, because if this is a Great Society, I'd hate to see a bad one." And James Forman scorned "Lyndon Bloodbath Johnson," "who sent napalm to burn our brothers and sisters in Vietnam."[77] In Cambridge, Maryland, Rap Brown (probably the most creative critic of Johnson) shouted:

> Now we're gonna [And we got to] talk about Lyndon Johnson. Lyndon Johnson is the greatest outlaw going. He is a two-gun cracker. He(`s) killing black folks here and he(`s) killing them in Vietnam. That's Lyndon Johnson, your President. [That's your president, brother.] That's who he is. [That's who it is.] And they talk [tell you] about how bad Hitler was. At least before Hitler burned the Jews he killed them with gas. Lyndon Johnson is throwing napalm on human beings in Vietnam. Burning them to death. He(`s) burning babies. He(`s) burning hospitals. He can't be nothing but an outlaw. [He can't be nothing but an outlaw.] Any time a man sends a plane full of napalm over a village of children, [over school houses and blow them up and burn children, and] believe me, brother, the only reason he do [is doing] it, (brother), is because the Viet Cong is black, too.[78]

These critiques only intensified as the Johnson years wound down and the Vietnam war ramped up. Even with the passage of the Civil Rights Bill of 1968, Johnson's reputation was damaged, his political career finished.

Still, by rejecting Black Power and characterizing their own resistance to the new black consciousness as "white backlash," white liberals participated in the same kind of racist demonization that they felt morally superior to when they castigated conservatives for resisting integration. The pronouncements about Black Power's lust for violence and mobilization of the absurd notion of "reverse racism" become legible when we see the utility in projecting racism upon those victimized by it. bell hooks explains:

It is useful for white supremacist capitalist patriarchy to make all black rage appear pathological rather than identify the structure wherein that rage surfaces. At times black rage may express itself pathologically. However, it also can express itself in ways that lead to constructive empowerment. Black rage against systems of domination, particularly as it is expressed in black youth culture, is mirrored in the rebellion against the white supremacist bourgeois sensibility expressed by white youth.[79]

Sadly, even after watching the massive terrorism during the Mississippi Freedom Summer, after countless beatings and jailings and torture, after the massive FBI repression that began under the Johnson White House, and after the assassinations of the movement's major leaders, white liberals still could not understand why Black Power activists felt the presence of whites in the movement was a hindrance and not a help. Where integration sought, at least in part, to domesticate blackness as a way of making it less threatening to the racial hierarchies maintaining segregation, Black Power embraced the seeming permanence of white assumptions about blackness to resituate rhetorical and political resources towards new inventive possibilities. Marking the absolute otherness of blackness in this political landscape, Black Power intellectuals suggested that white liberals cannot and will not ever be so othered and, consequently, will never understand Black Power because doing so would force them to give up structural power. In this way, then, activists deployed multiple strategies to disidentify black activism from white liberalism, transforming the movement from civil rights to Black Power and inhabiting all of the fearsome stereotypes foisted upon them to try and take back control of their communities.

Finally, if increasing identification with whites is held as the benchmark for measuring Black Power's success, there is certainly an argument that the movement failed quite intentionally to create new, positive black connections with whites. But if the standard for movement success is creating new in-group consciousness about black resistance, then it is hard to find a better example of this kind of provocation directed internally towards black America. Black Power created news spaces for the reinterpretation of black relationships based on new ideas of blackness that were not predicated upon assimilation. In this way, dis-identification as a rhetorical strategy paved the way for a stronger, healthier black consciousness but only by pointing to the ways in which, as Stokely says, "the liberal really [only] wants ... to bring about change which will not in any way endanger his position."

Black Power advocates intentionally invoked "white liberals" broadly to create new nodes of black identification that pointed to the structural investments in white supremacy in the Democratic Party, a strategy that was new in the black freedom struggle. And while this kind of broad net blurred distinctions among better and worse white liberals from various avenues of American life, it did succeed in creating a political consciousness capable of making structural claims about oppression across various policy issues (housing, education, employment, voting, etc.). The vagaries of the critique helped to make it useful for in-group identification within Black Power circles even when they often collapsed into various personalities (LBJ being the most obvious target) as repositories for their disappointment, disagreement, and contempt for administration policies.

Johnson was an obvious site for disidentification because of his towering presence in the country after John Kennedy's assassination and for his presidential commitment to civil rights. As the country slid deeper into Vietnam and as the Democratic Party embraced conservative strategies of law and order with Johnson at the helm, political assassinations increased, repression of black activists increased, and dissatisfaction with Johnson as a partner in civil rights reform eroded. At the same time, King's death created a vacuum where activists felt that radicalism was the only path forward as a strategy of self-preservation. Their frustration, then, poured into Johnson and administration officials who continued to thwart more progressive racial initiatives while continuing to actively repress the movement as it adapted to the emergent conservatism of the last years of Johnson's tenure. Anti-white slurs and the kind of denunciations performed by Black Power leaders evinced a series of disidentification strategies focused on Johnson because he was the primary target of their political pressure and because a focus on the president helped to streamline in-group identification among Black Power advocates, suggesting that this movement strategy may emerge and re-emerge in moments when the executive cannot or will not collaborate with activists in ways that incorporate activists' goals into federal policy. Ultimately, scholars need to read these rhetorical strategies of disidentification as forms that emerged in a period where the triumphalism of rights policies by liberals is vexed by that own administration's repression of rights activists. Historical and rhetorical scholarship on Johnson's civil rights policy might be better served by the adoption of a self-reflexive attitude about the ways in which his capitulation to "law and order" culture reflected a much more damaging civil rights posture for black America than is generally acknowledged.

Notes

1. See, for example: Karlyn Kohrs Campbell and Katheleen Hall Jameison, *Presidents Creating the Presidency: Deeds Done in Words* (Chicago: University of Chicago Press, 2008); Leigh Anne Duck, *The Nation's Region: Southern Modernism, Segregation, and U.S. Nationalism* (Athens: University of Georgia Press, 2006); Vanessa Beasley, *You, The People: American National Identity in Presidential Rhetoric* (College Station: Texas A & M University Press, 2004).

2. Kennedy's assassination was especially critical in the reconstitution of the national body. See Barbie Zelizer, *Covering the Body: The Kennedy Assassination, the Media, and the Shaping of Collective Memory* (Chicago: University of Chicago Press, 1992).

3. See: Patricia Witherspoon, "'Let Us Continue': The Rhetorical Initiation of Lyndon Johnson's Presidency," *Presidential Studies Quarterly* 17, no. 3 (1987): 531-539; Kurt Ritter, "Lyndon B. Johnson's Crisis Rhetoric after the Assassination of John F. Kennedy: Securing Legitimacy and Leadership," in *The Modern Presidency and Crisis Rhetoric*, ed. Amos Kiewe (Westport, CT: Praeger Publishers, 1994), 73-90; John M. Murphy, "Crafting the Kennedy Legacy," *Rhetoric & Public Affairs* 3, no. 4 (2000), 577-601; Campbell and Jamieson, *Presidents Creating the Presidency*, 59; and, Ashley Barrett, "Lyndon B. Johnson, 'Let Us Continue' (27 November 1963)," *Voices of Democracy* 4 (2009), http://archive.vod.umd.edu/citizen/lbj1963int.htm#_edn43

4. Randall Woods, *Prisoners of Hope: Lyndon B. Johnson, The Great Society, and the Limits of Liberalism* (New York: Basic Books, 2016), 8.

5. Robert Dalleck, *Flawed Giant: Lyndon Johnson and His Times 1961-1973* (New York: Oxford University Press, 1998).

6. Doris Kearns Goodwin, *Lyndon Johnson and the American Dream* (New York: St. Martin's Press, 1976/1991), 181.

7. Bruce Miroff, *Presidents on Political Ground* (Lawrence: University of Kansas, 2016), 77.

8. José Esteban Muñoz, *Disidentifications: Queers of Color and the Performance of Politics* (Minneapolis: University of Minnesota, 1999), 4.

9. See: Lester G. Seligman and Cary Raymond Covington, *The Coalitional Presidency* (Pacific Grove, CA: Brooks/Cole, 1989); and, Craig Allen Smith, *Presidential Campaign Communication: The Quest for the White House* (Malden, MA: Polity Press, 2010), 6-8.

10. Julian E. Zelizer, *The Fierce Urgency of Now: Lyndon Johnson, Congress, and the Battle for the Great Society* (New York: Penguin, 2015), 8.

11. Woods, *Prisoners of Hope*, 12.

12. Woods, *Prisoners of Hope*, 12.

13. Doris Kearns Goodwin, *Lyndon Johnson and the American Dream* (New York: St. Martin's Press, 1976/1991), 180.

14. Robert A. Caro, *The Passage of Power: The Years of Lyndon Johnson* (New York: Knopf, 2012), xix.

15. Miroff, *Presidents on Political Ground*, 123.

16. Robert Dalleck, *Lyndon B. Johnson: Portrait of a President* (Oxford: Oxford University Press, 2005), 113.

17. Dalleck, *Flawed Giant*, 224.

18. Dalleck, *Flawed Giant*, 31.

19. Kenneth Burke, *A Rhetoric of Motives* (Berkeley: University of California Press,, 1969,) 55. Emphasis mine.

20. Kenneth Burke, *Language As Symbolic Action: Essays on Life, Literature and Method* (Berkeley: University of California Press, 1966), *28*.

21. Maurice Charland, "Constitutive Rhetoric: The Case of the *Peuple Québécois*," *Quarterly Journal of Speech* 73.2 (1987), 133.

22. Gary Gerstle, "Race and the Myth of Liberal Consensus," *The Journal of American History* 82, no. 2 (1995), 579–586.

23. Sidney M, Milkis, "Lyndon Johnson, the Great Society, and the 'Twilight' of the Modern Presidency," *The Great Society and the High Tide of Liberalism* (Amherst: University of Massachusetts Press, 2005), 1–50.

24. August Meier and Elliot Rudwick, *CORE: A Study in the Civil Rights Movement, 1942–1968* (New York: Oxford University Press, 1973), 412, 414–15.

25. Malcolm X, minister of the Nation of Islam's Mosque No. 7 in Harlem, was assassinated in the Harlem Ballroom on February 21, 1965.

26. Stokely Carmichael, "What We Want," *New York Review of Books*, September 22, 1966, 4.

27. Carmichael, "What We Want," 6.

28. Floyd McKissick, "The Way to a Black Ideology," *The Black Scholar* 1.2 (1969), 14.

29. William James Cooper and Thomas E. Terrill, *The American South: A History* (Volume 2) (New York: Rowman and Littlefield, 1995), 763.

30. "President Points to Radical Actions." *New York Times*, July 6, 1966. Qtd in Jeffery O. G. Ogbar, *Black Power: Radical Politics and African American Identity* (Baltimore, MD: Johns Hopkins University Press, 2004), 64.

31. Ogbar, *Black Power*, 64; Robert L. Scott and Wayne Brockriede, "Hubert Humphrey Faces the 'Black Power' Issue," *Speaker and Gavel* 4 (November 1966), 11–17.

32. Evan Thomas, *Robert Kennedy: His Life* (New York: Simon and Schuster, 2002), 324.

33. Manning Marable, *Race, Reform, and Rebellion: The Second Reconstruction in Black America*, 3rd Ed. (Jackson: University Press of Mississippi, 2007), 93.

34. Jack Newfield, "Robert Kennedy's Bedford-Stuyvesant Legacy," *New York Magazine*, 16 December 1968, 30.

35. Adam Clayton Powell, *Adam by Adam: The Autobiography of Adam Clayton Powell, Jr.* (New York: Kensington Press, 1971/2008), 246.

36. Ogbar, *Black Power*, 64.

37. Grace Elizabeth Hale, *A Nation of Outsiders: How the White Middle Class Fell in Love with Rebellion in Postwar America* (Oxford: Oxford University Press, 2011), 209.

38. Devin Fergus, *Liberalism, Black Power, and the Making of American Politics, 1965–1980* (Athens: University of Georgia Press, 2009).

39. Kevin Boyle, *The UAW and the Heyday of American Liberalism, 1945–1968* (New York: Cornell University Press, 1995), 218.

40. Harry L. Feingold, *American Jewish Political Culture and the Liberal Persuasion* (Ithaca: Syracuse University Press, 2013).

41. Julian Bond, "Black Power: Its Meaning and Its Measure," *Negro Digest*, November 1966, 81.

42. Peter Carroll, *It Seemed Like Nothing Happened: America in the 1970s* (Newark: Rutgers University Press, 1990).

43. James A. Colaiaco, *Martin Luther King, Jr.: Apostle of Militant Nonviolence* (New York: Palgrave Macmillan, 1988), 173–175; Jon Rice, "The World of the Illinois Panthers," in *Freedom North: Black Freedom Struggles Outside the South, 1940–1980* (New York: Palgrave Macmillan, 2003), 41–64.

44. Muñoz, *Disidentifications*, 25.

45. Judith Butler, *Bodies that Matter*, 219.
46. Muñoz, *Disidentifications*, 5.
47. Muñoz, *Disidentifications*, 4.
48. Muñoz, *Disidentifications*, 4.
49. Mark McPhail, *The Rhetoric of Racism Revisited: Reparations or Separatism?* (New York: Rowman & Littlefield, 2001), 165.
50. Lisa M. Corrigan, *Prison Power: How Prison Influenced the Movement for Black Liberation* (Jackson: University Press of Mississippi, 2016).
51. Robert L. Heath, "Dialectical Confrontation: A Strategy of Black Radicalism," *Central States Speech Journal* 24.3 (1973), 169.
52. Grant Farred, *What's My Name? Black Vernacular Intellectuals* (Minneapolis, MN: University of Minnesota Press, 2003), 17.
53. John Louis Lucaites and Celeste Michelle Condit, "Reconstructing <Equality>: Culture-typal and Counter-Cultural Rhetorics in the Martyred Black Vision," *Communication Monographs* 57, no. 1 (1990): 5–24.
54. Corrigan, *Prison Power*, 7.
55. Muñoz, *Disidentifications*, 6.
56. Scott and Smith, "The Rhetoric of Confrontation," 5.
57. Corrigan, *Prison Power*, 8–9.
58. Corrigan, *Prison Power*, 9.
59. Stokely Carmichael, "Pitfalls of Liberalism," *Black World/Negro Digest*. August 1970, 91.
60. H. Rap Brown, "Speech at Cambridge," July 24, 1967, Maryland State Archives. Retrieved on 19 Feb. 2017, http://msa.maryland.gov/megafile/msa/speccol/sc2200/sc2221/000012/000008/html/speech1.html.
61. Steven D. Price, *Civil Rights, Volume 2 1967–68* (New York: Facts on File, Inc., 1973), 40.
62. Bryan Burrough, *Days of Rage: America's Radical Underground, the FBI, and the Forgotten Age of Revolutionary Violence* (New York: Penguin Random House, 2016), 41.
63. SNCC press release, July 26, 1967; "Rap Brown Denounced Johnson as 'Mad Dog,'" *Los Angeles Times*, July 28, 1967.
64. Brown, *Die Nigger Die!*, 53.
65. Muñoz, *Disidentifications*, 6.
66. Eldridge Cleaver with Kathleen Cleaver. *Target Zero A Life in Writing* (New York: Palgrave MacMillan, 2007), 83.
67. Cleaver, *Target Zero*, 83.
68. Cleaver, *Target Zero*, 83.
69. William H. Grier and Price M. Cobbs, *Black Rage* (New York: Basic Books, 1992), 210.
70. Berlant, *Cruel Optimism*, 25.
71. Berlant, *Cruel Optimism*, 23.
72. Berlant, *Cruel Optimism*, 24.
73. Berlant, *Cruel Optimism*, 27.
74. Berlant, *Cruel Optimism*, 27.
75. Robert E. Washington, *The Ideologies of African American Literature: From the Harlem Renaissance to the Black Nationalist Revolt* (Lanham, MD: Rowman & Littlefield, 2001), 273.

76. Eldridge Cleaver, *Soul on Ice* (New York: Random House, 1968), 107.
77. William E. Leuchtenburg, *The White House Looks South: Franklin D. Roosevelt, Harry S Truman, and Lyndon B. Johnson* (Baton Rouge: Louisiana State University Press, 2007), 337.
78. H. Rap Brown. "Speech in Cambridge," 24 July 1967, Maryland State Archives. Retrieved June 8, 2017 from http://msa.maryland.gov/megafile/msa/speccol/sc2200/sc2221/000012/000008/html/speech1.html.
79. bell hooks, *Killing Rage: Ending Racism* (New York: Owl Books, 1995), 29.

Afterword

Reflections on Rhetoric and the Presidency

DAVID ZAREFSKY

The cover of the May 2018 issue of *The Atlantic* included a lead story on "How the Presidency Became Impossible."[1] The article suggests that many of the problems of the Trump presidency are not about Trump so much as about the presidency. It has grown, the author suggests, especially in the post-Eisenhower years to the point where it may be an impossible job for anyone to do. And yet the growth continues, because the acts any president initiates become expectations for his successor. The article closes with a series of prescriptions for making the office manageable again, most of them involving paring back its expectations and scope. There is some confusion in the article, because sometimes when the author refers to expanded *powers,* he really is talking about expanded *responsibilities* or *expectations.* In fact, the first major argument of the *Atlantic* piece might be reconstructed as: The expectations placed on the presidency today are beyond the powers of the president to fulfill.

That argument should sound familiar to readers of this volume, because it is akin to the explanation offered over thirty years ago by Jeffrey Tulis for the emergence of what Tulis called "the rhetorical presidency."[2] Contrary to the views of rhetorical scholars who rushed to embrace this term (asking "why didn't *we* think of that?") because they thought it exalted their subject matter, for Tulis the implications of the rhetorical presidency were not altogether benign. The term does not suggest simply that presidents give lots of speeches, although they do. At its core it is an argument about the match between expectations and power. The claim is that, at some point, the expectations Americans placed on the presidency grew beyond the limited view of the office represented in the Constitution. One can dispute about whether that occurred with George Washington, who thought the presidency embodied the centripetal forces making the Union possible; or with Andrew Jackson, who was expected to represent the will of the people; or with Martin Van Buren, with whom the president came to be viewed as the leader of a party; or with Abraham Lincoln, who invoked the idea of emergency powers and assumed the responsibility for national self-preservation; or—as Tulis believes— with Theodore Roosevelt and especially Woodrow Wilson, who saw a positive function for big government as a check on big business. Much ink has been spent, including by me, on the question of just when this gap between presidential expectations and presidential power manifested itself—whether it developed over time or was there all along. But the existence of such a gap is hard to dispute, especially when one recalls that, fearful of executive tyranny, the founders deliberately created a presidency of limited powers and intended for the legislative branch to be supreme.

The second part of Tulis's argument is that, confronted with this imbalance between responsibilities and powers, presidents sought to augment their Constitutionally-designated power with power that derived from other sources, and that the source on which they relied heavily was rhetoric. This did not necessarily mean "going public," or appealing directly to the people to urge them to put pressure on Congress to do what the president convinces the people are what they want. It can include anything from arguing "in the name of the people" (that is, arguing to the relevant decision-makers that the people support this or that action and the fact that they support it is reason for the policy-makers to take the action) to using resources of definition, metaphor, imagery, and other aspects of language to shape the frame of reference in which people understand this messaging in the first place.

Political scientist George Edwards III has argued prominently that presidential rhetoric cannot be shown to have significant effects.[3] This has offended many scholars of rhetoric because it has been taken as implying that their field is unimportant, and a remark by a rhetorical scholar that there is any merit in Edwards's position is taken as *prima facie* evidence of apostasy.[4] Now, to be sure, Edwards's very broad claims open him to legitimate criticism: he offers a very limited notion of what counts as "presidential rhetoric" and what counts as "effects." The former seems to be limited to presidential speeches about public policy; and the latter, to whether the measure of public opinion polls regarding that public policy changes from before to after the presidential speech. And Edwards can be faulted for failing to understand that humanists talk about effects in terms of broad cultural factors that cannot always be measured empirically. But he is on solid ground in admonishing humanist scholars of rhetoric not to employ causal language when they are not really making causal claims. Still, in making Edwards the focus of our attention, rhetorical scholars (myself included) are missing the relationship between his claims and the "rhetorical presidency" hypothesis.

For the third step in Tulis's argument is that the rise of the rhetorical presidency is not altogether benign. When he refers to my work, for example, showing how Lyndon Johnson was able to use the war metaphor to gin up support for a poverty program for which there was no pre-existing demand, he is not sanguine about the results. The rhetorical presidency disrupts the balance between republicanism and democracy that is the foundation of American government. It de-emphasizes deliberation in favor of aggregating often unfocused individual preferences. It makes public campaigns loom larger than the processes of management and implementation on which successful public policy depends. And it makes it harder to confine executive power within its constitutional limitations or to prevent the executive from usurping powers assigned to the legislature or the judiciary, causing those institutions to atrophy.

Now, if presidential rhetoric is as ineffective as Edwards claims, then how can it have such deleterious consequences for American government as Tulis implies? Figuring out this conundrum, in my opinion, entails the conclusion that Tulis and Edwards are not discussing quite the same thing. Tulis is discussing changes in institutional characteristics whereas Edwards is assessing the efficacy of presidential performance. This difference is similar to the distinction Martin Medhurst draws between the rhetorical presidency and presidential rhetoric. Edwards's claims could be true or false regardless of whether the institutional character of the presidency is changing, and changes in the institution of the presidency could be benign or malign whether or not the claims advanced by Edwards are true. This means, in sum, that attacks on Edwards's limited perspective and disputes about just when the character of the presidency changed are both largely beside the point of Tulis's central normative claim: that on balance, the advent of the rhetorical presidency has not been a good influence on American political life.

Let me return now to the essay in *The Atlantic*. Whereas Tulis examines the early 20th century, Dickerson focuses on our current moment, the presidency of the early 21st century. Dickerson believes there has been a huge expansion of the job of the president since about 1960, and that the expansion has occurred largely in rhetorical functions. One president's creative rhetorical invention, if successful, becomes an expectation for future presidents, thereby adding to the burdens of the office. One example Dickerson uses is the president's growing role in offering national consolation by offering personal consolation to the victims of national disaster or tragedy. Ronald Reagan may have initiated this role by speaking to the nation in the wake of the *Challenger* tragedy and then going to the memorial service and eulogizing the victims. Bill Clinton expanded the role by traveling to Oklahoma City to console families of the victims of the victims of the bombing of the Alfred P. Murrah Federal Building. Clinton found that this epideictic discourse also had a political function: it re-established his ethos as president after it had taken a severe beating in the 1994 midterm elections. In their essay in this volume, Jay Childers and Cassandra Bird explore this new role of the president as comforter-in-chief. This expectation did not exist before Reagan. In fact, Dickerson observes, Eisenhower chose not to interrupt his vacation to travel to Louisiana where there were major hurricanes. To see the difference, contrast the benign response to Eisenhower's decision with the intense criticism George W. Bush received fifty years later for surveying the damage caused by Hurricane Katrina from the windows of Air Force One at an elevation of 30,000 feet. It was not that Bush could have done anything on the ground, and he might have made the job of recovery more difficult by being in the way, but it nevertheless was an expectation that he failed to fulfill. Dickerson suggests that in order to restore the presidency to manageable size, rhetorical tasks like this that are not core functions of the office should be offloaded to others, say to the vice president or to the first spouse.

Another example Dickerson discusses at length is presidential vacations. These used to be private affairs, and they were longer, affording presidents the opportunity to relax and refresh themselves. But as the belief developed that the president embodies the people, the expectation developed that the people would have constant, although vicarious, access to the president who, after all, worked for them. The people were not able to take frequent or long vacations; why should their employee? So there developed the norms that presidential vacations were "working" trips, that the president should not be seen enjoying them too much, and that a steady stream of news should issue from the presidential vacation spot. This is a rhetorical performance in which the president seeks to convince people that he is always "on task." In the process, the president may lose the physical and psychological benefits of vacation.

Perhaps the clearest villain Dickerson identifies is the collapse of the distinction between campaigning and governing, so that the former usurps the latter. As recently as 1968, it was customary for presidential contenders to announce their candidacy in the year of the election. It was thought unusual when Eugene McCarthy announced that he was running on November 30 of the previous year, and that was explained because he was a fringe candidate running on a single issue. The first three years of a president's term were for governing, calling for policy analysis, deliberation, and dialectic. The campaign, largely an exercise in public rhetoric, would intrude at the end but would not last so long that the country would suffer election fatigue. But a variety of factors, including election-law reform, the geometrically increasing cost of a campaign, and the advent of cable news, as well as the competitive desire to get ahead of others by starting early, has stretched the distinction between campaigning and governing to the breaking point. Sidney Blumenthal coined the term "the permanent campaign" during the 1980s, calling attention to the fact that no policy decision occurred in a campaign vacuum.[5] Even in a president's second term, when the incumbent is constitutionally ineligible to run again, attention is paid constantly to how the next election is shaping up. Most presidents wish to influence the choice of their successor, thereby to shape their own legacy. The logical conclusion of the permanent campaign was President Donald Trump's decision to file for re-election on Inauguration Day, 2017.

President George H. W. Bush defended the unusually negative campaign of 1988 by saying that that was part of campaigning, a genre of discourse that could be forgotten about when the election was over and he could turn to governing, an activity he much preferred. Dickerson takes a similar view and complains about the fact that campaigning has usurped governing. He blames this tendency for a variety of problems. Presidents come to office experienced in campaigning and do not realize that they are (usually) inexperienced in governing. They then overestimate their own efficacy because, after all, they just won the election. They assume they will be able to cajole Congress because, after all, Lyndon Johnson was able to do it—disregarding the highly unusual circumstances Johnson faced. Experienced in hyper partisan conflict, they are neither prepared nor disposed for the longer and harder work of building and nurturing coalitions on particular issues. And when they are stymied, they have no sense of a "Plan B" other than to blame the opposition and thus further intensify partisan conflict. Now, the distinction between campaigning and governing is not self-evident, but that does not change Dickerson's argument very much. He could deny a sharp distinction yet still maintain that the contemporary presidency unfortunately elevates certain types of campaigning over others.

Dickerson offers a set of prescriptions for improving the presidency. He does not describe them in just these terms, but many of them involve shrinking the rhetorical presidency by re-examining and reversing some of the ways in which rhetorical performance has enabled presidents to enhance their power and influence, in the process creating expectations that subsequent presidents must try increasingly hard to fulfill. Among the proposals: offload many of the epideictic functions of the president to someone else (as noted above), legally require transition planning by both candidates throughout the general election campaign, have a more systematic process for selecting key staff and for onboarding the president, reverse the congressional tendency to defer policy-making authority to the president, regard governmental experience as an asset once again, rather than a liability, devalue speaking ability relative to other criteria when evaluating pro-spective presidents, and so on. One is inclined to regard many of these proposals as impractical if not farfetched, or to see the evolution of the office as going in the opposite direction—until one fully realizes how much the Trump administration is shattering norms of presidential behavior. New norms are likely to emerge, or long-neglected ones to re-emerge, out of the current chaos and confusion. Right now it seems less likely that they will go in the direction of the institutional presidency Dickerson favors than in the direction of right-wing populism, if any-thing exacerbating current difficulties, but who knows? It depends on whether whatever follows the Trump presidency will seek to build upon or to reverse its emphases.

I focus on the Dickerson article because it is at least obliquely related to many of the essays in this volume (and directly related to some, such as Childers and Bird, as I have noted) and because it gives a sense of urgency to the future of the rhetorical presidency. Like any collection of essays, there are differences within this set regarding the clarity of their relation to the central questions. The editors invited contributors to (1) bring their particular focus or perspective to bear on the presidency if that is not usually the focus of their research, or (2) take up a different aspect of the topic, or a mediating institution affecting the presidency, if presidential discourse *is* the scholar's normal focus. I shall discuss the essays not in the order in which they appear, in order to bring some of them into conversation with one another or to suggest underlying themes or continuities.

Most of the studies are U.S.-centric in their materials. There is one essay deal-ing with Chilean President Michelle Bachelet that mentions the value of com-parative studies and provides interesting insight on the Chilean experience, the gender variable, and the justification of action by reference to previous commit-ments. It hints at precisely the issue that Dickerson develops—how a president can maneuver in a situation in which expectations of performance exceed presi-dential agency. But the key variable of "commitment" is under-theorized, and how this single non-U.S. case will permit generalization to presidential rhetoric as a genre, is an asked but unanswered question.

Two essays examine elaboration of new (for their time) modes of presidential rhetoric. Barney examines the use of maps. In the early days of World War II, Franklin Roosevelt asked his audience to obtain a map and bring it with them to listen to his radio address, but the Cold War presidents Barney examines developed their own maps as presentational aids. They were able to make several choices, such as where to locate disputed points, how to use color, how to arrange a series of static maps so that they told a story of movement and reaction, and the like. As Barney acknowledges, these choices are not neutral but affect the audi-ence's perception and understanding of the topic. The presidential choices also reflect the influence of Cold War ideologies on presumably (but not really) neutral representations.

Prasch addresses the contemporary significance of rhetoric *in situ*, exploring what the decision to speak in a particular place contributes to the rhetorical strength of a president. This is one of the oldest presidential uses of rhetoric, with George Washington's travel to different parts of the country intended to embody the claims that the nation was united and he was president of all the people. Numerous examples of this concern with place can be found. It was important for President Eisenhower to return to the White House from his vacation in Newport, Rhode Island, so that he could be surrounded by the symbols of presidential authority when announcing that he was sending federal troops to Little Rock, Arkansas to enforce the desegregation orders of the U.S. courts. Eisenhower not only spoke from the White House but during his speech explained why he was doing so. Both John F. Kennedy and Ronald Reagan spoke in Berlin about the significance of that city. Lyndon Johnson stressed continuity by choosing to sign the Medicare legislation in 1965 in Independence, Missouri, in the presence of former President Harry Truman, who had first proposed it. Recent presidents enacting the "comforter-in-chief" role have found it valuable to speak from the scene of the tragedy they memorialize. Prasch uses the case of President Barack Obama's 2016 speeches in Cuba to talk about how the acknowledgment of place strengthens his appeal about the importance of re-establishing relationships that had been blocked for over half a century. President Trump is giving a new dimension to this issue by selecting places more for their political than for their substantive significance—speaking in swing states, for example, or in locations that he won in the last election. The topic of place is also one that could be examined within the framework of Dickerson's argument. Presidents can travel wherever they wish, and this fact constitutes a rhetorical resource. Is it also a constraint by creating the expectation that subsequent presidents will need to travel to whatever site seems important to a subject or issue? Conversely, can we imagine that a future president will *decline* to travel, as several early presidents did, announcing that he or she will not venture outside the confines of Washington?

Technology has been a significant aid to presidential discourse, and presidents have tended to be early adopters of new communication technologies—Lincoln with the telegraph, Rutherford B. Hayes with the telephone, Franklin Roosevelt with radio, both John F. Kennedy and Ronald Reagan with television, Barack Obama with the Internet, and most recently, Donald Trump with Twitter. The rhetorical force of communication technology is twofold: it gives the president new resources for interacting with the American and global audiences, and it allows the president to normalize new technologies, treating them as something the president would use as a matter of course. This creates the expectation that subsequent presidents will do the same. I can think of no president who has chosen to forego technology used by his predecessors, except perhaps when the technology has been superseded.

One way in which presidential use of technology is normalized is by seeing it from the perspective of earlier technologies. Heidt and Pfister illustrate this with respect to Twitter. On its face, the presidential tweet appears to be a completely new means of communication. And in a sense it is: Heidt and Pfister note that it undercuts the time required for deliberation, attracting attention without stimulating deeper engagement with the topic of a message. The resulting "short circuits" activate immediate drives that find temporary satisfaction, analogous to the impulsive buying of consumer goods. This is a perceptive characterization of Twitter discourse. But the authors do not stop there. They see in Twitter manifestations of the ancient form of the diatribe, a resistant message that conveys cynicism about the civic culture in order to disrupt it. The disruption serves to critique its excesses and outrages. Heidt and Pfister regard Twitter exchanges as micro-diatribes. They accomplish their goals within the space of 140 or 280 characters. The brevity of the message abets the short circuiting of the public's energies. Heidt and Pfister suggest that the press has not yet figured out how to report on the tweets, treating them as if they were official presidential communications, investing the texts with more meaning and authenticity than they probably warrant. This framework, they conclude, is good for campaigning but bad for governing. They raise a question noted above, whether any meaningful distinction remains between the two. In short, these authors have examined seriously a new form of communication and found in it a new manifestation of an old genre. They pose the question of whether our understanding of the old can be stretched to account for the new. This is a most timely question in the aftermath of President Trump's Twitter "storm" following the 2018 meeting of the G-7 group of industrialized nations.

Another essay that tries to interpret older categories through newer lenses is Ryan Neville-Shepard's study of third-party norms of campaigning. Like Heidt and Pfister, he takes the Trump presidency as the object of study and contributes to emerging understanding of Trump's seemingly undisciplined communication. Rather than treat the president as *sui generis*, he argues that Trump's "outsider style" is a recurrent feature of American politics, usually found among third-party candidates. In their quest for press coverage and public attention, they transgress generic expectations and create public spectacles in order to craft a form of nontraditional authenticity. To be sure, Trump was not a third-party candidate, but he acted like one both on the path to the Republican nomination and in the general election campaign. He rejected traditional positions of both parties, alienating many mainstream Republican leaders in particular. The premise of Neville-Shepard's essay is that we will understand Trump better if we see him in the pattern of a renegade than if we see him as rudderless. Successful third-party candidacies often result not in election to the presidency but in absorption of the party's platform by one of the major parties. It seems that the Republican party of 2018 is quite different from that of 2016, and its remaking can be credited largely to Trump. His party largely absorbed his renegade positions, *and* he was elected to the presidency. He followed the third-party model and did even better than a third-party candidate.

The essay by Ortega and Stuckey calls for modification of our understanding of presidential rhetoric itself. Earlier scholarship understood it as presidential appeals to the mass public, often over the heads of established politicians and elites. Ortega and Stuckey suggest that there also is a discourse within the Executive Branch and among the elites, audiences that have their own motivations and cannot be taken for granted as supporters of the president *a priori*. They argue that discourse fragments are created for secondary audiences from primary texts. The case Ortega and Stuckey examine is the contest regarding ratification of the Panama Canal treaties during the Carter administration. They emphasize that presidential rhetoric has effects other than moving the needle of public opinion polls. For example, they suggest that it signals to elites how they should frame a topic for broader public discussion.

Studies of rhetorical strategy writ large sometimes neglect attention to the micro-level dynamics of language. Two of the essays in this volume seek to avoid that problem. Harris addresses the appeal of the concept of *home* as sanctuary, a site of belonging and safety. She maintains that nations can be understood by extension from the familial home; they should embody the same values and protections. Strengthening the familial home, then, necessarily will strengthen the national home. Working from these premises, Harris examines speeches by Theodore Roosevelt and Woodrow Wilson to identify early 20th-century views about the role of women in public affairs. Both presidents held that woman, through her position in the familial home, was critical to the nation. The national interest lay in enabling her to fulfill her duties in the home, not to step outside it. The civic training provided to their families by women in the home would contribute positively to the strength of the nation. By contemporary standards, this vision was constraining. Although Harris focuses intently on one time period, surely her method can be applied to other uses of *home* (periodic calls for the nation to "come home" from foreign entanglements come immediately to mind) as a way of exploring at the level of language the persistent conflicts between involvement and isolation—such as the current controversy between globalism and nationalism as guiding principles for America in the world.

Another essay rooted in language is Lemuel's study of Richard Nixon's war on drugs, which offers insight into the metaphors of contagion and war. Lemuel suggests that these metaphors laid the foundation for Nixon's thought and action regarding drugs. For example, Lemuel suggests that Nixon fuses medical and legal approaches to the drug problem and creates a mutually constitutive relationship between rehabilitation and compulsion such that each goal sustains the other. For the most part, however, this essay is several steps removed from the analysis of actual discourse, and for that matter from the presidency, focusing instead on a disciplinary debate about the nature of rhetorical criticism. The utility of this effort is weakened by Lemuel's uncritical acceptance of what he calls the postmodern assumption that presidential rhetoric is fragmented into digestible sound bites and recirculated in public discourse.

To be fair, neither Harris nor Lemuel is concerned primarily with the workings of language; I have read that focus into their essays. Both of their studies are concerned with the particular historical moments and topics they chose to examine. But by reading them together, one can see the significant role of presidential language.

At least three other studies also look at particular moments but with insights that transcend them. Johnson looks at what he calls "the debt ceiling debacle" of 2011, when the United States teetered on the brink of financial default because of congressional reluctance to raise the nation's debt ceiling. In the course of his analysis, Johnson introduces the concepts of "presidentialism" and "cruel optimism." The former refers to the belief that the chief executive is a synecdoche for the entire country, covering over constitutive differences. The latter refers to the notion that desiring something can actually be an obstacle to obtaining it. Seeing the president as the embodiment of the country, for example, depends on citizens' being able to identify with him, and in the case of Barack Obama this was difficult for many who obsessed over the fact that Obama did not "look like" previous presidents and did not evince masculine braggadocio. The "cruel optimism" of his presidency, and perhaps of any contemporary presidency other than in moments of national crisis, was that his calls for national unity served to emphasize existing divisions and to make unity harder to achieve. Johnson applies these constructs to the crisis over the debt ceiling as it played out in domestic politics. Seeing Obama as unlike them and hence not identifying with him, many Republicans saw his request to raise the debt ceiling as a mortal threat to the nation's economic security and a harbinger of national destruction. For these results to be averted, Obama had to lose this struggle, which was seen as a zero-sum game. Their refusal to compromise was, on this view, not irrational intransigence but principled witnessing. Johnson's theoretical apparatus could be better digested and its link to the case be made more explicit, but his essay offers valuable insight.

Corrigan explores the demise of interracial unity during the late 1960s in the civil rights movement. Her larger claim is that white liberals participated in racial backlash by denouncing Black Power as "black racism." This fractured the "liberal consensus" that had strongly supported President Johnson in 1964 and 1965. This fracturing had little to do with Johnson directly, except that he advocated "American democratic power, with a small 'd'" as transcending both black power and white power.[6] Corrigan's essay is not centrally linked to presidential rhetoric, and it accepts some questionable judgments as if they were facts, but it offers a powerful example of how once-united organizations can fragment and thwart the prospects for unity. In this respect it is a valuable companion to Johnson's study of the debt ceiling.

Ceccarelli examines President George W. Bush's discourse about science, claiming that Bush's anti-science rhetoric prepared the way for the more thorough and frontal attack on science during the Trump administration. "Prepared the way" is not offered as a strictly causal term in the sense of claiming that Bush's discourse was a sufficient condition for Trump's. Rather, it created a rhetorical trajectory into which Trump's later discourse would fit "naturally." In this sense, it says that Bush's discourse created conditions that easily could accommodate the later rhetoric of the Trump administration. It did so by exploiting the fact that science deals in probabilities, not certainties. This enabled Bush to magnify the uncertainty of scientific findings and to place judgments that put consensus judgments of scientists on a par with the doubts of isolated skeptics. Scientific consensus can be rendered untrustworthy by contending that scientists are tainted by vested interest and premature commitment to their positions, failing to keep an open mind.

I come finally to two essays that are difficult to characterize or to compare to others. Greene and Frank examine issues related to the presence of chemical weapons in Syria during the civil war aiming to overthrow Bashar al-Assad. They claim that one "becomes presidential" through talk about international norms and the responsibility of the United States to enforce justice in the world. They examine President Obama's address to Congress about Syria as he performance of duty through speech, and they conclude that appeals to duty foreclose deliberation and thus create a "post-rhetorical" presidency. Several of these ideas are interesting and provocative, but they need to be developed into an argument that coheres throughout the essay.

Abbott addresses the pressing and contemporary question (as of this writing) of how the presidency of Donald J. Trump has been articulated. His claim is that Trump has rearticulated the presidency in terms of white male privilege by reasserting authoritarianism. This was made possible, Abbott believes, by a backlash against the Democratic Party's emphasis on pluralist democracy, embodied in 2016 by the candidacy of Hillary Clinton. Abbott uses the theoretical notions of articulation and subject positions to explain the emergence of a white populist nationalism that evidently was just strong enough to carry Trump across the finish line. This by now familiar account resonates with much of what we know about 2016. Yet it raises questions about whether the analysis is overdetermined. How might it have explained the opposite result, the one nearly everyone expected? And is it a sufficiently nuanced account to explain the variety of factors that contributed to the final result, ranging from the slight drop in turnout among women in suburban Philadelphia to the late intervention in the campaign by FBI Director James Comey? And, finally, was the articulation of authoritarianism unique to 2016? That election was such a perfect storm that any simple or single-factor explanation of the results is suspect.

Taken together, then, these essays show the continuing vitality of older approaches to the study of presidential rhetoric, as well as adaptations in theory and method to encompass the changes of the contemporary presidency. One thing they do not do, however, is to suggest that the concept of either presidential rhetoric or the rhetorical presidency is itself outmoded. That suggestion depends on a very limited notion of what presidential rhetoric is, equating it with public speaking or oratorical performance. That mode of presidential communication does seem to be on the wane—although it is worth remembering that, as I write, Barack Obama, widely acknowledged for his rhetorical prowess, left office less than 18 months ago. But are not visual demonstrations also rhetoric? Are not tweets also texts? Are not impression management techniques a contributor to *ethos*? We are witnessing today not alternatives to the rhetorical presidency but new forms of rhetoric.

The volume resulting from the first Presidential Rhetoric Conference at Texas A&M University was titled *Beyond the Rhetorical Presidency*.[7] I do not take this title to suggest that "the rhetorical presidency" has become outdated as a characterization of the office, nor that presidential rhetoric is a major activity of the presidency. Rather, I take the title to suggest the need to get beyond labeling and categorizing in order to advance theoretical and analytical work. That goal is not achieved by repeating that there are many types of presidential rhetoric or that the rhetorical is an important dimension of the presidency as an institution. We need to consider how that observation affects our understanding of individual presidencies and how the study of specific cases refines the theoretical concepts themselves. Several of the essays in this volume point to ways of doing that.

Surveying the landscape of presidential rhetoric about a decade ago, Mary Stuckey observed that scholarship was necessarily constrained by the rather homogeneous character of the occupants of the office: "our understanding of power ... has been inflected by upper class, straight, white male expectations and practices."[8] That still remains the case. Of the 44 occupants of the office (Grover Cleveland served twice), only one has been African American. None have been women. Only one has been a Catholic and none have been Jews, Muslims, adherents of other religions, or nonbelievers. Only one has been unmarried; only two have been divorced. So far as we know, all have been straight, although there are rumors to the contrary in at least one case. In understanding the presidency, the point is not that gender, race, religion, marital status, or sexual identity are essentialized; indeed, there is much variety among these demographically homogeneous figures. For example, there has been considerable diversity in age, geography, educational attainment, and ideological disposition. But the range of knowledge that can be obtained by studies of individual cases is limited by the limited diversity of the cases. This limitation can be mitigated to some degree through comparative studies of U.S. presidents and those of other nations and cultures. Stillion Southard offers an example of such studies in her work on President Michelle Bachelet of Chile, although the utility of her study would be enhanced if the comparative dimension were more explicit.

One of the smarter books on the presidency I have read in recent years is Bruce Miroff's *Presidents on Political Ground.*[9] Miroff comes down somewhere near the middle of a continuum between belief in presidential agency (the view that underlay many early studies in public address) and institutional determinism, but he argues that the degree to which individual presidents have agency is heavily influenced by the political ground on which they must act. His ensuing analysis is similar to the position taken by Dickerson with which I opened this essay. He maintains that the political ground on which presidents act has shifted so as to make it harder for them to exercise power than in earlier times. He identifies five elements of the political ground: the media and spectacle, the economy, assembling political coalitions, navigating domestic policy, and the conduct of foreign policy. He explores how specific presidents since Franklin Roosevelt have found each of these grounds progressively more constraining.

Our concern is primarily with Miroff's first dimension, the media and presidential spectacle. This is the ground for "the presentation of character and the deployment of gestures that claim, in defiance of critics, to demonstrate presidential virtue."[10] Early on, television gave presidents great latitude for this performance, but recently, as viewing options have grown and suspicions about the president have increased, what originally was a boon has become as likely a presidential liability. The opportunities for critique and counter-spectacle may have nullified the president's original advantage. Case studies of Kennedy, Reagan, Clinton, the second Bush, and Obama are offered to trace this path of seemingly unbounded possibility yielding to constraint.

If the opportunities for presidential spectacle are limited by the shifting media ground, one response is to de-emphasize or abandon the production of spectacle in favor of some other means of exercising presidential power. That is, after all, what is implicit in many of the remedies Dickerson proposes. But another response is to double down on spectacle, offering seemingly ubiquitous spectacle, so that the president seeks to dominate every news cycle, to personalize every difference of opinion, to forego consistency or even truth if necessary, in order to stay in the public eye. Is this not what we are experiencing during the Trump administration? Miroff's analysis offers a lens for examining President Trump as the precipitant of hyper-spectacle. Such an examination might yield explanations of the Trump phenomenon that go beyond the polarized celebration and castigation that mark our contemporary moment.

Miroff's work has but one major flaw—the reductionist view of rhetoric I have noted above. He remarks that spectacle is to be distinguished from rhetoric, which he regards as the preparation and analysis of oratorical texts. He equates rhetoric with what traditionally was its paradigm of practice, excluding the many different manifestations rhetoric has assumed in an increasingly multimodal world. It would be as if the field of politics were confined to reports and analyses of election results.

But this category error should not blind us to the insightful case studies and generalizations Miroff offers. Slightly modifying his nomenclature, we could say that presidential rhetoric is a significant ground on which presidents seek to enhance their *ethos* and expand their power, and on which countervailing forces both institutional and otherwise contest those efforts, both to preserve the principle of separation of powers and to enhance their own power. That is the larger frame into which the studies in this book might be placed, revealing the ongoing tension between invention and constraint in both historical and political time. These studies help us to appreciate why that tension has persisted since the presidency began and why it is so central to an understanding of American politics.

Notes

1. John Dickerson, "The Hardest Job in the World," *The Atlantic*, May 2018, 46–63.
2. Jeffrey Tulis, *The Rhetorical Presidency* (Princeton: Princeton University Press, 1987). The argument of this volume was previewed in an earlier essay: James Ceaser, Glen Thurow, Jeffrey Tulis, and Joseph M. Bessette, "The Rise of the Rhetorical Presidency," *Presidential Studies Quarterly*, 11, no. 2 (1981), 158–171.
3. See especially George C. Edwards III, *On Deaf Ears: The Limits of the Bully Pulpit* (New Haven, CT: Yale University Press, 2003).
4. See, for example, Davis W. Houck, "Of 'Very Few Men' with 'Unusual Gifts' and 'Acute Sensitivity'—Whither Wichelns, Black, and Zarefsky?," in *The Effects of Rhetoric and the Rhetoric of Effects: Past, Present, Future*, eds. Amos Kiewe and Davis W. Houck (Columbia, SC: University of South Carolina Press, 2015), 282–296.
5. Sidney Blumenthal, *The Permanent Campaign: Inside the World of Elite Political Operatives* (Boston: Beacon Press, 1980).
6. Johnson made this statement in a press conference in 1966. See *New York Times*, July 6, 1966, 18.

7. Martin J. Medhurst, ed., *Beyond the Rhetorical Presidency* (College Station: Texas A&M University Press, 1996).

8. Mary E. Stuckey, "Rethinking the Rhetorical Presidency and Presidential Rhetoric," *Review of Communication*, 10, no. 1 (2010): 38–52.

9. Bruce Miroff, *Presidents on Political Ground: Leaders in Action and What They Face* (Lawrence: University Press of Kansas, 2016).

10. Miroff, *Presidents on Political Ground*, 7.

About the Contributors

Blake Abbott is Assistant Professor of Communication Studies at Towson University. He specializes in rhetorical theory and criticism, public argumentation, political rhetoric, and cultural communication, particularly as they relate to the intersections of citizenship and investment. He teaches courses in argumentation, and rhetorical theory and criticism, and intercultural communication. His work appears in *Argumentation & Advocacy*, *Communication Quarterly*, and *Journal of Contemporary Rhetoric*.

Timothy Barney is Associate Professor of Rhetoric & Communication Studies at the University of Richmond. His research looks at how geopolitics informs political communication, particularly through the visual rhetoric and public address of the Cold War and post-Cold War eras. He is the author of *Mapping the Cold War: Cartography and the Framing of America's International Power* (2015), and has been published in journals such as *Quarterly Journal of Speech*, *Rhetoric & Public Affairs*, *Communication and Critical/Cultural Studies*, and the *Journal of International and Intercultural Communication*.

Cassandra C. Bird (PhD, University of Kansas) is Assistant Teaching Professor in the Department of Communication at the University of Missouri. Her research interests include news media representations of violence and mental health as well as understanding how various publics use discourse to explain and cope with mass trauma.

Leah Ceccarelli is Professor in the Department of Communication at the University of Washington, Seattle, and Director of that university's interdisciplinary Science, Technology, and Society Studies Graduate Certificate Program. Her research and teaching specialties are the rhetoric of science, rhetorical criticism, and American public address. She is a recipient of the National Communication Association's Douglas W. Ehninger Distinguished Rhetorical Scholar Award. Other research awards have been conferred on two of her articles and on each of her two books, *Shaping Science with Rhetoric* and *On the Frontier of Science*. She serves on the editorial boards of five journals, and co-edits the book series *Transdisciplinary Rhetoric* sponsored by the Rhetoric Society of America and Penn State University Press.

Jay P. Childers is currently Associate Professor and Chair of Communication Studies at the University of Kansas, where he also holds a courtesy appointment in political science. His research focuses on the ways that discourse, from political rhetoric to public debates, shapes understandings of democratic citizenship in the United States. Most recently, he has been exploring the ways in which public violence can lead to policy change through the rhetorical struggle to define violent acts and the people who commit them. He is the author of *The Evolving Citizen: American Youth and the Changing Norms of Democratic Engagement* (2012), and the co-author of *Political Tone: How Leaders Talk and Why* (2013). He has also authored a number of essays, including pieces that have appeared in *Rhetoric & Public Affairs*, *Presidential Studies Quarterly*, *Quarterly Journal of Speech*, and *Western Journal of Communication*. He is on the editorial boards of *Communication Quarterly*, *Quarterly Journal of Speech*, *Southern Communication Journal*, and *Western Journal of Communication*.

Lisa Corrigan is Associate Professor of Communication, Director of the Gender Studies Program, and Affiliate Faculty in both African & African American Studies and Latin American Studies in the Fulbright College of Arts and Sciences at the University of Arkansas. She is the author of *Prison Power: How Prison Influenced the Movement for Black Liberation* (2016), which won the 2017 Diamond Anniversary Book Award and the 2017 African American Communication and Culture Division Outstanding Book Award, both from the National Communication Association. Along with Laura Weiderhaft, she co-hosts a podcast called Lean Back: Critical Feminist Conversations, which was named the top podcast in Arkansas and one of the top thirty-five podcasts in America in 2017 by *Paste* magazine.

Jay Alexander Frank is a PhD candidate in communication studies at the University of Minnesota. His research focuses on the role of scientific counsel in both government institutions and popular cultures. His current project examines the United States government's efforts to develop science-based policy responses to global warming through the United States Global Change Research Program. His work has also appeared in the proceedings of the NCA/AFA Conference on Argumentation and the proceedings of the International Society for the Study of Argumentation.

Ronald Walter Greene is Professor and Chair of Communication Studies at the University of Minnesota. His research investigates the material modalities of rhetorical practices as they guide institutionally situated judgments about the conduct of persons, people and populations. He has been awarded the Charles H. Woolbert Research Award from the National Communication Association (NCA), the Distinguished Scholar Award from the Critical and Cultural Studies Division (NCA), the Daniel Rohrer Memorial Outstanding Research Award from the American Forensic Association, and an outstanding article of the year award from the Critical and Cultural Studies Division (NCA). He is the author of *Malthusian Worlds: US Leadership and the Governing of the Population Crisis*. He currently serves on the executive board of the Rhetoric Society of America.

Leslie J. Harris is Associate Professor in the Communication Department at the University of Wisconsin-Milwaukee. Her research concerns issues of rhetoric in public culture, especially with respect to issues of gender and race. Her current research concerns the ways in which women exist within and create meanings of national space. Her most recent book is *State of the Martial Union: Rhetoric, Identity, and Nineteenth Century Marriage Controversies*, and her research has been published in journals such as *Quarterly Journal of Speech*, *Rhetoric Society Quarterly*, *Women's Studies in Communication*, and *Immigrants & Minorities*.

Stephen J. Heidt is an independent scholar based in Southern California. He specializes in the study of public discourse, particularly in terms of its institutionalization in government and the American presidency. His work focuses on issues of war and peace, the rhetorical dimensions of the Cold War and the War on Terror, and the power of the executive to manage foreign relations. He is also interested in the constitutive dynamics of the circulation of presidential rhetoric. His current book project, *The Mobile Savage: Presidential Management of the National Interest in an Era of Global Hegemony*, explains how presidents manipulate images of the enemy to reconfigure American power at the end of war. His work has appeared in *Rhetoric & Public Affairs*, *Southern Communication Journal*, and several edited volumes.

Paul Johnson is Assistant Professor of Deliberation and Civic Life in the Department of Communication at the University of Pittsburgh. Drawing on a mixture of work in rhetoric, political theory, gender studies, and queer theory, his research interrogates American national identity and political sovereignty, often through the lens of the modern conservative movement, thinking particularly about the intersections between race, gender, and populism. More specifically he is working on a book length project called *I, The People: The Rhetoric of Modern Conservative Populism*, which seeks to establish the historical—rather than recent—centrality of victimhood to American conservatism and its supporting role in helping conservatism to define "the people." His work has appeared in *Critical Studies in Media Communication, Argumentation and Advocacy*, and *Women's Studies in Communication*.

Joel M. Lemuel is Assistant Professor and Director of Forensics at California State University, Northridge. He earned his PhD in Communication from the Annenberg School for Communication and Journalism. His work focuses on the rhetoric of health and medicine, argumentation and public deliberation.

Ryan Neville-Shephard is a rhetorical critic who specializes in contemporary American political communication, with an emphasis on presidential rhetoric and its influence on the public sphere. He is the author of several journal articles, including pieces appearing in *Communication Studies, Western Journal of Communication, Argumentation & Advocacy, Southern Communication Journal, Communication Quarterly*, and *American Behavioral Scientist*.

Milene Ortega is a lecturer at Auburn University. She holds a PhD in Communication from Georgia State University and specializes in political communication focusing on presidential rhetoric, civic engagement, rhetorics of dissent, affect, conflict, and incivility. More specifically, her academic interests are situated in the intersection of governmental discourses and discourses of resistance, taking into consideration the role of affect in civic engagement. Her past research investigated incivility in presidential debates, as well as affective rhetorics that resist presidential discourse. Her current book project examines presidential responses to hecklers as opportunities to access the "affective presidency."

Damien Smith Pfister is Associate Professor of Communication at the University of Maryland. His work examines the confluence of digitally networked media, rhetorical practice, public deliberation, and visual culture. Pfister is the author of *Networked Rhetorics, Networked Media: Attention and Deliberation in the Early Blogosphere* (2014) and co-editor of *Ancient Rhetorics + Digital Networks* (2017), as well as numerous essays appearing in such journals as *Philosophy & Rhetoric, Argumentation and Advocacy, Environmental Communication, Rhetoric Review*, and *Social Epistemology*.

Allison M. Prasch is Assistant Professor of Communication Studies at Colorado State University. Her research connects methods of close textual analysis and archival research with contemporary scholarship on space/place and public memory to interrogate the relationship between oratorical texts and their physical, spatial, and historical contexts. Her current book project, tentatively entitled *To the Front Lines of Freedom: Cold War Presidential Rhetoric on the Global Stage, 1945–1989*, examines how U.S. presidents linked their foreign policy objectives to particular geographical locations and, in so doing, extended the United States' physical and metaphorical presence in the world during the Cold War. She is the recipient of the National Communication Association's 2017 Golden Anniversary Monograph Award for her theoretical work on deixis, and her research has been published in the *Quarterly Journal of Speech*, *Rhetoric & Public Affairs*, *Presidential Studies Quarterly*, the *Southern Communication Journal,' Women's Studies in Communication*, and *Voices of Democracy*.

Belinda A. Stillion Southard is Associate Professor in the Department of Communication Studies at the University of Georgia. She holds a PhD in communication and a women's studies certificate from the University of Maryland. Her research and teaching interests are grounded in the public address tradition and are guided by questions regarding gender, transnationalism, and citizenship. These interests are reflected in her book, *Militant Citizenship: Rhetorical Strategies of the National Woman's Party, 1913–1920*. The book is the winner of the 2012 Marie Hochmuth Nichols Award, presented by the Public Address Division of the National Communication Association. It also received an Honorable Mention designation for the 2012 Winifred Bryan Horner Book Award given by the Coalition of Women Scholars in the History of Rhetoric and Composition. Belinda's second book, *How to Belong: Women's Agency in a Transnational World*, centers on how women conceptualize belonging in the contexts of regional movements, the nation-state, and supranational organizations. Belinda's research has also appeared in *Quarterly Journal of Speech*, *Communication and Critical/Cultural Studies*, *Communication Quarterly*, *Rhetoric & Public Affairs*, *Rhetoric Society Quarterly*, *Advances in the History of Rhetoric*, and elsewhere.

Mary E. Stuckey is Professor of Communication Arts and Sciences at Penn State University. She specializes in public argument, especially as it pertains to the American presidency, presidential rhetoric, and political communication. She is also interested in issues of political power and the national media, and especially how both affect minority groups. She is the author of or editor of thirteen books, including, *Political Vocabularies: FDR, the Clergy Letters, and the Elements of Political Argument, Voting Deliberatively: FDR and the 1936 Presidential Campaign, Rhetoric: A Presidential Briefing Book, The Good Neighbor: Franklin D. Roosevelt and American Power*, and *Defining Americans: The Presidency and National Identity*. She is a recipient of the NCA Distinguished Scholar Award, Roderick P. Hart Outstanding Book Award, the

Marie Hochmuth Nichols Award, the Bruce E. Gronbeck Award for Political Communication, and teaching awards in both political science and communication. Her articles have appeared in *Quarterly Journal of Speech, Rhetoric and Public Affairs, Presidential Studies Quarterly, American Indian Culture and Research Journal,* and numerous other places.

David Zarefsky is Owen L. Coon Professor Emeritus of Argumentation and Debate, and Professor Emeritus of Communication Studies, Northwestern University. His publications include six books and over 120 scholarly articles concerned with American public discourse (both historical and contemporary), argumentation, rhetorical criticism, and public speaking, and books on the Lincoln-Douglas debates and the rhetoric of the war on poverty during the Johnson administration. He was president of the Rhetoric Society of America, and is a past president of the National Communication Association and the Central States Communication Association. He currently is working on two book-length projects, one concerning President Johnson's speech in which he announced his withdrawal from the 1968 Presidential race, and the other on the Texas annexation controversy of the 1840s as it affected the slavery debate.

POLITICAL COMMUNICATION

FRONTIERS IN

General Editors
Mitchell S. McKinney and Mary E. Stuckey

At the heart of how citizens, governments, and the media interact is the communication process, a process that is undergoing tremendous changes as we embrace a new millennium. Never has there been a time when confronting the complexity of these evolving relationships been so important to the maintenance of civil society. This series seeks books that advance the understanding of this process from multiple perspectives and as it occurs in both institutionalized and non-institutionalized political settings. While works that provide new perspectives on traditional political communication questions are welcome, the series also encourages the submission of manuscripts that take an innovative approach to political communication, which seek to broaden the frontiers of study to incorporate critical and cultural dimensions of study as well as scientific and theoretical frontiers.

For more information or to submit material for consideration, contact:

Mitchell S. McKinney: McKinneyM@missouri.edu
Mary E. Stuckey: mes519@psu.edu

To order other books in this series, please contact our Customer Service Department:

(800) 770-LANG (within the U.S.)
(212) 647-7706 (outside the U.S.)
(212) 647-7707 FAX

Or browse online by series:
WWW.PETERLANG.COM